LOCAL LITERACIES

'One of the best books on literacy I've read in my career. I can see myself going back to this book again and again, learning more each time I read it. You can't leave the book without new insights about the nature of literacy in people's lives.'

Local I centra[...]on-[...]ow people use literacy in their day to day lives.

This exploration provides a description of literacy at one point in time, and also reveals the nature and significance of communication to people, households and communities.

Local Literacies is both a theoretical work and a practical book. It provides stimulating and informative reading for anyone interested in the nature of literacy today, particularly students, teachers and researchers. It includes notes on how to use the book and guidance for carrying out individual research. As a detailed ethnographic study it also includes extensive quotes from individual people and asides providing broader contextual information. It is accessible to practitioners, parents, community workers and the general public.

Both authors are based at Lancaster University, where **David Barton** is Senior Lecturer in the Department of Linguistics and **Mary Hamilton** is Senior Research Fellow in the Department of Educational Research. They have worked together on several projects including *Worlds of Literacy* (1994) and are founder members of the national network, Research and Practice in Adult Literacy (RaPAL).

LOCAL LITERACIES

Reading and writing in one community

David Barton and Mary Hamilton

London and New York

First published 1998
by Routledge
11 New Fetter Lane, London EC4P 4EE

Transferred to Digital Printing 2003

Simultaneously published in the USA and Canada
by Routledge
29 West 35th Street, New York, NY 10001

Typeset in Baskerville by
M Rules

British Library Cataloguing in Publication Data
A catalogue record for this book is available from the British Library

Library of Congress Cataloguing in Publication Data
Barton, David, 1949–
Local literacies: reading and writing in one community/
David Barton and Mary Hamilton.
p.   cm.
Includes bibliographical references (p.   ) and index.
1. Literacy – Social aspects – England – Lancaster – Case studies.
2. Sociolinguistics – England – Lancaster – Case studies.
I. Hamilton, Mary, 1949–   . II. Title.
LC156.G72E53   1998
302.2'244'0942769–dc21   97–39774

ISBN 0–415–17150–4 (pbk)
ISBN 0–415–17149–0 (hbk)

CONTENTS

APPENDICES

ASIDES

FIGURES

FOREWORD

I have had the advantage of hearing about the research reported in this book while it was being conducted. Bits and pieces were reported at various conferences over the past five years and I was able to talk with David Barton and Mary Hamilton and their colleagues about it. They were motivated at first by a dissatisfaction with the grand, abstract theories constructed by earlier generations of literacy researchers. As they learned more about what people did with written language and how it was a part of them and where they lived, Barton and Hamilton began to construct understandings that went beyond the abstract definitions and constructs dominant in the field. They shared the view expressed by Jay Robinson in 1987:

> It will no longer do, I think, to consider literacy as some abstract, absolute quality attainable through tutelage and the accumulation of knowledge and experience. It will no longer do to think of reading as a solitary act in which a mainly passive reader responds to cues in a text to find meaning. It will no longer do to think of writing as a mechanical manipulation of grammatical codes and formal structures leading to the production of perfect or perfectible texts. Reading and writing are not unitary skills nor are they reducible to sets of component skills falling neatly under discrete categories (linguistic, cognitive); rather, they are complex human activities taking place in complex human relationships.
>
> (1987: 329)

But where Robinson had stated the case in negative terms ('It will no longer do . . .'), Barton and Hamilton have showed reading and writing as complex human activities, inseparable from both people and the places involved. With the publication of *Local Literacies* it is no longer possible to describe literacy credibly without also describing the people involved and places in which it occurs.

There is something very appealing about the title of this book – *Local Literacies*. It suggests a sense of place, of community, of home, a groundedness that seems so absent in contemporary society. It forces us to look around where we are and see the local literacies that make up our lives.

Sitting at our kitchen table I see the notices and reminders stuck on our

xii

make-shift bulletin board: emergency medical telephone numbers, the number to the poison control center (left over from when our children were very small and would put anything they could grab in their mouths), shopping coupons, announcements about upcoming events at our synagogue, my sons' high school soccer schedules (I've got two sons and two soccer schedules to attend), and my daughter's track schedule. There's a list of my sons' school mates and their addresses and telephone numbers and a notice of a fiddle contest in Franklin. Hanging off the bottom are greeting cards, pictures, and a list of restaurants we cut from the newspaper that we thought we might try out if we ever get a Saturday night and enough energy and money to go. Stuck underneath some coupons is a torn envelope flap with a return address of a friend from England who I haven't seen in four years and with whom I lost contact because I lost his new address. I have no idea whether the address is still current, but I can't throw it away because then I would surely forget to write. There's a picture of Ayodella, my goddaughter, chewing a book. You can hardly see per picture so much is tacked to the bulletin board, you have to know it is there. There's a cartoon making fun of the proposed 'English Only' amendment and a reminder to do what I said I would for the National Yiddish Book Center.

It's my life – at least in part – on that bulletin board, except for work and bills and the government (taxes and the monthly junk mail we get from our representatives and civil servants). These don't get to go on the bulletin board. Work papers are kept on my desk or at the office, bills and taxes in a special folder out of sight (so I don't have to think about them until the end of the month), and the government junk mail in the waste basket.

Each piece of paper on the bulletin board leads to people and connects me with them – if not directly (as in attending my sons' soccer games), then emotionally (such as my friend's outdated address on the torn envelope). These are connections that we have made and chosen – my family and me. What's on this bulletin board is *our* use of literacy to make *our* world. Even if we do not have absolute control of how we define ourselves through literacy at home or in our communities, we have a sense of at least enough control to feel efficacious. (Clearly there are those who have limited or no control over how they define themselves or their world at home or in their community, and their uses of literacy reflect it. This lack of control is part of the abuse they suffer, whether or not the abuse is physical (see Rockhill 1993). And clearly, that we feel efficacious may be little more than an illusion.)

Like everyone, I am faced with bills, taxes and government junk mail. Those are connections that others are making. Through these literacies I am defined as consumer, as debtor, taxpayer, worker and citizen subject. At work, it is more diverse, but not more complicated. Administrators, students, colleagues, use writing to define me as suits their needs and their views of the academe (teacher, worker, researcher, expert) – and I do the same to them. In these spheres – business, government, work – we rarely get the chance to use literacy to define ourselves or our world. It is *others'* uses of literacy to define us and place us in their world; and we are often complicit in this agenda, sometimes even aggressively so.

Local Literacies follows in the tradition of ethnographic studies of literacy that have made people and places visible as the authors simultaneously push forward new ways of understanding reading and writing as part of people's social and cultural lives: Shirley Heath's (1983) *Ways With Words*, Denny Taylor and Catherine Dorsey-Gaines' (1988) *Growing Up Literate*, Judith Solsken's (1993) *Literacy, Gender And Work*, and Guadalupe Vald's (1996) *Con Respecto*, among others. Yet, *Local Literacies* is also reminiscent of life history research that has focused on reading and writing, including Carol Steadman's *The Tidy House* (1982), Jane Miller's *Seductions* (1990), Mary Catherine Bateson's *Composing a Life*, (1989), Mike Rose's *Lives on the Boundary* (1989), among others. That is, although *Local Literacies* is not life history research *per se*, the book introduces us, especially in Part II, to specific people who think about and talk about what they do with reading and writing, how it is, and how it is bound up with all they do.

Building on these two traditions allows Barton and Hamilton to suggest a different epistemology for understanding literacy. Rather than understand literacy in terms of a knowledge base built up by isolated studies over years and aggregated from all over the globe, coercing people and places and what they do with written language into unifying theories and overarching laws of social science, literacy needs to be understood locally and historically (both in terms of the histories of individuals and in terms of the histories of the places and the social relationships in which they find themselves). Stated in other terms, rather than focus on what is universal about literacy practices, research on literacy practices needs to focus on the particular. Following a line of argument that builds on Clifford Geertz (1983), among others, the kind of knowledge building we need is not that which seeks the resolution of difference through technological and abstract, scientific processes of truth divining and dispute settlement (although there is a place for that), but rather a knowledge building which holds difference and disagreement as fundamental, as the nature and condition of a knowledge building that has something to say about people and places; and in so doing moves beyond just local knowledge. Geertz states it this way:

> We need, in the end, something more than local knowledge. We need a way of turning its varieties into commentaries one upon another, the one lighting what the other darkens. . . . The primary question, for any cultural institution anywhere, now that nobody is leaving anybody else alone and isn't ever again going to, is not whether everything is going to come seamlessly together or whether, contrariwise, we are all going to persist sequestered in our separate prejudices. It is whether human beings are going to

continue to be able, in Java or Connecticut, through law, anthropology, or anything else, to imagine principled lives they can practicably lead.

(Geertz 1983: 233–244)

And that, in the end, is what *Local Literacies* does.

David Bloome
Nashville, Tennessee,
USA
October, 1997

References

Bateson, M. (1989) *Composing a life*, New York: Atlantic Monthly Press.

Geertz, C. (1983) *Local knowledge*, New York: Basic Books.

Heath, S. (1983) *Ways with words*, Cambridge: Cambridge University Press.

Miller, J. (1990) *Seductions: Studies in reading and culture*, London: Virago.

Robinson, J. (1987) 'Literacy in society: Readers and writers in the worlds of discourse'. In D. Bloome (ed.) *Literacy and schooling*, Norwood, NJ: Ablex.

Rockhill, K. (1993) 'Gender, language and the politics of literacy'. In B. Street (ed.) *Cross-cultural approaches to literacy*. Cambridge: Cambridge University Press.

Rose, M. (1989) *Lives on the boundary: The struggles and achievements of America's under-prepared*, New York: Free Press.

Solsken, J. (1993) *Literacy, gender, and work: In families and in school*, Norwood, NJ: Ablex.

Steedman, C. (1982) *The tidy house: Little girls writing*, London: Virago.

Taylor, D., and Dorsey-Gaines, C. (1988) *Growing up literate: Learning from inner-city families*, Portsmouth, NH: Heinemann.

Valds, G. (1996). *Con respeto: Bridging the distances between culturally diverse families and schools: An ethnographic portrait*, New York: Teachers College, Columbia University.

PREFACE

This book is a study of the uses of reading and writing in Lancaster, England in the 1990s. In writing this book we have three overlapping aims. Our first aim is to offer a detailed, specific description of literacy practices in one local community at one point in time. Secondly, the book makes a contribution to the theoretical understanding of literacy by linking literacy to a more general understanding of social practices and how people make sense of their lives through their everyday practices. The account that results from this project is often at odds with the public image of literacy to be found in the media and much current policy discourse. The book draws attention to vernacular literacies which are often hidden literacies, devalued and overlooked. In this way, it contributes to our final aim, which is to offer an alternative public discourse which foregrounds the role of literacy as a communal resource contributing to the quality of local life.

In finding a way to write this book, we have paid a great deal of attention to what kind of book it is and how to make it accessible to readers with different purposes. There are many ways of 'telling the tale', and it has taken some tjme to create and tell a story in a way which relates to our three aims. Much of the book is concerned with describing the details of people's lives and situating reading and writing within their worlds. We are aware that our story contains many voices, especially those of the people we interviewed, and we have been conscious throughout that the voices of other people are always mediated by us. We have tried in various ways to bring this to the attention of the reader through the ways in which we have presented the material, and by commenting as honestly as we can on how we have selected and transformed the data in the process of researching and writing. Our concern about whose version of literacy is getting represented in this book is central to our aim of challenging discourses of literacy that are dominant and simplifying.

To complement these voices we should provide some details of ourselves, making it clear in what ways the lives we describe overlap with our own experiences and orientations to literacy. We are not from Lancaster, nor even from the north of England. We moved to Lancaster sixteen years ago to jobs at the university, having been brought up in the south and the west of England and having worked in the United States. David has a background in Linguistics and has been a volunteer tutor at the adult college and elsewhere. Mary was trained as a social psychologist and now works in a department of educational research, where she carries out research in adult learning. She has also worked as a part-time teacher and volunteer in adult literacy and numeracy. We came to the research with the advantages and disadvantages of being to some extent *outsiders* to the community we have been studying, in terms of both our geographical origins and our educational background. To the people in the study we are identifiable as middle-class academics and teachers.

At the same time, we live in one of the neighbourhoods of Lancaster, adjacent to the one we have studied, and it is not unfamiliar to us. We are both part of the first generation in our own families to study in higher education. We participate in local activities and our son was born and has been brought up in Lancaster. We have shared in momentous events such as the central market burning down in 1986 and in long-running arguments about traffic problems and pollution, changes in taxation and the reorganisation of public services. In these ways we have the knowledge and difficulties of being *insiders* to the research we have been doing. The research has grown into our lives and affected our perceptions of literacy in permanent ways, plaguing our friends, neighbours and colleagues, who are all now adept at pointing out interesting literacy events to us.

Our first debt is to the people we interviewed, who freely and generously gave us their time, whether for ten minutes on the doorstep, for an hour in their offices or for many hours over several months in their homes. The interviews are the backbone of the study, and we are grateful to Sarah Padmore, who worked on the project from 1988 until 1992, carrying out much of the interviewing and participating fully in the project. Like us, Sarah is not from Lancaster. Before joining the project she worked for several years as a tutor at the Adult College, Lancaster; she has been an organiser of the Lancaster Literature Festival and now works with teenagers on creative writing.

Many other people have contributed to this study. We are grateful to Carol Squire who transcribed and word processed many hours of interviews, and to Gill Plant, Fiona Ormerod and Kathy Pitt who helped with the analysis of parts of the data. During the research an informal Steering Group met several times and provided support and ideas; we are grateful to Nigel Hall, Roz Ivanic, Meriel Lobley, Wendy Moss, Sue Nieduszynska and Brian Street for their help. Other members of the Literacy Research Group at Lancaster have also contributed, including Marilyn Martin-Jones, Rachel Rimmershaw, Simon Pardoe, Karin Tusting and Anita Wilson. We are grateful to David Bloome, Fiona Frank, Peter Hannon, Gaye Houghton, Roz

Ivanic, Jane Mace, Janet Maybin, Juliet Merrifield, Wendy Moss and Mukul Saxena for reading and commenting on parts of the manuscript.

The book is based on a study entitled *Literacy in the Community* which was supported by the Research Fund at Lancaster University from 1988 to 1989, and then by the ESRC from 1989 until 1992 through two grants (R00023 1419) and R00023 3440). We thank them for this support.

Acknowledgements

We are grateful to Manchester University Press for permission to reprint extracts from the autobiography of William Stout, and to Lancaster Leisure for the map in Figure 3.1. The photographs in Figures 3.2, 7.1 and 7.2 are courtesy of Lancaster and Morecambe Newspapers Ltd. The photographs in Figures 3.3 and 3.8 are by Phil Keen. All other photographs are by members of the Literacy Research Group at Lancaster University.

Part I

1

UNDERSTANDING LITERACY AS SOCIAL PRACTICE

Introduction

Literacy is primarily something people do; it is an activity, located in the space between thought and text. Literacy does not just reside in people's heads as a set of skills to be learned, and it does not just reside on paper, captured as texts to be analysed. Like all human activity, literacy is essentially social, and it is located in the interaction between people. This book is a study of what people do with literacy: of the social activities, of the thoughts and meanings behind the activities, and of the texts utilised in such activities. It is about how a particular group of people use reading and writing in their day-to-day lives. Of necessity, the book is particular; it sets out from individual people's lives and particular literacy events at a certain point in history. At the same time, it is also about the general nature of literacy and about the state of literacy in the world at the end of the twentieth century. This book explores contemporary uses and meanings of literacy in everyday life and the ways in which these are changing. It is based upon an ethnographic study which documents in detail literacy practices at one point in time and space: the time is the final decade of the twentieth century, the place is Lancaster, a town in the north-west of England. We look backwards at the history and cultural traditions on which these practices rest, as well as examining the constant change affecting people's contemporary practices.

The book draws upon and extends new views of literacy. It develops the field of literacy studies which has come into being in the past few years. Several studies have examined the literacy practices of individuals and groups, including people's uses and meanings of literacy and the value it holds for them; these studies have contributed to a theory of literacy as social practice and collective resource. We will refer to some of these studies later in this chapter but will keep more detailed discussion of much of the work until the third section of the book when integrating and extending ideas about the nature of literacy.

As described in the preface, we wish to contribute to this field in three distinct ways. Firstly we offer a description and an investigation of literacy in one local community. Secondly, the book represents a contribution to the

3

theoretical understanding of literacy, and more generally to the understanding of social practices and how people make sense of their lives through their everyday practices. In doing this we find that we provide an account which is often at odds with other public images of literacy such as media images, and we draw attention to vernacular literacies which are often hidden literacies. This leads to our final aim, which is to contribute critically to public discussions on literacy, education and the quality of local life.

This book is based upon an empirical study. Whether or not it is made explicit, all empirical studies start from many theoretical assumptions. All research has a theory underlying it. In approaching our study of literacy, we brought a clear set of propositions about literacy – a theoretical framework. This oriented us towards particular ways of working and particular approaches to data collection and analysis. The theory has been further refined and amplified as we have carried out the study, analysing and reflecting on the data. We wish to make this theory explicit. The main part of this first chapter is concerned with describing our theory of literacy. We also introduce other concepts we have made use of and explain some of the motivation for this research.

This theory of literacy we put forward implies a certain approach to research, demanding particular research methods and data. It is an ecological approach, where literacy is integral to its context; this is what Barton (1994) refers to as 'an ecology of written language' and Lemke (1995) has called an 'ecosocial' approach to human communities. The theory also provides a rationale for the structuring of the book: because literacy is situated socially, we need to devote the next two chapters to describing the context of the study. This means historical context as much as contemporary context. Chapter 2 provides some of the literacy history of the city and its institutions, with glimpses of literacy in Lancaster at the turn of the eighteenth century and at the turn of the twentieth century. Chapter 3 is concerned with locating the study, as a contemporary study based in Lancaster, England in the 1990s. Lancaster is a distinct city with its own idiosyncrasies, and the 1990s are a particular point in history, not least in terms of the changing nature of literacy.

In terms of methodology, we carried out interviews, we observed activities and we collected documents. We refer to the study as an ethnography; it is an ethnography of a set of cultural practices, those concerned with literacy. It is an ethnography in that the study consists of detailed examination of a real situation, working, as Clifford Geertz puts it, 'by the light of local knowledge' (1983: 167). A variety of methods are used and people's own perceptions are highlighted. This is a critical ethnography in the important sense that we are trying to reveal and question the traditional assumptions which frame literacy, to expose the ways in which it is ideologically constructed and embedded in power relationships (see Kincheloe and

McLaren 1994). In so doing, the study contributes to a more critical debate and understanding of literacy practices, both in and out of education.

Our study is also a critical ethnography in that we are committed to uncovering and documenting everyday literacies which are often unrecognised in dominant discourses about literacy. In this way, our research has affinities with feminist methodologies and other research with marginalised groups (Harding 1987). Our research has, in Kincheloe and McLaren's terms (1994), a transformative, emancipatory aim. However, it is not directly action-oriented. Implications for education and cultural action can be drawn out of this study, but we have deliberately not set out from educational concerns or agendas for change. Other aspects of our research programme focus more directly on these action outcomes, as in Ivanic and Hamilton (1990); Barton and Hamilton (1996). Our approach has been strongly shaped by the insistent voices of practitioners and adult students in community-based adult education who reject definitions of literacy in terms of skills, functions and levels which do not fit their experiences, nor their visions of the power of literacy in everyday life (see Mace 1992a).

This is an ethnography of a limited set of cultural practices, those concerned with literacy. Therefore, in traditional terms it may be more accurate to say that we utilise ethnographic methods or that we take an ethnographic approach, rather than to say that this is a full ethnography of the whole of people's lives (see Green and Bloome 1996). In Chapter 4 we describe the research methods and their rationale, raising issues about qualitative research methodology and the relations between researcher and researched.

These first four chapters provide information which creates the setting for the empirical study, covering theory, historical background, contemporary context and methodology. The second section of the book consists of four chapters each of which provides a detailed picture of the literacy life of an individual person. Harry Graham, the subject of Chapter 5, is a retired firefighter with strong views on education and who is trying to write his memoirs of the Second World War. Shirley Bowker, in Chapter 6, is concerned about her children's schooling and cares passionately about social issues. In Chapter 7, June Marsh, a part-time market worker, keeps detailed household accounts in order to survive financially and utilises a wide range of media. In Chapter 8, Cliff Holt is worried about his health but he enjoys betting and gets pleasure from writing.

The third section of the book consists of six chapters which explore particular themes about literacy and draw upon data from the full range of people we talked to and the observations we made. In these chapters we examine how literacy is a communal resource utilised by families, by community groups, and by individuals. Chapters 9 and 10 are concerned primarily with the range of reading and writing which goes on in the home, exploring first of all its diversity and then looking at patterns related to gender, numeracy practices and practices in a multilingual household. Chapter 11 addresses the relationship between everyday practices and learning, covering the informal learning of new literacies, as well as relationships between home learning and more formal learning of educational institutions. The next chapter, Chapter 12, examines the role of literacy in the many local organisations which people belong to, and how literate activity is one of the roots of local democratic participation.

Chapter 13 describes how people use reading and writing to make sense of the world and to become experts in particular domains. Chapter 14 brings together some of the threads of the earlier chapters and in it we identify a range of vernacular literacies, or local literacies, in people's everyday lives, exploring their definition and contemporary significance. An afterword, Chapter 15, reflects on how the findings from this local study can be related to literacy practices in other times and places. The Appendices contain further information and notes on some educational implications of the book. Throughout there are boxed Asides, mainly covering a variety of extra material which the reader may want to pause at or return to selectively at a later stage. This material includes detailed quotes from interviews and fieldwork observations, discussions of methodological points, and statistics which provide some national context for the findings of this local study.

A social theory of literacy: practices and events

We present below the theory we employed as a set of six propositions about the nature of literacy. We explain each one, making clear how it shapes our study. The starting-point of this approach is the assertion that literacy is a social practice, and the propositions are an elaboration of this. The discussion is a development on from that in Barton (1994: 34–52), where contemporary approaches to literacy are discussed within the framework of the metaphor of ecology. The notion of literacy practices offers a powerful way of conceptualising the link between the activities of reading and writing and the social structures in which they are embedded and which they help shape. When we talk about practices, then, this is not just the superficial choice of a word but the possibilities that this perspective offers for new theoretical understandings about literacy.

Our interest is in social practices in which literacy has a role; hence, the basic unit of a social theory of literacy is that of literacy practices. Literacy practices are the general cultural ways of utilising written language which people draw upon in their lives. In the simplest sense literacy practices are what people do with literacy. However practices are not observable units of behaviour since they also involve values, attitudes, feelings and social relationships (see Street 1993: 12). This includes people's awareness of literacy, constructions of literacy and discourses of literacy, how people talk about and make sense of literacy. These are processes internal to the individual; at

---

Aside 1.1   Literacy as social practice

- Literacy is best understood as a set of social practices; these can be inferred from events which are mediated by written texts.
- There are different literacies associated with different domains of life.
- Literacy practices are patterned by social institutions and power relationships, and some literacies become more dominant, visible and influential than others.
- Literacy practices are purposeful and embedded in broader social goals and cultural practices.
- Literacy is historically situated.
- Literacy practices change, and new ones are frequently acquired through processes of informal learning and sense making.

---

the same time, practices are the social processes which connect people with one another, and they include shared cognitions represented in ideologies and social identities. Practices are shaped by social rules which regulate the use and distribution of texts, prescribing who may produce and have access to them. They straddle the distinction between individual and social worlds, and literacy practices are more usefully understood as existing in the relations between people, within groups and communities, rather than as a set of properties residing in individuals.

To avoid confusion, it is worth emphasising that this usage is different from situations where the word 'practice' is used to mean learning to do something by repetition. It is also different from the way the term is used in recent international surveys of literacy, to refer to 'common or typical activities or tasks' (OECD/Statistics Canada 1996). The notion of practices as we have defined it above – cultural ways of utilising literacy – is a more abstract one that cannot wholly be contained in observable activities and tasks.

Turning to another basic concept, literacy events are activities where literacy has a role. Usually there is a written text, or texts, central to the activity and there may be talk around the text. Events are observable episodes which arise from practices and are shaped by them. The notion of events stresses the situated nature of literacy, that it always exists in a social context. It is parallel to ideas developed in sociolinguistics and also, as Jay Lemke has pointed out, to Bahktin's assertion that the starting-point for the analysis of spoken language should be 'the social event of verbal interaction', rather than the formal linguistic properties of texts in isolation (Lemke 1995).

Many literacy events in life are regular, repeated activities, and these can often be a useful starting-point for research into literacy. Some events are linked into routine sequences and these may be part of the formal procedures and expectations of social institutions like work-places, schools and welfare agencies. Some events are structured by the more informal expectations and pressures of the home or peer group. Texts are a crucial part of literacy events, and the study of literacy is partly a study of texts and how they are produced and used. These three components, practices, events and texts, provide the first proposition of a social theory of literacy, that: *literacy is best understood as a set of social practices; these can be inferred from events which are mediated by written texts.* Our study is concerned with identifying the events and texts of everyday life and describing people's associated practices. Our prime interest here is to analyse events in order to learn about practices. As with the definition of practices, we take a straightforward view of events at this point, as being activities which involve written texts, but we return to this term for further discussion. An example of an everyday literacy event, cooking a pie, is to be found in Aside 1.2.

Aside 1.2   Cooking literacy

When baking a lemon pie in her kitchen, Rita follows a recipe. She uses it to check the amounts of the ingredients. She estimates the approximate amounts, using teacups and spoons chosen specially for this purpose. The recipe is handwritten on a piece of notepaper; it was written out from a book by a friend more than ten years ago. The first time she read the recipe carefully at each stage, but now she only looks at it once or twice. The piece of paper is marked and greasy by having been near the cooking surface on many occasions. It is kept in an envelope with other handwritten recipes and ones cut out of magazines and newspapers. The envelope and some cookery books are on a shelf in the kitchen. The books range in age and condition and include popular ones by Robert Carrier. Sometimes she sits and reads them for pleasure.

Rita does not always go through the same set of activities in making the pie. Sometimes she makes double the amount described in the recipe if more people will be eating it. Sometimes she cooks the pie with her daughter, Hayley, helping her where necessary. Sometimes she enjoys cooking it; at other times it is more of a chore, when time is limited or she has other things she would rather do. Rita has passed the recipe on to several friends who have enjoyed the pie.

Rita does not always follow recipes exactly, but will add herbs and spices to taste; sometimes she makes up recipes; at one point she describes making a vegetable and pasta dish similar to one she had had as a take-away meal. She exchanges recipes with other people, although she does not lend her books.

Our work complements other studies, primarily in Linguistics, which focus on the analysis of texts. The study of everyday literacy practices points attention to the texts of everyday life, the texts of personal life; these are distinct from other texts which are more usually studied, such as educational texts, mass media texts and other published texts. Work in the field of literacy studies adds the perspective of practices to studies of texts, encompassing what people do with texts and what these activities mean to them. In our work, practices remain central and we are led to examine how texts fit into the practices of people's lives, rather than the other way round. Nevertheless, we see the full study of written language as being the analysis of both texts and practices.

Once one begins to think in terms of literacy events there are certain things about the nature of reading and writing which become apparent. For instance, in many literacy events there is a mixture of written and spoken language. Our study has print literacy and written texts as its starting-point but it is clear that in literacy events people use written language in an integrated way as part of a range of semiotic systems; these semiotic systems include mathematical systems, musical notation, maps and other non-text-based images. The cookery text has numeracy mixed with print literacy, and the recipes come from books, magazines, television and orally from friends and relatives. By identifying literacy as one of a range of communicative resources available to members of a community, we can examine some of the ways in which it is located in relation to other mass media and new technologies. This is especially pertinent at a time of rapidly changing technologies.

Looking at different literacy events it is clear that literacy is not the same in all contexts; rather, there are different literacies. The notion of different literacies has several senses: for example, practices which involve different media or symbolic systems, such as a film or computer, can be regarded as different literacies, as in *film literacy* and *computer literacy*. Another sense is that practices in different cultures and languages can be regarded as different literacies. While we accept these senses of the term, the main way in which we use the notion here is to say that literacies are coherent configurations of literacy practices; often these sets of practices are identifiable and named, as in *academic literacy* or *work-place literacy*, and they are associated with particular aspects of cultural life.

This means that, within a given culture, there are different literacies associated with different domains of life. Contemporary life can be analysed in a simple way into domains of activity, such as home, school, work-place. It is a useful starting-point to examine the distinct practices in these domains, and then to compare, for example, home and school, or school and work-place. We begin with the home domain and everyday life. The home is often identified as a primary domain in people's literacy lives, for example by James Gee (1990), and central to people's developing sense of social identity.

Work is another identifiable domain, where relationships and resources are often structured quite differently from in the home. We might expect the practices associated with cooking, for example, to be quite different in the home and in the work-place – supported, learned and carried out in different ways. The division of labour is different in institutional kitchens, the scale of the operations, the clothing people wear when cooking, the health and safety precautions they are required to take, and so on. Such practices contribute to the idea that people participate in distinct discourse communities, in different domains of life. These communities are groups of people held together by their characteristic ways of talking, acting, valuing, interpreting and using written language. (See discussion in Swales 1990: 23–7.)

Domains, and the discourse communities associated with them, are not clear-cut, however: there are questions of the permeability of boundaries, of leakages and movement between boundaries, and of overlap between domains. Home and community, for instance, are often treated as being the same domain; nevertheless they are distinct in many ways, including the dimension of public and private behaviour. An important part of our study is clarifying the domain being studied and teasing apart notions of home, household, neighbourhood and community. Another aspect is the extent to which this domain is a distinct one with its own practices, and the extent to which the practices that exist in the home originate there, or home practices are exported to other domains. In particular, the private home context appears to be infiltrated by practices from many different public domains.

Domains are structured, patterned contexts within which literacy is used and learned. Activities within these domains are not accidental or randomly varying: there are particular configurations of literacy practices and there are regular ways in which people act in many literacy events in particular contexts. Various institutions support and structure activities in particular domains of life. These include family, religion and education, which are all social institutions. Some of these institutions are more formally structured than others, with explicit rules for procedures, documentation and legal penalties for infringement, whilst others are regulated by the pressure of social conventions and attitudes. Particular literacies have been created by and are structured and sustained by these institutions. Part of this study aims to highlight the ways in which institutions support particular literacy practices.

Socially powerful institutions, such as education, tend to support dominant literacy practices. These dominant practices can be seen as part of whole discourse formations, institutionalised configurations of power and knowledge which are embodied in social relationships. Other vernacular literacies which exist in people's everyday lives are less visible and less supported. This means that literacy practices are patterned by social institutions and power relationships, and some literacies become more dominant, visible and influential than others. One can contrast dominant literacies and vernacular literacies; our study is concerned more with documenting the vernacular literacies which exist, and with exploring their relationship to more dominant literacies.

People are active in what they do, and literacy practices are purposeful and embedded in broader social goals and cultural practices. Whilst some reading and writing is carried out as an end in itself, typically literacy is a means to some other end. Any study of literacy practices must therefore situate reading and writing activities in these broader contexts and motivations for use. In the cooking example, for instance, the aim is to bake a lemon pie, and the reading of a recipe is incidental to this aim. The recipe is incorporated into a broader set of domestic social practices associated with providing food and caring for children, and it reflects broader social relationships and gendered divisions of labour.

Classic studies of literacies in the home, such as Heath (1983) and Taylor and Dorsey-Gaines (1988), have offered classifications of the functions and uses of literacy for individuals. This approach can be revealing in providing an overview of the range of literacy practices in a community and, in doing so, links back to Richard Hoggart's classic work from 1957, *The Uses of Literacy*. In practice, however, it is often difficult to identify discrete functions, what is counted as a function is inconsistent, and they overlap a great deal (as discussed in Barton 1994: 152–4; see also Clark and Ivanic 1997, chapter 5). In the current study we move beyond this approach, to examine how literacy activities are supported, sustained, learned and impeded in people's lives and relationships, and the social meanings they have. It is very clear from our data that a particular type of text, such as a diary or letter, cannot be used as a basis for assigning functions, as reading or writing any vernacular text can serve many functions; people appropriate texts for their own ends. Just as a text does not have autonomous meanings which are independent of its social context of use, a text also does not have a set of functions independent of the social meanings with which it is imbued.

A first step in reconceptualising literacy is to accept the multiple functions literacy may serve in a given activity, where it can replace spoken language, make communication possible, solve a practical problem or act as a memory aid – in some cases, all at the same time. It is also possible to explore the further work which literacy can do in an activity, and the social meanings it takes on. For instance, we discuss ways in which literacy acts as *evidence*, as *display*, as *threat*, and as *ritual*. Texts can have multiple roles in an activity, and literacy can act in different ways for the different participants in a literacy event; people can be incorporated into the literacy practices of others without reading or writing a single word. The acts of reading and writing are not the only ways in which texts are assigned meaning. We return to these issues later in this chapter, as well as in Chapter 14 when identifying the range of vernacular literacies in the community.

It is important to shift from a conception of literacy located in individuals to examine ways in which people in groups utilise literacy. In this way literacy becomes a community resource, realised in social relationships rather than a property of individuals. This is true at various levels; at the detailed micro level it can refer to the fact that in particular literacy events there are often several participants taking on different roles and creating something more than their individual practices. At a broader macro level it can mean the ways in which whole communities use literacy. There are social rules about who can produce and use particular literacies, and we wish to examine this social regulation of texts. Shifting away from literacy as an individual attribute is one of the most important implications of a practice account of literacy, and one of the ways in which it differs most from more traditional accounts. The ways in which literacy acts as a resource for different sorts of groups is a central theme of later chapters in this book, which are devoted to how families, local communities and organisations regulate and are regulated by literacy practices.

Literacy practices are culturally constructed, and, like all cultural phenomena, they have their roots in the past. To understand contemporary literacy it is necessary to document the ways in which *literacy is historically situated*: literacy practices are as fluid, dynamic and changing as the lives and societies of which they are a part. We need a historical approach for an understanding of the ideology, culture and traditions on which current practices are based. The influences of one hundred years of compulsory schooling in Britain, or several centuries of organised religion, can be identified in the same way as influences from the past decade can be identified. These influences are located partly in the literacy practices themselves, complemented by family memories which go back to the beginning of the century and earlier. There is also a broader context of a cultural history of five thousand years of literacy in the world, and the ways in which this shapes contemporary practices.

A person's practices can be located also in their own history of literacy. In order to understand this we need to take a life history approach, observing the history within a person's life. There are several dimensions to this: people use literacy to make changes in their lives; literacy changes people and people find themselves in the contemporary world of changing literacy practices. The literacy practices an individual engages with change across their lifetime, as a result of changing demands, available resources and people's interests.

Related to the constructed nature of literacy, any theory of literacy implies a theory of learning. Literacy practices change, and new ones are frequently acquired through processes of informal learning and sense making as well as formal education and training. This learning takes place in particular social contexts, and part of this learning is the internalisation of social processes. It is therefore important to understand the nature of informal and vernacular learning strategies and the nature of situated cognition, linking with the work of researchers influenced by Lev Vygotsky, such as Sylvia Scribner, Jean Lave and colleagues (Scribner 1984; Lave and Wenger 1991). For this it is necessary to draw upon people's insights into how they learn, their theories about literacy and education, the vernacular strategies they use to learn new literacies. We start out from the position that people's understanding of literacy is an important aspect of their learning, and that people's theories guide their actions. It is here that a study of literacy practices has its most immediate links with education.

Studies of community literacy

The starting-points for our study are three distinct studies of literacy carried out in the 1970s, those of Shirley Brice Heath; Brian Street; and Sylvia Scribner and Michael Cole. In her well-known study Heath (1983) contrasted three Appalachian communities in the south-eastern United States in a study over several years which used ethnographic and sociolinguistic methods to provide detailed descriptions of people's uses of reading and writing in the home and the relationship of home practices to school practices. The sociolinguistic notion of literacy event is central to her work. Street (1984) studied Islamic villagers in Iran; he lived there as an anthropologist carrying out ethnographic fieldwork. He observed two literacies being used side by side in the community, one commercial and one not. He documents how the commercial literacy was taken up with the development of oil in the region, while the other more traditional literacy was not of value in that situation. Street utilises the idea of literacy practices and contributes the useful distinction between autonomous and ideological theories of literacy. Also developing the notion of literacy practices, Scribner and Cole (1981) studied literacy among the Vai of West Africa; these researchers used a battery of cross-cultural psychological tests, along with interviews and detailed observations of the community. Scribner and Cole contrast different literacies associated with three cultural traditions, Koranic, Western and indigenous, and they provide detailed descriptions of literacies which are learned informally and which exist outside the educational system.

The two terms which are the starting-point for the present work, literacy practices and literacy events, come from these earlier studies. In their separate ways these studies also show the value of detailed investigations of particular communities. Each of the studies is located in a different intellectual tradition with a distinct methodology: Heath's is primarily in sociolinguistics and education; Street comes from social anthropology and Scribner and Cole from cross-cultural psychology. The two terms, literacy practices and literacy events, therefore also come from different intellectual traditions. There may be some tension in combining them, and there is no reason to expect them to fit together in a neat and easy manner. To us events are empirical and observable; practices are more abstract and are inferred from events and from other cultural information.

Since these original studies, there have been several detailed studies in different parts of the world including Niko Besnier's study of Pacific islanders (1993) and Daniel Wagner's study of Arabic speakers in Morocco (1993). In the United States, studies have usually been of minority communities as in Moss (1994), often with a specific educational focus, as in Stephen Reder's work with Inuit, Hmong and Hispanic communities in the Pacific North-West (1987; 1994). In Britain, ethnographic research has primarily been on the uses of literacy in minority bilingual communities, including studies by Mukul Saxena (1991); Arvind Bhatt, David Barton, Marilyn Martin-Jones and Mukul Saxena (1996), Michael Baynham (1993) and Eve Gregory (1996). There is also a recent study of writing by participants in the Mass Observation Archive (Bloome, Sheridan and Street 1993). A study of community literacy in Australia is found in Breen *et al.* (1994). Several contemporary studies from South Africa are reported in Prinsloo and Breier (1996). Other research has been on the influence of specific social institutions, such as two studies of religious groups: Andrea Fishman's study of writing among the Amish of Pennsylvania (1988, 1991) and Cushla Kapitzke's study of Seventh-day Adventists in Northern Australia (1995). In addition, further studies of specific aspects of community uses of literacy are reported in Barton and Ivanic (1991), Hamilton, Barton and Ivanic (1994), Street (1993), Dubin and Kuhlman (1992).

These studies have in common the fact that they have focused primarily on the literacy practices of adults in their homes and communities, rather than investigating literacy in relation to children and their schools. Some ethnographic studies have been concerned primarily with children and their literacies at home and at school, such as Solsken (1993) and those reported in Schieffelin and Gilmore (1986). In addition, Luis Moll's work with Hispanics in the southern United States links up community practices and school practices (1994), contributing the notion of the 'funds of knowledge' which families and communities can draw upon. There have been further studies of literacy within families, focusing on parents and children, most notably those associated with Denny Taylor (Taylor 1983; 1996; 1997; Taylor and Dorsey-Gaines 1988). Studies of children's non-formal literacies in and out of school include work by Miriam Camitta (1993), Gemma Moss (1996) and Janet Maybin (1997). Studies of other domains, such as the work-place (Gowen 1992; Gee, Hull and Lankshear 1997), and ones which focus on particular aspects of life, or with particular historical periods, will be brought into the discussion where necessary. Together these studies provide a way of locating our work and a map of the field to which the current study contributes.

Theorising local social relations

The concept of community

Although most of the above studies are called studies of communities, there has been little discussion of this term in the literature on literacy (but see Heath 1995). The first point to make is that the term usually has positive connotations. As Raymond Williams puts it in a discussion of the word **community**, 'unlike all other terms of social organisation (state, nation, society, etc.) it seems never to be used unfavourably' (1976: 76). As a word which can have both positive and negative connotations we might add the term *family*. Williams was writing in 1976; since then the favourable connotations of the word community have been used by the British government, trying to name the much disliked poll tax the community charge, and with notions of community care and, in one of the rare uses of the term community in our data, that of a community policeman. We return to this later.

The original title of our research project was *Literacy in the Community*, using the word community in a general unanalysed sense. We are aware of the variety of meanings of the word community, its general positive connotations, the fact that the term implies homogeneity, and the problems of defining community boundaries. Despite these complexities it provides a useful starting-point. We initially defined our community in two ways: firstly in geographical terms, as a small town and as a neighbourhood within that town; and secondly in social class terms, as a working-class community. Soon we became aware of the complexity of the term as we contrasted community with family and with neighbourhood, and as we uncovered many *communities of interest* which cross geographical boundaries. In carrying out the research it was in fact useful not to have a precise definition of community at the beginning. Ideas on this developed during the study. We return to definitions of community in Chapter 14 and also contrast the term community with family, household and neighbourhood.

Community literacy is often taken to mean the literacy practices of minority communities, and most of the studies of literacy practices in Britain and North America have been of minority communities. Whilst the literacy practices of minority communities are of importance in themselves, community does not necessarily mean minority community. Often a contrast is made or implied with mainstream literacies. In these studies mainstream literacies, or the literacies of the researchers' own cultures and discourse communities, are often assumed and taken for granted; they are not seen as objects needing to be researched. Nor is the notion of mainstream defined clearly. Our study is of a mainly white working-class community, and it is our assumption that all social groups are part of communities.

The notion of community is enduring, and it remains useful for dealing with what Crow and Allan (1994) refer to as the realm of 'local social relations' which mediates between the private sphere of family and household and the public sphere of impersonal, formal organisations. Many of the literacy practices we describe in this book occur in this context of local social relations, and there is a constant movement of focus back and forth between private households, local community and the institutions of the wider public sphere, such as school and work-place. We want to explore these relationships.

Networks and roles

To describe how people relate within social groups we have drawn on the concept of **networks**. In the cookery example in Aside 1.2 the recipe was passed around a network of friends and relatives. Within such networks people take on specific roles and assert different identities as they participate in different literacy events. Our concern is to describe the social relationships which characterise literacy practices and the power and identity dimensions of these. The idea of networks is a first step in this. The strength of the notion of networks is that it provides a simple way of moving beyond a focus on individuals and individual encounters, towards one which shows how literacy links across people and localities. The significance of networks in the study of literacy is emphasised in the work of Arlene Fingeret (1983) and Linda Ziegahn (1991) in the United States. They have studied adult literacy students and the social networks they establish, paying particular attention to the different roles people take within such networks.

We utilise the idea of networks in several places. One of our informants, Harry, has a range of informal networks in his daily life. Another person, Shirley, uses private and public networks to get things done in the community. We can see networks in family life and in the workings of local organisations. During the research we have moved from a generalised idea of networks to a more differentiated one, distinguishing between different kinds 'of networks and their functions, seeing how some are more public, formal, official and structured than the more private and informal everyday networks (as discussed in Barton 1994: 42–3). We see in our research how networks have a function for people in many activities: in getting things done in groups, when finding out information, in providing mutual support. We utilise the concept in several chapters, gradually developing a more complex view. In addition, we see how networks can also involve coercion and exclusion, and can be normative and controlling. Network, like community, is a cosy and beguiling word, but closely structured local social relations can also be oppressive, disruptive or resistant to individuals' needs for change. This arises, for instance, with family resistance when people have wanted to return to education, and with one of our informants, Eddie, and his membership of gangs. We see ways in which networks have negative aspects as well as positive ones, and they can be constraining as well as supportive.

Within the home there are unequal power relations, including those between adults and young children. More generally in society there are inequalities, such as those associated with social class and gender. These structure people's participation in literacy events. There are also issues concerning adults who are labelled as having problems with literacy. In addition, many of people's activities are related to social institutions where literacy is located in formal hierarchies: this is true of institutions such as schools, religion, the welfare system and the legal system. Literacy between equals is just one sort of literacy. It is necessary to develop ways of incorporating the unequal nature of many social relations into understandings of literacy. This also includes the relationship between researcher and those being researched.

Stephen Reder and Karen Reed Wikelund's notion of 'practice engagement theory' (Reder and Wikelund 1993; Reder 1994) is helpful in accounting for the fact that participants may engage with literacy practices in different – and often unequal – ways. They use notions of domains of practice, roles and participant structures. They identify three aspects of literacy practices: technology, function and social meaning, and they suggest that people may engage with any or all of these three aspects in a particular literacy event. They define social meanings as 'beliefs about who should engage in a particular literacy practice, in what situations and under what circumstances – that is, the propriety of participation – as well as the social distinctions marked by use of literacy in a particular context (Reder and Wikelund 1993: 179).

If literacy is often located in unequal social relationships, this inequality is most apparent in the access to literacy resources which people have. The idea of access is therefore related to the important concepts of control and power. We discuss these later under the heading of the 'social regulation of texts', a phrase used by Gemma Moss (1996) and implicit in Dorothy Smith's work on the constitutive role of texts in social institutions (1988). Literacy practices involve the social regulation of texts, that is who has access to them and who can produce them. The resources people have access to can be seen in terms of technical skills and equipment, as well as sites and supports for learning. These may be institutionally based or informal. Resources consist of physical resources as well as people (see Giddens 1984), and include collective or shared resources for literacy in households, neighbourhoods and publicly available in the community more generally, such as in bookshops, libraries, educational institutions, advice centres for dealing with bureaucracies and other literacy-related problems. The notion of discourse communities, mentioned earlier, is useful here: a given person may or may not have access to membership of such groups and their discourse.

Literacy is often treated as functional, something people use to get things done in their lives. A social view of literacy extends the notion of literacy by including other facets of the cultural practices of literacy. A first extension is that identified by Kathleen Rockhill (1987; 1993) and by Jennifer

Horsman (1990; 1994), who point out the emotional dimensions of literacy. They discuss how literacy constitutes both desire in the lives of women returning to education and threat to the men in their lives. We broaden this and identify other ways in which literacy represents threat and desire in people's lives. A simple example is that threat and desire come through the letter box in the morning: the opening of mail in the mornings can be experienced as threatening as people deal with bills; other letters, in the form of love letters and consumer catalogues, can also embody dreams, fantasy and desire. Niko Besnier (1993) has shown how written texts can encode emotion just as strongly as it is expressed in face-to-face interactions. Often in our discussions, people express other strong feelings about literacy, including disapproval, triumph, control or mastery, stigma, fear; the subject is charged with emotion. In order to talk about literacy people tell us about their *ruling passions*, and this has become an important organising concept in analysing people's interviews.

The bureaucratic, record-keeping functions of literacy have been frequently identified by others, for example, by Goody (1986). We can extend this by identifying ways in which literacy has other public functions, the many ways in which it is used as evidence, evidence of being educated or qualified, of being a certain sort of person, of belonging to particular social groups. Related to this, literacy is often used as display, for example when wearing logos on clothes, and as ritual, where it has a role in events such as seasonal celebrations, competitions and marking achievements. As well as having a legal function, the uses of signing ceremonies at weddings, in political treaties and business deals also have huge ritual and symbolic significance.

All these observations show that there are many different ways of engaging with literacy beyond a utilitarian functionalism, that as well as being active readers and writers, people can be passively incorporated into literacy practices, as when free advertising is put through the letter box or they carry home their shopping in plastic bags emblazoned with supermarket logos. Throughout this book we offer examples of the many different ways in which people engage with literacy.

Theories of culture

Social theory

Literacy studies is essentially an interdisciplinary endeavour, and in the process of articulating what is really an aspect of a theory of culture we have become aware of parallel concerns elsewhere in the social sciences. From a variety of different starting-points, many social scientists are aiming to redefine the relationship between the individual and the social, developing new concepts to express the links between the micro interactions which make up experience of everyday life and the large-scale social formations which shape and are shaped by this local realm. Depending on whether they start from the micro world of social interactions and discourse or the macro world of social institutions and global change, different disciplines have elaborated different parts of the relationship between action and structure.

The sociological and historical approaches of theorists such as Giddens (1991) and Foucault (1972; 1977) start from social systems and the ways in which social practices are structured and regulated through particular configurations of knowledge and power. What these perspectives can contribute to literacy studies is an understanding of how to locate the notion of literacy practices within more general social practices and processes of social change, how these are constituted in specific social institutions and, in turn, how people's sense of personal identity is shaped by them.

A very clear description of how concepts from Foucault's theory can be applied to literacy practices in one domain is given by Cushla Kapitzke (1995: 8–20) in her discussion of the religious practices of Seventh-day Adventists. She draws particularly on the notions of 'discursive formations' and the 'disciplinary techniques' that are used to enforce social rules in everyday life. She shows how these can be helpful in revealing the broad and persistent patterns which underlie the local details of literacy practices and how people make sense of them. We can see the relevance of these concepts in the interpretation of our own data, although our own starting-point is rather different in that we are looking at the interface of a range of dominant discourses of literacy with the vernacular, rather than focusing on practices in one dominant domain as Kapitzke does.

Another perspective on our work is provided by theories of language and discourse which pay attention to social theory, such as Norman Fairclough's elaboration of critical discourse analysis (1989), Gunther Kress's social semiotic theory (Kress and Hodge 1988) and the work of both James Gee (1990; 1992) and Jay Lemke (1995) on discourse and social processes. As mentioned earlier, literacy studies contributes to such work by its emphasis on analysing practices as well as analysing texts, and by providing practical ways of doing this. More generally it can contribute to social theory by emphasising the importance of written texts in the discursive formations of powerful institutions (as in Smith 1988; 1993).

Media and cultural studies

A further area in relation to which we locate our study of print literacy is recent ethnographic work on the use of other media and technologies, such as television, video and computers in the home. New perspectives on literacy are suggested by these investigations of the social and cultural contexts in which communication media function. For example, taking reading in a broad sense, Gray (1992) points out that there are continuities in people's reading preferences and habits across the media: women's viewing of television, film and video genres echoes their consumption of print texts. Media studies research in an ethnographic tradition also examines the way different media are used together, or complement each other, and how their use is structured in the home by domestic routines, priorities and technologies. Such research looks at leisure patterns, how these are changing and how they are structured by, for example, gender or employment. It asks how and why adults regulate children's behaviour.

In parallel with literacy research, ethnographic audience research debates the relationship between mass-produced media texts, the reader (or viewer) and the context of viewing, and it identifies active, differentiated readers who construct meaning and appropriate texts according to different social contexts and cultural knowledges (as in Morley 1992: 15–16). This has included how readers react to and interpret texts, not just analysis of the text itself (see Radway 1987). Reading and writing can be viewed as extensions of people's identities, interests and roles, as James Lull (1988) has discussed with reference to family viewing of mass media.

Whilst we find many useful parallels, comparisons between literacy studies and media studies also reveal the limitations of each: mass media research has tended to focus mostly on viewing, not producing, and only in the context of leisure. Few parallels with writing, such as popular production of video, photography, local radio participation or CB use, have been studied. Because the mass media are largely consumed in the domestic environment, media research has been fascinated by home life and by the behaviour of adult viewers as well as children. Studies of print literacy, on the other hand, have focused largely on educational contexts and children's learning.

The public narrative on literacy

One motivation for developing new views of literacy has been many researchers' unease with more traditional characterisations of literacy, both academically and in public and educational debate. More complex views have developed out of dissatisfaction with purely psychological characterisations of reading and writing as autonomous skills. One feature of this developing field is the way it is moving beyond ideas of literacy as something solely located in people's heads as cognition. These studies contribute to ways of talking about literacy which properly acknowledge its situated nature and therefore offer the possibility of representing the multiplicities of literacies which exist in any culture. Potentially these studies can contribute to public and educational debate by providing an alternative discourse of literacy.

However, much public discussion and political debate still draws upon and supports simplistic views of literacy which treat it as an autonomous skill. The media narrative on literacy is an autonomous one, focusing largely on methods of teaching and learning and attributing blame. We wish to challenge this narrative. We refer to it deliberately as a narrative. It is a way of talking about literacy but it is more than just a particular set of words or a particular discourse. It is a narrative in that is a continuing story of literacy, told over several years and which each newspaper article, radio commentary and television interview contributes to. In the media narrative on literacy the autonomous view of literacy usually provides the framing of what are regarded as possible or reasonable questions to pose and it limits what might be possible answers.

There are many recurrent themes within this narrative. There are debates about declining standards, fuelled by surveys of problems and failures, where correlations are turned into causalities. There is an obsession with teaching methods, polarised as phonics versus real books, and with the blaming of teachers; and endemic in much media discussion of family literacy is the blaming of parents. There are fears of a decline in reading, of new technologies and of their effects on the culture of the book. Deborah Cameron (1995) and others refer to such fears as 'moral panics'. The interest in new technologies is fuelled by a sense of anxiety as well as one of possibility, but it is often simplistically defined in terms of negative effects, the dangers to children and the effects on education practice and on reading and book buying.

The issues raised by these debates can be considered in a new light by taking on the perspectives offered by the social practices account of literacy. We intend that our work should feed into public discussions and educational discussions. For example, our approach assumes that children's progress in achieving literacy is strongly influenced by the cultural and linguistic experience they bring into school from their lives at home and in their local community. Detailed ethnographic accounts can identify the many ways in which reading and writing are used and valued outside of educational contexts – or ignored for more highly valued alternatives; at the same time such accounts demonstrate the need to understand more fully the ways in which adults make use of literacy, providing the models and support that initiate children into literacy practices.

Within the field of education there is a new willingness to look across the boundaries of formal educational institutions, schools and colleges, to understand informal learning strategies and the resources which people draw on in their lives outside of education, recognising that schools are just one specialised context in which literacy is used and learned. Ideas about lifelong learning, flexible and open learning and notions of critical pedagogy which consider the role of formal education within its broader cultural and political context all have implications for the study of literacy.

A final root of this study is a concern with educational opportunities for adults to develop their literacy. Another study based at Lancaster (Hamilton and Stasinopoulos 1987) used very different methods to pursue this issue. This research analysed computer data from a large-scale longitudinal study of a sample of the population of Britain, the National Child Development Study. The research focused on self-reported difficulties with reading, writing and numeracy. The study provided a national overview of reading and writing problems which people perceived to be important in their everyday lives. Its breadth provides a useful context for the detailed ethnographic approach utilised here. It was a concern with adult literacy, with how adults with difficulties in reading and writing are portrayed in the media, compared with our first-hand knowledge of their diversity and strengths, and with the paucity of educational provision for adults which originally motivated our interest in the field.

2

LOCATING LITERACIES IN TIME AND SPACE

(1) A history of literacy in Lancaster

A time and a place: Lancaster, England

Literacy events are located in time and space. Reading and writing are things which people do, either alone or with other people, but always in a social context – always in a place and at a time. To make sense of people's literacy practices we need to situate them within this context. When Cliff Holt or Mumtaz Patel (these names are pseudonyms – see Aside 4.3) or any of the other people we interviewed walk to the library, they walk through a town which has roots going back two thousand years, whose city centre streets were laid out in medieval times. They set out from Victorian houses, and in visiting the library they go to an institution established in Lancaster in the eighteenth century and whose practices date back much further. We want to explore these details of people's literacy lives later in the book. First, we need to situate them in a place, Lancaster, and in a time, the 1990s. In this chapter we will provide some historical details of literacy in Lancaster in earlier times. In the next chapter we provide general description of Lancaster today from the point of view of our interest in literacy, including details of the main institutions associated with local literacies.

There are many Lancasters throughout the world and, according to an article on the front page of the *Lancaster Guardian* about planning a millennium event, there are nineteen Lancasters in the United States. This includes Lancaster, Pennsylvania (where the study of Amish literacy mentioned earlier was carried out). In Britain the name Lancaster evokes the Wars of the Roses, the incomprehensible government post of *Chancellor of the Duchy of Lancaster*, Burt Lancaster, the Lancaster Bomber. To a language teacher in Tokyo or Kuala Lumpur it may be known primarily as a university. It is also the name of a brand of cosmetics. Lancaster hosted the famous trial and execution of the Pendle Witches in 1612, when the city was still the judicial and legal centre for the surrounding region. (Note that we use the words 'town' and 'city' interchangeably when describing Lancaster.) It achieved momentary national notoriety in the early 1980s for being the site of the grisly handless corpse trial, additional atmosphere for the court case deriving from its location in a medieval castle on a hill.

Three decades earlier another celebrated court case was that of Buck Ruxton, a local doctor, who murdered his wife and his housekeeper in 1935. One older resident we talked to had a certain pride in having had such a colourful character as his family doctor.

There is evidence that the Lancaster area has been inhabited since the end of the last Ice Age, around twelve thousand years ago. The earliest writing which has endured includes Latin inscriptions on milestones and dedication stones dating from AD 100. They were left by the Romans, who established a garrison and river crossing here in the north-west of England on the narrow flatlands between the Pennine hills and the coast. They built the castle and a settlement on the banks of the River Lune. The Romans named the city as the castle on the Lune – although, contrary to popular local belief, the name of the river comes not from the Latin for moon but from the Welsh word 'llawn' meaning 'full', another clue from the past to the origins of the town. The language of the Romans, Latin, is still a compulsory subject for twelve-year-olds at the boys' Grammar School, and it has a role in the city today on gravestones, inscriptions and school mottoes.

The castle was rebuilt in Norman times and extended in the Middle Ages. It is now partly a prison and partly a tourist attraction, and can be seen from much of the city. The Duke of Lancaster became King Henry IV of England at the end of the fourteenth century, and the ensuing Wars of the Roses were between the royal houses of Lancaster and York. Lancaster was, and is, the Red Rose city. People still grow red roses in their small front gardens, and schoolboys wear a red rose on their school blazers.

The town became the legal and business centre of the county. It also became and has remained a market town, selling produce from the surrounding rural areas and providing goods and services in return. Lancaster had always been a small port using the river for local trade, and this encouraged many local industries to develop. In 1688 there were six companies of tradesmen registered in crafts ranging from plumbing, leather work and metalwork to weavers, carpenters, rope makers and dyers. In the mid-eighteenth century the port expanded, and raw materials were imported from North America, the West Indies and the Baltic, including hardwoods and cotton for local industries.

William Stout of Lancaster, 1665–1752

A glimpse of the literacy practices of one person in Lancaster three hundred years ago is provided in the autobiography written by William Stout, a local tradesman who kept a diary throughout his life. It is unusual to have a first-hand account of everyday life three hundred years ago, and we offer this as one point in Lancaster's history which may help us visualise the continuities between then and now. We have been through William Stout's autobiography, noting all references to reading and writing, and using this information to build up a picture of his literacy practices. The quotations are taken from Marshall (1967), who has kept the original spelling but has added punctuation. In the opening lines of the autobiography William Stout locates himself in terms of a family tree, a practice that is still popular today:

> *In the beginning of a booke with a parchment cover, of this size and volume, I entered the names of my father and mother, brothers and sisters, and their sevrall marriages and habitations and children, and all their ancestors, so farr as I had certaine information.*

Many of his references to reading and writing concern his education and that of his family. These are collected in Aside 2.1. Though his mother was illiterate, his parents ensured he had an education. The free school which he attended was the forerunner of the current boys' Grammar School (now a selective secondary school entered at age eleven), attended by some of our informants. The first reference to reading and writing outside of education was when his father on his deathbed drew his family around him and recited quotes from the Bible to them, *exhortations which he caused me to put in writing.*

Stout describes reading and writing in his daily life, including at work: . . . *in the shop, where, when out of necessary business, I passed my time in reading; or improving myselfe in arethmatick, survighing or other mathamatikall sciences, which I was most naturally inclined to. And made some progress in more than my present station required, but was of some service upon some occasions afterwards.*

He describes his religious life, including a record of the establishment and persecution of the Quakers. He was impressed with the Quakers he met and he therefore *retired much and read, and meditated in the scriptures of truth.* And as a result of this reading and meditation, although he was aware that it might count against him in terms of business contacts, he became a Quaker. His diary contains much detail of Quaker life in Lancaster and oppression by the government and the established church. He records in 1681 how William Penn established Pennsylvania and how many Quakers in Lancaster took the opportunity to move there and set up farms. At one point the mayor of Lancaster locked the door of the meeting house and impounded the goods of Quakers. Although this intensified the resolve of some to stay, many others went. It may well be that Stout knew some of these people who moved to the new world and established Lancaster, Pennsylvania.

There are many references to Stout's business trade with America, importing sugar, tobacco and other goods, including trade with Philadelphia. He describes a range of work-place literacy practices. In the fourth month of each year (presumably at the end of the financial year) he made an estimate of his effects and worked out what he had gained or lost over the year. He also corresponded to keep up his business of buying and selling merchandise. *At my beginning I was too credulos and too slow in caling, and seldom made use of atturney, except to write letters to urge payments, always being tender of oppressing*

Aside 2.1 Learning to read and write in the seventeenth century

Our parents were very careful to get us learning to read as we came of age and capacity, first at a dame schoole and after at the free schoole at Boulton [Bolton-le-sands]. *But my sister was eaarly confined to waite on her brother, more than she was well able . . . But our sister was early taught to read, knit and spin, and also needlework . . . As to my selfe and brothers, as we attained seven years of age we were sent to the free schoole at Boulton . . . till I was 14 years old . . . As we attained to the age of ten or twelve years, we were very much taken off the schoole, espetialy in the spring and summer season, plow time, turfe time, hay time and harvest, in looking after the sheep, helping at plough, going to the moss with carts, making hay and shearing in harvest, two of us at 13 or 14 years of age being equall to one man shearer; so that we made smal progress in Latin, for what we got in winter we forgot in summer, and the writing master coming to Boulton mostly in winter, wee got what writing we had in winter . . .my father minded to get me constantly to schoole to get learning in order to be placed to some trade or other imployment.*

In the spring of the year 1678 my father took me to the schoole at Hearsom [Heversham] *in Westmorland, where Thomas Lodge, a native of Boulton and our kinsman, then taught; and then reputied the best schoole and master in these north parts . . . I continued at that school till the 10th month 1679, at what time the said schoole master removed to Lancaster to the master of the free schoole there. I made some progress in the Lattin there, and was entring for the Greek grammer, but I was not so forward in learning the Lattin and Greek as many of my age might; my genius, as they tearme it, not leading me that way. Nor did I make any great progress in writing, although much taught, by reason I was naturaly left handed, and could not be steady in my right hand; and then it was suposed that one could not learn to write legably with the left hand, which was a mistake, for I have seen much writing with the left hand as perfect and regular as any right hand writing. And I would tell any who has left handed children to teach them to write with that hand if they intend that they should write fine, in order to be clarks or booke keepers to merchants.*

The two months next before my father's death, I continued to learn at Lancaster Schoole under the aforesaid master, Thomas Lodge, and for three weeks after my father's death I went to a scrivener, to learn to write, half, and the other to arethmatick. As for writing I made not much improvement; but in half that time I got so good an entrance into arethmatick that by my industry I made good progress in it, without any instruction other than books; my inclinations always leading to the learning arethmatick, surveying and the mathematicks.

(Marshall 1967: 68–74)

poor people . . . He took on apprentices, and took responsibility for their education, sending one *to the free schoole for at least fower years, and he learned well to the entring into Greek, and could write well.*

As executor for a friend, John Johnson, he took responsibility for the education of Johnson's children *and borded them out and kept them to the schoole – Edward to Latin, writing and arethmatick till he was about 15 years of age, and then designed him for some shop trade.* The daughter, Margret, stayed at home at first, *she was a good reader, and could repeat whole chapters in the New Testament, off book* (i.e. by heart). Later, she *was kept to schoole to write, sawe, knot and other nessesary imploy . . . till she was about sixteen years of age . . . And soon after she writt to me that I might not expect her return.*

In examining this autobiography we can see the importance of literacy in someone's life two hundred years before the coming of compulsory schooling. There is evidence of a range of practices related to school, religion, work and everyday life. The account touches on themes still relevant today, such as the relationship between literacy, schooling and employment, the gendered patterns of reading and writing, and theories about literacy learning.

The nineteenth century

By the 1820s, if we move forward a hundred years, Lancaster was in decline as a port since more accessible ports such as Liverpool and Manchester were nearby. Lancaster still maintained its position at the centre of transport networks. In 1797 a canal running north to south was opened, and in the next half century mills were built along the canal. The mills were owned by James Williamson and the Storey brothers, and they were used for the manufacture of cotton for table baize and oilcloth. Factories were also built alongside the river. On the basis of the wealth from the mills Williamson's son, who became Lord Ashton, built the Ashton memorial which overlooks the city from the east. The country's main west coast road between London and Scotland, the A6, went through the centre of Lancaster. The railway came in the nineteenth century linking London and Scotland, and the M6 motorway in the mid-twentieth century. The Ashton memorial is the glimpse of Lancaster which drivers get from the motorway. With road, railway, canal and motorway the city has always been part of the western route north, and issues of transportation and traffic through the city are as much a part of the local agenda as they have been for maybe hundreds of years.

During the latter half of the nineteenth century Lancaster underwent considerable expansion as its industries grew and prospered. The town expanded eastwards towards the moorlands with rows of tightly packed stone-built Victorian terraced houses built up the hillsides for the manufacturing and cotton workers. These form distinct neighbourhoods; one of these, which we refer to as Springside, is the site of our case studies. Villages to the north and the south were incorporated into the city's boundaries. In the twentieth century Lancaster continued to grow, with new areas of housing being built.

The turn of the twentieth century is important in terms of literacy, as people born then were often the first generation to have had formal schooling. Aside 2.2 provides recollections about reading and writing from an oral history study of people born at this time.

Aside 2.2 Everyday literacy at the beginning of the twentieth century

This is a summary of what we learned about literacy practices from an oral history study of working-class people born around the turn of the century in Lancaster and neighbouring districts. (The interviews were carried out and transcribed by Elizabeth Roberts as part of a larger oral history study (Roberts 1984); further details on literacy are in Barton 1988.)

Firstly, the people interviewed had all been to school and could read and write to some extent; they were a schooled generation. However, often their parents were not literate. They give sympathetic accounts of their parents' abilities and do not attach any particular stigma towards their parents' illiteracy; it was explained in terms of their lack of opportunity of schooling. Often one parent was remembered as literate but not the other, and some respondents were not sure whether or not their parents were literate; some recall reading to their parents from books or newspapers.

Most homes had few books; typically these were the Bible and other religious books. Religion usually had a central role in people's upbringing, and this was an important context for literacy. If they had more books, they recalled themselves or their parents reading novels, biography and technical information books. Sometimes these were received as Christmas presents; often they were Sunday School prizes:

> *Of course, when you did get a Sunday School prize you took the trouble to read it because it had taken you twelve months to acquire it . . . they were always on about this demon drink, what happened to urchins who sat outside on the front doorstep while their parents were drinking and now they were deprived of shoes on their feet, then how the lad vowed he would never drink, sort of like turn again Dick Whittington. All the books that you got were like that.*

Libraries were used extensively, and there were several in the town. As well as the public library, there were private libraries which made a small charge. These were located in shops or the post office, Sunday School or work-place. However, one woman remembers her mother's hostility to the library:

> *My mother didn't agree with libraries, you got germs. You weren't allowed to join the library.*

People also bought books second-hand, borrowed from each other and exchanged books at a stall in the local market, something which still exists today.

> *You could get quite good paperback books from the market. I can remember that if you went for them the boy had a big long handle and a tin scoop and the book came on that and you put your money in the scoop. They had them on all the market stalls then.*

Newspapers featured prominently in their homes – often people took a national morning paper and a local evening paper. Significantly, they did not count newspaper reading as reading – real reading involves books. Sometimes one member of the family regularly read out to the others from the paper. Although they took both national and local papers, the topics people recalled reading in the papers were sometimes national such as *where the troops were in the Boer War*, more usually local news was mentioned: births, deaths and marriages, the weather forecast etc.

> *Got Daily Mail in morning, Evening Mail at night. Sunday paper. With Dad being in bed we used to try and get the paper ourselves and you'd go creeping up the hall and he'd know what the time was and you'd be standing there reading the paper and he'd shout 'Fetch that paper up'. He knew very well what time it was and he had to have the paper first. You couldn't have a bit of the paper until he'd read it. We used to be saying 'Have you finished with the middle yet?' 'Have you finished with the outside?' You used to read it like that, the front and the back and the inside so that we could dole that piece out.*

With books, magazines and papers available, there was certainly reading in many childhood homes. This can be contrasted with the very little amount of writing that is reported. It was hardly mentioned, and what writing there was was very functional. It was also noticeable that who counted as a good writer was someone who wrote neatly:

I used to be a good writer at one time! In them days it was two fingers on your pen. The teacher would hit you if you only had one finger on your pen. The down stroke had to be thick. You had to do it properly!

Neatness was all that counted, and there is no mention of the processes of writing such as composing. One image which came over strongly is that some people are born writers: either you were or you were not *a writer*.

When and what did people read? Reading was construed as a leisure activity, and many people reported that their parents did not have time to read, except maybe on a Sunday. The rest of the week when not at work or school parents and children were busy with housework. One woman in a family of nine children recalled her sister being *a reader* and neglecting household chores. Reading was not work but it was better than doing nothing:

If there was anything to do we had to do it rather than read, but she would rather we read than did nothing. But she didn't make it a priority.

A recurrent theme in people's recollections was that their parents controlled what, where and when they read. Newspapers, especially Sunday papers, were heavily censored in the childhood home. Sometimes all books were vetted, but more often particular types of books were acceptable, such as only religious books or most novels, and certainly not comics. Library books were vetted and even returned to the library if they were deemed unsuitable. Children responded spiritedly in what must be universals of literacy – they hid books and they read in the two places of privacy in the Western family, the toilet and under the bed covers.

In the social aspects of literacy, one common phenomenon was the asymmetry of abilities and how this affected the roles people took. Firstly, within the family, people often recalled one parent being able to read and write but not the other. Often it was only the father who read, but sometimes it was the mother. When only one person was literate, this person would take on roles which needed literacy:

Q: *Did you know a lot of old people who couldn't read or write?*
A: *None of them could. I used to go and read the letters for many a one in Hindpool. They were old married women.*
Q: *Did your mother write letters for them?*
A: *She did for all of us. Any letters that were written m'mother always wrote them because she was a beautiful writer, she used to do lovely writing.*

Sometimes people recalled that they used to read to their non-literate parents. Often it was mentioned that a non-literate person had other skills, such as numeracy.

Q: *Why did your mother never go to school?*
A: *I think they had to pay to go to school and it was probably too expensive. She couldn't read, she couldn't write but reckon money up you couldn't beat her. You couldn't have diddled her out of a ha'penny.*

They often learned to read and write from each other, with relatives, with neighbours, at work, in church. One person recalls her father, a postmaster, actually teaching his customers to write:

My father taught lots of people to read. When the old aged pension first started [in 1909] *a lot of them couldn't write so he taught a lot of his customers just to write their names so they could sign their pension book.*

The significance of literacy for these people was that it helped them in their everyday lives. They valued literacy where they could see a use for it:

They tried to make me read but I didn't see it any good to me, but now I miss it. I should have done. I quite agree, learn what you can while you're young, and this is where I tripped up. If I'd have known the world was going to go as fast I would have been different today to what I am. Learn while you can, it's a fool that doesn't.

They did not particularly talk about literacy in relation to their jobs and they did not attribute having jobs to literacy. The modern gloss we would put on it was that their literacy was functional, but that it also enabled them to cope with change, and go beyond their current lives. Nevertheless, there was an ambivalence towards the power of literacy. It is a form of exploration; it is exciting but dangerous:

it runs in my mind that they were putting things into your head because they weren't in our class.

if you started reading books, where would it all end!

Aside 2.3 Literacy rates in the eighteenth and nineteenth centuries

Historical evidence about literacy is based on public records such as the signing of marriage registers and the sales of publications. Statistics are produced which are then used to make generalisations about literacy rates in communities or geographical areas. Although the validity of using measures such as signatures can be questioned, they can nevertheless be used to discuss differences between communities or changes over time. (See discussion of this *nominal* literacy in Vincent, 1989.) The limitations of the data and the patterns they reveal inevitably lead to questions about the social basis of literacy.

The requirement that all people getting married should sign the marriage register dates from 1754. Before that, data on literacy rates is less reliable, but it is still based on signature evidence. National figures for England and Wales suggest that in 1714, at the time of William Stout, 40 per cent of men and 25 per cent of women were literate. The mid-eighteenth century appears to have been a time of accelerating literacy in the north of England, especially among the commercial classes, to which Stout belonged, rather than among industrial workers. In the second half of the eighteenth century literacy rates actually declined in manufacturing towns, while in other places it was still rising. This reflects the population growth and shifts accompanying industrialisation.

Literacy rates, as measured by signatures on marriage registers, were rising throughout the nineteenth century, and a large percentage of the population had some basic literacy even before the introduction of compulsory schooling. The rates varied according to geographical location and type of community. The strongest link is with occupation; there are large gender differences, but also variation due to family culture and individual interest and predilection. By the mid-nineteenth century, in the years before compulsory schooling was introduced in the 1870s,

History of education

The history of literacy in Lancaster is a particular instance of literacy in Britain, a particular mixture of more general influences of schools, churches, libraries, and adult institutes. These are some of the more tangible of the institutions which have contributed to local literacies in Lancaster. However, the literacy of home and community is also influenced by additional literacies, ones deriving from the activities of local clubs, trade unions and associations. It is these latter which we will be focusing on in some later chapters, and the mix of local literacies will become more apparent as we provide examples of the lives of individual people.

literacy rates were substantial and increasing, although they still show disparities between women and men.

Percentage of people signing the marriage register in Lancaster (figures in parentheses are for England and Wales as a whole)

	Men	Women	All
1856	77	63	70 (65)
1866	85	77	81 (74)
1871	84	81	82 (77)

The figures for children's attendance at school, however, seem to be systematically lower than these adult literacy rates. In Lancaster in 1851, out of a population of 14,604 children aged five to fourteen years, 13 per cent were registered in day schools and 18 per cent in Sunday Schools. Day school attendance was higher than the average for Lancashire (10.6 per cent) and slightly higher than the national average of 11.7 per cent. The proportion of children attending schools in Lancaster at this time was, therefore, much lower than the proportion of the adult population who were literate enough to sign the marriage register. (School attendance rates are common measures of literacy internationally.)

Although we do not have detailed data for Lancaster, figures for the county show that in 1851 64 per cent of children attending school were registered in Church of England day schools. A further 24 per cent were in Dissenting schools and 12 per cent in Catholic schools. If we look at the figures for Sunday Schools, Dissenters are in the majority (57 per cent) while 37 per cent were attending Church of England Sunday Schools and 5 per cent were attending Catholic ones.

All figures are taken from Stephens (1987).

The development of formal education in Lancaster has been affected by the changing legal framework in Britain as a whole. This has been played out in Lancaster in a particular way according to its specific development. Until the end of the nineteenth century when state involvement began, education was either funded by endowments from wealthy citizens or sponsored by churches. One of the earliest schools in Lancaster, the Free School, set up under the terms of the will of a former mayor of the town in 1472, and attended by William Stout, was the forerunner of the present-day boys' Grammar School. It provided basic education for boys who had already learned to read and write from private tutors. Another was the George Fox

School, established as the Friends' School before 1690 and associated with the Quaker movement. (This closed in 1988.) Tutors and private academies also existed although little remains of them. Many of these 'dame schools' were run by women in their own homes and were often short-lived. In the eighteenth century a boys' and a girls' Charity School also existed to educate and train poorer boys and girls; girls were trained for domestic service and boys were apprenticed to a trade at the age of fourteen years.

More and more schools gradually opened in the second half of the nineteenth century with the help of charitable societies such as the British and Foreign Schools Society (BFSS) and the National Society. Although the school reform acts of the 1870s made universal schooling possible, Lancaster did not elect a School Board until it became compulsory in 1893. Lancaster became a Local Education Authority in 1902, again as a result of national legislation. This part of a general pattern whereby developments in public services in Lancaster, particularly those relevant to women, occurred in response to legislation from central government, rather than from local initiative (Winstanley 1993). The girls' Grammar School, which some of the women we interviewed attended, was not founded until 1907.

By 1982 Lancaster had fourteen primary schools, including three Catholic ones, and seven secondary schools. Although grammar schools were turned into comprehensives in most parts of the country in the 1960s and 1970s, the city held on to them until they were back in favour when the Conservatives returned to government in 1979. In 1990 new government legislation allowed the schools to vote to opt out of local authority control and become maintained by grants from central government, and both grammar schools did this in 1990. There are also a number of private schools around Lancaster, but these did not feature at all in the lives of the people we interviewed, none of whom had the means to pay for their own or their children's education.

Apart from the two single-sex grammar schools, the schools in Lancaster are mixed. Around half the schools are religious, some being Church of England and others being Catholic. The result in Lancaster is a strange historically induced amalgam of single-sex grammar schools along with religious schools which in their prospectuses specify the criteria by which places will be allocated to families of different religious persuasions. The religious basis of schools makes school choice fraught for Muslim, Quaker and atheist alike, as our interviewee Mumtaz found. (See Chapter 10.)

Less visible are the opportunities for children to get extra classes outside of formal schooling. The voluntary Dyslexia Association provides extra support for children who have problems with their reading and writing. A tutoring agency provides private coaching for children. A mosque provides after-school classes for Muslim children, as described in Chapter 10. There are schools of dancing and music, theatre groups and sports organisations where children can pursue these activities beyond what is offered at school.

Children can leave school at the age of sixteen and many go on to take vocational courses at the College of Further Education.

If we turn to the education of adults, we find that Lancaster was one of the first towns to establish a Mechanics Institute (see White 1993: 174–76). It began in 1823 with proposals to open a library and reading room. One of the mill owners, Sir Thomas Storey, enlarged it and reopened it as the Storey Institute in 1891, housing a Technical School, School of Art, Public Library, Museum and Art Gallery and News Room. Students could attend both day and evening classes. This was the forerunner of the College of Further Education and the College of Adult Education, both of which still exist. In the 1970s, as part of a national campaign, the adult college began providing classes for adults with problems in reading and writing. These were free and offered a range of provision, including small classes and individual tuition at the college or in people's homes, often using volunteer tutors (see Hamilton 1996). Private training and tuition are also provided in Lancaster. In 1990 one such college, Victoria College, offered courses in office- and business-based skills including typing and word processing; another, Lindow Tutors, offered private tuition in a number of subjects for both adults and children.

In 1963 a Church-of-England-based teacher training college was founded, and in 1964 Lancaster University was opened; this occupies a purpose-built campus in the countryside three miles south of the city. It employs around two thousand people. In 1990 its student population was 6,300 and by 1996 it was over ten thousand. It has many different sorts of link with the town. As well as students and academics from the rest of Britain and from other countries who move to the town, local people go to the university as mature students. Many students are tenants of Lancaster and Morecambe landlords and landladies. The university is also a source of employment for many people, both short-term and long-term, as secretaries, print operators, porters and labourers. These links were mentioned frequently in our interviews. For example, one of our interviewees, Patrick, commented, *I did a few years at the university – not studying, like, but building it.*

Lancaster has a long unbroken historical tradition which shapes the literacy practices that people engage in. New traditions have also entered as the population changes, new groups enter and employment patterns change. Traditions from Lancaster have also been carried out to other places, as when the Quaker refugees set up new communities in North America, taking their traditions and religious beliefs with them though the roots of these may be invisible. We can already begin to see in Lancaster a microcosm of change and continuity in literacy practices, which is happening on a wider scale all around us.

LOCATING LITERACIES IN TIME AND SPACE

(2) Lancaster today

Lancaster today

Traces of the past exist today in the sort of houses people live in, the land they own, the jobs they do and the practices they engage in. In Lancaster the physical layout of the city centre is not unlike that in the Middle Ages. The nineteenth century leaves its imprint where the junior school still has a separate boy's entrance and girl's entrance etched in stone above the doorways. In outlying villages buildings which were libraries or men's reading rooms can still be found by the enquiring tourist.

The city itself has a population of around fifty thousand people, which rises to one hundred thousand if neighbouring areas such as Morecambe are included. At the beginning of 1990 the official unemployment rate in the Lancaster area was around nine per cent, similar to the rest of the north-west of England as a whole and around 2 per cent higher than the national figure. These figures hide pockets of extreme poverty, however, and one area of Morecambe had the highest unemployment rate in Lancashire at 30 per cent.

In appearance Lancaster is a typical north Lancashire mill town, comprising terraces of grey stone houses rising steeply up the hilly moorlands to the east, with a much older town centre built around the River Lune and the castle. The river cuts across the north of the city with only a few bridges, creating both a physical and a psychological barrier. The mills closed over thirty years ago, as these manufacturing industries moved overseas; some mill buildings have been torn down to be replaced by housing or car parks; others have been transformed into small businesses or student accommodation. Lancaster is joined to the coastal town of Morecambe and it is within an hour's drive of the Lake District to the north and the cities of Manchester and Liverpool to the south.

The centre of the city is a large oval-shaped area, largely pedestrianised and within a one-way system of traffic, *an island in a sea of traffic*, as one person said. The city centre streets and alleyways had a similar layout in 1990 to that experienced by William Stout three hundred years earlier, and is shown in Figure 3.1. The central crossroads of Lancaster where Market

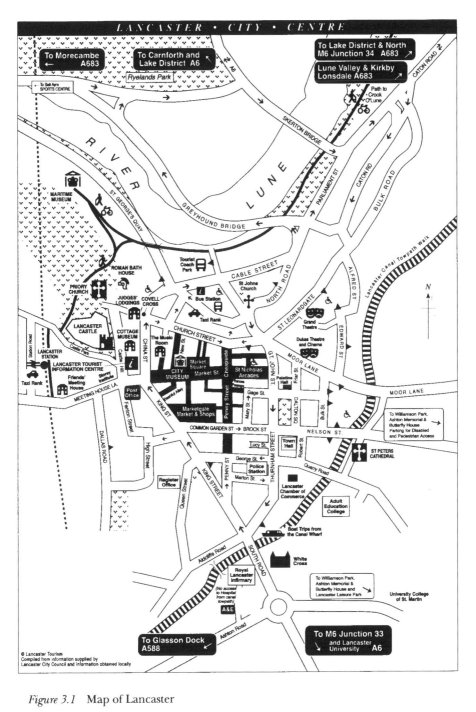

Figure 3.1   Map of Lancaster

Street meets Penny Street is once more pedestrianised. Stout lived and worked in various buildings on Market Street between Market Square and Penny Street. The street names remain the same except that St Nicholas Street has become St Nicholas Arcade and Pudding Lane has become Cheapside. The town hall is now the museum. The open market which Stout refers to would have been in the current Market Square. Three hundred years later, it has a fountain sponsored by Nuclear Electric, which youths fill with detergent on Saturday nights, but it is still a focus for shopping, public protests and begging. In our study, Harry and his wife going to the library to look up details of their family tree would have passed the site of William Stout's business on Market Street. June on her shopping trips uses the same streets and alleys as Stout would have done, and when walking her dog she might walk along the banks of the Lune, as Stout did.

Ravaged by development, the city centre is in constant change, with nothing ever finished, stores constantly opening, closing and changing places, old buildings being refurbished for new uses. The university was built three miles south of the city in the 1960s, and during the same period a teacher training college replaced the military barracks. The huge rectangular buildings of two nuclear power stations on the coast at nearby Heysham now vie with the memorial and the castle to dominate the horizon from afar.

A social profile

Since the economic boom of the nineteenth century, Lancaster's manufacturing and industrial base has declined steadily during the twentieth century, and the city's employment reflects a national shift towards the service sector. In the 1960s the local economy was buoyant, owing mainly to the new university, the teacher training college and the two nearby nuclear power stations. By 1987 an employment survey carried out by Lancaster City Council found that 15 per cent of Lancaster's workforce were employed in the manufacturing sector, and only 5 per cent in construction. This compares with 70 per cent employed in the service sector. Ninety per cent of all women employees worked in the service sector, over half of them part time. Major employers of service workers are the University, local colleges and the health service. Education, health care and public administration account for nearly a third of Lancaster's total employment. These patterns will be seen in the jobs of the people we interviewed and their friends and families.

In terms of social class, it is largely a white, working-class town. There are small minority groups of Polish-speaking Catholics and Muslim Gujarati speakers. Within the middle classes there are two overlapping groups: 'locals', born and bred in Lancaster, and 'incomers', who move here for career reasons. Business people are often locals while doctors, lawyers and academics are often incomers. This distinction between local people and others was often voiced by the people we talked to and is apparent in our data in several ways. In this distinction many Gujarati and Polish speakers are locals. It is also true that those who move to Lancaster as adults, for example academics at the university, find that their children are locals, proud to be Lancastrians and to have a local accent (see also Constantine and Warde 1993: 235).

Three major regional hospitals have been important employers in the town, often employing several generations of people from the same families. The Moor Psychiatric Hospital is now much smaller as a result of the policy of relocating former residents in the local community, and there are plans to build executive homes in part of the extensive grounds. The Royal Albert Hospital, a long-stay psychiatric hospital founded in the 1860s, closed in 1996 and has now reopened as a private boarding school for Muslim girls.

During the nineteenth century the politics of the city were dominated by local business and aristocracy, and it has returned a Conservative Member of Parliament throughout most of the twentieth century. The local council changes, and currently it is Labour-controlled. Lancaster does not have a history of strong trade unions and, historically, wage levels in the mills were lower than comparable jobs in the nearest, much larger town of Preston. Several of our informants commented on the non-militant traditions of working people in Lancaster using the derogatory term *cap-doffers*, and they attribute this to the legacy of the nineteenth century when, as a small, isolated community dominated by a few major employers, Lancaster was almost a company town. Williamson forbade union activity in his factories and, as a local politician himself, he kept a watchful eye on the political allegiances of his workforce. Dissent would put jobs on the line (Constantine and Warde 1993: 209–10).

Although Lancaster is not noted historically for its political activism, the 1970s, 1980s and 1990s saw the local development of the peace movement, the women's movement, environmental groups and road protests, reflecting the movements which were ascendant in the country as a whole. Since many people locally are now employed in the shrinking public service sector, concerns about jobs in health and education were widespread. In the early 1990s, Lancaster had its share of poll-tax protests as in many other towns around the country. Our research picked up echoes of all these popular movements as they were played out in people's lives.

For a town of its size, Lancaster supports a wide range of leisure activities. There is a cinema, a theatre and a dance studio. A regional theatre, the Dukes Playhouse, has films and a theatre; in the summer it produces plays in the park, using the Ashton Memorial. There is an annual literature festival. Locally there is a thriving music scene in pubs and clubs with dances and sessions with local musicians. Interest in music ranges from Irish-influenced ceilidhs and an annual folk festival to a music co-operative and a community music school run on Saturdays supporting youth orchestras.

The visual literacy environment

The external, public image first apparent to the visitor is a visual impression, and it is revealing to provide this in terms of literacy. The visual literacy environment provides traces of literacy practices, and we will add to this description later as we move inside people's homes. For drivers to Lancaster from the south, *Lancaster 35 miles* is marked on the motorway route signs. Around 1990 the city was first designated *The Historic City* by signs on the motorway and other approach roads to the town, marking a new enhanced image for the town aimed at tourists. As one comes into town from the south, there are advertising hoardings, sometimes imaginatively defaced. At the first roundabout home-made banners can often be seen hanging on the railings at the edge of the roundabout, usually announcing birthdays or engagements, but sometimes advertising local events such as meetings or jumble sales. These are tolerated by the council; they appear regularly, and are regularly cleared away.

This is unusual in an environment where most public notices are official or commercial, as can be seen from the ways in which they are produced

Figure 3.2   A sign at the roundabout

Figure 3.3   Fly-posting in 1990 and 1996

and designed, where they are placed and by the messages they purvey. In historical photos of Lancaster the most common traces of literacy were election posters and signs above shop fronts. These days there are a plethora of traffic and other regulatory signs, including, in 1996, those explaining the complexities of parking a car in the city centre. Direction signs for pedestrians have been added as the city becomes a tourist city. Businesses pay for the rights to advertise publicly; political organisations, entertainers and others often work at the boundaries of this, by fly-posting as a way of reaching potential customers. In local neighbourhood shops and in the front windows of houses there can be found a range of notices. These might advertise local organisations, items for sale, or descriptions of missing cats and dogs. Occasionally they refer to neighbourhood campaigns.

Some aspects of the visual environment, such as road names, are reasonably permanent; others are more ephemeral, such as advertisements on hoardings, posters advertising local events or even the mobile advertising of supermarket plastic bags as people carry them around the streets. During the course of this study there have been waves of graffiti reflecting current political activities and campaigns, including the defacing of advertisements by those wanting to put across counter-messages about gender, war, the poll tax, a proposed road building programme and animal rights. The public visual space of the city is dominated by those who have the authority and money to use it to put across their messages. They serve either public or commercial interests. Every so often this official face gets interrupted and there is a struggle to keep the unofficial messages at bay with the council cleaning service clearing away graffiti and fly-posters. Sometimes an accommodation is reached between council and public, as with the banners on the railings of the roundabout.

The visual literacy environment is a useful starting-point as it provides evidence of a range of literacies. There are traces of literacy practices related to commercial activities, entertainment, political campaigning, information-giving and legal practice. Many official signs, including traffic signs, are regulatory and designed to control people's behaviour. They are part of a framework of assumptions about social relations and obligations into which people are incorporated and which, like the legal principle of consent, go unnoticed until they are violated or challenged in some way. Just as road signs offer traces of regulatory literacy practices, hoardings and posters are part of the commercial literacy practices of selling and advertising, whilst graffiti and hand-made, unofficial signs of celebration or entertainment

Figure 3.4 City centre graffiti

Figure 3.5   People with messages

are evidence of vernacular literacy practices. Attending to these visual traces, therefore, offers us a useful source of information about literacy practices in the community.

Contemporary institutions of literacy

Lancaster Public Library is in the centre of town in Market Square, in an old building formerly a police station and a fire station. There is a lending library with books, newspapers and CDs downstairs, with a reference library upstairs. Although the children's library is physically the same building, the entrance to it is in another street, and people see them as two separate libraries. Within the district there are ten branches of the library, along with two mobile libraries and branches in the hospitals and prisons, and links with schools and day care centres. In 1990 there were over six hundred thousand issues of books. Forty per cent of the population of the district are members of the library. Next door is the museum, with extensive archives about the city.

There is also a public library in Morecambe town centre, and a travelling library bus visits local villages. There are academic libraries at the University and at St Martin's College. Earlier in the century there were two or three private lending libraries, including one in Boots the Chemists. The earliest library, first documented in the seventeenth century, was in the Friends Meeting House (Haines 1981). Remnants of it are still there in a large wooden bookcase, including George Fox's journal.

There are several bookshops in Lancaster, and many other shops which sell books. Waterstone's, a branch of a national chain, is clearly a bookshop. Smiths, the most often mentioned bookshop in our study, is in fact a city centre newsagent's, bookshop and stationery and record store. It is also difficult to be precise as there has been a significant amount of change with bookshops opening, closing and moving. One bookshop, backing on to the market and with a good children's section, the City Bookshop, closed during our study. Cut-price bookshops which sell new books at discount come and go in the city centre, with more appearing just before Christmas. In addition there are several second-hand bookshops and the second-hand books stall in the market which sells and exchanges books. (This is a continuation of one which existed there in the nineteenth century, mentioned in Aside 2.2.) Bookshops have a seeming permanence, and the amount of movement and change was surprising to us. Three large second-hand bookshops in the town centre owned by one person closed just before the project started. In 1996 a radical bookshop and two charity-run second-hand bookshops opened.

Specialist bookshops include The Paperbook Back Shop [sic], which concentrates on science fiction and fantasy books, and a Christian religious bookshop. Other shops such as car shops and health food shops have specialist books, as do gardening shops and the hard-to-find scout shop. There are rows of false books on the shelves of bookcases in furniture stores. Charity shops usually have a shelf or two of books, as do general second-hand shops. Jumble sales and car boot sales have book stalls, and other stalls often have a box of books on the ground. There are magazines and some children's books in supermarkets; this has increased considerably since 1990. Books are sold at Christmas fairs, and school fairs sell children's books. (See Aside 9.5 for the national picture.)

There are newsagents throughout the town and in each neighbourhood. Apart from the city centre newsagents they deliver daily papers to people's homes. They also carry a range of magazines. As with books, magazines are available in a range of different shops, including a range of radical magazines in the whole-food co-operative. Similarly, postcards and greetings cards are available in a variety of places, and there are two specialist greetings card shops. Free brochures, magazines and leaflets are available at travel agents, the tourist information office, the city council information booth, and the Citizen's Advice Bureau. At the bus station and the railway station there are free timetables.

Lancaster's first local paper, the *Lancaster Gazette*, began publishing in 1801. Now there are several local newspapers; the daily evening paper, *The Lancashire Post*, covers the north-west region. The weekly *Lancaster Guardian* comes out on Fridays: when people in Lancaster talk about reading something in *The Guardian,* they are more likely to mean the local one than the national one. Several free papers exist, such as: the weekly *Citizen,* delivered to people's houses; *Off the Beat,* a free events listing; and *Star Buys,* which contains classified advertising. Local newspapers complement the homes, pubs, clubs, corner shops, hairdressers, markets and work-places where news is shared and the web of everyday life reasserted.

There is a central post office where, in addition to matters concerned with mail, people pay their car tax, deal with passports, do their banking and collect a range of forms concerned with finance and benefits. There are plans for it to be closed and for its services to be moved to a shop in town. As well as the central post office, most neighbourhoods have their own local post office; this may double as a chemist, an off-licence, a general store or newsagent's. These local post offices are important for pensions and savings, as well as for collecting child benefit. For many people they are a crucial part of neighbourhood life. Whenever planned changes to the system of sub-post-offices have been proposed, there have been campaigns to save them.

Education obviously shapes and influences local literacy, but it is only one influence on it. Local literacy is also much more than books in bookshops and libraries. There is other institutional support, for example in religious institutions. Religious institutions assert a major influence through the schools they run. They also support particular literacy practices around worship in the values they assign to the written word. In addition they are involved in teaching in Sunday Schools, and may provide informal help for adults with difficulties in reading and writing. A list from the local Tourist Office names thirty-two churches in Lancaster, including several Church of England churches, the Catholic cathedral and churches, several Methodist churches, Quakers, Jehovah's Witnesses, Mormons and a Spiritualist Church. The list does not include the Polish Catholic church near the cathedral, nor Muslim mosques in private houses. Lancaster has a lively history of religious dissent, particularly identified around Catholicism and Quakerism. Religious interests still dominate the school system in the town, which maintained selective secondary grammar schools throughout the 1970s when most parts of the country adopted comprehensivisation.

There are at least twelve small printing businesses in Lancaster. Many are hidden away on light industrial estates on the edge of town; there are also two print shops in the centre where people go for photocopying or the printing of wedding invitations. These also print magazines and newsletters, and even locally produced books, often about some aspect of life in Lancaster.

A sense of place

People have a clear sense of living in Lancaster and being from Lancashire. People refer to themselves as Lancastrians, meaning coming from Lancaster, as much as meaning from the much more extensive Lancashire. There are distinct Lancashire accents, and old rivalries with Yorkshire still remain in the jokes which are told and in attitudes towards accents. Lancaster is held together as a recognisable coherent community by diverse threads, including a local paper, the local council administration and a town centre. The psychological edges are blurred: a reference to Lancaster sometimes includes Morecambe, at other times excludes it; it sometimes includes the surrounding countryside, at other times excludes it. People see Lancaster as a small town, but it is special. People identify with the city. Many students who arrive to study for a course find themselves staying on after they have finished their studies.

The sense of place is also created by the identity which the city has on paper. There is a public identity in the postcards which are produced of the city, and which are mainly for tourists, and in the booklets and leaflets produced by the Tourist Office. There is another identity in the booklets produced by the Council for prospective business people. A more vernacular identity is constructed in the local magazines and newsletters which are produced by local churches, schools, sports clubs and other organisations.

Another contribution to Lancaster's identity on paper exists in the ways in which it is documented in books. Various books have been written about Lancaster, the first one probably being William Stout's autobiography. Other early books include *An Historical and Descriptive Account of the Town of Lancaster* by C. Clark, which was self-published in 1807, and *History and Antiquities of Lancaster* by R. Simpson, published in 1852. In the twentieth century there have been a range of local books, often printed in the northwest, including specific histories of the city, local life, natural history, guidebooks and booklets of walks in the area. Books exist documenting the history of specific buildings, local tradesmen, transportation, regiments, a theatre, schools and businesses. There are also books of photographs, and maps of Lancaster. These are available in local bookshops, which often have a section entitled *Local Interest*. The coming of the university has affected the documentation of the town, and a Centre for North West Regional Studies at the university has brought out its own booklets on the social, economic and historical life of Lancaster and its immediate surroundings. The university has also spawned papers and dissertations on the city, coming from many departments including History, Geography and Sociology. There have been substantial oral history studies by Elizabeth Roberts (such as Roberts 1984; 1995). Local organisations and trade unions have brought out their own booklets, as has the city museum. In addition there are sections on Lancaster in books on Lancashire or north-west England, as well as in national guidebooks. The museum has over twenty-five books and booklets on Lancaster and district for sale in its bookshop. The library has more.

The sense of place which exists on paper is of a city with a history, a working-class small town with local tradespeople and Victorian terraced houses; it is a place from where people go out on country walks at the weekend and where there are some places of interest to the tourist. Physically, the place on paper is usually the urban area and it does not include the rural areas which are nevertheless part of the administrative area of the city of Lancaster. Nor does it normally include Morecambe, which is seen as a distinct town. The administrative boundaries of local and national government, including the parliamentary constituencies, do not necessarily have an identity for people. Sometimes Lancaster is the setting for short stories by people on Creative Writing courses or members of writers' groups or song-writing projects. Academics may situate themselves here: for example, in Myers (1996), an article on Science and Technology Studies, the author situates the article as being written in Lancaster where he had views of the Lake District and of the nuclear power station. Our research and the way we disseminate it also contribute to this sense of place for Lancaster.

Springside

Lancaster consists of a number of identifiable, named neighbourhoods, often with a post office and other local shops, a pub, a primary school and other facilities. The ones closest to the city centre are clusters of Victorian terraced houses; further from the centre there are more recent estates. As well as considering Lancaster as a whole in our research, we focused on one neighbourhood, which we refer to as Springside. The reason for concentrating on one area was in order to give more detail and to get closer to people's lives; more on the rationale for the choice of neighbourhood is given in the next chapter, and, for the moment, we provide a description of the neighbourhood.

The Springside area of Lancaster is situated about three-quarters of a mile from the city centre. It is an area of low-cost terraced housing built across a steep hillside in the 1880s for the industrial and mill workers of the town. There are 660 houses, built of local stone and slate-roofed, of two and three storeys. The area is well defined on all sides and is hemmed in by college lands, industrial lands and a small park. Springside itself has no internal

Figure 3.6   A neighbourhood street

open or recreational space; most houses have small rear yards, with a path, or ginnel, running between the backs of the houses. Around a quarter of the houses have small private front gardens, the rest open directly on to the street. Most of the interior streets are totally enclosed with no open views, although since they are on a hill, some upstairs rooms have views over the city. Open space is provided on its borders by the college, the Council allotment land on the eastern edge, and the park.

It is probably useful for later chapters if we give a description of the individual houses. A typical house opens directly on to the street. The small front room is used as a lounge; it leads into a back room, which is sometimes the kitchen. The bathroom may be beyond this room. There is a back door leading into a small yard which has a gate into the back lane running between the rows of houses. Stairs between the back and front rooms lead up to the first floor which has a front bedroom and a small back bedroom. Some houses have three floors, in which case there is just one bedroom and the bathroom on the first floor and one or two rooms on the second floor. Some houses have a cellar. Aside 3.1 provides an estate agent's description of a typical small house in Springside being offered for sale in 1996.

Aside 3.1 A house for sale in Springside

* PEDESTRIAN FRONTED MID TERRACE HOUSE *

* TWO BEDROOMS * ONE RECEPTION ROOM *

PRICE £35,950

GROUND FLOOR

LOUNGE	11′3 x 9′10 (3.429 × 2.998) Fitted gas fire in stone fireplace.
KITCHEN	7′10 × 7′4 (2.388 × 2.236) Single drainer sink unit. Base and wall units. Part tiled walls. Gas cooker point. Window to rear. Staircase to first floor.
REAR PORCH AREA	Plumbing for automatic washing machine.
BATHROOM	Panelled bath, pedestal wash hand basin and low level wc. Part tiled walls. Gas water heater.

FIRST FLOOR

LANDING

BEDROOM ONE	10′2 x 9′4 (3.099 × 2.846) Window to front.
BEDROOM TWO	9′ x 6′10 (2.744 × 2.083) Window to rear. Electric storage heater.

OUTSIDE

Rear yard with shrub border and garden shed. Rear service road.

* ESTABLISHED RESIDENTIAL LOCATION *

* SUITABLE STARTER HOME *

* EARLY VIEWING RECOMMENDED *

Figure 3.7 A neighbourhood shop

It is harder to get information about a particular neighbourhood such as Springside than about the city as a whole. A Lancaster City Council survey of the Springside area undertaken in 1980 gives some information concerning both the properties and the residents. The population in 1980 was 1,500 people, excluding seventy students who were not counted as full-time residents. According to the survey there were almost equal proportions of all age groups. Around 10 per cent of the population are minority-language speakers, mostly Gujarati Muslims and Polish-speaking Catholics. Almost a third of the population had been resident for longer than twenty years – more than half of these were elderly households. Another third of the population of Springside had become resident within the last five years. The low market value of the houses makes them suitable for first-time buyers – people buying their first house. Most of the houses are owner-occupied, with around 10 per cent rented out by private landlords. In another survey for the 1987 Lancaster City Council Declaration Report, a smaller survey of 180 houses in the area, 16 per cent of all household heads were registered unemployed; 7 per cent of all households were classed as single-parent families.

The 1980 report looked into the structural conditions of the houses in the Springside area and estimated that, although the majority were structurally sound, about one-third were in need of substantial repairs. Ninety households lacked one or more amenity, such as a bathroom or internal toilet. By 1990 twenty-four houses were without a bathroom, according to the Housing

Action Project. The 1987 Declaration Report claimed that nearly half the houses in a smaller survey were in need of substantial improvement and repair, and a quarter were classed as unfit for human habitation owing to disrepair or dampness.

Fifty years ago neighbourhoods such as Springside were dotted with corner shops of every description, and many houses at the end of streets have extra-large windows as proof of their former use. The neighbourhood still boasts two corner shops, one of which is also an off-licence; there is also a newsagent's, a butcher's, a hairdresser's, a fish and chip shop and a launderette. There is a nearby post office in the adjoining neighbourhood. There is a public telephone box and a telephone in one of the shops. A pub, a church and a men's club completes the institutions. Edna Worthington and Ida Mason (see Appendix 1) are two of the oldest long-standing residents of Springside, and they remember in detail the old shops, especially the co-operative grocery shops, the bake-houses where residents could take their own bread and pies to be cooked, and the selling-out shops, forerunners of the off-licence, which sold everything *from a pin to an elephant*. Even

Figure 3.8 Signs in a neighbourhood shop

**Aside 3.2   1990 in Lancaster, summarised from headlines
in the Lancaster Guardian throughout the year**

One of the main issues in Lancaster during 1990 reflected the national
controversy caused by the poll tax. The rate was set at £385.50 in March
1990; this sparked numerous protest marches and demonstrations,
including one organised by a local hairdresser from Springside. It also
caused a power struggle in the City Council, which was hung between the
Conservative and Labour parties. Eventually a compromise was worked
out. Labour assumed control during the first part of 1990, and the
Conservatives took over in October for the next six months.

Local issues included the Lancaster City Plan and the proposed
Western by-pass road to link the M6 with Heysham via a new bridge over
the Lune. Both schemes looked to be in jeopardy by the end of the year.
The by-pass scheme was threatened by lack of central government funding, and was also the subject of much opposition from environmentalists.
The city centre redevelopment plan, previously scheduled to be well
under way by 1990, might now be delayed by up to three more years. The
developers blamed the economic recession and soaring costs. A less ambi-
tious revised plan might yet be adopted; and the market might stay on its
present site. Plans to move the market were the basis of many of the
objections to the original plan.

Both the boys' Grammar School and the girls' Grammar School voted
to opt out of local education authority control after months of controversy. St Martin's teacher training college announced its ten-year plan to
expand and was granted planning permission to extend its car park; this
was approved despite opposition from local residents who wanted to
retain the green fields and who were also worried about increased traffic
on' surrounding roads. Springside residents were affected by County

---

Edna's granddaughter remembered the selling-out shops from the early
1970s.

The Housing Action Project which we discuss later occupies the site of
one of the former small general stores, originally run by the co-operative
society. The Housing Action Project was one of twenty-four such projects set
up around the country in 1989 as part of a central government policy
designed to encourage home owners to improve their properties in run-
down neighbourhoods and increase people's commitment to their locality
(Leather and Mackintosh 1990). The project had just become established
in Springside when our research began, and our interviews with residents
were peppered with references to the 'enveloping' scheme, whereby certain

Council plans to sell off local allotments to property developers; a compromise was eventually agreed, with some land sold and the rest retained by the allotments. The City Council announced the end of Housing Action Areas which involved council-funded maintenance and repair of private housing.

Promises were made to reduce and even eliminate the smell from Nightingale Farm's animal processing plant with a new filter system which was installed in 1990. Other environmental issues included: the long-called-for release back to the wild of Rocky the dolphin in Morecambe's aquarium; fears over radiation in the River Lune reaching Lancaster owing to contamination from Sellafield nuclear reprocessing plant; more opposition and concern over a proposed nuclear dump to be built either at Sellafield or Dounreay and its effects on Lancaster and Morecambe; and the rejection of a proposal by North West Water to build a pipeline to discharge raw sewage into the sea near Fleetwood.

More job losses in the area were announced during the year as Lancaster faced the new recession. The brickworks north of the city announced a rationalisation of their work-force with thirty-eight job losses. A local shoe factory received a last-minute reprieve from closure and the loss of seventy jobs. The Dukes Theatre and Cinema was continually threatened with bankruptcy and closure but managed to survive the year. Lancaster's Chamber of Commerce was also threatened with the loss of at least seventeen jobs when the government-sponsored Employment Training programme moved to Preston. A report by the North Lancashire Child Poverty Action Group claimed that up to eleven thousand people in the district were living in poverty. It also stated that people in the Lancaster District were much more likely to become unemployed than the average UK citizen. The plight of the homeless featured in the local news, as the lack of housing in Lancaster reached critical levels.

properties in the neighbourhood were eligible for grants to have windows replaced and the outsides of houses re-pointed. A quarter of the houses, starting from the bottom of the neighbourhood, were eligible. The enveloping was sponsored by a mixture of private building contractors and government grants; in fact it caused a good deal of controversy and disruption among residents, not least because initially only the properties along one side of some streets were eligible for the grants: administrative boundaries cut across neighbourhood boundaries. People were also unhappy that they had no say in the design of the new windows they were being offered. The project had two paid workers, and its local office in Springside was used as a resource and advice centre for the neighbourhood.

Aside 3.3　Finding out local information

We carried out a random door-to-door survey of sixty-five people in Springside to identify local issues and to ask how they found out local information. The local issue mentioned most commonly was that of traffic in the neighbourhood; two concerns were about the amount of through traffic using the local roads, and the difficulty with finding parking spaces for cars. Traffic was mentioned by twenty-five out of the sixty-five people we talked to. The other commonly mentioned local topics were issues about the building work in the area and issues about street lighting. Further topics mentioned by at least five people were: play provision for children; problems with cats and dogs; worries about the poll tax; and worries about noise from neighbours or the pub.

In terms of finding out local information, most people said that their main source of information came from talking to other people; reading local papers and notices came second, with information from regional television or local radio coming third. Two-thirds of people said they read the local newspaper and more than ninety per cent read something from the free newspaper. Around half the people said they sometimes cut things out of local papers, usually items of personal or family interest. More than half the people sometimes listened to local radio, and nearly a quarter listened to it regularly. Ninety per cent of people sometimes watched local television news, and two-thirds of the people watched it regularly. A quarter of people had no phone in their homes and used the public phones or one in the local shops when necessary.

When asked about junk mail, twenty-two people said that it went

---

One of the aims of the Housing Action Project was to involve the local community in developing its own activities and groups, and soon after the project began in Springside it helped set up a residents' association. As well as developing community activities, the residents' association acted as a conduit for residents' views on issues to do with the building work being carried out through the project. It was run by volunteers, who organised meetings and social events, distributed newsletters and information and canvassed opinion on various local issues. They had no resources or premises of their own, so made use of the project to provide these. For example, while one of the residents edited the newsletter, it was typed up by one of the project employees on the word processor in the office. Meetings were also held in the project office. After giving some Springside houses a major facelift, the project closed at the end of 1990 when funding was not renewed. Although the residents' association protested against the closure straight in the bin; twenty have some organised system for sorting it and keeping coupons or offers. Eleven people expressed some feeling of getting too much junk mail. More women than men dealt with the junk mail. The range of material which came through the door included adverts for commercial products and services, some national, some local; free samples – recent examples included small sachets of mustard, and round tea-bags; catalogues; charity appeals; and a range of newsletters and notices. The newsletters included ones from the church, the school, local associations, political groups and the residents' association.

We asked people about their local links. Seventy per cent had been born in Lancaster or the north-west and 10 per cent had actually been brought up in Springside, the neighbourhood where they now lived. Around half have other family in the Lancaster area, beyond their household.

National figures suggest that most people rely on local papers as their main source of local news, with 81 per cent of people naming a paper as one of their first three sources (Gunter *et al.* 1994: 56). Television and radio come next. Talking to people was mentioned by 40 per cent of respondents as a major source of local news. In comparison with these figures, Springside residents claimed to rely much more heavily on talking to people as a source of news, but local papers do play an important role in Springside. In this respect, finding out about local news is different from national news, where people in general rely more heavily on television (see Aside 7.6). Telephone ownership in Springside, at 75 per cent, is lower than the national average, which in 1990 was already 88 per cent and increasing annually (Central Statistical Office 1993).

and carried on meeting in the pub for a few months after, it did not survive the collapse of the project.

1990 and the 1990s

We have included a broad sweep of Lancaster's literacy history to indicate how the present is made up of the past. The main case studies were carried out in 1990 and our interest has continued more than six years beyond 1990 into the present. It is important to pin down a precise period in order to locate these practices in time. The year 1990 was a particular point in history, distinct from a few years earlier or a few years later. This is true in terms of new technology, for instance. Many offices in town had computers, but very few homes in Springside did. Similarly, fax machines and mobile phones were not apparent. It was that point in time, that brief window in history, when a word processor was used for the local newsletter, but it was treated as if it were just a typewriter; thus, Shirley handwrote items for the newsletter and then someone else copy-typed them using a word processor. At the doctors' surgery in town, in 1990 all patients' records were kept in untidy brown file envelopes, clogging up the main office of the surgery. Prescriptions were handwritten, personal and illegible; now, in 1997, they are computer-generated, impersonal and legible, and handwritten only if the doctor writes out the prescription on a home visit.

It is possible also to pinpoint 1990 in terms of the social and political issues of the day, such as the poll tax and unemployment. To give a flavour of the year 1990 from the point of view of Lancaster, Aside 3.2 summarises the headlines and stories from the front page of the *Lancaster Guardian* throughout the year. This is one public view of Lancaster in 1990. Another view could have been drawn from the pages of official notices, the small ads or the jobs in the paper. Still other, more personal views are recorded in personal diaries kept by Lancaster residents.

To provide a more local glimpse of issues, Aside 3.3 has details of the local issues which people identified to us as important in our door-to-door survey of Springside. It includes some figures which provide a broader context to this local data. In the survey the national issues which were on people's minds included standards of reading in schools, the Gulf War, Margaret Thatcher and national politics, and, above everything else, the poll tax. We return to some of these issues in later chapters, approaching them in terms of literacy. Nationally, one symbolic day in 1990 was the day that the Prime Minister, Margaret Thatcher, resigned. People remember this and can recall what they were doing when they heard about this, just as locally they, and we, can recall the day that Lancaster's Victorian market hall burned down in 1984.

Since 1990 there have been many changes in Springside, the most noticeable being traffic calming measures on the roads and the demise of the Housing Action Project. Nevertheless, we will fix upon 1990 as the present time of this narrative, although we will also benefit from the hindsight provided by the last few years, and include more recent perspectives. A time and a place come together in our study of Springside in 1990. An understanding of the social practices of the allotment association meetings or the production of the local newsletter depends on an understanding of the history of the place and of the current point in time. This understanding brings together many of the threads of this chapter, including knowledge of what technology was available and what access the community had to resources, both in terms of material resources such as word processors and in terms of access to people and their knowledge.

4

ETHNOGRAPHY IN PRACTICE

The idea is not so much to prove one's existing hypotheses as to try to reach beyond the old problematics . . . to look at societal phenomena from fresh, unprejudiced, yet well-founded points of view . . . and to call into question the self-evident.

(Alasuutari 1995: 145)

Introduction

The research goal in this study is to uncover patterns and regularities in the organisation of one aspect of cultural life. Our aim is to be explicit about the methods used in this research, by describing what we did, and by explaining why we did it. The point has already been made in Chapter 1 that having a social theory of literacy, as something which is contextualised in time and space, implies that certain research methods are appropriate. Methods which take literacy out of its context of use are not appropriate. Instead, methods are needed which enable us to examine in detail the role of literacy in people's contemporary lives and in the histories and traditions of which these are a part. Our study has begun by indicating some of the historical roots of contemporary practices and describing some of the contemporary environments in which people are carrying out their everyday lives. We continue now by describing how the interviews and observations were carried out, analysed and written up.

In terms of methodology, this research draws heavily upon ethnographic research traditions, as developed by anthropologists and utilised in several fields including education. Traditionally there are four aspects to this approach (see Goetz and LeCompte 1984: 3). Firstly, ethnography studies real-world settings; we do this by focusing on a particular place at a particular point in time. We deal with people's real lives: we never ask anyone to take a decontextualised test and we never stage a photograph. Secondly, the approach is holistic, aiming at whole phenomena; the phenomenon we are studying is this cultural artefact, literacy. Thirdly, the work is multi-method, drawing on a variety of research techniques; we combine extensive interviewing with detailed observation and with the systematic collection of documents. Fourthly, ethnography is interpretative and it aims to represent the participants' perspectives; we endeavour to do this by highlighting the actual words people use and by discussing our data and our interpretations with them. Contemporary ethnography is not without its intellectual and methodological debates and reflections upon how it is written (as, for example, in Clifford and Marcus 1986; Atkinson 1990), and we intend to contribute to these discussions. In designing our study we also drew upon other named traditions of qualitative research, including case study research and oral history.

Rather than just naming an approach we describe carefully what we did in our study and provide some rationale for each step. One reason for this is that many of the terms used, including basic terms such as ethnography and qualitative research, have different meanings to different researchers. In addition, the way these meanings are turned into a practical research strategy is frequently only vaguely described, often deliberately so: ethnography has a tradition of not being explicit about methodology. We make our methodology explicit, in order to provide some possibility for it to be evaluated by others, but also in order to aid others who wish to do similar work. In doing this we have to address issues such as sampling procedures, the nature of the database, validity, reliability and generalisability. These are terms which are transformed and challenged by qualitative research, but which need to be addressed in some way if research is to be evaluated. (Since we began our work, a growing number of books on qualitative research methodology which address some of these questions have been published, including Brymon and Burgess 1994; Dey 1993; Hammersley 1990; Mason 1996; Silverman 1993.)

An additional reason for being explicit is that we were not taking one specific well-tried methodology off the shelf for this project. Significant methodological decisions were made as the research progressed, allowing the topic of the research to shape the methods, adapting and evolving new strategies over time. We are consciously developing methodology in this research. We have already indicated some parts of our methodology, by being explicit about the orienting theory and by providing historical background and contemporary contextual descriptions. In this chapter we outline how we chose the participants for the study and the methods used for collecting data. Throughout we draw attention to some of the methodological issues faced in carrying out this work. Aside 4.1 summarises the main areas of data collection; further details including lists of the people included in the study are given in Appendix 1 at the end of the book.

Aside 4.1 Summary of data collected
(See Appendix 1 for further details)

Adult College data
 Twenty interviews with students at The Adult College Lancaster
Survey data
 Door-to-door survey of sixty-five households in Springside
Case study data
 Twelve in-depth case studies of people in Springside
Other neighbourhood data
 Further interviews
 Case studies of community groups and organisations in Springside
Collaborative data
 Five people from the Adult College group and five people from the
 case studies
City centre data
 Observation in Lancaster, including photographs and collection of
 documents
 Interviews and observations of access points for literacy in Lancaster

---

The data

Adult College data

As background to the main study, twenty adults who had attended part-time Basic Education classes at the local Adult College were interviewed. We had some background of involvement in adult basic education as teachers, volunteers and researchers. The interviewees were contacted by Sarah Padmore, who had been teaching at the college and who already knew many of them. They were chosen by personal contact and represented a convenience sample (as in Cohen and Manion 1994).

The interviews were semi-structured. Following procedures used in oral history there was a checklist of themes or topics to cover, such as: borrowing and owning, public and private, household roles, and networks. Within these headings we devised more than 160 topics to ask people about. These covered many topics to do with people's everyday reading and writing: where, when and with whom they read and wrote; what they did with pens, papers, books and other artefacts; their use of libraries, links with religion, memories of childhood literacy including schooling, and much more. This list was revised during this period; details are given in Appendix 2.

The questionnaire was used as an *aide-mémoire*, there was no attempt to follow the list of topics in a precise order. The interviews were kept fairly informal to give people space to talk about other aspects of their literacy lives.

New themes emerged from individuals' stories. This period was also used to explore other techniques, such as group interviews involving other members of the research team.

This was the starting-point. However, it was important to move beyond the Adult College. We were interested in broadening our study to include the majority of adults who do not define themselves as having literacy difficulties and examining how reading and writing is embedded in their day-to-day lives. We also wanted to move on from the familiar education-defined world to working with people in the local community, who may or may not define themselves as having difficulties with literacy, and who may not think very much at all about reading and writing as they carry on their lives. We wanted to find out more about home literacy, to talk to people about links with literacy at work and at school, and to explore networks of support between friends, neighbours and relatives. To do this we needed to find a rationale for talking to people about literacy that did not start from education or from educational institutions.

The survey data

When working in the local community, we decided to limit ourselves to one neighbourhood within the city. This would offer a shared context of a very local, everyday kind for a series of case studies of people in their households. As described in the previous chapter, Lancaster consists of a number of identifiable, named, neighbourhoods, and between us we walked or cycled round all of them, mapping the range of neighbourhoods in order to decide on one to use as the focus for the study. We decided on the neighbourhood which we refer to as Springside (see Aside 4.2), one easily characterised as an area of Victorian terraced housing, with clearly defined physical, geographical boundaries and a variety of inhabitants including many with long-standing connections in the area. Therefore, initially, the community we were studying was defined in physical geographical terms.

After considering several possible methods of reaching a cross-section of people within the neighbourhood, we decided to knock randomly on doors and to carry out a small survey on an accessible topic to do with everyday uses of literacy. We prepared a brief survey questionnaire, asking people about their ways of finding out about local information. (This is reported in Aside 3.3.) This was used as a lead in to the topic of reading and writing. We knocked on the door of every fifth house in Springside until we had carried out sixty-five survey interviews. If no one answered the door we returned to the house several times at different times of the day, in order not to bias our sample towards people who are home only at certain times. Most of the survey interviews were conducted on the doorstep, and they lasted from three minutes to thirty minutes. With one or two exceptions, noted below, this can be regarded as a survey of a random sample of households in the neighbourhood.

Aside 4.2   Home, family, household, neighbourhood, community

In Chapter 1 we introduced the terms *home, community* and *family*, which we use along with *neighbourhood* and *household* as different but overlapping frames which can be placed upon our data. It is important to bear these different frames in mind as they all recur in the following discussion, and we move between them. In the fieldwork we deliberately did not start with families but with individual people, nearly all of whom were contacted by random knocking on doors. We knocked on the doors of *households*; households were the groups of people who shared living space and, usually, ate together in a home. Often they were related, and sometimes they were not. (We excluded students from the study and so excluded the most common group of non-related households in the neighbourhood.) In the research, *home* had a very physical existence. When we visited people it was normally in houses where the front door was on the street and opened directly into the front room, then we either stayed in the front room or went into the room behind it. One of these rooms would be the nerve centre of the home.

From this starting-point, we became involved with other people in the families and households, depending on their individual circumstances. The range of households can be seen in the lists of people in Appendix 1. Some were married couples with children living at home, such as Jeff and Brenda, Shirley and Jack. June's husband, a lorry driver, was away much of the time and she had a grown-up daughter living with her. Eddie and Janette split up during the period of our study and Eddie went to live with his mother and aunt, while Janette became a single parent with school-aged children. Cliff lived with his mother and teenage son and partly shared his household with his half-sister, Rose, who lived nearby. Terry, in his early twenties, lived alone. The people in each of these very different households in turn told us about their networks of extended family members, neighbours and friends, people at work and school or college, those they shared specific interests and activities with.

In analysing the data what is important is whether or not the categories *household, family, neighbourhood, community* are useful in describing people's literacy activities. The validity of the terms becomes an empirical question, and this is addressed in Chapter 14.

The case study data

The central focus of the study is life in the neighbourhood of Springside, as lived by the people who participated in the case studies. This is the core data, and all other data exists in relation to this. It is therefore important to make clear how we chose the twelve people who participated in the case studies. The sixty-five people we interviewed in the survey formed the pool from which we selected the people for the case studies. The criteria for selection for the case studies were that at least one adult in the household had lived on Springside for several years, had attended local schools and had left school at the minimum leaving age. This excluded most university students and other short-term residents, as well as the small number of well-educated professional residents who were not from the area. At the end of each survey, we asked respondents who fitted our criteria whether they would be willing to talk to us in more depth over a longer period of time.

Forty-two of the sixty-five people fitted our criteria and thirty-two of them were interested in participating in the case studies. We chose our case studies from these. We wanted a range of family types, including working people, retired people, unemployed people and people living alone, in couples and with other family members. We also wanted the group to be fairly representative of the residents of the neighbourhood in terms of age, gender and ethnicity. Thus the selection of people for the case studies was deliberately motivated and can be regarded as theoretical sampling, in Cohen and Manion's sense (1994). For example, around one in ten of the households in Springside consists of Gujarati speakers of Indian origin: we therefore included one such household in the case studies. At this stage we had no idea if most people were confident about reading and writing or not, and we did not choose households on the basis of literacy-related criteria. We chose twelve'households to work with; we invented pseudonyms for people (see Aside 4.3) and began the case studies.

At the same time as carrying out the door-to-door survey we were making approaches to other people in the neighbourhood. We met the workers at the Housing Action Project and announced the survey and ourselves in the residents' association meeting so that people would know who we were and what we were doing when we were seen taking photographs in the street or were standing in the fish and chip shop talking to people. This helped us build up more information about the social composition of the neighbourhood. The manager of the Housing Project suggested we interview the person we refer to as Shirley Bowker who was the editor of the residents' association newsletter, and her name came up in conversation with several other people. We included her but she was one person who was not contacted randomly through the survey. In terms of ethnography she is more of a 'key informant', someone who knows the area well and talks about the whole community. We did not want to rely on a key informant, as we did not

Aside 4.3   Confidentiality, anonymity and voice

Places called Roadville, Murrayville and Pleasantville define the land-scape of research on language and literacy, often having greater reality to students than strange-sounding real places like Martha's Vineyard. Ironically, fictions are invented in order to get closer to 'the facts'. We have added Springside to the mythology, but not without some hesitation.

In terms of anonymity we identify two conflicting traditions, both of which we are sympathetic to. Firstly, there is the tradition in social science research that people have a right to anonymity and to the knowledge that what they say will be treated as confidential, and respected as such. At the same time there is another tradition, common in community education and adult education work, that people have a right to be heard and named in research, and that research writings can give voice and prominence to people's lives.

Since we wanted to explore the connections literacy has to other aspects of people's lives and we wanted to be free to talk about all areas of life, it was important that we should guarantee people confidentiality. In consultations with our informants we therefore invented a pseudonym for each person we talked to. In fact people shared many intimate aspects of their lives and we have respected their confidentiality. We learned some things that we have not reported and some small details of people's lives have been changed.

At the same time, it seemed impossible and undesirable to try to hide the identity of the city we were studying, especially when we explored publicly known historical details or information about the structure of the schools. It is also central to our approach to literacy that reading and writing are anchored to particular times and places. We are not talking in generalisations, but are talking about particular people's practices in particular places. Therefore, this study is openly about Lancaster, a real town in the north-west of England. Having made this decision, we then found that in between the city and the individuals there were a surprising number of decisions which had to be made about anonymity. To protect the anonymity of individuals, we gave the neighbourhood we studied a pseudonym, Springside, and roads and schools around it also have invented names. We also decided not to use photographs of people in the neighbourhood. However, we decided that institutions in the city centre and people we interviewed in public social roles, such as the managers of shops or councillors, should be identified by their real names, as should other schools which are part of the history of Lancaster. As a result of these decisions some names in the text are real names and others are invented. Details are provided in the Appendices.

Aside 4.4   What ethnographic interviews offer as a research tool

Unlike some ethnographies which rely more on participant observation, this study makes much use of interviews. We set out to explore the shape and meanings of certain activities directly with informants and chose interviews as an appropriate way of doing this. Our intention was to generate data which reflected vernacular interpretations and theories of literacy in a more direct way than is possible from research which does not involve asking questions but relies on the interpretations of an outside participant observer.

The traditional notion that this participant outsider, the ethnographer, can study a culture, 'describing it . . .from the participants' point of view,' as Spradley (1979) claims is based on a naive view of the role of the ethnographer. Such a description is not really possible unless the researcher is in every sense a participant too. Even the use of interviews which generate accounts from informants in their own words is a process significantly shaped and filtered by the ethnographer, at all stages, and we comment on this at relevant points throughout this book

The character of the interviews we used changed across the course of the study. In the case studies we used long, repeated interviews and over time these became less structured, allowing the interviewees to tell the stories which seemed important to them in the context of literacy, rather than responding to a set of questions. The importance of repeated interviews in allowing this process to unfold is described in the fieldworker's notes:

---

want to make the assumption that there is a homogeneity of views and meanings in the community. Nevertheless, there are different ways in which our informants are positioned within the community, and Shirley's perspective is an important one. We see in the data both examples of how she represents the community and examples of how she is at odds with the community.

In terms of social class, the people we interviewed would be regarded as working-class. Such terms are not precise, and a clearer idea can be provided by giving details of their jobs: these include psychiatric nurse, care assistant, fire-fighter, cleaner, market stall assistant, office worker, two factory workers. Most houses in Springside are privately owned; many residents are owner-occupiers and some are renting privately. While people were often extremely short of money and faced many difficulties in their day-to-day lives, we were not researching the poorest and most marginalised people in Lancaster.

One thing our methodology has taught us is that initial interviews – one-off interviews with respondents – are not enough. However thorough they appear at the time, they can prove to be superficial to the point of being misleading. If we had not involved people in [the process of repeated interviews], *we would, in some cases, have had a very limited overview of their literacy practices; and might well have held inaccurate beliefs about their values.*

This is not a case of people's attitudes and practices changing over time, although this had obviously happened too. People simply began to open out about areas of their lives they hadn't talked of before; they lost some of their inhibition about being tape-recorded; they began to get a sense of the range of our literacy interests, and to feel more free to initiate topics. A couple of people commented that they had felt shy the first time round – they hadn't been used to being interviewed. And being interviewed in their homes must have made a difference too.

Interview data is essentially self-report and it is important to be clear about the status of this material and that it needs to be complemented or triangulated with data from other sources, such as observations. An interview offers the researcher one participant's reporting of events, what they think it appropriate or comfortable to tell us or can remember, what they define as literacy and what they think the interviewer is interested in hearing about.

The case studies involved several extended visits in people's homes. These began with semi- structured interviews based on the ones we had used earlier. These were normally tape-recorded. Often they took more than one visit to complete. Subsequent interviews were less structured and drew on the particular interests and practices of individuals (see Aside 4.4). We pursued particular topics with different people, according to their interests and their life activities. To some extent each person set their own agenda. In some households we talked only to the original person we had contacted; in others several members of the household became involved. Maps were used with several people to plot where they went on a regular or occasional basis, who they communicated with, what areas of physical and social space they identified with. Some people saved letters from school or one week's worth of their junk mail; two people kept month-long diaries of their literacy practices; one couple recorded their bed-time reading sessions with their daughter and invited the researcher to family tea; one man was accompanied to the library and on to his regular café. We also met these people at social events, in the pub and at meetings; sometimes these were planned encounters and often they happened by chance. The additional areas pursued with each person are summarised in Appendix 1.

The collaborative data

When we had finished data collection for the case studies we concentrated on transcribing the interviews and analysing and understanding the data. With the benefit of further funding we returned to some people more than a year later to share parts of the data and analyses, and to collect further data. We refer to this stage of data collection as the *collaborative ethnography stage.* We wanted to explore new ways of involving informants in the interpretation of data. In part this was to check the validity of our analyses. Crucial to a social approach to literacy is the fact that people make sense of it and that their conceptions of the nature of reading and writing affect their learning and use. The collaborative methodology is a logical extension of this approach. Ten of the people we had already worked with participated in this phase. Five were people who had been studied as part of the Adult College data and five were from the Springside case studies, as described in Appendix 1. As with the case study data, we tried to get a range of people and our choice was theoretically motivated, but we were also limited in terms of who was available to work with us further. This was a year after the case studies had finished and more than two years after the Adult College data had been collected.

We returned to them with two sorts of information. Firstly, there was a transcript of about ten pages of typed extracts from transcripts of earlier interviews with them; we refer to this as *the short transcript* or simply as *their words.* Secondly, there was our analysis of their practices. We summarised this in about ten typed pages for each person, and refer to it as *the themes,* or simply as *our words.* In order to have a description of each person in their own words we also asked them to provide a pen-sketch of themselves. Three visits to each person were planned for the collaborative phase, although in practice it took more visits, and the research developed in a different way for each person. A further discussion of how participants in the study made sense of these research relationships is given in Appendix 3. (See also Barton and Hamilton 1992b; Hamilton 1998.)

Further observations, interviews and case studies

At the same time as these case studies on households were being started, we were also gathering data in other ways. Beginning with published studies, we collected a wide range of contextual information about Lancaster and Springside. Much of this has already been provided in Chapters 2 and 3 when giving the general social and historical profile of the city and the neighbourhoods. Alongside this, we carried out a series of interviews of people working in organisations which have some relation to literacy. These are organisations which either deal specifically with literacy or are involved in providing advice and information of some sort, or places where people have to deal with the written word. They include schools and colleges, bookshops, libraries, greetings card shops, travel agents, post offices, the tourist information office, Citizen's Advice Bureau, Dyslexia Association. Separate questions were used in each interview. We wanted to find out such things as the formal and informal literacies involved in the work: how these organisations saw their roles and how they viewed their clients or customers. They were asked about the services they provided; the literacy involved in attracting custom and dealing with the public; and to what extent they were aware of literacy difficulties.

Over the time of this project we have added other information collected in much more informal and ad hoc ways as events developed, ranging from documenting the banners placed at a main roundabout to announce birthdays and engagements, through to observing what happened on the day that Margaret Thatcher resigned, and tracking a summons to court about poll tax. We became especially interested in documenting the visual environment using photography. We took many pictures of signs in the public environment and some of people doing things with literacy. (See Barton *et al.* 1993 on photography both as a source of data about literacy practices and as a reflective tool for developing theory.)

While many of these observations centred on the whole city, others concentrated on Springside. This distinction became less clear-cut since we went round the city with people from Springside and, at the same time, local issues arising in Springside affected the whole city. Within Springside we carried out case studies of community groups and organisations through observations in the neighbourhood; through attending monthly residents' meetings, and other meetings. We were in regular contact with the Housing Action Project on Springside, and collected data for a case study on that organisation. When a neighbourhood issue arose, such as the planned selling of allotment land for housing, we attended meetings, interviewed participants and documented events as they unfolded.

Analysis and writing

Even though analysis and writing takes up more time than the collecting of the data, reports of qualitative research often leap from the data to the finished written product as if there are no intermediate steps, or as if themes and analyses simply emerge from the data. The reality, however, is somewhat less mysterious and more mundane than this. There are common steps in analysing the data, and we want to give some indication of the steps we took in making sense of our data.

The database

First, we should describe the database on which the analysis is based. The activities of talking, observing and collecting documents and artefacts generated data of various sorts. The records we kept and collected from these activities constitute the database for the analysis. To begin with, all the tape-recorded interviews were transcribed on to the computer, using a broad orthographic transcription; notes of interviews which were not recorded were also put on the computer. There are more than one hundred and forty interviews, most of them around ten thousand words long. These form a significant database in their own right. In addition to the interviews, there is a range of field notes, consisting of observations, impressions and reactions written at the time of each interview. These too form part of the database, as do our individual research diaries. The other written record is the handwritten project log book which was filled in at weekly project meetings and which is a mixture of plans, decisions and odd notes.

We collected a variety of artefacts and documents, such as the residents' association newsletters, posters and signs, one year's issues of the local paper, letters home from schools. Some artefacts and documents were created or collected for us by our informants, such as the diaries which we asked people to keep, or the junk mail. This data also includes our photographs and the background books and documents about Lancaster which we collected. Finally, we should stress the importance of head notes, the memories and interpretations which remain in our heads and which never reach the written form (Sanjek 1990). Memories and prior knowledge as well as written notes form the basis of the analysis and write up; they are crucial in integrating and making sense of the data, and we wish to acknowledge this. To summarise, the analysis and write-up are based on four sorts of data: transcripts; diary and field notes; documents; and head notes.

Analysis

Analysis is about looking for patterns in the data. Our approach to analysis is based upon grounded theory, following Glaser and Strauss (1967). This is not a methodology in itself but a set of principles, an epistemological stance, where the discovery of theory comes from data systematically obtained and analysed. It is based upon principles, such as the constant cycling back and forth between data and theory. These principles are interpreted in concrete ways when they are applied to individual research projects. In the following section we will describe how we have interpreted and operationalised the process of developing grounded theory.

We started with an orienting theory, described in Chapter 1, a theory of literacy which provided a framework for designing the study and initially viewing the data. As we got to know the data better, new elaborations and changes to the theory were developed. Data analysis began as soon as we had any data, and it continued throughout and beyond the period of data collection. In addition, we did not start all the case studies at the same time, but refined the methodology with each one. The methodology and the analysis were developing throughout the study. There are several practical strategies in analysing the data which we can identify.

(1) The first practical strategy for analysing the data is *reading* and re-reading the transcripts and notes and making notes on them, an activity we refer to as *memoing*. This begins with established themes which are part of our orienting theory, looking for example at the gendering of literacy events, at networks of support, at how people deal with problems they encounter and how people learn new literacies. By means of this process we articulate and amplify existing concepts, or change and modify them. Gradually we develop new themes and concepts by constant reading and re-reading. We then investigate them by further reading and memoing.

(2) There is a constant process of *selecting*, choosing some parts of the data as more significant than other parts. Each act of selection involves interpretation and is a reduction of the data. This is happening at every stage of the research, from the initial decisions about who to talk to and what to ask, right through to the final decisions of what to include and emphasise in this write-up of the research. Recognising this constant interpretation is the hallmark of qualitative research. With each transcript, and with each person's data, it was often useful to do simple *summarising*, and to identify significant themes.

(3) A major step in interpreting and reducing the data is *coding* and categorising, saying that different instances are all examples of similar phenomenon. We carried out various forms of coding of the data. The initial Adult College interviews were all coded systematically for all one hundred and sixty items in the questionnaire. Other data sets were coded for particular topics under investigation.

(4) One of the most important ways of evaluating themes, both existing ones and new ones, is by cycling back and forth between theory and data in order to identify patterns and regularities. Ideas developed in relation to one part of the data are checked out in other parts; new instances are located in relation to established patterns. This cycling between the data and the themes is done constantly at many levels: it involves making comparisons, looking for similarities and differences in different parts of the data. An important step is *linking*, making connections between different parts of the data. *Sorting* data is another way of examining similarities and differences, using different dimensions of the data, whether themes, people or documents such as photographs.

(5) Sometimes the analysis concentrates on one individual person, such as Harry or June, and we try to make sense of their practices; sometimes the analysis concentrates on a particular theme, such as the use of new technologies, and we check it across all people. A useful way to conceptualise this

is to think of the data as a matrix, with people or cases in the columns and themes or concepts in the rows. A vertical slice, then, is everything about one person; this leads to a profile of that person and information about relationships between practices and their overall coherence to that person. A horizontal slice is everything about one concept and how it is realised across a range of people. Sometimes we are doing horizontal slicing and sometimes vertical slicing. In the rest of the book, for instance, Chapters 5 to 8 each make sense of one person's practices and the relations between them. These can be seen as four vertical slices of the data. The remaining chapters look across as many people as possible and deal with particular themes; these can be seen as horizontal slices.

(6) In looking for patterns in the data there are basically three distinct forms of analysis which we can use on texts such as the interview transcripts: the first two are concerned with analysing the content of the texts, either in terms of the actual words in the text or in terms of coded categories which we apply to the text. The third form of analysis is to look at the broader aspects of the interview as a social interaction. We use all three forms of analysis in different places, often in combination. For example, all three approaches might provide clues as to how the informants make sense of the research, as in Appendix 3. At some points we contrast analysis of actual words and phrases with theme analysis, referring to the use of *their words* and *our words* respectively.

(a) Analysis of words and phrases in the interview data and examining how they are used. This means dealing with people's actual words as representing something significant about literacy. One example is that Harry often uses the words *educated* and *uneducated* when referring to people. We are able to trace this usage across different interviews and make sense of this distinction which is very salient to him. As another example, we traced the use of the word *community* and found that it was rarely used by the people who were interviewed; it was used more by us as interviewers than by our informants, and when it was used it was often in set phrases such as 'a sense of community' or 'community policeman'.

(b) Theme analysis: this has been mentioned already. It involves using our categories, such as networks of support or gendered relationships. These are our social science categories, our interpretations of the data. Transcripts have to be coded for such categories and themes can be traced and explored across the data.

(c) Analysis of the broader discourse of interviews: this includes all forms of analysis which look at the broader dynamics of the discourse, using simple narrative analysis, for example, to examine the stories which people tell. This includes examining the structure of the interviews, and issues such as which topics are taken up or ignored, the role the interviewer plays in prompting and shaping responses, what kind of encounter it represents, and the sense which informants make of the interviews. We notice, for example, that most

people sometimes told rehearsed stories. These are the stories which it is apparent they have told before, and probably many times. They may be repeated in different interviews, using similar words and phrases. Rehearsed stories are important because they are a part of an identity, and intrinsic to the way that person presents themselves to others. There are other types of story, including the *stranger on the train* stories described in Appendix 3.

(7) The acts of reading, memoing, coding and developing themes are all aided by the use of the computer. Having all interview transcripts stored on the computer, along with other field notes and diary notes, meant that a wide range of analyses could be carried out. Using the word processing package and concordancing packages, simple searches could be carried out across the data, as in people's usage of the word *community*. We found that the word processor was useful for much simple data organisation and manipulation. For systematic coding we used particular qualitative analysis packages including *Ethnograph*. Our higher-level analysis was a more fluid linking and memoing set of activities and we sometimes used Hypertext facilities and visual mapping with packages such as *Inspiration*. The computer enabled us to treat an individual transcript as a text, or to work across several transcripts.

(8) We were constantly evaluating the reliability and the validity of the analyses. Although all steps in research involve acts of interpretation, we wanted to evaluate the reliability of our analyses, whether the inferences we were making from the data were similar to those which other researchers working in the same paradigm would make. This was done in several ways. By constant dialogue in research meetings we were able to compare the perspectives of different members of the research team, getting corroborating perspectives for our claims. By comparing different sources of data, it was also possible to check the reliability of the data; we refer to this as the *triangulation of data* from different sources. At various point in the data analysis we set up systematic reliability checks, where three people would all transcribe the same piece of text, for example.

We were also interested in the validity of our data, how our interpretations fitted with the reality of participants' perspectives and the reality of other studies. One way of investigating the relation of our work to participants' perspectives was in the collaborative ethnography phase when we shared parts of our analyses with the people who had been interviewed.

(9) There were different stages in the analysis over time. At first we pursued the themes we had set out to explore, such as networks of support; gradually we shifted to themes which arose from the data, such as sense making and the importance of local groups and organisations. This shift is evident in the later chapters of the book. The method of argumentation and the way we can back up what we say changes to some extent. Inevitably there are some gaps in this data as we move on to themes which were not part of our original interests and which may even have been identified after

all data collection had finished. Nevertheless, whenever we have made a point based on one person's data we have attempted to examine whether it is supported by what other people said.

(10) Each stage of analysis involves selection; this is particularly true at the point of writing up the work where there is further interpretation, selection and organisation. This will be apparent in the remainder of the book. The final product is two people's construction, a report by just two social scientists studying a phenomenon. At the same time, it contains many other voices: we have included many quotes from informants, their words, and have included details from Sarah's diary notes. However, these are our choices and our selection from the mass of data and details. It is important to stress that other people's voices have always been mediated by us. The words have a 'double articulation', in Bakhtin's sense (1953/86). We are uttering the words of others, and in some senses they have become *our words*. The distinction between their words and our words exists but their words are always selected by us and contextualised in the text by our words.

What can be learned from an ethnographic study of literacy

This research starts by describing the particular. It is also about connecting the particular to a larger context of patterned practices, how specific things, people and processes are related, how the specific is connected with its social and historical context. This relationship between local activities and global patterns is described differently by different disciplines where people are working to understand the social construction of technologies and how cultural systems operate (as in LaTour 1993; Silverstone *et al.* 1994; Myers 1996). LaTour refers to a 'thread of practices and instruments, of documents and translations' which 'allow us to pass with continuity from the local to the global' (p. 121). In this research we are engaged in tracing the threads of literacy practices through contemporary social life.

There are many ways of relating a local study, a finding or an explanation to broader entities, including referring to statistical studies, to other literature, concepts and theoretical traditions, and appealing to the relevance of an explanation. It is the task of the researcher to specify in what ways the data relates to broader entities (see Alasuutari 1995). We make links beyond the research in Part III of this book. At various points we contextualise the findings by juxtaposing other studies which offer different sources of information. These include national survey data and other studies of literacy.

We do not need to prove to our readers the existence of literacy, but we are trying to interpret and explain the data we have collected – to make these examples of everyday literacy intelligible within the framework of cultural practices and social theory which we have adopted, producing classifications, conceptual tools and theoretical explanations which can be used to extend understandings of literacy in other contexts. Such theoretical explanations are essential to empirical study of any kind, and without them, data, whether quantitative or qualitative, cannot be interpreted. Ultimately, this study will be evaluated in terms of the ways in which it fits in with the theoretical frameworks we make use of, with other research data on literacy, and, not least, its relevance to our readers' concerns about literacy.

Part II

Each of the four chapters in this section of the book concentrates on one person and presents an in-depth profile of their literacy life and history. We introduce, in turn, Harry Graham, Shirley Bowker, June Marsh and Cliff Holt. They are four of the twelve people, listed in Appendix 1, who participated in the neighbourhood case studies; they also participated in the collaborative phase of the research a year later, and they have seen early versions of the analyses. We chose these four people to represent a range of different ages and interests and to get a gender balance. The people vary in the importance they attach to reading and writing and the roles it plays in their lives and also in the extent to which they identify difficulties with reading and writing in their everyday lives. We did not choose these four people as being somehow more special or more interesting than the other case study people; any of the twelve could have been chosen and would have revealed the similar richness and range of issues which arise in these four case studies.

Each chapter is structured to begin with general aspects of the lives of these individuals and moves on to cover their literacy history and life, the ruling passions which were apparent in their accounts and particular themes to do with literacy. The aim at this point is to provide a high proportion of their own words talking about literacy issues and to represent their voices in as many ways as possible, including reporting the pen-sketches which people provided of themselves. The chapters are not identical in style but to some extent reflect the ways in which these people talk about themselves, their skills as story tellers and the importance they place on literacy.

These in-depth profiles represent one approach to our data, that of trying to understand the meaning of literacy to a particular person. This approach gives the best and closest sense to you, the reader, of what the case study data was like in its 'raw' form and how we worked outward from the detail of individual lives to more general interpretations covering the other people. Part III brings together the whole range of people we interviewed by approaching the data from another direction, organising it by themes across all informants.

5

HOW THEY'VE FARED IN EDUCATION

Harry's literacy practices

We first came in contact with Harry Graham when knocking on doors randomly as part of the door-to-door survey in Springside; he was immediately interested in what we were doing and was happy to be interviewed further. In order to build up a picture of him, we will begin with how he describes himself, and then move on to our descriptions of him and his literacy history.

As we did not want to impose our own descriptions of him, right at the end of the research we asked him for a description of himself. He was reluctant to write anything down; nevertheless he was happy to talk and the interviewer wrote it down as he spoke; every so often he was read back what had been written and then he would add more detail. This description is given in his pen-sketch in Aside 5.1; all the words are his words. When asked how he would describe himself physically, Harry was at a loss for a while and then he said, *I'd be lost in a crowd of three. Nondescript.*

Another way of getting an idea of Harry is to listen to him talking about reading and writing. Selecting from the hours of interviews with him, the quotes in Asides 5.2 – 5.6 are illustrative of some of the things Harry said about himself and his literacy. Two further ways of visualising Harry and his life are provided firstly by a short description of him taken from background notes, and then by an extract from diary notes of a visit to his house. Sarah described him as follows: *Harry is neat and dapper and has sailor's blue eyes. Despite poor physical health there is something agile and youthful about him . . . He's an alert thoughtful man . . . sociable and lively.* The diary notes come from a visit when he has been left a transcript of a previous interview, and the notes include a general description of his living room:

> *Room: dark red raised tufted carpet. Glass coffee table with copy of the Daily Mirror. A settee with wooden arms against the wall opposite the front door; fireplace to left as enter. Alcove between fireplace and far wall, contains modern stereo music centre. Collection of records and tapes: war songs. Next to music centre, shelves with Harry's files, notebooks and a black pottery sports car. Colour photos of kids. TV.*

Aside 5.1   Harry's pen-sketch

I'm sixty-six . . . How would I describe myself . . . I don't know really. I like to be liked and so I do everything to encourage people to like me. I help people and do things like that. My personality is I can't be serious about anything. Happy-go-lucky me. I can't be serious. Like to look on happy side of everything.

I haven't altered anything since my wife died. She died two years ago. I've never altered. She used to play pop at me about helping people . . . putting myself out. She used to say, 'bloody fool' and I still do that now. I always do anything on an impulse me. It just comes in my mind and I do it irrespective of what the cost entails. That's me. I don't hold any grudges against anybody.

The thing I enjoy doing most is being in company . . . men's company. I like men's company for the talk and I'm always out of place when there's women about.

One of the loves of my life is I love children. The house is full of them when school comes out. I like me kids, aye . . . all round they come in here . . . do what they like. They know more about me house than what I do. I'm invited to all the birthday parties. I never go but I get a piece of birthday cake. Daft really but I enjoy owt like that. It keeps you young having kids about. Everyone of them knows that I'm twenty-one. Ask any kid around here. They all call me by my first name, Harry. I hate being called Uncle or anything like that.

Harry had used the pens as asked [using specific colours for different changes] *and appeared to have understood and enjoyed adding to the transcript. His initial reaction to working on the script was, in his actual words: 'I tell you what, it sounds queer if you type it as you talk . . . And there's some things that I just couldn't alter it if I tried. It's right and that's it . . . I mean, it's me, isn't it?'*

His daughter had laughed when she read the script and remarked, 'It sounds just like you, Dad'. Harry was surprised by the way he speaks on the transcript but not bothered. He said he had kept reading and rereading the transcript, 'must have looked at them a thousand times'.

Harry's literacy history and literacy life

So far we have given Harry's description of himself and have heard him talking briefly about his literacy. We now turn to our making sense of his life. He has lived in Lancaster all his life. His father was a machinist at Williamsons, a local factory, and his mother worked in the canteen there. They were short of money and his memory of holidays was of going to the beach at Morecambe for the day, walking there and back (a distance of six miles), and loving it. He recalls both his parents reading a daily paper which his father used to bring home from work. This would have been in the 1930s. Harry remembers waiting expectantly, so that he could read the daily cartoon strip. He also recalls swapping comics with other children in the neighbourhood, and his parents buying him an annual every Christmas. Apart from these, he remembers no other books in the home.

Aside 5.2   Writing on a slate

Oh! Well I can't understand it. The length of time they do at school now and all this new stuff that they teach them. And all the modern aids they have. I mean my teeth are still sat on edge now when I think about it. When I were writing on a slate with one of them things. And ee . . . and it still makes my mouth water, writing on a slate.

He attended a local infants school and junior school. He recalls writing on a slate and remembers the transition to exercise books (Aside 5.2). As the anecdote about the Grammar School (Aside 5.3) indicates, he passed the examination but his parents could not afford the cost of the books and uniform for him to go there. (The school, the examination and the uniform all still exist.) He went instead to Lune Street school which at that time was a *through school*, combining both primary and secondary age pupils. While at school he worked part time as an errand boy for a local butcher and left school at the age of fourteen to work there full time.

Aside 5.3   My education was nil

My education was nil actually. I did pass the exam for the Grammar School when I was ten years old but as my mother said, 'I can't afford to buy you the cap, never mind the uniform and books', so the opportunity was missed, I must have had the potential though. And I know I can put things into sentences and start new paragraphs in the proper places. But it's the ramblings in between instead of getting down to the nitty gritty. Somebody that was educated would probably say in two sentences what it would take me two pages.

He had around fourteen jobs from then until the age of seventeen when he entered the Royal Navy as an ordinary seaman. He remained in the navy until the end of the Second World War, when he joined the fire service in Lancaster. He moved up through the ranks of the fire service and stayed there until he retired. He has lived in several parts of Lancaster and moved to Springside to be near his daughter; he explains how *she was bottom in everything*, left school at sixteen and went on to *the college of knowledge*, the College of Further Education, where she took a two-year course in hairdressing. She owned a local hairdresser's, which she sold recently in order to go to college to train to be a nurse. She has two children, one of whom has just left the girls' Grammar School and is also taking a nursing course. Harry's son, who lives a mile away across town, went to the boys' Grammar School and on to university, although he left before completing a degree, and is a nurse at the Infirmary. He comments that there have been nurses from his family at the hospital ever since it was built a century ago. His wife died a few years ago and Harry lives alone, maintaining a network of friends and relations in the city.

Aside 5.4   Learning at work

I'm not illiterate. But I think it's a . . . something you've got to be trained at really. I always remember my fire service training. When I was doing the hotels and boarding houses. We had to do these fire precautions. Had to go round all the hotels and boarding houses from here to Barrow and issue a paper to them telling them what requirements were needed you see. I knew what they wanted but it was putting it into these words. So I went through all the old files and got . . . and I made a play on words. I put my words into their . . . my requirements into their words you see. Until I got it off where I could do it from memory. You know, like I could just do it parrot fashion and . . . But it was a struggle.

After the first contact, he was visited at his house and interviewed several times over a period of a few months. As well as the interviews and visits to his home, Harry also collected his junk mail for a week for us. He seems to have quite a regular routinised life. He goes to the local library at least once a week, and Sarah also went there with him. We also interviewed him with an old friend, Ted. Harry lives alone but he has regular contact with other members of his family. His sister-in-law does his shopping, and his son who lives nearby helps him in other ways.

Aside 5.5   Reading in the library

Oh well, I like to live in the past. I'm very interested in things that happened years ago . . . I'll go and say 'Can I have the Guardian for 1940?' And they bring you the big book, you see [referring to the local newspaper upstairs in the Reference room at the library]. *You've got all the Guardians there for twelve month. And I just . . . I'm away. And I'll stop there till I've read it all. I spend many a happy hour up there. And seen my own name many a time* [laughing]. *That brought back memories. I live in the past. I never look to the future, me.*

We gradually built up a picture of his life and the role of literacy in it. There are many examples in the transcripts of Harry using different literacies. For a retired person who might be seen as leading a fairly quiet local life he reports a wide range of different literate activities. He has a keen interest in local history and keeps magazines and newspapers associated with this; he spends time reading about this in the library, often taking notes from books. Connected with this he has books, photos and records to do with family history, and says that he and his wife traced his family back to the 1600s, looking up names in church record books and going round cemeteries. He reads a lot, usually about the war and is *never without a book*. Every night he reads in bed for an hour before going to sleep. He only reads *authentic war books*, meaning factual books, and never fiction. He borrows books from the library, going there every Thursday morning, and also buys second-hand books and swaps with friends. Despite not seeing himself as *a writer*, he sometimes writes letters and has written a story for a magazine about his war experiences; during the period we were studying his literacy practices he started writing his life history. Sometimes he refers to writing as *a struggle*, feeling he lacks the necessary training, although at other times he is more positive about it. He always writes letters out in rough first, he is concerned about *proper English*, and sometimes he tears up letters he has written rather then send them.

He uses literacy to keep up with current affairs and local issues. He reads a national daily paper sitting on the settee after breakfast *first thing in the morning, cup of tea and read the paper*. On Fridays he reads the weekly local paper, cutting out and keeping some things for reference. He also reads the local free newspaper which is delivered to the door, church newsletters and the residents' association newsletter, as well as watching television and listening to local radio. Literacy has other roles in his everyday life: his sister does much of his shopping and he keeps money-saving coupons for her to use; reading and writing have a role in organising his finances and paying bills; he has used medical reference books to check on his health, and his son's train timetables to plan holidays; he keeps a diary for future appointments and birthdays; and he takes phone messages for his son who does not have a phone. He helps neighbours with some aspects of literacy, such as helping them with their tax forms, and in turn is helped by others, for example when his son helped him write a job reference for a former colleague.

This kind of help can be seen as part of a complex system of support and reciprocity extending over many years. Within the family, Harry recalls that he began supporting his son's literacy development when he was little. His son would sit on his knee and pick out words from Harry's newspaper, for example: *what we used to do was give him a pen and tell him 'Ring all the "thes" or the "ands"'. That's how he got started, sat down with newspaper.* When his son went to grammar school, he began studying subjects such as Latin which Harry couldn't help him with. So Harry then supported him through finding others *in the circle* who could help him. His wife used to read the children stories, and his son sometimes helped his daughter with her maths. Now Harry's grand-children often do their homework in his house; neighbours' children often come round and he has sometimes helped them with their homework.

Aside 5.6   Helping others with writing

Oh aye. I've been asked. People come across, 'Will you make me tax form out for me?' And they've fetched all the papers and I've managed the tax forms for them, you know. Things like that.

On reflection I think this was because I was an officer in the Fire Brigade – people must have thought I was an academic, but I got my rank with hard work in studying for the exams, the last and hardest one was when I was fifty-two years old. Well I must be. And I must look the part. I've had people come round for what-do-you-call-its . . . to get a job. References. I've had people come round for references. And I gave them a reference. I gave one lad a reference. He was a fireman and he wanted a job. And he came round to me 'cos I used to be his Officer and asked me for a reference. And I give him one you see. And my lad came round . . . I always take a copy. And my lad come round, who's very well educated and he started laughing at it. I said, 'What's to do?' He said, 'That's no good'. He said, 'You don't do things like that'. And he wrote a proper one out you see. So that I got in my car right away and I took it round to this fellow and I said, 'Give us that one back and have this'.

It was rambling, you see. Instead of getting down to nitty gritty. Oh no, I didn't feel bad about it. No, because what did they expect of me anyway? Well I said, I wrote down what I felt about him and it was all true. So what more do they want. And yet, my lad laughed at it. Well, I read his and he actually said as much in a few words you see. That's what annoyed me. I wish I could do that.

One particular literacy event which is a regular part of his life is that Harry and Ted meet each week on a Wednesday morning to read through and discuss the local newspaper. They sit in the front room of one of their houses, drinking tea and discussing local politics and people they know, *generally putting the world to rights*, as Ted puts it. Sometimes they compose letters to the paper; they plan them together, then Ted writes them out and sends them off. These are *critical contentious letters* aiming to *expand people's opinions a wee bit*. If these letters are accepted by the newspaper, they are published on the letters page of the paper as unsigned anonymous letters coming from *A local resident* or *A taxpayer*. This is a type of letter which is common in local newspapers. These weekly meetings, then, represent a fairly complex literacy event, involving several stages and a range of technologies.

Other current activities he mentions involving literacy include shopping, paying bills, leaving messages, health care, holidays and entertainment. In these activities the networks operate in both directions and are part of broader social patterns of reciprocity. People help Harry and in the same way people have approached Harry for help, with tax forms and other forms. At the working men's club men discuss the war, and sometimes exchange and discuss books and magazines on the subject. This would be part of other networks of support at the club, so, for example, Harry has a friend who mends his car. There are also examples of support at work; when he was in the fire service, a colleague helped him to revise for exams, teaching him the idea of how there is a formula for passing exams, a way of answering questions. Harry used to accompany his wife to graveyards and the library in their search for information about her ancestry. Harry's sister-in-law helps Harry with his shopping sometimes. She takes tokens he has collected for money off various items. She also sometimes walks his dog. When his wife was alive, she and her sister used to shop together.

Having given an overview of Harry's literacy practices, we now turn to making sense of them, looking for patterns and meanings within Harry's practices. In later chapters we will be looking for patterns across different members of the community, and putting them in the explanatory framework of a broader social context. Beginning with making sense of Harry's practices, we will explore them through three themes which appeared prominent in his data.

Ruling passions

The starting-point for understanding Harry and his contemporary practices is the war, the Second World War which he experienced as a young man over fifty years ago. We've called this his ruling passion. He often turned the conversation round to the war; many of his stories were about the war and his interests were linked to it. When we went to interview people *we* wanted to find out about reading, writing and literacy practices. Unfortunately, it seemed, the people we interviewed often wanted to talk about something else; each person had a ruling passion, something *they* wanted to talk about and share with us. We talked to them about literacy, it seemed, and they talked to us about their lives. Often this appeared to have no relation to reading and writing, and we were tempted to say, 'No, don't talk about that: tell us about where you keep your books; tell us if you use the library'. In fact as the interviews continued, we found that when people told us their stories, they ended up telling us much more about literacy.

Examples of Harry's literacy practices which have been given already have links with his ruling passion. He has been reading *authentic war stories* – the phrase recurs – ever since the war finished, joining a number of different libraries in his search for more and more new books on the subject. He discusses and exchanges war books with friends. They are his main reading interest; they have titles like *In Danger's Hour, The Longest Battle, The War at Sea, The British Sailor, Fly for Your Life.*

Harry has also given us interesting information about literacy activities during the war. He kept a diary, although it was confiscated since, for security reasons, service personnel were not allowed to write diaries in wartime. He described the pleasure he got from receiving local newspapers, parcels of pens and paper, and letters from friends and relatives when he was at sea. Letters were sent and arrived in monthly batches. All mail was checked and parts cut out with razor blades. The post took three months to come and the waiting was *unbearable.* He has talked about the letters he wrote home, often written standing while on watch. He found it difficult to write, knowing it would be read by an outsider. Sailors were not allowed to say where they were or what the weather was like; Harry described the coded messages he sent to his mother to describe his location: the first letter of each paragraph spelled out the place where he was. He never told anyone about this and he was never discovered.

In talking about the war Harry speaks of *pumping adrenaline* and the comradeship amongst the men serving. He seems to feel real nostalgia for some aspects of war, but he is also haunted by memories of horror. When he went round the library with Sarah, he pulled a particular book off the shelf and turned to diagrams of a battle he had been involved in; he explained the details to her. (See Aside 5.7.)

Recently, his ruling passion has also motivated Harry to write, in several different ways. He has been trying to make contact with another serviceman who served on the same ship. He has been pursuing this by writing letters to *The Soldier* magazine and a veterans' association magazine. Harry took great care over writing the first letter. It was important to him; he was scared of adopting the wrong tone or failing to communicate what he wanted to say. He rewrote it several times. He has started a correspondence with one old shipmate who wrote an article in one of the magazines.

He also wrote a story for *Landing Craft* magazine. He was invited to do this after attending a meeting of the veterans' association which brings out the magazine. It took him *an hour to write it out, and then about an hour to go through it crossing things out and putting things back in again.* A friend across the road typed it out and he sent it off. It was his first time in print. Part of this article is shown in Aside 5.8 to give an idea of his style of writing.

During our research Harry began to write his own *authentic war story.* When we first talked to him he said he did not enjoy writing at all, but a year later he was surprised to discover that he actually got a great deal of pleasure from writing. He started this partly because of the landing craft article and also has been encouraged by his son and other people. He is enjoying this kind of writing: *it brings back memories and it's one of the pleasures of my life.* When writing about the war he questions what style he should use: should

---

Aside 5.7   Diary notes: Harry in the library

We walked past the computer – 'Ever used that?' 'No call to' – and on round the corner to the history section. A small sign at the top of the shelves read WAR STORIES. 'This is where I come . . . nowhere else.' Not wanting to inhibit his search for books I started to browse a bit, half watching him. He has very swift movements. He pulled books out, glanced at the covers, put them back. This went on for about five minutes. Then he pulled one out and started to leaf through it; he appeared to be looking at pictures in it – diagrams and photographs. He replaced it. I pulled out a Laurens van der Post. He came over. 'That's a good author', he said. I was surprised. I didn't imagine he'd like someone like that but I didn't comment. 'Mind, it's not a patch on the real stuff – too much writing in it' (it was a slim book) '. . . the author not the people, if you know what I mean.' 'Description?' I asked. 'Yeah, description, that's it. I like the words people said . . . out of their mouths . . . not all this word play, or florification [sic]. There's a lot glorify it.' He was staring at the shelves and pounced on a book. 'I'm in this one.' He flicked through it and found a diagram – some sea battle – lots of lines and little ships. He pointed to one, 'That was me. I was in on that.' I looked at the diagram. I saw a flat line drawing which evoked nothing in me. 'Makes me tingle looking at it,' he said. This is an extreme example of a literacy event which was both shared -- we were both looking at a diagram in a book – and, at least at the time, interpreted so differently by the two of us, it could not possibly be called a shared literacy experience.

---

he keep his story fairly light and amusing for the reader – *there's plenty of humour in war* – or should he describe the darker side and the dirty side of things as well? Would this shock or disturb people? In many ways he needs to make sense of everything that happened. He writes it out by hand and his son will type it for him and will *flower it up a bit . . . not the actual thoughts of the words but flower it up a bit . . . like the dawn broke. It was cloudy, rainy, anything like that, you see.*

The first way of understanding Harry's literacy practices, then, is to locate them in the war, his ruling passion and something not immediately connected with literacy. A second way is to examine how Harry talks about reading and writing, the frames he puts upon it. There are two theories of Harry's which seem to structure his view of literacy; they are the way in which he uses the dimension educated–uneducated and his attitude to reality and fantasy.

Educated and uneducated

When we asked people about their home and community literacy practices, they often replied in terms of education, providing memories of their own

---

Aside 5.8   Saga of the Landing Ship

LST 304 PARTY MONKEY DRAFT

It was late May 1944, I was rotting in Chatham Barracks again, having just been 'paid off' a destroyer, which we had just given to the Russians. Ginger Leonards and I were old hands, no one could put one over on us. We were not green, falling in for morning parades was not for us. Too many rotten jobs were handed out, plus there was a big enough workforce, without our help. About 15,000 ratings milling about nowhere to sling ones mick, long queues for meals, no money, no prospects.

I had a shovel, Ginger had a brush which we hid every night. Each morning we collected our tools and strolled around the Barracks, brushing here, shovelling there whenever anyone of rank appeared. It was a monotonous life. One morning sat in our usual chairs, the 30 seater heads, a P/O came in, heard us dripping and said 'How would you lads like a good draft'. Don't read on if you know whats coming. 'We are opening a new shore base in Grimsby and there is 7 days leave with it'. It gets worse doesn't it. 'What have we to do to get on it?' 'Just knock on the back window of the Drafting Office and ask for 'Party Monkey Draft' hurry there are only two places left'. 10 seconds later we handed in our station cards, we were in, couldn't believe our luck. 'Listen to the pipes' the wren said. Sure enough the next day Monkey draft fell in on North Road. The Chiefy shouts 'When I call your name, I will give you a number. Fall in on the rating holding the board with that number'. Ginger and I both got 304. Hand in your kitbags and hammocks, steaming bags only. Boarding the train in the barracks it puffed its way with many stops until eventually it stopped in Pompy Barracks. What an odd way to get to Grimsby. We fell in – we fell out – fell in again until finally we boarded a ferry which delivered us to a thing called LST 304. What a let down. What had we 'volunteered' for?

Party Monkey Draft turned out to be an RN Medical Party headed by Surgeon Lt. CDR French, 3 Sur.Lts, 12 sick berth attendants, 20 seamen with a P/O in charge. When the ship unloaded on the beach it was turned in to a hospital ship run by the above, it had none of the fineries of a proper hospital ship, in fact none at all, but it served its purposes . . .

---

education or details of their children's education. Talking about education was the easiest way into talking about literacy for them and it was often a frame they used to make sense of our research. This was true of Harry. A theme which kept recurring in Harry's transcripts was the distinction

Aside 5.9 Quotes on education by Harry

- *Good heavens I must have been illiterate when I left school.*

- *And I went in front of the Officer who dealt with all these things and his first question was, 'Where was you educated?' I told him the Marsh School and Dallas Road Elementary School. He said, 'I'm sorry but you haven't got the education for this job.'*

- *And so I'd no education.*

- *Well don't you think that's a lack of education in the first place?*

- *I've exactly the same feelings but lack of education. I can't express myself in words like Ted can. I can't even write letters where I can express myself.*

- *I get my son to write it out 'cos he was educated and I wasn't.*

- *But he's well educated and he can put in two words what it would take me a sheet of paper. I know what I want to say but I can't put it in words. And that's with my opinions as well. I have strong opinions on a lot of things but I just can't express them right.*

- *I was Secretary of that* [the club] *for a few years. And I used to have to write and write. Write the minutes out and I'd come home and I'd write them all out. And then I had to put notices on the board and notices everywhere. And it's very trying when you don't want to make any mistakes. I'd try and put it into the proper English. Except my education doesn't go that far.*

- *And in the Fire Brigade when it come to hydraulics and all these formulas, it were foreign to me but I had to learn them. And I studied for hours and hours over them. Trying to catch up on education which I never had. Especially on arithmetic and hydraulics and . . .*

- Helping children with homework: *Oh yes. But it got . . . it was embarrassing really. 'Cos they were far and away ahead of me. Because my education was nil really.*

- *And accept me as you find me, that's it. That's how it should be. It's been a problem all my life. This education business. They come out with things now even at bloomin' junior school. And I never did them at senior school.*

- *Because my education wasn't all that good. In fact, it was blooming awful.*

- *Then me son who has a lot better education than me can type it out and put it into better . . .*

- On the point of the research: *Is it to do with education? Right from start to the finish, getting people from different walks of life to see how they've fared in education.*

between *educated* and *uneducated*. He frequently uses the two words when referring to people, as in Asides 5.2, 5.6 and 5.9. Getting a place at the Grammar School, but not being able to afford to go, has been a lifelong disappointment to him. It has also affected his working life. He recounts that when he was in the navy, he was denied access on to a training course because he didn't have *the education*. He also describes how this has affected his work opportunities, particularly speed of promotion in the fire service.

Harry appears to view the world as being divided between educated people and uneducated people. It seems to be his yardstick for talking about people, including himself. He often talks of his own lack of education, and suggests that the occasional difficulties he has with writing tasks are due to this. He left school at fourteen. In contrast Harry talks of others who are educated, in particular his son who gives him support with some writing: there is the example in Aside 5.6 of the son helping Harry re-write a reference for someone; also typing up and *flowering up* Harry's Second World War story.

Harry contrasts himself with his son who is *educated*. His son went to the Grammar School, and on to university. He dropped out of university. Harry has mixed feelings about *the educated*. He respects his son's literacy skills, which he appears to see as being superior to his own. His son can write concisely and during nursing training wrote a case study on a patient which has now become part of a training manual. His son is very good at exams. Harry has no doubt that his son could pass the exams in the fire service with ease, exams Harry struggled over; but without any knowledge of the actual practicalities of the job. This is something which annoys Harry. He sees a clear distinction between practical expertise and educational or academic expertise.

He talks more than once about how educated people are people who are good at exams, good at paperwork, but how those skills are not necessarily the most important in working life. Harry comes across as practical, quick-witted and calm. Those things are important in the fire service. Any educated person might be able to revise for fire service exams and pass them, but that would not mean they would necessarily be any good at the job.

So, although he feels uneducated and although he still feels a sense of injustice about not having had the passport of a grammar school education to help him in his working life, he does not actually seem to aspire to being an *educated person* or to feel any great respect for those who are. Harry identifies strongly with working people who do practical jobs, and dirty jobs. He has spent his working life in dangerous, dirty and stressful situations. Cutting bodies out of mangled vehicles in motorway accidents, and continually risking life to save others, or pulling corpses from burning buildings, is perhaps the least enviable of all jobs. Fire-fighters keep a low profile. Harry is modest, and quite unselfpitying, but he is very aware that practical expertise is undervalued in society. When he is talking about people from the university there is a respect for them but it is always tinged with some sort of *but*: there are things that they can't do.

Harry's views on how people learn also derive from this division. The skills which were vital for his job were not skills which anyone could learn from books. He thinks apprenticeship is the best form of training and contrasts this with book learning: *Books can't teach you anything . . . nothing like that . . . it's daft. I've told my son he could pass the exams on the fire service with no problem. He's great at book learning . . . he'd come out top. But he wouldn't be able to do the job 'cos it's nothing to do with book learning.* He also criticises the lectures he had to attend on training courses, where he kept his *eyes open with match sticks,* and he has never enjoyed giving talks at meetings.

Harry says that he *must have been illiterate when I left school . . . I had the potential . . . but I never got any further with it.* At one point in the navy he was refused a particular job because he was told he didn't have the education for it. It was in the fire service that he studied hard to catch up on *the education which I never had.* There was an entrance test and exams for promotion. He studied hard for these. Part of the job was to read and keep up with technical bulletins, informing others of incidents and industrial changes. Information about new chemical hazards, equipment, changed procedures was displayed on notice-boards and they were expected to read these. As he was promoted there were more literacy demands at work, including writing reports and providing statements as a witness to accidents

He provides a good example of changing work practices leading to new literacy demands. From the early 1960s, new government legislation made fire authorities responsible for overseeing fire safety and carrying out inspections of businesses. The Fire Brigade in every town had to go round offices and shops, checking fire precautions and issuing certificates. Later on it included hotels and boarding houses and it took three years to certify all the buildings in the area: *And every one you went to, it was miles and miles of paper, written reports explaining why and how.* Harry and Ted described all this, and how as a result of the inspections attitudes to the Fire Brigade changed. Fire Officers were expected to impose and enforce an Act which they did not fully understand at first. They learned about it as they went along. This involved training centres being set up and officers going on courses; many of them were not interested in this, they had joined *to fight fires not to do office work.* On the courses they were taught about the new acts; how to inspect premises; and how to communicate with the public. They were not taught how to actually write the reports. Harry recounts how he learnt by reading and copying from old reports filed in the fire station: *you took out the bits that was relevant to yours and you wrote that in. And then after a few weeks you started developing your own . . . your own little way of doing it. It was a play on words really. You can write a sentence out ten different ways with different words but all meaning the same.* He chuckled when he thought about how other people would now be using his old reports as models and copying out bits of them.

Harry and Ted were also active in various committees in the Fire Brigade and in the local working men's club. This involved a range of literacy practices. When asked about minute-taking, Ted reported *and we strictly observed the rules of permitted procedure which are standard, you know. And we drew up agendas and appointed officials annually. And they were all like conducted, by and large, on standard committee procedure and rules.* The procedures were all handed down from the past. All the committees kept to the same old rules whether or not they were relevant to today. Harry was secretary for a while; he had to write minutes and put up notices. He found all this very difficult, wrote them all out at home, trying *to put it into proper English.*

Despite his feeling on being uneducated, it is clear that Harry participated in a wide range of complex literacy practices both in his work life and in his community life. It is also clear that he learned them as an adult and picked them up informally. This first theme, then, is an attitude to education which reflects early childhood experiences, and which structures how he sees the world today, how he deals with people and how he feels about literacy.

Fiction, truth and reality

This theme emerged slowly. For Harry the only stories worth telling or reading are *authentic*, real-life stories. He seems to look down on novels. His wife used to read a lot of novels and also stories to the children. He didn't understand what she saw in the stories. Harry appears to feel a clear distinction between reading factual books and reading fiction – one is educational, the other almost a waste of time. Interestingly, Harry received praise at school for his imaginative stories. It was fine as a child, but not as an adult. He accepts that a child reading a novel might be learning something from it, but there is an edge to what he says which somehow implies that some other activity might be preferable. Also, it is fine to have his own imagination, but he does not want anyone else's. This view is also apparent in his television viewing. He'll watch documentaries or quiz programmes but not soap operas or plays. When questioned, Harry suggested imagination was a dangerous thing – *the last thing you want in wartime.* He also talked of not believing in dreams and fantasies: *they get you nowhere.* Harry was not the only man we interviewed to express a preference for reality and a hostility to fiction, and we return to this theme in Chapter 10 when we discuss some of the differences in the meanings of literacy to women and men.

When we returned Harry's transcript to him in the collaborative ethnography phase of the research, he was pleased with it and read and re-read the script. As the diary quote at the beginning of the chapter makes clear, he was pleased with the way it sounded and at ease with his own voice.

The life story that Harry is now writing is for himself and for other seamen like him (See Aside 5.8). It is important to him that he writes in his

Aside 5.10 Imagination and reading

HARRY: *Well I've got a book upstairs . . . The Longest Battle . . . The War at Sea '39–'45. Which obviously impressed me because it's fact. And because I was there at the time, it's interesting . . . And that's the only books I read is factual.*

INTERVIEWER: *You don't read novels?*

HARRY: *Oh no. I can't be interested. No. Other people's imagination. I'd sooner read the real thing . . . I don't really like reading tripe. But then again if they [children] read a novel, they're learning something from it, aren't they?*

INTERVIEWER: *Do you think novels are tripe?*

HARRY: *Oh yes, aye. It's somebody's imagination. I couldn't read anybody else's imagination. I'd sooner read the real authentic thing, you see. As it happened.*

. . . Oh aye. We used to have compositions . . . and I always had to go and read mine out because I had the best imagination in class.

INTERVIEWER: [laughing] *Well this is rather strange isn't it?*

HARRY: *Aye. It is, yes.*

INTERVIEWER: *So, why do you feel so little respect for imagination then? If you were good at it.*

HARRY: *Well my imagination . . . I mean it's all right to me but I wouldn't want to read anybody else's . . . I remember as a kid I had a very vivid imagination. I could write compositions about anything that . . . just all made up. Never anything true to life.*

INTERVIEWER: *What do you think changed that? Just leaving school?*

HARRY: *Probably, aye. I don't know really. You could go into a lot of blarney about the war really. When you go in as a boy and come out as a man. It certainly makes a man of you. And that's where imagination's worse thing ever.*

INTERVIEWER: *Do you think it's dishonest?*

HARRY: *Oh aye. And it's bad for you anyway. You can imagine all sorts of things. And it never happens. There's nowt as good as true life, is there?*

It's a queer attitude I've got really. I can't go along with anybody else's imaginations. I don't mind my own [laughs].

INTERVIEWER: *Quite a few . . . particularly men I've spoken to have said that.*

HARRY: *Yeah, aye. I suppose men are a lot different to women. Women fantasise a lot.*

. . . Oh if it's a novel of somebody's own imagination, I won't even look at it. No, I could make my own story up better.

INTERVIEWER: *So is that what it is? That you feel that really you could do better?*

HARRY: *Oh yeah, aye. In fact the people at work said they'd like me . . . to put down my life story, you see. Because I've had a right good life you know, and all that. And I wish I had the ability to do it.*

own voice, a voice other men like him can relate to. He is a compulsive reader of *authentic* war stories, but has no interest in reading books by officers. Harry feels his own reading has given him a good sense of how to approach this writing, but he lacks confidence in some aspects of the project. He feels confident about the structure of the story, the technical information, the language of seamen and writing dialogue. His memory of the war is very vivid. But he feels he needs to include more literary passages, with descriptive language to convey atmosphere and weather, to conjure up storms with. This links up with the educated–uneducated theme where he is going to pass his writing on to his *educated* son to *flower-up* for him. There is no sense of this being a failing or an intrusion on his son's part. It seems to be a collaborative venture which is agreeable to them both. It is the point at which the educated and the uneducated meet on mutual ground and share literacy skills.

There is a connection between this theme and his ruling passion. Harry's passionate interest in the war fifty years later seems in part to be a search for the truth. This is not so much a political truth but a need to rediscover, or recreate the real experiences of servicemen like him.

He is using literacy to make sense of his own life. He is doing this through both his reading and his writing; his reading about the war is to make sense of his experiences, his writing makes sense of his experiences and communicates them to other people. The writing also validates the experiences and provides a voice for *ordinary people.*

6

GETTING THINGS DONE IN THE COMMUNITY

Shirley's literacy practices

Aside 6.1 The petition

INTERVIEWER: *Can you tell me about the petition?*

SHIRLEY: *Well . . . it started off about two months ago which would be what . . . July. When I was listening to various people and they were going on about the housing action area and that it wasn't going to be covering their homes higher up the Springside area. So, when I mentioned to various people about getting a petition sorted, they decided, 'Yes, it would be a good idea to get one sorted'. But nobody seemed to want to make the initial move. So I set to and started it off.*

INTERVIEWER: *Who did you talk to? When you first thought of it, who did you talk to? Did you just talk to people . . . ?*

SHIRLEY: *Well no. I'd spoken to a lot of the residents first and they were most disgruntled about . . .*

INTERVIEWER: *Was this just casually meeting people in the street?*

SHIRLEY: *Yes. Yes, when they were talking about the housing action area and the work that was being done on the houses and, you know, 'We're not getting the housing action area coming up this far but we're putting up with the muck and everything else from the other part of the area'. So I then had a chat with a chap from the Environmental Health Department, and asked him whether he thought it would be a good idea for them to petition.*

INTERVIEWER: *How did you get in touch with him?*

SHIRLEY: *He was coming to visit some of the residents that were going to have the work done. Because it's an Environmental Health Scheme that is going on. And he said that he thought it would be a wonderful idea to petition the Council and to encourage it as much as I could. So I went round anybody who then mentioned to me that they were angry that their house wasn't going to be covered under this housing action area. And I then said to them, 'Well, I've been chatting to this chappie from the Environmental Health and he said to encourage you all to send in a petition'. But as I said, nobody wanted to started it off. So I got . . . well more and more*

> *frustrated. After sort of finding out whether it would be worth doing and all the rest of it and nobody wanted to make the first move. So I typed up a simple phrase that said that the people that had signed the petition were very angry that their homes were not going to be covered in an enveloping scheme as had the other houses in the area. I then got one or two people . . . after I'd started it off with a few signatures . . . then got people then 'cos I'd started it off, to take it over a little bit. And then they went to some other streets for me.*
>
> INTERVIEWER: *So, who were those people? Were they . . .?*
>
> SHIRLEY: *Well, one was a lady who lives on Williams Street whose house is just outside of the housing action area . . . She actually said if ever I wanted anything doing that she would be quite happy to help. We were talking one day and she said whether it was delivering the newsletters or whatever, she'd be quite happy to do that. So I collared her to do the petition and she did Williams Street and a couple of the others. And somebody on the opposite side of Springside Street that hasn't been done took it for me to Moss Street. And then I went door to door to the other streets.*
>
> *. . . So as I say, we covered every street.*
>
> INTERVIEWER: *Have you any idea how many houses you didn't get answers to?*
>
> SHIRLEY: *Oh no. I know there have been a lot of people ringing up my office and saying 'I believe there's been a petition going round about the housing action area and I haven't seen it. How can I sign it?' But a lot of them . . . we just didn't have the time to go back to houses where there wasn't people in.*

Shirley's literacy history and literacy life

Shirley Bowker is in her mid-thirties. She lives with her partner, Jack, and two sons, aged nine and ten years. Shirley was brought up in Lancaster and went to local schools, leaving with some basic qualifications. When she left school she worked for eighteen months in a printer's. After a brief period working in London she returned to Lancaster and moved to Springside. She has done a variety of paid part-time jobs since her children were born, including catering, barwork and being a slimming and aerobics instructor. She was not in paid work when we met her. Jack is a trained electrician but, like Shirley, he has done many different jobs, including deep-sea diving. For the last thirteen years he has worked as a labourer, based at a local hospital. This is his second marriage and he has grown-up children who live elsewhere.

Shirley was mentioned to us when we first visited the Housing Action Project office to talk to the Manager about the project. He suggested that if we wanted a short-cut to a key community figure we should approach Shirley Bowker. He talked of her in glowing terms, saying *she knew the area like the back of her hand, knew just about everyone and could be relied upon to stir up interest and get things done.* She was already editing the residents' newsletter at that time, and liaising between residents and the office. Other workers in the office backed him up, saying she was *a great character as well,* and *would do anything for anyone.*

Aside 6.2   Shirley: how others see me

How do I think others see me? Who knows? I suppose it depends on who you ask. I would hope I haven't crossed anyone that they would wish me the worst they could, but I'm also no saint, and have ruffled a few feathers, mainly by not doing what others wanted, but I don't think I've hurt anyone to the extent that they feel any malice toward me.

The boys see me in different lights. I'm sure they think I'm mad, they know my sense of humour which they see as being a bit off sometimes. I may say something very seriously and it's only when they see me grinning that they realise it's a joke. I do have to watch this sometimes though, I have almost hurt their feelings. It does boil down to moods at the time. Their view or opinion of me is quite important to me. I know people who have grown up hating their parents and resenting them for one reason or another. I hope my boys don't grow up feeling like that about me or Jack.

So from the boys – fun, loving, supportive and understanding. A friend.

From Jack – expressive, supportive, a partner and friend, an ally.

From others – think of me with dread in their hearts, a listener, a helper, a fighter of causes, someone who will go where they probably wouldn't have thought of, an advice giver, trouble shooter.

I hope.

We had not intended seeking out a key figure. In fact we had doubts about recommendations of this sort, as we say in Chapter 4. We were not certain at this stage in our research what role the Housing Action Project played in Springside's community and wondered if someone who appeared to be a key community figure to a formal organisation, staffed by people who were not actually residents themselves, might be seen differently by locals. But we kept Shirley in mind. A few days later Sarah met her at a touring play about dyslexia in a local college. She was immediately interested in the project and was happy to be interviewed in her home. We interviewed her and her husband and also observed her at the residents' association meetings and at other social functions. Extracts from her pen-sketch are given in Asides 6.2, 6.4, 6.6 and 6.7; unlike other informants, she wrote this for us as a set of responses to the themes we initially wrote about her.

She lives in one of the terraced houses of Springside. The house is very much a family house and the front door opens into the lounge. The house is described in Aside 6.3.

Aside 6.3   Field notes: first visit to Shirley's house

Two two-seater armless settees upholstered in rough orange and brown striped fabric. Pale mushroom-coloured wallpaper with a silvery leaf pattern. A small fireplace with a mirror above it, and an oblong appointment calendar with a design of bluetits on it hanging from a nail left of the mirror. To the left of the fireplace there is what looks like a 1930s figurine – a woman in a green dress; it could be a light. This stands on a shelf beneath several wall shelves of books and records. There are also about twenty letters, opened envelopes on this shelf. They are arranged in an orderly looking way, standing upright like books. But there is a clutter of odds and ends to the left of them; and the floor space beneath the shelves is also cluttered: old magazines, papers, books (these are stacked on the floor against the wall), plastic bags, a white china mug with crimson roses on it full of biros and felt tips – about twenty pens with tops on.

Between the two settees there is a table, invisible under piles of paper and books and kids' toys. Two children's Ladybird books on top of the pile have cardboard markers sticking from them. One settee is in front of the window, which is painted white, the other runs from the hall door to the window. Above this one there are perhaps a dozen photographs of Shirley's two boys – professional-looking photographs; some are framed. On this settee there is a cat basket.

Around the tiled fireplace, on the carpet, there are lots of bits and pieces; fire lighters and other packets, old slippers, paper bags etc. To the right of the fireplace there is a glass-fronted bookcase, two shelves of books arranged in a fairly orderly sort of way but there are lots of other things in with them – bits of paper and odds and ends.

The sense of chaos, things bursting out of cupboards and sliding off tables, is misleading. It seems that Shirley knows exactly where everything is. The pen pot she retrieves from a nest of towel and cat fur behind the settee almost certainly lives behind the settee.

Through the archway there is a dining/working area. Shirley's knitting machine is set up in this end of the room. She is currently knitting sweaters for a haulage firm. Black words with the name of the firm on grey wool. This is for friends. There is a table and chairs where the family eat, more shelves of oddments, a back boiler, bags and boxes on the floor, and a witch mobile hanging over the window.

Shirley proved to be invaluable to our research. The fact that she was a key figure was apparent in our door-to-door survey where her name was mentioned spontaneously in connection with local advice-giving. It was also clear through visits to the Housing Action Project and in residents' meetings that Shirley really was a key figure locally, known by many people not just for her involvement in official organisations but through her informal activities and networks too.

Aside 6.4 Shirley: key figure in the community

'Key figure in the community.' Phew! What a title to live up to. Well I suppose I try to do more than some but I don't do as much as others. Yes people do know me for the involvement with all sorts of things, probably because I've badgered them on one thing or another. Perhaps I'm lucky that I make friends easily and appreciate any help anyone gives me and will express my thanks. I don't or try not to take others for granted which I think others appreciate that in me. Down to earth? Unshockable? I suppose on reflection, I am both of these, and yes I do have strong views on things and am not afraid to voice my opinion, but I won't try to ram my views down anyone's throat and will always try to find a compromise if a stalemate is reached on any issue. Who do I turn to? It depends on the problem. I have friends and acquaintances and will contact the one I feel can help the best.

Shirley is active in a number of ways in the local community. She has a reputation as a general advice-giver, someone people take their problems to. Occasionally she has been approached by friends for help with reading and writing – both for themselves and for their children. In fact many of her social concerns are to do with children's welfare. One resident described her as *Springside's Dr Spock*; another referred to her as *the local dyslexia person.* She has many contacts in the neighbourhood as she sold goods from a catalogue for several years. She is also known for her machine knitting; she knits for friends and designs machine patterns in the form of graphs for them, something she taught herself to do. She also has a regular stall at car boot sales. People pass books on to her for her stall, which she runs as a book exchange:

> *When I was doing car boot sales . . . I found that if I sold nothing else I always sold books. And because we are quite prolific readers, books were something that we always had hundreds of and so I decided to have a clear out of bookshelves to get rid of the ones that had been sat there maybe for a few years and I thought, 'No, perhaps I'm not going to read that again'. You know. And then my mother-in-law did the same thing. She decided to have a good clear-out. Partly because her sister had died and it shook her 'cos she found out what a hoarder her sister had been. She decided she didn't want to be like that. So she gave me boxes and boxes of books because she had really been hoarding books and because there were so many different types of books in what she gave me as well, I decided that perhaps it would be a good idea to do an exchange with them.*

People pass on magazines with things in which might interest her – articles on dyslexia or knitting patterns. In turn, Shirley lends people her personal books and passes on magazines sometimes. She is an avid reader with wide-ranging tastes.

> *Prima* [magazine], *I do actually keep every copy. I've got every copy since I started buying it. Sometimes people will give me other ladies' magazines that they think, you know, 'Oh, Shirley would like this because it's got such and such in it'. They'll give me that. Sometimes I will only cut out the section that they've given me the whole magazine for, and then throw the rest of the magazine out.*

Shirley does not feel she has any problems with reading and writing herself and reads and writes a great deal in her day-to-day life. She says she has *a lousy memory* and because of this relies on written records:

SHIRLEY: *I do keep an appointment diary. 'Cos if I don't, I forget appointments. I do write . . . I have a diary now but I only write in it you know, things that I must remember. Birthdays . . . I'm terrible with birthdays. So I must write down birthdays. And if I have any meetings for Springside Residents or whatever to do with that then I write those down so that I don't forget.*

INTERVIEWER: *You've also got a calendar on the wall which you write dates in on.*

SHIRLEY: *I do. Again because of this lousy memory. I need as many reminders as possible!*

One of Shirley's sons has difficulties with reading and writing; he now has a statement of special educational needs as being dyslexic. Shirley is aware of a strong literacy tradition and values, particularly from her father's side of the family. Her father *was the secretary for the local branch of the St John Ambulance Brigade. So he used to do an awful lot of writing. He doesn't do as much now because he's had to give that up for health reasons. But he still, given half a chance, will pick up a book and have a read.*

Shirley sees her family as being strong and close-knit. She explained that they have mutual interests, and support one another. They discuss issues with the children and play family board games together. When the children have problems they are taken seriously, examples being Ben's dyslexia and Sam's confrontation at secondary school. Shirley explained that, being at home more, she deals with the household correspondence, bills etc. She writes to Jack's family, including to his grown-up children. She writes the letters and cards to mutual friends and relatives on both sides. Shirley enjoys letter writing and she said that her handwriting is easier to read than Jack's. Shirley helps Ben with his reading and writing and reads to the children at night sometimes. Shirley and Jack seem to be united in their educational beliefs and general outlooks. They share common interests; both are interested in drawing and painting, although Shirley does little these days. The children also enjoy art, and at one point Sam said that he wanted to be a

---

Aside 6.5   Family traditions of reading

SHIRLEY: *I've got one sister and one brother.*

INTERVIEWER: *And as a family you were all readers were you?*

SHIRLEY: *Not so much as a family. My father did a lot of reading. My mother doesn't because my mother is like Ben and has dyslexia. So she doesn't read very much at all. But my father did. He doesn't as much now but he did. My sister reads quite a lot now. She didn't read a lot when she was younger . . . neither of us did. We used to read something if we had to read it because it was part of school or something like that. But we tend to read a lot more now.*

INTERVIEWER: *Is there anybody in your family who's considered sort of a bookworm? Somebody?*

SHIRLEY: *My grandmother. Yes. She is a bookworm. She reads Mills and Boon so . . . But, no . . . she doesn't just read Mills and Boon but she does read an awful lot. She has a mobile library that goes to her once a fortnight . . . and she gets maybe six books and will read all six books plus any that somebody else has given her.*

INTERVIEWER: *Is she ever criticised for that?*

INTERVIEWER: *No, no, no. Not at all. You don't criticise my granny at all [laughing]. Not at all. Jack's Mum is a big reader as well. She can read half a dozen books a week. She will sit up . . . 'cos she has problems with arthritis and things like that. If she's in a lot of pain she will sit and read. If she's in pain and she can't sleep.*

---

sculptor. As a couple they enjoy a similar taste in novels although Shirley doesn't read Jack's war books.

Shirley says that she and Jack never buy newspapers. For regional and national news she relies on the television, which she watches regularly. For local news she relies on word of mouth: *I'll listen to Granada Reports and things like that. I watch that on the TV. Most of it's word of mouth. You know, somebody will read the Visitor and they'll say 'Did you see the Visitor?' which I never buy anyway, then they'll say 'Oh, there's such and such a thing happened at such and such a place', you know.*

She gives two reasons for not buying papers. Firstly she feels that journalists present biased views and that they harass people to get their stories. *I find a lot of journalists tend to twist a lot of the facts. So no, I don't read them. I object to journalism especially when it comes to specific incidents. Like when my friend's son drowned, obviously she was quite upset that he had drowned and things like that and all the local journalists were on her doorstep hammering on the door and saying, 'Could you make a statement for the press?' And, you know, obviously she wanted to be alone in her grief and she was being hounded by journalists who just wanted what they classed as a sensational story.* The second reason she gives for not reading newspapers is that the news is old by the time it reaches the newspaper: *it's easier to watch the news on the TV and get it as it happens or whatever, rather than wait twenty-four hours to get it.*

Ruling passions: fighting injustice, making changes

Just as we found a key starting-point for understanding Harry's accounts of his life, so we did for Shirley. Shirley seems to have a very strong sense of justice. This is evident in her personal life, in her dealings with her children's education, and in her community role. She doesn't just complain, she acts – if something needs sorting out, she will get on and do something about it. She will encourage others to do the same. In her own words, she is *willing to set a ball rolling.* She has strong opinions about local issues and a desire for change.

She described a string of activities that she had been involved with, many of them prompted by her concerns as a parent: she had edited the newsletter at the nursery school; she had tried to start a parent–teachers association at her child's primary school and she has helped out at the school; she fundraises for the local dyslexia association, and has been their press officer; she has tried to organise a pressure group to improve the play space in the neighbourhood; she got a neighbourhood watch scheme set up in Springside and has lobbied the council about traffic calming measures. Most recently, she has become newsletter editor for the newly formed residents' association and organised a petition to get more households included in the enveloping scheme to do with house improvements. Shirley's active roles in these initiatives are all evidence of her commitment to justice and her belief in community action to make change.

Aside 6.6   Shirley: helping out

There are many things I feel passionately about, and if I can do something to help sort out a problem either mine or someone else's, be them family, neighbours or friends then I won't turn anyone away. Perhaps I'm a sucker for a sob story, it has been said in the past. But the thing I have learnt to do is help people stand on their own two feet rather than allow them to use me as a crutch. I would rather fight for something with someone than for someone. I will also try to recruit people to help me fight for a cause if I think the cause is worth fighting for.

During the period of our research, Shirley's life seems to have been in a continual state of change and development. The support which she has given to friends and neighbours on an informal basis appears to have extended to a wider range of people in the community.

Shirley is interesting and unusual among our case studies in that, as well as having strong personal networks in Springside, she is confident to approach key figures and officials in other places and organisations. She makes links between these informal networks and the more official ones, mobilising resources both for herself and on behalf of other people to get things done in and for the neighbourhood. This is where her strength and importance lies as a community figure. It is not just literacy that enables her to do this, but literacy is an important tool among others that she does not hesitate to use to get things done. She is confident about her own skills in written and oral communication but also confident about asking for help from and giving help to others. This makes her a very effective campaigner in dealing with official institutions and using their procedures and rules.

During the project we caught her in transition between being a local community figure, active mainly in informal local networks, and being a more public figure. Someone had suggested to Shirley the previous year that she would make a good councillor. She was tempted to stand, and said that she hoped to in the future, but at present she felt she had too many family commitments to consider it. She wanted to get the boys settled into secondary school first. In fact by the time we finished this book she had become a local councillor and chair of the local Labour Party constituency group.

As discussed above, many of her original concerns come directly out of Shirley's experience as a parent, and these have acted as a springboard to her wider involvement in the community. Recently she has been thinking about broader issues such as racism and the way women are treated. She has been involved in personally removing racist stickers put up in the neighbourhood by the British National Party.

Aside 6.7   Shirley: my life is changing

I hope my life is changing, if it wasn't I would probably do something to change it. I am not a stop at home, clean the house, do the laundry, be a good wife and mother type. I believe women do have a role to play in the great scheme of things, and that a woman's place is no longer in the house, women can be good jugglers of roles and play many. And I hope or think I manage this fairly well and get support from my family and friends with whatever I try to do. If I didn't have their support I'm my own woman and still have a choice.

Dyslexia, home and school

This theme crops up repeatedly in the transcripts. The subject of dyslexia is one of Shirley's main reading interests. She reads books on the subject and magazine articles since her own son was diagnosed as dyslexic. Shirley's mother also has some writing difficulties, and Shirley has researched the possibility that there is an inherited tendency to dyslexia through several generations of her family, talking to her own parents and grandmother about their experiences of reading and writing. This is probably one of the reasons she was interested in taking part in the research project with us – a strong interest in reading and writing difficulties prompted by her son's experiences at school. Shirley helps her son after school, and takes him to the Dyslexia Association every fortnight (see Aside 6.8). She used to go into school and work with him. Now she goes in regularly to discuss how he is getting on.

At first Shirley had some problems with the school, in getting them to recognise that Ben was having difficulties with reading and writing, but she has worked hard at developing a good relationship with the head teacher. She talked at great length about this in the interviews, and it had obviously been a major focus of her attention over several years when Ben was very unhappy at school. Her stories include detailed descriptions of the teaching methods at the school, her ways of supporting Ben at home and the kinds of difficulties Ben had in his reading and his writing. Shirley had to fight to get a support teacher for her son, and the head teacher helped her with this, helping her draft a letter pushing for her child's need for urgent support and advising her whom to send it to for maximum effect.

SHIRLEY: *I wrote it . . . a rough copy of it first by hand. Then re-read it and changed it and reworded it and then rewrote it again and if I still wasn't happy with it which I wasn't, I wrote it three times until I felt that I got . . . said what I wanted to say.*
INTERVIEWER: *Did you read it out to anyone?*
SHIRLEY: *I actually showed it to* [the head teacher] *up at school because it was done with her approval as well and she pointed out that I'd misspelt a word which was quite good of her to do.*

Shirley copied the letter to two local MPs, educational officers and school governors and even sent a copy to the Department of Education. Although she only received two replies, from an MP and from the school governors, they took her case up with the education office and very quickly she heard that the final statement for Ben had been approved:

SHIRLEY: *So, lo and behold next thing that arrives is a proposed statement, which I was quite shocked about, I didn't expect it to happen quite so soon..*
INTERVIEWER: *What does it look like?*
SHIRLEY: *Well, it's sheets and sheets and sheets of paper in various colours and, each one is a report from either the medical he's had; or a report from the Reading and Language Services; there's a report from* [the head teacher] *in it, there's a report from the educational psychologist in it, there's a report from his class teacher in it, and it's all done in various colours, for each section. So like, the yellow pages are the medical report, and the pink pages are the Reading and Language Service's report, and, you know. And then I got the final statement, which, was just a copy of the white pages, with a covering letter, which I received just over a week ago.*

Aside 6.8   Dealing with dyslexia

INTERVIEWER: *Had you got any idea that Ben might be dyslexic?*

SHIRLEY: *Yes, yes. Looking at his work two years previously, I noticed that there were mis-spellings. Not so much mis-spellings . . . the letters were there but they were in the wrong order. The reversals of letters was quite prominent. Sometimes it wasn't just an odd letter that was reversal, a whole word would be reversed. So when I went to various parents' evenings and things like that, I always mentioned to it to his teachers and asked if he had dyslexia tendencies. Which at the time, they said, 'Well, it's possible but most children grow out of reversing letters and things like that' and that there are letters that all children will reverse no matter what. But I had a feeling that Ben was not going to grow out of it. It was too . . . prolific I suppose is a good word. But the amounts that he was reversing was far greater than what you'd class as the norm. Yes, he did, yes. He didn't like writing. He still doesn't like writing. Reading was another thing. He didn't like reading either. His reading is still poor although it is coming up to the correct standard I suppose that is laid down in the curriculum. But, no, his reading and writing are still very poor and his spelling is atrocious.*

INTERVIEWER: *How did you know that those things might mean something like dyslexia? Did you know about dyslexia already?*

SHIRLEY: *Yes. Because my friend's son a few years ago had dyslexia, and . . .*

INTERVIEWER: *Is that somebody local?*

SHIRLEY: *They were yes, at the time . . . And my friend's son had been diagnosed as having dyslexia, and . . . one of the deciding factors actually of me choosing Springside School was that her son went to Springside School and when they discovered he had these learning difficulties, there was actually somebody there who understood dyslexia and was trained in it.*

. . . I have various teacher's books what I've borrowed from the Dyslexia Association. Spelling Made Easy is a range that is devised specially for children with learning difficulties. And they do from introductory level up to level 4 I think it goes up to . . . We try to do it basically for . . . between ten and thirty minutes depending on his mood. If he's in a really bad mood and can't be bothered then we only do ten minutes. If he's in a good mood and wants to have a go, then we'll do half an hour. We don't do anything more than half an hour because I don't want him to get to the stage where he's really cheesed off with doing it all. So we do that and we tend to do that four or five times a week and it's normally straight after school while he's still in that frame of mind. 'Cos if he's had the chance to go out and play and then comes in to do it, he's not interested.

Aside 6.9   Dyslexia as a cultural belief

Shirley is part of a growing group of parents, teachers and psychologists in the UK who use the term 'dyslexia' to explain many of the difficulties that children and adults experience with reading and writing. The Lancaster Dyslexia Association had been running for about ten years when we interviewed Shirley, offering out-of-school-hours tuition for children, counselling and support for parents, and advice to them about how to help their child at home. More recently, tuition has been offered to adults as well. We talked to the founder of the local association who explained: *we started as a support group for parents only, thinking that parents had these children and they needed to know what was the matter with them and be told. They also needed to be helped with how they could cope with them at home and how to do the right things with them.* It was only later that the group began to offer direct tuition to children.

The belief that difficulties with reading and writing are often caused by a scientifically proven condition called dyslexia is a controversial one that is struggling to be accepted among teachers and others in the education system (see Young and Tyre 1983; Herrington 1995). In many countries, including the United States, the concept is less accepted than in Britain (as in Pikulski 1996). *Dyslexia* is a difficult term to define. It is based on a medical or psychological definition of reading and writing difficulty (rather than a cultural one which might look for explanations within the educational or home environment). According to the founder of the association, dyslexia takes many forms with a variety of *symptoms* but the basic condition is *a disorganised brain* which needs a highly structured teaching approach to remedy. This teaching approach is usually based on phonics and is associated with traditional ideas about schooling and discipline, including helping the child cope with behaviour and emotions which get in the way of learning to read and write.

Our main interest here is dyslexia as a cultural belief about literacy that is promoted by some educational professionals and lay people, such as parents, and is on the margins of scientific respectability. What role does the Dyslexia Association play in the local community and why do parents feel the need for it? Why do people believe so fervently in the idea of dyslexia when it is so hard to describe or explain what it is?

Our interviews with the founder suggest some answers to these questions. Firstly, she clearly describes the role of the Dyslexia Association as a go-between for parents and schools, usually where parents have identified a problem with their child's literacy that they are finding it hard to get the school to recognise or deal with. She emphasises that parents are often frightened of approaching teachers or do not know effective ways to put pressure on them: *I don't think it's all teachers' fault, I think it partly goes back to that if you're not used to going into school, you remember yourself at school. All the bad times when you were in trouble with the teachers, so immediately you go through a school door, you're in that position, before you've started.* The Dyslexia Association takes parents' worries and knowledge about their child seriously. It validates their point of view, offers counselling in what is often a highly emotionally charged situation, including speaking on behalf of parents to the school, and it may sort out the problem immediately without the need for a diagnosis of dyslexia.

Where a diagnosis of dyslexia is made, it is often greeted with relief by parents and accepted as a much preferable explanation to the alternatives – that the child has general learning difficulties, and is seen as *thick*; or has behavioural problems, and is seen as *bad* or *lazy*. Dyslexia is still presented as a disability, but it is one that has some dignity associated with it and one that is associated with the hope of a successful programme of remedial teaching, with very specific instructions for what to do with the child. The fact that such a service has grown up in many areas raises many questions about the ways in which children's literacy learning is supported inside schools, about the length of time it takes to sort out any problems that arise and about communication between teachers and parents. Later examples in this book confirm that parents feel confused and shut out of their children's schooling, especially where they feel that their child is not progressing happily, and will often look for other resources to help them solve these problems.

Once Ben's reading and writing had improved and he didn't need Shirley's help any more, she shifted her energies to fundraising for the local Dyslexia Association so that other children could get the support that her own had benefited from. This is a good illustration of how Shirley's personal starting-points become generalised to others in the community. Shirley's investigation of dyslexia is also a good example of the way in which someone becomes a local expert on a topic of importance to them, and we pursue this more generally in Chapter 13.

Editing the residents' association newsletter: linking public and private

We have seen a number of examples above of how Shirley works at linking public and private contacts to get the things she wants done. At first these links were motivated by personal concerns, such as when she got her first job through a friend's mother. They developed through her concern as a parent for her own child, learning how to put pressure on the education office to speed up the statementing process, and gradually widened out to issues such as the petition for play space which affected other parents and children in the neighbourhood. As Shirley became more involved in organisations, such as the residents' association, the Labour Party and neighbourhood watch, she has had a more formal role to play, as a contact person – someone who will liaise between members of the community and the council, or the local media, for example, and sort things out. As part of becoming more of a public figure, she had become conscious about choosing her words carefully, both spoken and in writing:

Well, I am quite well known for being blunt in some of the things that I say. I'm learning very rapidly that my bluntness can be hurtful although sometimes I get quite cross with people. I tend to be a good compromiser and if people aren't prepared to compromise then I lose my temper. I will at least listen to someone else and I might not agree with their views but I will perhaps then say 'Well look, if we're not going to get this we perhaps go for this instead. Are you happy with that?' So, yeah, I do think that I am learning very rapidly to be a bit less blunt and to the point . . . Calling a spade a spade is one thing but if you call it an object for lifting dirt or whatever from one place to another, it's a much nicer way of putting it.

What Shirley says here about her awareness of choosing words carefully, and emphasising compromise rather than conflict, links in very solidly with evidence we have elsewhere of the everyday writing she does. She says that she never redrafts personal letters, but has done so very carefully, and in consultation with others, when writing the important official letter to the education office about her son. Such awareness is also evident in her astute descriptions of oral strategies she has learned in order to deal with difficult and influential people. An example of this is when she talked about trying to persuade her child's head teacher to make a change by making it seem as if an idea had come from the head teacher herself. On another occasion she talked about an editorial dilemma in the residents' association newsletter about whether to publish material which she felt would polarise opinion and accentuate negative feelings.

Shirley's formal roles in organisations have involved her in much writing, and it is interesting to look at these more public literacy practices she engages in, and the differences and continuities between them and her personal literacy life. The interviewer noticed, for example, that Shirley's paperwork for the residents' association was quite orderly, in contrast to her personal paperwork which appeared to be chaotic. She keeps the residents' association papers in a leather satchel which acts as a file for news sheets and minutes of meetings. Past news sheets are dated in red pen and are kept in order inside it in a plastic see-through wallet.

As editor of the residents' association newsletter, Shirley regularly wrote the editorials, as well as much of the content, of the newsletter. We have examined thirteen newsletters, covering one year, studying the *text world* she creates and how she uses the newsletter to bridge private and public worlds. This analysis is given in Aside 6.10. In the analysis we are interested in the text world which Shirley creates on paper and how she positions herself and others, and moves between public and private. We focus on the details of the texts she produced, and discuss them in relation to the context of how and why they were written which we know from other sources in our study – observations and interviews. We think the newsletters are particularly revealing because they are a kind of public writing that has no fixed, official format, and is therefore influenced a great deal by the personal style and purposes of the editor. They are an interesting form of vernacular text in their own right, and looking at them reveals more about Shirley's literacy practices and her identity as a community activist.

The residents' newsletter was physically produced by Des, one of the paid workers in the Housing Action Project office. He typed it on to the office word processor, pasted it up by hand and duplicated it. It was then hand-delivered by volunteers to all households in Springside. Shirley's editorials are just one part of the text of the newsletter. She wrote them out by hand and gave them to Des in the project office for him to type out. An example is given in Figure 6.1. Some features of the newsletter are that from the type-face it does not look like a professional publication; and that it includes cartoons and other graphics along with contributions by Housing Action Project workers, occasional residents' letters and a mixture of news and information. We get the impression from the cajoling tone of Shirley's editorials that it was not always easy to fill the newsletter, so editorial decisions about what to include are generally not hard to make. It is more a case of persuading people to write for it, as in her plea: *please, please send in items for the Newsletter . . . Come on, put pen to paper.*

We have noticed that in her editorials Shirley frequently makes public points using personal examples, and moves frequently between official and unofficial voices. In interviews with her she articulates a strong perception of herself as crossing boundaries and linking public and private domains. This seems to be very characteristic of her practices in the neighbourhood, where she frequently mobilises her personal networks for public ends and, conversely, makes use of 'official' contacts to achieve personal and family goals. She links people with resources and with each other whether it is in running a book exchange, getting a job or organising a petition amongst her neighbours. The idea of being able to cross between domains, bring people together, is a crucial part of her strategies for getting things done.

We have used the newsletter editorials to focus on the identity issues that

Aside: 6.10   The text world of Shirley's editorials

We examined thirteen newsletters covering the year 1990. Figure 6.1 is the editorial from one of these newsletters. The others are similar in their presentation, length and content, and the same kinds of textual practices can be seen throughout. We have studied the *text world* of Shirley's editorials, the *textual practices* and the *expressions of identity* contained in them.

The text world of the newsletters is a list of the people represented or discussed by Shirley in her editorials and what they are doing. These are all the people, real and fictional, who are mentioned in the thirteen texts, along with the activities which are ascribed to them. The list includes two policemen, residents, non-smokers, councillors, children, people with dyslexia. The people are thinking, thanking, seeing, noticing, missing, coming to meetings, taking time out of busy schedules, calling in. We can see that it contains primarily local people and family members. It also includes some officials from public worlds who are usually named, such as *Mr Ken Hartley, Private Housing Officer*, as well as mass media people such as Jason Donovan, Mork and Romanian babies, illustrating Shirley's intertextual drawing upon assumed shared knowledge with her readers.

This is the world on paper created by Shirley. It is not the definitive guide to what is actually happening in Springside, it is Shirley's version as editor and as represented in the texts of the newsletters. Each person we have interviewed constructs their own different, though overlapping, world of Springside in their interview texts. Shirley's world as seen through interviews with her is not identical to the one she constructs as editor. The world that we glimpse from minutes and observations of residents' meetings is again different from what is presented in the newsletters. For example, we know from our interviews with her that Shirley is aware of racism and conflicting self-interests in Springside, but in the newsletter she addresses the residents as one coherent community, all with the same interests at heart. The editorials obliterate or downplay possible differences of interest. Shirley chooses carefully who and what to include in this text. We know from our observations that residents do not participate evenly in the public life of the neighbourhood: meetings are not always well attended and people do not always come with a single agenda. From all these different sources we can begin to see the interplay of perspectives and the different voices that interrupt our working notion of an unproblematic *community* of Springside.

Shirley is in some sense at the centre of her text world, since she has created it and chooses who and what is represented in it. Our next step was to look through all the texts to see what Shirley is doing, how she is making the text work for her purposes: her textual practices. In her editorials Shirley introduces and thanks people. She encourages and berates others, often evaluating behaviour. She informs people about local news. This is a mixture of personal and official news, including the pancake day party, the shopkeeper's heart attack and imminent builders' deliveries. She represents people. At some times she represents the local community, passing on information and requests to the officials; at other times she represents the official world, addressing the local residents; she tells stories and personal narratives about local activities.

These stories are of particular interest as they usually have a moral to them concerning local life. She tells a story about her son walking into a disused lamp-post; she uses the anecdote to request that the lamp-post be removed. The point of a humorous story about two young men urinating in a back alley is to stamp out such activity. She personalises local community concerns and introduces serious issues in a humorous way. She frequently uses her editorials to mobilise people to get things done, whether in the neighbourhood or raising money for Romanian babies. At some points in the editorials she claims authority to represent other people and in the interviews she strongly articulates her interest in being able to do this: *As a councillor I would be able to do more than what I do now.* What she does now in various ways is to try and bring local people together to influence the Council to do things in the neighbourhood: whether it is introducing traffic calming measures, getting children's play space, defending allotment land or getting more resources for building work. Her positive view of the councillors comes over in her editorials and relates to aspects of her identity where she is aspiring to their role as a more official representative of the local community.

One general point to be made about these textual practices is that they draw heavily on the discursive conventions of addressing a meeting orally, and in fact to Shirley this is a familiar context where she regularly meets other residents as a group. She is adapting these oral conventions to the written form of the newsletter.

In carrying out these textual practices Shirley is constantly shifting identities and positioning herself and her readers in different ways. This can be clearly seen in the different ways in which she deploys the pronouns *I, me, we, us* and *you* throughout the text. These detailed shifts of voice are textual evidence of the complex ways in which Shirley is positioning herself in relation to other people in her text world, and they provide additional support to our interpretation of her role in the community which has emerged from our other sources of data, the interviews and observations. In particular, they give evidence of Shirley's active stance in bridging the public and private spheres in her neighbourhood, and her desire to act as a catalyst in community activities and to represent the interests of others.

SPRINGSIDE RESIDENTS GROUP

❁　　　❁　　　❁

Newsletter

IN PARTNERSHIP— WITH

PROUD OF SPRINGSIDE

Hi Everyone!!

Yes, it's me again! So before you skip to the next item can I thank everyone who came to the meeting - I don't think I have seen as many at a meeting since they first began and it was great to see the return of some very familiar faces whose absence had been noticed and very much missed.

It was also very enjoyable to meet our two community Policemen, P.C. Andy Currant and P.C. Paul Greenhalgh, who took time out of their very busy schedule to come and introduce themselves to residents, and have promised to come to the next meeting. They also ask that if you have a problem that maybe the Police can help you with, do not hesitate to contact them in person at the Police Station or through the HAP Office as they will be calling in there on a regular basis.

And now my hearts and flowers bit!! Please, please send in items for the Newsletter, in the past many people have promised items which HAVE NOT materialised and often cannot find things to put in, so if you want to tell us about an organisation you belong to or have a good moan about something, please let us know. Also, if you live in the area and want to advertise something, appeal for something, sell something, find something or congratulate someone on any occasion - engagements, weddings, exam passes, driving tests, birthdays or anniversaries, all these things will be put in the Newsletter FREE OF CHARGE and we are happy to receive them. So come on, put pen to paper and let us get your announcement to all the people in Springside! As I said, these advertisements are if you live in Springside.

And before you fall asleep.................

My final announcement is the Meetings are now to be NON-SMOKING!!! So all you non-smokers have no excuse - you can come to the meetings without worries about walking into a fog.

I would like to take this opportunity to thank OUR Councillors Paddy and Eileen for attending our Meetings whenever they are held. It is good that we have such representatives on the Council who are interested ALL OF THE TIME AND NOT JUST WHEN THEY NEED OUR -VOTES!!

THE NEXT MEETING WILL BE TUESDAY 6 MARCH 1990 at 7.30 pm - SEE YOU THERE.

AND DON'T FORGET THE PANCAKE DAY PARTY ON 27 FEBRUARY 1990 7.00 pm at THE PROJECT- OFFICE

EVERYONE WELCOME, INCLUDING CHILDREN!!

If you have an item for the Newsletter, please let either me or Kev at the HAP Office have it NO LATER THAN 13 MARCH. ITEMS RECEIVED AFTER THAT DATE WILL NOT BE INCLUDED IN THE MARCH ISSUE.

Shirley Bowker,Editor
81 Fortune Street,Springside,Lancaster.

Figure 6.1 The newsletter

are particularly interesting in relation to Shirley and the positioning of the residents' association in the Springside community. These issues are not the only features of the newsletters that could have been pursued: we could have used them to examine other issues, such as the cohesion of the Springside community, the range of social and commercial activities residents engage in, the way local information is disseminated and discussed, the ways in which people participate unevenly in local social networks of this kind. We will take up some of these issues in later chapters, in particular in Chapter 12 where we examine the ways in which people use literacy to get things done in groups.

7

LIVING A LOCAL LIFE
June's literacy practices

We first met June Marsh at the beginning of the door-to-door survey of Springside. On a clear winter's day three of us, Mary, Sarah and David, were going – with some trepidation – from house to house along Fairview Street. We had undertaken to do ten interviews each, and we planned to stand on the doorstep of each house and ask our questions. When I, David, knocked at June's house, she came to the door with a small barking dog. She put the dog into the back room and returned to invite me in. The door opened straight into her front room; I was quickly catapulted into June's world. My survey notes read as follows:

> *TV on, CB radio on and crackling away. Gas fire, warm. Birds in cage and washing drying on rack. Talked a lot, she explained CB radio to me and how it's useful for her husband telling her when he's coming home, and for reporting accidents. She recognised a man's voice on the CB and said he's retired, living in Morecambe, and directs truck drivers to addresses, etc. Junk mail just delivered was in the bin. When I asked her about junk mail, she pulled it out to look through, it was unopened and she obviously hadn't read it before.*

What should have been a ten-minute doorstep interview in fact took nearly half an hour. She made links with the rest of the neighbourhood. She told me about the planned anti-poll-tax march, the first in the town, and how it was being organised by her hairdresser, Janice, as in Aside 7.1. Although she seemed very busy and not to have much spare time, she was very friendly and was happy to take part in the longer study; Sarah interviewed her several times over the next few months.

We gradually built up a picture of June's life. Her parents had moved to Lancaster when she was two years old. Her father worked as a telephonist and her mother worked first in the mills and later did office work. June went to local schools and left school when she was fifteen, without taking any exams, but coming top of her class in maths. She worked in the office of a local factory and later became a cleaner. She tried going to night school at

---

Aside 7.1 The first anti-poll-tax march in Lancaster

Janice, the local hairdresser, was shocked at how distressed her customers were about the poll tax, a newly introduced and much-hated national tax, which had to be paid in the next few months. Many did not have enough money to pay it and were becoming very upset. She had never organised anything like a march before and did not know what to do. According to June, she phoned the university – unsuccessfully – to ask the Students' Union for advice on how to organise a march and she put up home-made posters in shop windows around Springside. When she saw her customers, mainly local women, Janice told them that the following Wednesday they were going for a march from Springside to the Town Hall though she did not say that she had organised it. People were to bring a banner if possible. June was unsure whether to go on the march, and in the end she did.

A small group, mainly women, marched to the Town Hall, where they were joined by other people who saw what was happening. They got coverage in the local paper, as in Figure 7.1. This was the first march in Lancaster against the poll tax, and was followed soon afterwards by other, larger ones, as in Figure 7.2. Two days after the first march, Janice was phoned by the local police, who warned her she would *get into trouble* if she organised another march. They also talked to her husband, who persuaded her not to do anything else. She stopped participating, but local political groups became involved, including the anti-poll-tax union, which had already been organising public meetings in community centres in other parts of the city, giving information and advice to people. It was active in supporting people when, as the year went on, those who defaulted on payments were summonsed to court. Members gave out locally produced leaflets advising people of their rights and offering to act as 'McKenzie Friends' by helping them prepare their defence.

---

the local college to learn shorthand and typing, but quickly gave up, and went for a while to private classes. This was her only contact with further education.

When she was eighteen, June got married and moved to her current house. She has four children and is a grandmother. Her youngest daughter in her twenties still lives at home. June's husband, a long-distance truck-driver, has never liked the idea of her working, and she has spent most of her married life at home; however, in the past few years she has worked part-time on a market stall, alongside two of her daughters. She is now in her early forties and enjoys her work.

To get a further idea of June, here is an extract from our field notes, with a first impressions description of her:

June is quite a tall broad woman with high colouring and dark eyes. She has windswept hair which she wears short . . . She looks like someone who would work out of doors, in a market garden perhaps, or on a farm. She is strong, thoughtful, interested in the world and has both a good sense of humour and a deeply serious side. She has a real gift for story telling, and stories, however serious, are always interspersed with a good deal of self-mockery and laughter.

Figure 7.1   Poll tax: 200 join protest

Another angle on June is provided in the pen-sketch which we asked each person we interviewed to provide of themselves. She appeared hesitant about describing herself and, as the interviewer records in field notes, *A sudden stupid brain-wave to get her going made me suggest she describe herself as if to a dating agency.* She agreed to this and here is part of the way she described herself on tape:

Yeah, yeah. Old woman . . . old woman. I would like to meet somebody to share interests in . . . going out walking in the countryside and a love of animals. Must like animals. Must enjoy nature. Would like to go out

occasionally for meals. Must be a smoker, can't give it up [laughing].
*Couldn't do without cigarettes. Well basically yeah, must enjoy conversation.
Must be able to talk to me. That's one, that would be a major thing. Yeah,
I like to talk to people. That's a big thing I think. Well I know it is. I don't
think about it, but it is. I'd like to go out cycling again. That's what I would
like. Somebody that'll take me out on my bike. Probably couldn't do it now.
I'd be out of puff before I got to end of street. Must like children. I know
because I'm snowed under with 'em. Oh I like kids. It'd have to be somebody
that would care as much as I do. And I do care. I care a lot. And I'm finding out all these things about me now that I didn't really know existed in me.
I didn't have all this . . . I didn't get all this with my own kids. And when
you say . . . everybody says, 'Oh you know, you enjoy your grandchildren
more'.*

Figure 7.2 'No Poll Tax'

June's literacy life

June reads the local newspaper, as well as watching television and listening
to the local radio, saying that she reads everything in the paper. Although
she throws away the junk mail, she reads other information which comes

---

Aside 7.2   Doing the accounts

June is explaining the records she keeps in a large book of her household expenditure.

JUNE: *See. This is what I've been paying out every week you see. I've got everything listed. Milk, Co-op, insurance, phone, water rates, washer, papers, hamper, petrol, club . . . and it goes right through. Getting less and less as my debts are getting less. Then look, this is where I'm at now. And I always have it a bit in advance.*

INTERVIEWER: *Oh I see. You draw out the days in it.*

JUNE: *Yeah. Weeks.*

INTERVIEWER: *Oh the weeks in it. It's a hard backed book with lined paper on the inside and paisley pattern on the outside. The paper's old isn't it?*

JUNE: *Oh it is now 'cos I started this book in 1988 . . . I don't know if I've got any other information in it. But I don't think so.*

INTERVIEWER: *Have you drawn the weeks in right up until the end?*

JUNE: *No. I just do a couple of months at a time. I've just done up to there. Then when I've nowt . . . nothing much to do I do some more. And then . . . you see this is bonus week. And I've put bonus . . . fourth week there. And I'm getting down now . . . 22nd this weekend. £7.50 for my milk, £10 for Brian's petrol, £16 for Great Universal Co-op . . . that's once a month now. My phone bill . . . £51. And down here I've got my cooker £41.30p. That has to be in for the 26th so it goes under 22nd to make sure it's all in the Bank. House insurance was £24.27p . . . I wonder why I've got them separated. I usually have them together. Car insurance there, look, every three months. Cooker £26 . . . Oh, 9th and 13th, gas and house insurance £43.11p.*

INTERVIEWER: *Everything to do with money going out of the house is in that book? And you deal with it all?*

JUNE: *I do everything.*

INTERVIEWER: *So what about the car. You don't drive do you?*

JUNE: *No.*

INTERVIEWER: *You deal with all that still?*

JUNE: *I do it all.*

---

through the door, including the free newspaper and newsletters from the church and the residents' association. She also enjoys reading magazines. She has written off for free magazines and also sent off for offers in the magazines related to her interests in wildlife. She collects coupons of supermarket offers for a relative. There were newspapers and magazines around the house, as well as leaflets she had brought back from places she had visited in the area.

INTERVIEWER: *Have you always done that since you got married?*

JUNE: *Oh yeah. Brian won't do anything.*

INTERVIEWER: *So does Brian . . . What happens to Brian's wages? Does he . . . ?*

JUNE: *They go into bank. It's all mine. I handle it all. I've two cash point cards and he doesn't even know number. He couldn't use a cash point machine. He hasn't a clue. He doesn't have to write a cheque.*

INTERVIEWER: *So his money goes into the bank but it's a joint account?*

JUNE: *Yes that's right. And I use it.*

INTERVIEWER: *Does he have any interest in the household budget?*

JUNE: *None whatsoever. No. Well he does. So far as 'why haven't we got any money?' You know, 'It's about time this . . .' and 'It's about time that we had this . . . We need a new carpet . . . We need a new three-piece suite.'*

INTERVIEWER: *What about money in his pocket?*

JUNE: *Well he gets £10. You see on bonus week I give him £15 and every other week he gets £10. So he gets £45 a month in his pocket. Now his petrol's £5 a week. So he gets what . . . well he puts £10 in about every three weeks. So he has . . . 15 . . . 25 . . . He has £15 a week. I buy all his cigarettes. I buy everything. He has nothing to buy. He doesn't go out. He never goes out.*

She goes on to explain how she keeps records not just of the weekly bills but also of the insurance policies on the car and house, and a life insurance policy she has arranged for her husband.

JUNE: *I sort everything out. And I've got poll tax. And I write them down in here so that I don't miss them. Water rates . . . when they're due you see . . . there . . . Weeks that I don't have to pay it, you know, I don't put it in.*

INTERVIEWER: *If you weren't here, how would Brian cope?*

JUNE: *He'd be knackered [laughing]. He'd be knackered. He couldn't do it. He couldn't. It's took me a long time to do this. This is when I started doing this in 1988. So that's like four years. But up until then I used to get in an awful pickle . . . I found this was a lot easier. A lot better. And I can do it weeks ahead, so I know how I'm doing with my money, and that's mainly what these books are for.*

She writes letters and cards to friends and enjoys browsing through cards for sale in shops, reading all the words. The words are important to her. There were some books around the house and she explained how she used the encyclopedia to resolve arguments with friends. She also keeps magazines and catalogues. During one interview she pulled out a magazine containing an article about endangered animals being bred in captivity; she did this in order to explain something which had come up in the conversation about the Siberian tiger.

At home she also keeps detailed records of everything she spends each week, with a records book she devised. In the quotation, Aside 7.2, she explains to Sarah how she keeps the records. This quotation is rich in themes about literacy, including gender, home record-keeping, learning new literacies and the links between literacy and numeracy. She once worked out that she was owed a pay rise and she wrote everything out to be sure she hadn't made a mistake, before approaching her boss. She enjoys doing the mathematics involved in record-keeping, even though at first she was nervous about it. At work on the market stall, she has to do adding up, as well as weighing and measuring. She writes shopping lists before going shopping. The act of writing the list organises her shopping and it does not then matter whether or not she takes it with her.

Aside 7.3   Buying cards for the boss

JUNE: *And I went for one for the boss on last Friday, for her boyfriend's dad. She says, 'Get me one if you can with pheasants on', you know. So, there was this one with pheasants on but it had no words in. She said 'not a lot of sloppy words or anything'. It had no words in at all. It was a beautiful card, quite reasonable, recycled paper they're made from, only 95 pence, you know . . .*

They're lovely. And there was these three pheasants picking around in this heather, and I thought how beautiful. You know, it didn't even say Happy Birthday in it, so I got her one with kingfishers on side of the river, and that just said Happy Birthday, but I said, 'Can I change it? I'll tell her about the other one but can I change it if she'd prefer the other one?', you know. Anyhow I told her, but she liked the kingfishers, she said 'because he's a farmer', you know, she wanted something to do with countryside.

INTERVIEWER: *She doesn't like cards with sloppy words in?*

JUNE: *Oh she does like cards with sloppy words in, yeah, but this was for her boyfriend's dad.*

INTERVIEWER: *Right, so it wasn't appropriate?*

JUNE: *No. If it was for her boyfriend it would be as sloppy as you could get, you know what I mean, but she sends you to get, she won't go for herself, you have to . . .*

INTERVIEWER: *So you get things for her boyfriend as well?*

JUNE: *Oh yeah she sends me or daughter, you know, well both daughters work on there now, but she'll send anybody except herself.*

INTERVIEWER: *That's quite trusting as well.*

JUNE: *Yeah, but I don't like doing it.*

She did not think of many examples of helping other people or being helped with reading and writing. At work people sometimes hand her their shopping lists and ask her to cross off the things they've bought; sometimes they also proffer a handful of change for her to take the correct money from. She also refers to a man whom she noticed *because he was reading from a shopping list and men don't do that, women do.* One example of doing things for other people is that she has sometimes been sent to buy magazines and greetings cards for her boss. June's boss sends her when she wants cards for her boyfriend and her boyfriend's dad. June feels uneasy about this, choosing the picture and the words for someone else, and feels put upon, as she explains in Aside 7.3. Another example of helping other people, and one she is happier with, is that she sometimes helps Maggie, her neighbour and long-time friend, with filling in forms. June and Maggie also let each other read some personal letters they receive.

Living a local life

When we came to identify themes in the interviews with June, there was not one obvious ruling passion which came out of the interviews with June and the observations of her practices. There were a set of interconnected themes which may not appear to be primarily concerned with literacy; they are more concerned with how she lives her life. Nevertheless, they are revealing in the way in which they clarify how literacy fits into her life. They are concerned with living a local life. Most of what she talked about referred to her life and to life around her. She uses the local shop *every five minutes* and the local hairdresser's. This is possible in a small neighbourhood which has corner shops and where the centre of town is just a walk away. She places special value on *talking to people*, which she mentions in her pen-sketch, and which was apparent in her willingness to be interviewed at length despite her busy schedule. At one point when a visitor interrupted one of the interviews, she explained this research as being about *communications* – she was probably the only person we interviewed who did not construe it as being about education.

In answer to questions June often told stories, as did Harry and Cliff. However, these stories seemed different in kind. Some related to news items or stories in magazines, but many of them revolved around her life and the lives of people she came into contact with. She located them in local life and often they were about relatives. Often they were wry comments on experience, and frequently they were humorous in tone. She told the story of the family in Moorby, another neighbourhood of Lancaster, who kept a horse in the back garden:

> *It used to go in house. It used to go in front door and out into back garden. Mind you that sort of family . . . they had tortoises running . . . everything*

was running wild round house. If you went in you'd to watch where you were walking [laughing]. *I said, 'What you taking him through house for?' She said, 'He just comes in. I can't keep him out.' Just couldn't stop him going in. Used to take him out and into back yard and in back garden and hose him down.*

Another story concerned the photographer at her daughter's wedding who is the brother of a neighbour, Mumtaz. He lives in Springside and, as a friend of the family, he was arranging all the photos. He borrowed a pair of doves for wedding shots and was worried about how to return them, *and they said, 'Just let them go and they'll fly back.' And this was for doves of peace or whatever. And there's a photograph, she's kneeling down on the floor with a big white wedding dress and she's letting these doves go and her hands are up like that and these doves are just flying.* June recounted this as an example of the quirkiness of everyday life, but also as part of something very important and moving to her.

If there is a ruling passion it is her interest in animals; she is passionate about animals, she has a household full of them and many of her stories of local life involve animals, such as the two stories just mentioned, the horse in the back garden, and the doves of peace for the wedding photos. She uses the pet shop in town as a reference point when describing locations and she stops off to feed the ducks in the canal on her way into town each day. She has magazines about animals and watches television programmes about them. This is her ruling passion in the sense that, as with Harry and others, it is what she wanted to talk about, and it seemed to us that her interest was getting in the way of our interview until we started listening to the stories. Listening to her stories we learn about how she finds out information, her use of different media for this and how she utilises reading and writing for sense making, a theme we pursue in Chapter 13.

Two smaller themes connected with this arise when talking about how she leads her life. Firstly, there are several ways in which the discussion revolves around ideas of being organised in her life. Related to this are comments on the many constraints on her everyday life. June's daily life is closely organised. This is clear in the way she organises time and manages the household, and this idea is captured in the quotation in Aside 7.2, above, where she discusses the household accounts. Doing the accounts is one of many household chores she takes responsibility for, although this was not the pattern she had grown up with, which she has bad memories of:

My Dad does everything. He still does. Yeah. Mother used to have to hand her wages over to him. I had to hand mine over. Tight as a fish's backside he is. Terrible . . . the times I've seen my Mother heartbroken. Because my Dad . . . he would go into town. He wouldn't ask her. He came home, he said, 'I've ordered a new three-piece suite'. Well, she was struggling to make ends meet. And when it came it was the most abominable thing you've ever seen. She sat down on it and cried. Same when he got a television . . . 'I've ordered a television . . . it's coming tomorrow'. You know, and she was in tears. He never even consulted her. You know, I find it hard to believe.

As a woman with many domestic commitments, doing the accounts is one more chore which June juggles into her limited spare time, but at least it gives her some control over her life and ensures that she is involved in the decisions that she and her husband, Brian, make about spending. She uses literacy to organise her life; she has to do this to ensure that she does not get into debt. Writing also comes in where she finds it crucial to write a shopping list in order to *get organised*, although, as mentioned earlier, it then does not matter whether or not she takes the list with her when she goes shopping. Another example of being organised in her life arose when we used maps to prompt discussion of where she goes in Lancaster. She follows a regular route into town when she walks to work in the morning, stopping to feed the ducks in the canal; she describes this in the quotation in Aside 7.4, pointing out that if something changes this routine it upsets her.

Aside 7.4   The route into town

JUNE: *I always plan a route, I have to know what I'm doing. I'm all right if I'm just going down, oh well, I'll just go and have a look round town, it doesn't matter. But if I'm doing me shopping I've got to know where I'm going and in which order I'm doing it. I'm really organised . . .*

INTERVIEWER: *But in your head you've got a map of just where you're going?*

JUNE: *That's it, down to paper shop to pay me papers, down to canal, feed the ducks, down to traffic lights, through Boots's, to Electric Board we used to go 'cause it was up that way. Then back down to Superdrug, then into Wilkie's, then through alley at the side of where Halifax was, then into Market, collect wages, do a bit of shopping in market, go into Littlewoods, get me shopping in Littlewoods, and back into market. Then we used to go down alley at side of Marks's, used to always put money in Halifax for hamper for Christmas, and then into Marks's, and then up to Ventura for a cup of tea. And that was it, as long as I knew I was planned I'm right. Then when I had a shock of me life a couple of weeks ago. I couldn't go that alley and I said, 'Oh no, what's happening?' You know, re-plan everything. It threw me really off, I think I forgot half me shopping, it's stupid. I did, I came home with only half of what I wanted. And I went in all the shops.*

   . . . I always write a list, even if I go without it. As long as I've written it, basically know what I want, you know.

In general she carries out her life in a regular way and is at ease with it but is thrown by changes. An example of a new experience which confused her was when she visited a travel agent's. She told us this as part of a complex story about trying to find a long-lost sister-in-law. Brian and June have been trying unsuccessfully to trace her, and the woman suddenly phoned up from Ireland, not having had any contact for thirty-five years. She phoned up as she had heard from someone else living near Lancaster that June and Brian were trying to contact her. After the initial surprise, June recounts how she thought of visiting this relative, who lives in Northern Ireland, but has no idea how to get there, nor how to find out how to get there. *I hadn't a clue where to start, or how to go set about it, honestly I still haven't.* She went into a travel agent, for the first time in her life, but could not get an answer to her simple question of how much it costs to go to Ireland. Firstly, the travel agent has two shops in town – having taken over another travel agency – and June is confused that the first branch cannot help her; she is re-directed to another branch which deals with ferries in order to get an answer to her simple question. In the second branch she doesn't get an answer to her question as firstly they need to know what time of the year she wants to travel, what time of the day and which route she wants to take. Her question is too general for the people in the travel agent's and she does not get an answer. The conclusion to this story is that they drop the idea of going to Ireland as June's daughter announces that she is about to get married and June works out that she cannot afford to go to Ireland as well, *That's when daughter announced she were getting married and that was it, you know. Now we've got poll tax so I don't suppose we'll be going again now.*

June's difficulty with the travel agent is not particularly a literacy-related one but is an example of a more general problem faced by people when they need advice but are not sure where to start in asking for it and they are not familiar with the procedures which bureaucracies impose upon them. When we interviewed a Citizen's Advice Bureau worker about people's difficulties with filling forms, for instance, she saw this as a familiar problem. In addition, a common difficulty with forms is that they often present many complex options because they are designed to be generally relevant to all cases. People find it hard without help to isolate the information that applies to their own specific case.

There are many different constraints on June's life. She is a busy person with very little spare time or money. Not having enough money recurs as an issue in her life and two or three times she explains how *money's tight.* Family and work seem to dominate her life. Other people, including her husband, her boss, her daughters, her grandchildren, her friends all seem to depend on her and to make demands on her time and energy, physical and psychological. She doesn't seem to have much time for herself at all, or to know people who share similar interests. Although she was always keen to be interviewed and to take part in the research, frequently there was some disruption of people coming and going, and others' needs which had to be met. These were often to do with various family problems, which were mentioned during the first interview and which were apparent throughout the time she was interviewed. Her youngest daughter still lives at home and suffers from epileptic fits. Her second daughter has two children, and at one point June was looking after Carly, aged three, while the younger child was being kept in hospital in Manchester, sixty miles away, with a suspected heart problem. Despite these concerns, June took part in an interview, with daughters and their boyfriends coming and going through the house. When she does do something for herself such as reading the paper in bed, or watching wildlife films on television or listening to music, her husband is not interested, and puts pressure on her not to do whatever it is. In relation to literacy, burying her head in a newspaper or magazine is seen as *not spending time with him watching television.*

Using media

From the first meeting, when there was a television on, and a CB radio, and newspapers and magazines strewn around the living-room, it was clear that media and communication are very important to June. As we have already said, June reads newspapers and magazines regularly. She reads a national newspaper, the *Mirror,* and the local papers, including the *Lancashire Evening Post* and free papers in which she reads the ads and horoscopes; when reading the local paper she says she reads everything in it *from cover to cover, starting with the sports,* especially cycling, which she is keen on. She reads newsletters which come through the door, and when we asked she named ones associated with churches, political groups and the residents' association. She mentions leaflets from the local video shop and from the window cleaners, and she collects coupons for offers in the supermarket; as we have seen, she draws a line between these and *junk mail* which she throws away without reading. She reads a range of magazines, including women's magazines, ones on wildlife, and commercial consumer magazines brought out by supermarkets and other stores, keeping a pile of old magazines on a shelf next to the fire.

Another example of written media concerns greetings cards. She buys commercial ones with pre-written messages. The words are important to her and she spends some time choosing appropriate ones for people. There are many ways in which choosing the words in a card is writing, not merely reading, and that it is a active process, as in Padmore (1992). The manager of one of the city centre card shops that June uses confirmed that many people spend time choosing cards on the basis of the words printed inside and would sometimes come into the shop and ask for a card expressing particular sentiments. This use of pre-written texts which are then customised for a particular occasion has parallels in other contexts; in the work-place, for example, writing business letters often involves choosing and assembling parts of existing texts.

June watches television, including morning programmes, and usually has it on *for company* when she is at home. She watches soaps, wildlife programmes, programmes about people and news: *I'm addicted to news*. She plans what to watch, and our interviews had to be scheduled around television programmes. The television is deliberately left on for visitors, and was frequently on throughout our interviews. From time to time the interview transcripts have seemingly random comments in them from June, which are actually comments on what was happening on the screen as the interview was going on (see Mace 1992b). She uses it as an important source of information, and television programmes are often the basis of conversations.

June listens to the radio, including local radio, for an hour every morning, and again she talked of following the news. As already mentioned, she has a CB radio, and this was often on during interviews. It is used for keeping in touch with her husband when he is away driving trucks, and she has a whole social life that involves conversations with truckers, for example by giving them directions – she says she has made a lot of new friends. She got the idea of having a CB from her daughter who used one. Now it was an integral part of her life. This is clearly shown in field note extracts in Aside 7.5, where she has to change the fan belt which is broken in the vacuum cleaner; she does this following instructions over the CB radio from her husband many miles away.

Other media June uses include photographs used as a record of events. In one interview she spent considerable time going through the wedding photos from her daughter's wedding, which were in an album kept in the living room. They were taken by the local photographer. She went through the photos one at a time, commenting on each one and telling stories based upon them, including the story about the doves mentioned earlier. It is clear from her comments that she believes this visual record of a landmark event is highly valued not only by herself but by many other people; at one point she recalls *a terrible story* that appeared in a local paper where an incompetent photographer had produced wedding photographs which cut off the heads and feet of the guests. A wedding is seen as a critical point in both personal and family history, hence the importance of the photographic record as a document, a stimulus to story telling and recall, and as a source of aesthetic pleasure in its own right.

As with everyone we studied, we captured one particular time in June's life at which she would be faced with a mixture of established literacy practices and new demands. The wedding is an example of people encountering new, or at least infrequent, literacy demands, involving the invitations and the guest and present lists; the ceremony; arranging the reception at a local

---

**Aside 7.5   Field notes on mending the
vacuum cleaner**

*When I arrived, the television was on, the CB was crackling and there were
faint voices on it. Like listening to radio in a taxicab. The Hoover was upside-
down on the floor and there were wires everywhere. June said she'd been having
problems. She said she'd thought something had happened to the Hoover. She
suspected the fan belt had gone and she was really annoyed because she'd been
meaning to get everything done today. She'd been doing some sort of spring
clean on the house. And she sat down on the settee, pulled the Hoover up on to
her lap upside-down and she got a screwdriver . . . She'd just been on the CB
to Brian . . . And she'd asked him how to change a fan belt and he'd told her.
I think she'd watched him do it before but she'd never done it herself. So she got
the screwdriver that he'd told her to get which was on a shelf next to the settee
and she was trying to unscrew these screws but the screwdriver was too small
and kept slipping. So she picked up the hand piece to the CB and she got
Brian and said, 'The screwdriver isn't working.' It was just as if she was talking to him in the room. And he said 'Oh have a go with the other one.' And he
described what the other one was like. And it was also on the shelf next to the
settee. And we both looked towards the shelf and saw it, the one with a white
handle. She tried the screwdriver and it worked, and Brian was talking as she
was doing it. Saying 'How's that? Is that better? Is it going in?' And she was
saying, 'Yeah, this one seems to be working now.' And she undid the screws and
pulled the casing off the back and dug out all the fluff and pulled out the
broken fan belt and got another one and put it on. And we both discussed how
to put it back in. She had a bit of trouble at first. Brian had gone off. And then
he came on again and said, 'How's it going?' And she said, 'Oh I've fixed it.'
And he seemed pleased. And she said, 'Now I'll have to call off now Brian 'cos
I'm going to get on with my Hoovering.' So it sounded like she wasn't telling
him that I was there. And after that she said that she was 'right chuffed' that
she'd done it ' 'cos it was the first time'. And she felt good to have coped.*

---

hotel. Although June must have been involved with a whole set of wedding
literacy practices, it is the pictures that she focuses on and tells her stories
about.

   The different media June uses are all integrated into her life within the context of particular events. Discovering her husband's missing relative involved
writing letters, making phone calls, asking people. She also uses a range of
media in an integrated way *to keep in touch* and to find out what is going on in
the world. Combine this variety of media use with the people she regularly
talks to and the situation becomes more complex. She places a high value on
communication; literacy is part of this, but only a part. Her relation to the

---

**Aside 7.6   The national context on uses of media
in the home**

The period from 1990 onwards has been one of increasing choice and availability of different media. Some of these changes are the result of new technologies becoming available. For example, forty million CDs were sold in 1989 in the UK, overtaking sales of records for the first time, and by 1990 sales of CDs were more than double those of LPs. Ownership of home computers and videos is increasing (see Aside 10.1). The increasing availability of satellite and cable television has meant more choice of channels, although it has not led so far to increasing hours of television watching. The trend has been for terrestrial channels to lose audience time to satellite and cable television.

Ninety-nine per cent of UK households possessed at least one television in 1990. Almost two-thirds of households had a video recorder in 1990, and video viewing at home now takes up a significant amount of people's prime-time television viewing. In 1990 thirty-eight million videotapes were purchased and over seven million were rented each week. A quarter of households with a video recorder hired a video in any one week, mainly from specialist shops, and the rest from newsagents, off-licences and garages.

Some households are 'media rich': a household with a video recorder is more likely to have satellite and cable television as well. Higher social class households tend to have more media equipment, as do larger households and those with children. Television and radio audiences are measured in terms of 'reach', the percentage of people watching or listening in any time period. The monthly reach of television is 99 per cent of the population under 70 years of age. Weekly reach in 1990 was 94 per cent, and daily reach of television was 78 per cent. Figures for radio were 74 per cent weekly and 45 per cent daily.

The average time spent watching television in 1990 was 25 hours and

---

news and local information is very different from Shirley's, for example, and what she would count as *knowing what is going on* is very different.

June would not regard herself as politically active, she is not an active member of the organisations she belongs to. She approves of the residents' association, reads the newsletter, but did not get round to filling in the questionnaire which the association circulated. Her commitments are to her personal networks of friends and family and she joined in the poll-tax march largely because of her personal friendship with Janice who organised it. Nevertheless she calls herself *a news addict* and news pours into her living room from the television, radio, CB and newspapers.

33 minutes per week, including time-shifted viewing by video. Older people tend to view for more hours, as do those in lower socio-economic groups and unemployed people. Except for the oldest viewers, the reported hours of viewing show a slight decrease since 1990, especially for children.

Hours of listening to the radio have been slightly increasing since 1985. In 1990 the average was 10 hours 12 minutes per week, only 2 hours 26 minutes for children under 16, and highest for the 16 to 34 years age group at 12 hours 28 minutes.

There is a great deal of information available on how people decide what to watch on television. This shows strong gender and age differences in preferences for particular kinds of programmes such as detective, horror and action films, soaps, sports and wildlife. These preferences have continuities with the kinds of books and magazines which both children and adults choose to read.

Media programmes are structured to fit in with the real time of domestic routines such as tea breaks and children's bedtimes, and, in turn, structure them. Viewing competes with many other activities in the home, and much of the time people are viewing very casually. At other times they engage in sustained searching out and perusing of particular programmes. The habit of 'grazing' or 'surfing' the channels is well established, so many of those who do not regularly view a particular channel nevertheless probably see it from time to time.

More than two-thirds of people report that they rely on television as their main source of national news: 20 per cent rely on newspapers and 10 per cent on the radio news. However, although television is the main news source and more trust is placed in it, people spend more news time per day with newspapers.

Sources: Gray 1992; Gunter *et al.* 1994; Hall and Coles 1996; Central Statistical Office 1992; 1993; PSI 1993; Saatchi and Saatchi 1990.

June's use of media has to fit into her daily routines and priorities of work, communication with family and friends, and leisure. She adapts available technologies to her needs – most obviously the CB radio. She mentions video watching in relation to children's viewing, not just her own, and the television is used as a backdrop to her domestic life – on for many hours of the day, sometimes consciously attended to but often watched intermittently as other events and activities claim her main attention. The magazine reading, television viewing and other media uses that June reports are very similar to accounts given by women in other research (see Hermes 1995; Gray 1992) where they are integrated into domestic activities and frequently disrupted by them, with reading and viewing snatched as rare personal space among many competing demands.

There is a sense in which literacy is not important to June. In answer to a question about the relative importance of television and reading, she does at one point emphasise that it is important to be able to read and write: *if you stop reading and writing it's peril.* Nevertheless, literacy seems to be something she uses as it is needed in order to get things done. She does not go out of her way to do things with literacy and it does not particularly interest her. It arises in her daily life in an incidental way, when she draws on reading and writing in order to get other things done; or she uses it to pass the time, such as browsing in the bookshop by the bus stop. When she has time to herself, literacy activities seem to revolve around interests in news and wildlife – animals and plants. Although she is interested in information and watches television and reads magazines and leaflets, she is one of the few people we talked to who has never been to the library. She reads stories in magazines, but not novels. She took a short secretarial course in town after leaving school but has never been to the Adult College, nor have any other members of her family.

Despite probing, we did not identify any problems June has in her every-day life which are primarily literacy problems. Her problems with the travel agent are to do with not being familiar with the ways of travel agents and with a shortage of money, but these are not literacy problems. As our inter-view with the travel agent makes clear, travel agents are brokers who expect to deal with form-filling, booking procedures and interpreting brochures to their clients as part of their normal role – mediating the reading and writing involved in making travel arrangements. In fact, June helps others, such as her neighbour Maggie, with filling in forms and has developed her own complex system of recording financial information about her household transactions. As we have seen, June has many problems and there are many constraints on her life but literacy is not one of them. She uses literacy but it is not important to her. She is at ease with literacy, she is good at figures, and she immediately found her way around our maps. People can get by without revolving their lives around literacy.

June is an important person to include in this study precisely because she has little interest in literacy, has little to say about it and yet has no obvious everyday difficulties with reading and writing. Other people we interviewed, like Harry and Shirley, are easily included because they have a great deal to say about the difficulties they have identified with reading and writing, are relying on it extensively to get things done in their lives and are particularly interested in certain aspects of it. It is likely that there are many other people like June living local lives in Lancaster and in other communities. The casualness with which June makes use of literacy, and the ease with which she embraces other forms of communication and expression, are refreshing.

8

LEISURE AND PLEASURE
Cliff's literacy practices

Aside 8.1 Writing to Ken Dodd

CLIFF: *Well, yeah. I wrote to . . . I met Ken Dodd when . . . twenty-odd years ago at The Alhambra Theatre in Bradford. It was one Spring Bank Holiday Monday and if I remember rightly it was a very wet, cold, windy day. And I had two little girls at that time. And they'd be about four and five year old and we didn't know where to go. I hadn't a car in those days. And he was appearing at the Bradford Alhambra. And they'd seen him on television because he had a series, 'Ken Dodd and the Diddymen', on television. It was a children's programme. So I said I would take them down to see if we could see him at the stage door. We couldn't get in for the show because it was a complete sell-out.*

Anyway he came up and had a talk to us. And then he give the children a tickling stick each and said we had to keep in touch. So obviously being little girls they couldn't write. So I wrote for them. And I had one or two letters from him in the early days and then of course, we just started to go, and every time he came locally we'd go to the shows to see him. And then go back and see him backstage. And that's carried on for all those years. Right up to more or less the present time. I don't write as much now but if he's around anywhere locally I pop in and see him and have a word.

INTERVIEWER: *Do you enjoy writing letters?*

CLIFF: *Yeah I do, actually. I wrote to James Cagney. I got one back from him as well. When I write I put it down as I think it. I would write it as I'm talking to you. I would even deviate from what I'm saying and then come back to it again. Like I'm doing when I'm talking to you. That's how I would put it down. I wouldn't put blah, blah, blah . . .*

INTERVIEWER: *So you might write a long, long letter?*

CLIFF: *Oh I could write twenty pages and think nothing about it. I could write you a letter now and I could write you down twenty pages and never even stop to think what I were putting down. I find it that easy.*

129

Cliff Holt was keen to be involved in the research and had heard about it at one of the residents' association meetings. Sarah's notes on her first interview with Cliff describe how she felt uncomfortable with him at first, but that her impression of him changed as they both relaxed:

> *When I rang the bell the door was opened by an elderly woman in a blue overall. At first I thought I must have gone to the wrong house but she invited me in with a slightly quizzical look on her face and went to the bottom of the stairs to call Cliff.*
>
> *The front room was sparkling clean. The carpet was covered in cleaning equipment: Hoover with yards of wire, dust pan and brush, furniture polish and dusters. Cliff arrived downstairs in slippers . . . and we went through to the kitchen . . . The back kitchen was tiny – barely room to sit down. A small three-leaf table was folded against one wall opposite the sink and draining boards. Newspaper covered this table like a cloth. It was a spartan room; very little cupboard space but nothing on show. I sat back to the wall on a chair and Cliff fetched a stool.*
>
> *I felt nervous. Cliff didn't appear to go in for smiling. For the first fifteen minutes or so things were slightly sticky, and it took a while for me to realise that my first impression was wrong. Cliff was nervous too. Once we'd both relaxed, he started to open out.*

Cliff turned out to be a great talker, as he says of himself: *I can talk to inanimate objects, yeah. It doesn't bother me, you know. But some of this might be due to the fact that, being in hairdressing, I had to talk to the back of people's heads anyway. You know, I used to recognise people by the back of their heads. And I always have been a bit of a chatterbox.* He gave us four long interviews. We also interviewed his half-sister Rose, who was present during many of the visits. Both Cliff and Rose kept diaries of their daily literacy activities for a month during the research period. Sarah visited Cliff three more times during the collaborative phase of the research to collect his reactions to the transcripts and themes we had identified for him. During the final visit Cliff dictated the pen-sketch of himself, part of which is given in Aside 8.2.

He was used to hearing his voice recorded, and when we asked what he had felt on seeing his words written down in the transcript he replied: *It didn't come as such a great shock because I use a tape recorder for sending tapes to Canada so I know what I sound like. I seem to say a lot of 'yeah' . . . If that's what I say, that's what I say. I can't alter it can I? If that's the way you speak, that's the way you speak isn't it? You know, it's like some people are ashamed of having a regional dialect . . . but to me it would be a dreadful shame if regional dialects went because they're part of what you are, aren't they? You know, I mean Oxford English is nice but I like dialects.* There followed a discussion of regional dialects – which ones Cliff liked, which he didn't, *I suppose accents or dialects are like music and some are nice on your ears and some are not . . .*

Cliff's literacy history and literacy life

Cliff was born on Springside in his grandparents' home, just across the road from where he now lives with his mother. He says he was delivered by Buck Ruxton, the doctor who was hanged for the murder of his wife and his housekeeper. Cliff says his mother won't hear a word said against him. Cliff is amused by his connection with a celebrity like Buck Ruxton. Cliff's mother was a warper, and his father a spinner at a local mill. When he was very young the family lived with his mother's parents and his four uncles on

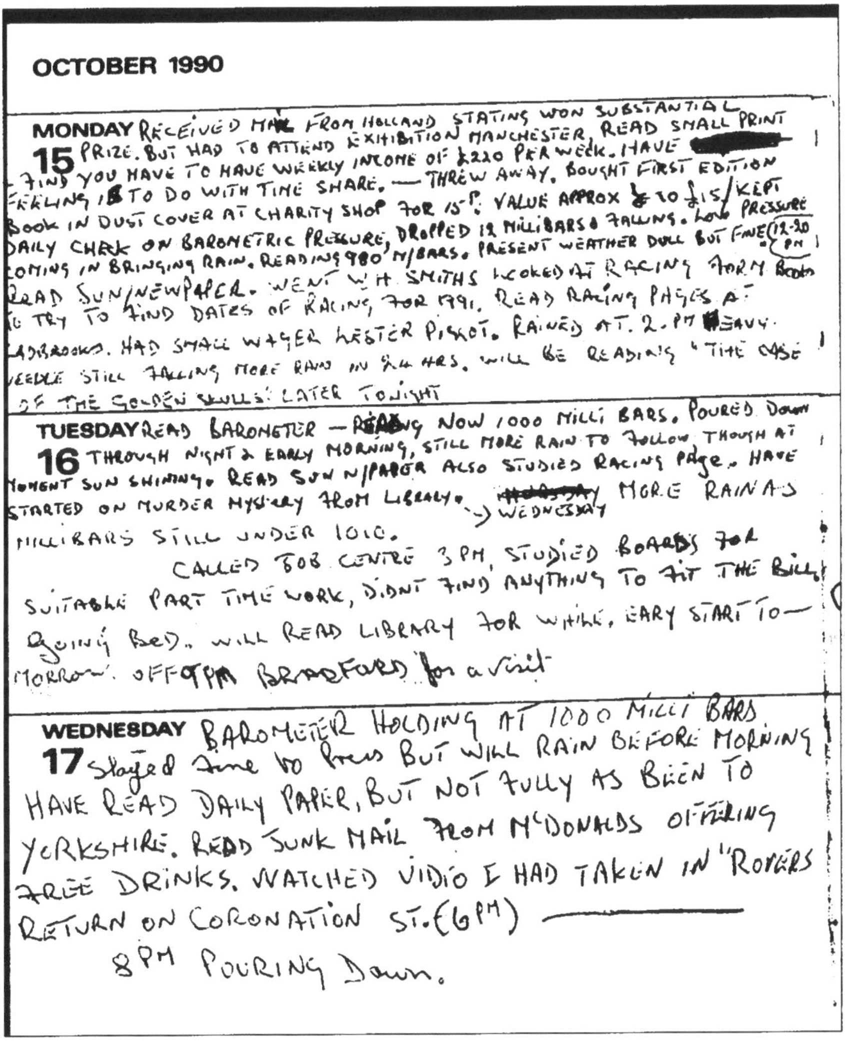

Figure 8.1 Extract from Cliff's diary

Springside. Later his parents moved out into a house of their own, a few streets away, but Cliff stopped with his grandparents who brought him up. His uncles were like brothers. He had a good relationship with his parents, but they were working and his grandmother had more time to look after him.

Aside 8.2   Cliff's pen-sketch

I've never had to do this before. I would probably say, 'I'm 5 foot 10, twelve and a half stone which is a stone and a half overweight, was fair haired but now going grey, 58 years old, got all my own teeth. I've a beard, a mischievous sense of humour when I'm that way out and usually take life fairly easily.' I usually, you know, can see the funny side of everything as a rule. At the moment obviously things are not funny because things are pretty desperate as you know, with my Mother being ill and everything. But I am a bit of a worrier. What else do you want to know? I'm not as fit as I used to be.

I like driving. I love driving. I could drive all day. I love to visit places and see things . . . see how the local people live and see the places of interest. Unfortunately, with Rose being bad with chronic asthma, there's a lot of places I can't go and daren't go. Because if she's taken poorly abroad it could cost me an arm and a leg. It could bankrupt us too, you know . . . And she can't stand the heat as well . . . I'll tell you where I'd really like to go. I'd like to go to Egypt to see the Pyramids and all the Valley of the Kings because I like Egyptology. Not that I know anything about it. I don't. And I would like to go to the Holy Land. They're two places I'd like to see. Or do a cruise up the Nile. And I'd like to go to Disneyland. That's the silly of the three. But not the one in France. I'd like to go to the original one and I'd like to go to Epcot. And there's a tour in America that takes in all the west coast . . . it goes right round Yosemite National Park, Arizona . . . all around that area . . . Nevada. It's like a triangular tour if you will. I like reading about that sort of thing you know. I want to see as much as I can before I fall off me perch. It's just unfortunately that I can't afford to do it without raiding the bank. Apart from that, as I say, Rose can't go.

Cliff started at Springside School, and went on to the Boys' National which later became St John's. Cliff was offered the chance of taking an exam at the Technical College but he refused; by the age of fifteen, he was keen to get out to work. In response to a question about whether he left with any certificates, he said *I never finished up with any. I must have been dumb.* His father fixed him up with a job at the local hairdresser's where he had his own hair cut. Hairdressing would not have been Cliff's chosen career.

After doing his national service, Cliff married and moved to Bradford where he set up his own hairdressing business and stayed in hairdressing for about twenty-five years. During this period he had three children, two daughters and a son. He trained to be an inspector for an engineering works in Bradford, and worked there for a couple of years until he got divorced, and moved back into Lancaster to live. He was unemployed for three months and then got a labouring job at the saw mills, where he worked for eight years and became a shop steward. The last job Cliff had was a part-time one at a local police station.

Since leaving this last job Cliff has been on invalidity benefit but talks of himself as being *unemployed*. He visits the Job Centre and scans the newspapers regularly for jobs. Although he didn't talk in detail about this, there would have been a range of different literacies associated with his different jobs throughout his working life, including running his own business, union activities as a shop steward and later his dealings with the benefit agencies.

When he moved back to Lancaster, Cliff went to live with his mother, who had re-married but been widowed. Her second husband had two grown-up daughters, Rose and Margaret. Rose, Cliff's half-sister, who had herself been married and had children, also moved into the household. When Cliff's youngest child, Robert, was thirteen or fourteen he left his mother and came to live with Cliff and his grandmother in Lancaster. He had learning difficulties and Cliff was keen to give him support. Robert still lives in his grandmother's home with Cliff. He is now nineteen, and works as a butcher. The three of them share the house, and much of their lives together, along with Rose, who now has a flat around the corner. They are a strong family unit, mutually supporting one another and linking with a larger extended family network.

As well as being a great talker, Cliff has enjoyed letter writing for many years. He corresponds regularly with his daughters and other relatives. When his marriage broke up, letter writing to his daughters was an important way of keeping in touch with them since he did not have a telephone. Letter writing is also part of his enjoyment of popular entertainment. He has been a Frankie Laine and Ken Dodd fan for about twenty-five years and started correspondences with these two popular entertainers. Both stars write to him. He writes long letters back and considers Frankie Laine to be a friend now. If he needs to, he checks his spelling by asking Rose or his mother. He also sends greetings cards at Christmas and has his own list in his head. He sends sentimental cards to Rose, who pays great attention to the words.

Cliff and Rose make frequent visits to the library, collecting leaflets on local events, looking up information and exchanging books. Cliff occasionally borrows books from the library for himself and also goes there looking for historical fiction for Rose and romantic fiction books for his mother. He feels uncomfortable about being seen taking out romantic fiction, though.

Rose has a broad interest in literature and history, reading widely, while Cliff seems to have more of a specialist interest, collecting Biggles books, a series for boys featuring a fictional airforce hero from the Second World War, and other adventure stories. However, both share a love of British detective stories. He and Rose frequently share books, and he reads his mother's copy of the *Sun* newspaper, although he is very critical of it as a newspaper.

Cliff says he collects books as an investment as well as a hobby. He searches the second-hand bookshops, car boot sales and charity shops for them. He keeps his books in a bookcase in his bedroom; his mother's house and Rose's flat are full of them. He has been collecting Biggles and Worrals (the female version of Biggles) books for about four years now. He reads them over and over again. He sees himself as an informed book collector; he knows what to look for and where to buy, he can spot a bargain at a glance.

He reads regularly, most nights, as do his mother and Rose. The three of them share newspapers and regular magazines, such as *Bella* and *Chat*. Cliff's son is not interested in reading, however. Cliff writes letters on the settee in the living room, and does not find it distracting to be writing with the television on.

Cliff talks a great deal about having a sense of commitment. This is evident in many areas of his life. It appears to be partly a practical concern, and partly an emotional concern, a sense of loyalty. He does not believe *in chopping and changing*. As an example of this, once he became a hairdresser, he stayed in it for twenty-five years. He built his own business up, although it was his father's choice and not his own; now he regrets going along with this and wishes he had stuck up for himself. There seems to be a struggle for him between *pleasure and leisure*, on the one hand, and the constraints and commitments that are the reality of his life. Constraints of both money and ill-health structure his life and his day-to-day activities, including his literacy practices.

Activities to do with shopping and being careful about spending were common topics during the interviews; these included spending on food, clothes, betting, the poll tax. Cliff and Rose travel considerable distances for bargains, to buy cut-price food, Christmas presents and greetings cards, which they buy in sales months in advance. They explain that *money is tight*, and they *have time on our hands*. They have researched Lancaster and the surrounding towns for value for money and they regard themselves as prudent shoppers. They are practical and resourceful, recording in detail the amount of money spent shopping and writing lists to keep Cliff *to the straight and narrow when shopping*, as Rose puts it. They also shop using catalogues such as *Kays* and *Freemans*; they leaf through catalogues together and Rose regularly orders clothes from them. Rose has always run a catalogue, ordering for friends and people at work, but now she only does it for herself and her relatives. They monitor their spending in several other ways, including checking gas bills and noting the petrol consumption on the car. Cliff does much of this, although

Rose is better at figures and enjoys working with them. Cliff keeps a close eye on his son Robert's finances too, and offers him advice; this causes some friction between them.

Despite these uses of literacy for organising life, Cliff give the impression of not being especially interested in such bureaucratic activities. He does not keep written records of birthdays or Christmas cards but keeps them in his head. We can deduce from what he tells us that he must be involved in the complex literacies associated with his claim for compensation for industrial injuries, and in claiming his pension, paying his poll tax and so on, but he does not dwell on the details of these during the interviews.

Cliff has outspoken ideas about education, general knowledge and intelligence. He takes part in pub quizzes, where he draws on his knowledge of local history. He says he has *a memory for trivia*. His views about knowledge and learning sometimes come out in direct statements but more often these are indirectly and repeatedly expressed through jokes. He has a store of anecdotes about *daft academics*, for instance, which illustrate his theories about learning. His stories reflect an ambivalence similar to Harry's on *educated people*, and which we have noted in several people we talked to.

There is very little in Cliff's interviews on his involvement with organisations or any broader neighbourhood connections. The picture he presents is centred on the close relationships with his immediate household, and he does not talk very much about his wider network of family and acquaintances. However, his and Rose's entries in their diaries give some glimpses of it, offering a wider view of their interactions than comes across in the interviews. For example, Cliff still occasionally cuts people's hair, such as that of an elderly man who is not able to get out any more. We know from our observations and interviews and from his diary entries that he goes to residents' meetings and wrote letters to the council about his irritation with the parking arrangements on his street.

Cliff's ruling passion: leisure and pleasure in life

In looking for a ruling passion in Cliff's life, we start from the frequent references he makes to his easygoing approach to life. He sees the funny side of things, enjoys novelty and entertainment, seeing new places and finding out about new things. He is an avid fan of popular comedy and music, and his interviews are peppered with humorous asides. He does impersonations of show-business personalities and sings songs in different voices to make people laugh. He invents words to well-known tunes to entertain others. He is a fan and collects records and books, as well as travelling all over the north-west to see his favourite stars, Ken Dodd and Frankie Laine.

Pleasure in literacy seems to us now to be the central theme in Cliff's image of himself, and he returns to it time and again in his stories. However, it was not obvious to us at first as a ruling passion, because it contradicts the

135

depressed and worried person that Cliff also appears to be from many parts of the interviews and his preoccupation with the constraints on his life. Just as Harry expresses in his interviews a central dichotomy of educated and uneducated, Cliff has a dichotomy of pleasure versus constraint and commitment; many of his stories illustrate the way he makes sense of his experience through these opposing ideas.

This dichotomy seems also to be linked to his interest in and dreams of seeing more of the world, as described in his pen-sketch. It seems that he feels part of a wider and more glamorous life through the connections he has made with his show business heroes. This is obviously part of the way he makes meaning in his life. We made the mistake of asking to see his letters to Frankie Laine, thinking that they were in some sense a public correspondence, but Cliff refused, saying that these were very personal letters: his relationship with Frankie Laine, to Cliff, is a very private and personal one. Also, he told Frankie Laine about being involved with this research and seemed proud of the links the research gave him to a wider world.

Although he did not spontaneously talk a great deal about literacy, when we asked Cliff in a later interview about his theories of literacy and how people learn, he responded with stories about the cruelty of teachers at his school when he was learning to read. His observation about literacy was that associating reading with punishment did not encourage him to learn, and he thinks that children probably learn better nowadays because schools are more enjoyable places. This seems to be consistent with the theme of pleasure, as is his statement about the fact that he likes to read children's books because they are easy and relaxing. Reading, in his view, should not be hard work and he does not like books which are *too drawn out*. Cliff seems to be more interested in writing than reading. He finishes letters, but quite often gets bored when reading. Cliff says he loves writing letters: *I write as I think, not as I think it should be written . . . and there's a difference.* Words spill on to the page effortlessly. He writes long letters, sometimes about twenty pages.

Cliff has kept diaries at various points in his life. He describes his diary writing as something he enjoys but which he can take or leave. He likes having a large desk diary to write in. Whether or not he keeps one depends on him coming across a diary, but he does not go out of his way to carry on when that one runs out. He is easily able to find a use for a diary, but it does not seem to be a central part of his life.

CLIFF: *I never kept a diary. But . . . when I went to work with the Police one of the things they gave me that we used to have to use at work was a desk diary.*
INTERVIEWER: *Is that like a big one?*
CLIFF: *Yeah. A Crime Prevention desk diary. And they gave me one as a Christmas present while I was there you see. So I started to put things down in it. What was happening daily. And also at that particular time this uncle I was telling you about developed lung cancer and was dying and I was looking after him basically*

Aside 8.3   Being a fan

There is a small literature within the much bigger area of mass media audience research which deals with fans and their culture (see Jenkins 1992; Lewis 1992). The attention paid to this area is slight in relation to the number of people who would count themselves as being fans and who actually engage in fan-like behaviour, rather than the passive watching that is the traditional view of the audience's role. This is especially true if all the popular media, music and sport and other areas of public life, such as politicians and royalty, that spawn adored figures and celebrities are included.

Significant literacy practices are associated with being a fan, including producing, reading and contributing to fanzines and participating in a collective fan-culture either at a distance through these publications or through actual meetings, clubs or performances and other public events. Other possibilities involve appropriating and remaking performances and textual material such as songs or scripts (as in *Star Trek*, the *Rocky Horror Picture Show*). Cliff primarily engages in sustained letter writing and collecting of memorabilia; he also sometimes goes to shows. He appears to be an isolated fan, conducting what is to him an intimate personal correspondence with his heroes.

There are parallels in being a fan with being an expert, a specialist, a collector, or an *aficionado* of high culture. They differ in terms of two important value dimensions involved here: one is to do with which aspects of culture are singled out as important enough to attend to and admire, and the second is the quality of the attention given. As Jenson points out, 'the literature on fandom is haunted by images of deviance: the fan is consistently characterised as a potential fanatic . . . fandom is seen as excessive, bordering on deranged behaviour' (1992: 9). The image of the fan borders on danger and harassment – as in the stalking of public figures. The stereotypical image of the fan is one who is young and female. Cliff does not fit this stereotype, but the image of the middle-aged fan is closer to that of the collector, perhaps regarded as nostalgic rather than dangerous. In fact, Cliff also collects books and pictures unrelated to show business. In terms of literacy practices all these activities can involve the sense making and communal group activities which are described in later chapters.

so I kept a diary on his condition day to day. And on what I'd done. And also made a note of what we'd have for a meal that night. So I was sort of writing out a menu. I'd also put down every Friday how much my mother spent at the Supermarket. Just as a general guide you know.

INTERVIEWER: *Was that . . . so you kept that up?*

CLIFF: *Till the diary ran out, but I never got another because being out of work I couldn't afford to be going out buying desk diaries. I was hoping to get another one last Christmas but I never. I got a mug and a pen instead.*

When we asked Cliff if he would keep a diary for this research, he filled up every page each day and spread out into the margins. During the research he recorded barometer readings, car mileage, activities to do with betting. He discusses the extent to which he included personal things – he had decided not to comment, but just to record his activities for us. When Rose's sister died unexpectedly during this time, he records *Jean Died today* without comment and moves on to other things. He used the diary for his own notes, including records on betting, as in Figure 8.2.

Cliff and Rose visit museums and places of historic interest. They go on jaunts in Cliff's car. One of their favourite spots is Cleveleys, about three-quarters of an hour's drive away on the coast. Cliff dreams of buying a bungalow there, saying that at Cleveleys the air is fresh and it would suit Rose with her asthma. In the summer they go away together often with other family members, including Robert and Cliff's mother. Cliff and Rose have no interest in lying on beaches. They have travelled around England and abroad to Germany, Belgium and the Netherlands. If they go abroad they want to find out about the places they visit, the architecture and the people.

Cliff's diary prompted a story about a trip to the Manchester Granada television studios with his mother, which somehow epitomises Cliff's enjoyment of popular media and interest in being linked with celebrity stars. He had written an entry in the diary that read *Watched video I had taken in Rovers Return on Coronation Street.* (The Rovers Return is the public house featured in *Coronation Street*, a long-running television soap about life in a northern town.) Cliff and Rose filled in the details of the story for Sarah, with Cliff appearing to be especially impressed by the illusion that the video created:

CLIFF: *Well, me and my mother went to Granada Studios and we had a video done of us talking to Mike Baldwin and Betty Turpin in Rovers Return. Laugh of the century, that is!*

ROSE: *She looks like she's looking into space. She's not looking at anyone.*

CLIFF: *Well she's reading off an idiot board you see . . .*

ROSE: *I'm just beginning to feel at home already.'*

CLIFF: *It starts . . . you get the headings and everything on it. And then Mike Baldwin gets out of his car and . . . Ivy Tilsley comes out of her house and they*

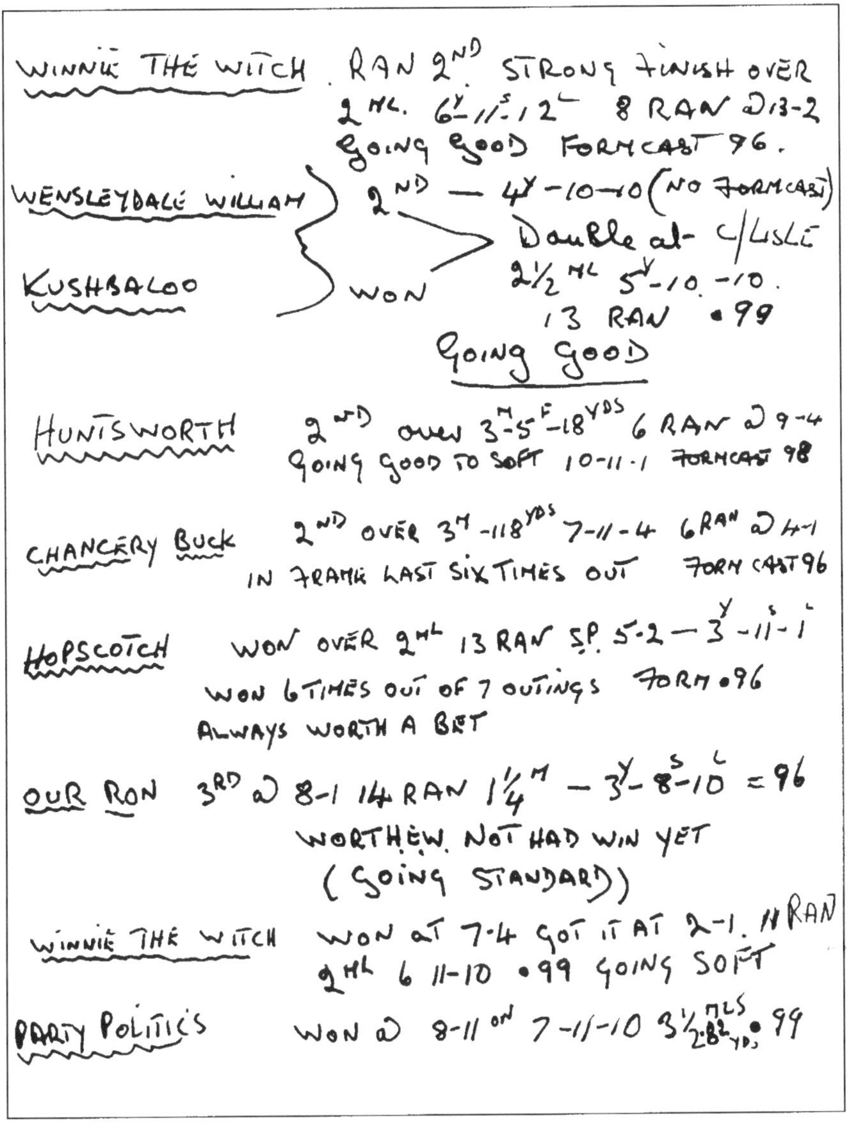
WINNIE THE WITCH RAN 2ND. STRONG FINISH OVER
2 ML. 6Y-11S-12L 8 RAN @ 13-2
GOING GOOD FORMCAST 96.
WENSLEYDALE WILLIAM 2ND — 4Y-10-10 (NO FORMCAST)
Double at C/LISLE
KUSHBALOO WON 2½ ML 5Y-10-10.
13 RAN •99
Going Good
HUNTSWORTH 2ND OVER 3M-5F-18YDS 6 RAN @ 9-4
GOING GOOD TO SOFT 10-11-1 FORMCAST 98
CHANCERY BUCK 2ND OVER 3M-118YDS 7-11-4 6 RAN @ 4-1
IN FRAME LAST SIX TIMES OUT FORMCAST 96
HOPSCOTCH WON OVER 2ML 13 RAN SP. 5-2 — 3Y-11S-1L
WON 6 TIMES OUT OF 7 OUTINGS FORM •96
ALWAYS WORTH A BET
OUR RON 3RD @ 8-1 14 RAN 1¼M — 3Y-8S-10L = 96
WORTHEW. NOT HAD WIN YET
(GOING STANDARD)
WINNIE THE WITCH WON AT 7-4 GOT IT AT 2-1. 11 RAN
2ML 6 11-10 •99 GOING SOFT
PARTY POLITICS WON @ 8-11 ON 7-11-10 3½ MLS 28 YDS •99

Figure 8.2 Notes on betting

both go into Rovers Return. And then she says something about looking at these new houses, 'cos they've built a lot of new houses on Coronation Street . . . proper ones. And he says 'I see some other people looking at them' and that's when me and my mother appear in Coronation Street and we're talking to Mike and Betty Turpin. And then it finishes and credits come up and your names come up as well. Guest appearances of . . . Well what it is, you go into a room and there's a bar in this room and on the wall is an idiot board with lines on. When the little red light lights up, you say what your line is and then when the light goes out you just stand there and when the light comes on again, the next person speaks their lines right? Now when it's played back you're actually stood in the Rovers Return.

INTERVIEWER: *So you're not really with Mike Baldwin?*

CLIFF: *Oh no.*

INTERVIEWER: *But it looks like it.*

CLIFF: *You're stood there, talking to him.*

INTERVIEWER: *But they look like ghosts, do they?*

ROSE: *Well it looks a bit ghostly, doesn't it?*

CLIFF: *Well it doesn't to me. It's just, I don't know really. It's not so bad.*

In the six months before we started interviewing, Cliff and Rose have developed a common interest in racing and betting, as described in Aside 8.4, and they go to as many races as they can. Recently they have been to Cartmel and Haydock Park. Cliff is fascinated by the tick-tack men; he tried to buy a book on how to learn to read tick-tack gestures but he was not able to find one. Cliff goes to the betting shop because it is too smoky for Rose; but they study the forms together and enjoy reading up about it. Rose loves working with the figures. They place small bets as they *have to be careful with money*. They have developed their own system of signs on the racecourse.

Learning to bet is trying to enter a set of practices which are largely passed on orally from one person to another. However, the practice of betting uses a wide range of written documents, including newspapers, tote books and betting slips, along with a range of other semiotic systems, including boards, the tick-tack signalling system and television and computer monitors. This example of learning to bet again illustrates the range of media Cliff draws on, his willingness to use literacy if it can help him, but also his willingness to incorporate other methods, such as non-verbal sign systems, if these will work better in a given situation.

One principle of Cliff's relationship with literacy, then, is that of entertainment and pleasure. He seems to use literacy intensely and actively in some contexts, such as keeping in touch with long-term pen-friends who are well-known people who have almost become his personal friends since he has been writing to them; he also reports intermittent diary keeping and reading to solve practical problems; however, literacy is not a central organising tool in his life. He is very much someone who puts literacy to use in his personal life, but he picks and chooses when and how, and he is not interested in *working at it*. He uses many different media, and seems equally at home with radio, popular music, television, video and theatre. He uses a tape-recorder but not a calculator; he uses the phone a great deal and has taken part in a radio phone-in on a health issue. He would like an electronic

Aside 8.4 Learning betting literacy

CLIFF: *We're not daft with money, are we? The only daft thing we do . . . well it isn't daft really, we back horses. Just recently, within the last six month, we've started picking horses out of the paper. Now when I say that, we don't put pounds on. We put shillings on. We do it for fun, just for something to do. Pick them out and next day see if they'd won. Just to see how lucky or unlucky we are. And we started off with a pound six month ago. And we're still playing with their money. We've never dipped into ours yet. We got it up to something like, what . . . twenty five, thirty quid in front?*

They all have their own tipsters. I mean . . . this one here. I've got no tips in this one. But I go down and look at . . . You see when I first went in, I was so embarrassed like Rose said, getting mixed up in company of people that know more than you. I didn't even know how to fill a race . . . a betting form in. And I didn't like asking. But now I go in and I've found out all sorts of things I didn't know before.

I waffled around and finally I had the nerve to say to somebody, 'Will you show me how to fill this in?' I mean a bloke of fifty-seven asking somebody how to fill a betting form in. I said, 'I've never done it before.' So we just did it each way. I asked 'em how to fill it in. And then if I wanted to do a double, I didn't know how to do a double. And I didn't know what the boards meant. It'd say something like . . . there'd be five numbers at say seven to four, ten to two, three to one, so many at odds on. And it would say bar six. And I didn't know what bar six meant. I hadn't a clue.

Now this is the way it works with the on-the-course bookies. Their prices are altering all the time. 'Cos tick-tack men are passing from one to the other what one is giving odds. So they all, more or less, have the same odds. But when you put a bet on with a bookie on a course, you get the price when that horse finishes . . . if you get it at twenty-five to one and it drops down to three to one, you still get twenty-five to one 'cos it's written in his book that when you put it on, he guarantees you twenty-five to one.

I went to try and pick a book up at the bookshop, to find out if you could learn how to read tick-tack men. So that I could keep my eye on them if I went to a race course. So that I understand what they were saying when they were doing all this business. But I can't find one anywhere.

INTERVIEWER: *But who teaches who then? How do they know?*

ROSE: *One passes it to the next.*

diary if he could afford it and uses the ready reckoner in his tote book. Knowing that his son finds writing difficult, he finds an alternative way of keeping in contact with a pen-friend by substituting a different medium, tape-recording, rather than forcing him to write letters.

Sharing lives and being a committed parent

As described above, Cliff's family are very close but not a straightforward nuclear family. His childhood family experience was not of a nuclear sort either, and neither was Rose's. Cliff and Rose are especially close. As we have seen above, they spend most of their time together, share a sense of humour and many interests including some that involve literacy. Cliff's concerns, his worries about his son and his mother, are Rose's concerns also. They give the impression that they discuss the family constantly and sort things out between them. Just as we have noted his sense of commitment in other areas of his activities, Cliff feels a sense of commitment to his children and a need to impress his values and understanding of constraints on them, and in particular on his son Robert. This leads to some tensions. Cliff is concerned that Robert does not share his sense of commitment. Robert is nineteen, with learning difficulties, and living at home. Cliff is worried that Robert is forever buying, selling and exchanging bikes. Cliff worries that he should do this at all, but he is especially worried because Robert does it in an uninformed way, and loses money. He makes his feelings clear to his son.

Cliff finds it hard to advise Robert, and he says that, like most teenage sons, Robert usually chooses to ignore him, but he has managed to persuade him to get a pension scheme going. Cliff is concerned that Robert should not end up like him relying solely on a state pension. Generally he feels Robert is careless with money, a spender not a saver. Robert would not put money by for his poll tax payments but managed to pay them off anyway with a tax rebate, a chance thing, which annoyed Cliff. Cliff describes his own marriage as *difficult*. After leaving his wife he communicated regularly with his children including by letter; but Robert had problems and, Cliff feels, was very neglected both at school and at home. When Robert was fourteen and came to live with Cliff, he did his best to support his son's education. He describes how he recorded tapes of tables for Robert's Walkman and tried to encourage him to read:

> *His times table wasn't so good. So I taped them for him. I taped him saying them about four times slowly. Like one two is two, two twos are four, three twos are six. I did it four times per table and then the fifth time I left the answer out. One two is . . . and I left a pause, two twos are – and I put them on a tape for him. And I used to make him put it on his head and walk around . . . people thought he was listening to music. In actual fact, he were learning his times table and up to a point it did sink in. And it's sunk in*

much now that he actually serves in the shop . . . at the butcher's shop and
he has no problems.

Over the last few years Robert has made progress. He works in a shop and is committed to his work. Cliff and Rose think he is a late developer; he has surprised them:

In fact, I think, he's a bit of a late learner. And he's a fast learner. He's
learnt his trade. He's good at his job. He's not as daft as everybody thought
he was, you know. And he's quite a . . . he's a tinkerer. He's always mon-
keying about. He's always taking his bike to bits and putting it back together,
and he's quite adept at doing things. He's put a fish pond in the back
garden and built a wall. And stuff that he's never been shown to do. He's
sorted it out and worked it out and done it. You know. He'll have a go. Even
if he makes a mess of it, he'll have a go. Now I wouldn't. This is where I fall
down. He's a lot more confident in that respect that I am. Rather than try
something and not get it right, I won't have a try. He will.

When Robert was younger the school arranged a pen-pal. He had difficulty writing and had little interest in contacting the pen-pal. Cliff was shocked by this. He insisted that, having committed himself, Robert should follow it up. Appreciating his son's difficulties he suggested Robert should communicate with her through tapes. Since then Cliff has started the tapes off and Robert has added bits.

My son is a typical teenager. The school wrote to one of the agencies that pro-
vide pen-friends and got a pen-friend in Canada called Holly Beecham. And
then does nothing about it. Now I don't like letting people down. And he
won't write letters so to try and get him off the hook I said 'Look, why don't
you ask her if you can send tapes rather than write letters'. It's easier for you,
you know. 'Cos it was, 'How do you spell this?' He's not all that brilliant . . .
his spelling, you know. And he's not all that good in putting down on
paper what he thinks in his head. So we do that. Having said that, if three
tapes go, three-quarters of them I'll have filled in and he'll have filled the last
little bit in, you know. And this is how it's gone on. I have to practically
stand by him to make him put anything on.

Another area of tension is Robert's relationship with a local girl. Cliff and his mother do not approve of the relationship and, in fact, they actively discourage it. Robert's girlfriend sends him notes by sticking them in the door to the passageway between Cliff's house and the next house. Robert goes there daily to put his bike away. He hides these notes in the house but he hides them in places which Cliff discovers, for example in the wardrobe which they share. Cliff is not just annoyed by the relationship but irritated by his son's lack of cunning. He talks of this with a half-affectionate sense of annoyance but his worry about the relationship seems to be serious: Cliff had an unhappy marriage and doesn't want his son to do the same.

Ill-health and depression

Issues to do with ill-health and dealings with medical services are another prominent theme in Cliff's literacy life. Ill-health was mentioned as a constraint and limitation on both practical activities and natural enjoyment of life, as we have seen in Cliff's pen-sketch of himself. Rose had developed asthma through working in a cotton mill and Cliff has suffered from migraines for many years. He has tinnitus, a constant ringing in the ears, and other hearing problems since working in a saw mill. Cliff's condition has often made him depressed. Within his overall theme of pleasure and constraint, Cliff talked about a number of instances involving literacy which show how his practices were shaped or motivated by his experiences of ill-health.

Tinnitus makes it difficult for Cliff to read or to watch television. He reads information that he gets from the Tinnitus Association, such as medical charts about hearing tests, and gets a certificate from his doctor when he is off work. He has to cover his ears when listening to information on monitors at the bookmaker's to avoid distortion. Rose's ill-health also affects their activities. She is good at picking winners, especially dogs, but they don't go to the dogs very often as Rose can't sit inside because of the smoke. Sometimes he sits inside and she stays outside; they developed their system of signals and lip-reading in order to communicate there.

As mentioned above, Cliff took part in a phone-in organised by the local radio station, Red Rose Radio. This was a programme involving a discussion about noisy working environments and he actually went to the studios. As a result of this, the radio station arranged for him to have hearing tests done and they put him in touch with an independent specialist and a solicitor. The solicitor had received a report from the specialist and was in the process of trying to get compensation for Cliff for damage due to a noisy working environment. Cliff describes how he critically evaluates medical advice and advertisements for hearing aids, and seeks out information about alternative devices. Rather than relying on Job Centre staff to select possible jobs for him, he reads the local paper employment section and the Job Centre boards himself. He feels he can judge the suitability of jobs advertised better than Job Centre staff, as they don't know how tinnitus affects him.

The examples Cliff gives of becoming embroiled in medical issues echo a number of other people's experiences in relation to their health which we will return to in Chapter 13. Every ailment has its support group and newsletter. People develop extremely detailed, technical and specialist knowledge about their own ailments and the treatments and services available to them, which include complex literate activities and vocabularies that are not necessarily present in other general areas of their lives. Here, for example, Cliff talks about how he used literacy to get information about ergotomine medication for his migraine:

CLIFF: *I was hairdressing when it started. And I can't put my finger on actually when it did start. But obviously for a long time when I had them, I didn't know what they were. I went to the doctor's and he just gave me various things. I never even questioned it. I know one period I went for a long time without having any sleep and he gave me two pills and he said, 'Take these. You'll sleep tonight. I guarantee it. But don't take them till you get into bed.' I got into bed and took them and I never even shut my eyes. He didn't believe me when I told him. So I went to read up about it and I found out that you could get smaller doses of this ergotomine. It wasn't as strong a dose as the pills or the other things, in a little aerosol spray. You couldn't take anything that would stop it coming on. But you could take things to nip it in the bud, once it started. And these little ergotomine sprays were only about a fourth of the strength of the tablets or the suppositories. But with it going into your lungs, it immediately got where it had to go straight into your blood stream. And I could guarantee that once I felt it starting, if I took one inhalation followed by another in five minutes, within fifteen minutes it started to lift.*

INTERVIEWER: *Right. And you read about it in the library. And then you went to a chemist?*

CLIFF: *No, no. To the doctor, and I asked him if I could have one of these sprays as I would find it more convenient. And he had a look in his little book and he said, 'Yes'. It never occurred to him I don't think. You know, I don't think he'd heard about them. And he read about it in his little book and he gave me one.*

INTERVIEWER: *Had you done that before? Had you been to look up medical conditions before?*

CLIFF: *No. Because I never suffered with anything before. No. The only thing was I've had this for twenty-odd years and it was getting on my flaming nerves.*

This outline of Cliff's activities suggests that a number of purposes and motivations lie behind his literacy practices. These include his own enjoyment, to entertain others, to initiate and maintain relationships, to affirm a sense of his own value and importance, to increase his own knowledge and control of things, and to help others to do this, to get everyday things done. Cliff's story foregrounds the issue of feelings around literacy and how people might want to avoid certain kinds of literacy, not because they find it technically difficult, but because it doesn't feel pleasurable and may be experienced as boring, with not enough action, as irrelevant, as threatening, or as a punishment. Cliff's life also gives an insight into how bound up a person's literacy preferences and activities can be with the other people whose lives are closely shared, such as Rose and Robert.

145

The key quotation on meeting Ken Dodd that we chose for the start of this chapter illustrates several important points. Firstly, it shows the close relationship between literacy and Cliff's enjoyment of popular theatre, comedy shows and music. At other points in the interviews he talks about other celebrities whom he follows on the television and through going to live shows. His meeting with Ken Dodd is part of a bigger fascination with celebrities and a bigger set of letter-writing practices – for example his encouragement to his son to write to a pen-pal. These practices reflect a strong *value* about literacy for sustained personal communication, but also complete acceptance of interchangeable media to accomplish the same end – hence his idea of taped letters as a substitute for written ones. Another important point made by the key quote is the obvious link between adult interests and the shaping of children's experience. Though Cliff says he was taking the children to see Ken Dodd, his own choices and enthusiasms are reflected in this event. We do not know whether his daughters were equally fascinated, but it is Cliff who kept up the correspondence over a period of years.

Part III

Having dealt with four individuals in some detail, we now approach the data in a different way, as we look for themes and patterns which link different people's experiences and perceptions. The analysis turns to the full range of people we worked with in the study. These include the rest of our case-study households, the people from the Adult College whom we interviewed in the first stage, and a range of other informants from throughout the town. Brief profiles of these people can be found in Appendix 1.

Our data collection strategy involved identifying several samples of individuals, and using several discrete approaches to them, as described in Chapter 4. However, these samples were not intended to be the basis of our analyses, so there are no results sections to mirror each of the samples. We integrate the information from all of these sources throughout the following chapters. We refer back to the concepts introduced in Chapter 1, and also to the wider literature that provides a context within which to locate our findings.

Chapters 9 and 10 provide an overview of everyday literacies in households, first documenting their diversity and then commenting on patterns to be found within them. Chapters 11, 12 and 13 explore three major strands of our findings about literacy: as a family resource, a collective organisational resource, and a resource for sense-making.

Chapter 14 draws all this together and develops our theoretical view of literacy as community resource and vernacular practice. The final chapter, Chapter 15, discusses how our findings from this local study can be related to literacy practices in other times and places.

9

EVERYDAY LITERACIES

(1) The range of practices

Diversity

We were struck by the wide diversity of literacies in the home. Literacy at home is tied in with daily activities. Often it combines many sorts of reading and writing as well as drawing upon spoken language, numeracy, other media and much more. People deal with shopping lists, television schedules and junk mail. They write and receive personal letters and cards; some keep diaries, some write poems or words for songs; they deal with official letters, bills and forms; they have notice-boards, calendars, scrap books, recipe books, address books; they read local newspapers, catalogues and advertisements; people keep records of their lives, and read and write to make sense of this complex world; they belong to community organisations and pursue leisure interests bound by a web of newsletters, notices, minutes and messages. Newsletters from local associations, and from national ones, arrive as part of the unsolicited mail which comes through the door, or may be picked up by people from events and meetings.

Written instructions accompany every consumer product and service, from a bicycle helmet to a gas bill; people are even told by written instructions how, when and where to put out the rubbish. Texts of all sorts circulate in the household – newspapers and books, magazines, advertisements, recipes and instruction manuals; they get passed around from one person to another and are treated in many different ways. Simply to state the diversity of people's engagement with literacy counteracts images of homes and people empty of literacy. But there was also coherence in this diversity. Not everyone did everything. Variation related to individual histories and cultural histories, and also to the range and pattern of activities which go on in households, including feeding, sleeping, leisure, budgeting, praying, repairing, consuming. Two influential sources of the structure of household routines are employment and having children in the household. Religion can be an additional important factor for some households, as can ill-health or financial constraints for others. Underlying all of these are the pervasive patterns of relations between generations and between genders. In this chapter we identify some of the diversity in home practices, concentrating first on writing and then on reading, and including discussion of adults who identify problems with reading and writing. In the next chapter we discuss particular examples of the patterning of practices. For details of other aspects of the range of practices in the home, see Barton and Hamilton (1992a; 1992b).

Writing in the home

In an earlier paper David Barton and Sarah Padmore reported on the writing done in the home (Barton and Padmore 1991). This data came from interviews with the twenty adults from the Adult College who had identified themselves as having difficulties with literacy. First, we will summarise the results of that paper and then move beyond it to examine home literacy practices more generally.

Barton and Padmore (1991) identified three general areas of writing carried out within the home: writing to maintain the household, writing to maintain communication and personal writing. In terms of the first category, people keep household records, writing appointments on calendars, sticking reminders on to notice-boards, writing lists of tasks which need doing, leaving messages for other family members on the stairs or stuck to the fridge with a magnet. Most people had a standard place for keeping scraps of paper for writing and there would be pens and pencils lying around.

The second category, writing to maintain communication, included the regular writing of letters to friends or relatives who did not live nearby. More common was keeping up relationships with people by the regular sending of cards. Several people reported keeping a Christmas card list and often a list of people's birthdays and other anniversaries. A number of people, especially the women we talked to, reported spending a considerable time choosing greetings cards with 'the right message', sometimes supplementing this with their own words. Choosing greetings cards can be seen as a form of writing: it is little different from copying the prepared letters from nineteenth-century etiquette books or using the late twentieth-century 'make your own greeting' computer programmes. Subtle layers of meanings, humour and double-entendre can be created by mixing the pre-written and the personal messages; for example, Rita, one of the people we interviewed, described this in the cards she composed to send to an ex-lover. (A brief description of Rita, along with the other people we interviewed, can be found in Appendix 1.)

Personal writing included the writing of poems, diaries and stories. We were initially surprised at the number of people who did some personal writing in their everyday lives. At least nine out of the twenty people we interviewed in this phase of the research had written a poem which had nothing to do with their college work; several wrote short pieces of fiction as a leisure activity; three people talked of writing down their thoughts; and two had kept personal diaries for around a year. Several others talked of having kept diaries at other points in their lives.

There are two aspects to literacy practices: the tangible, observable activities, on the one hand, and interpretative aspects such as attitudes, values and other social meanings which lie behind these activities, on the other hand. In terms of the tangible activities which people were involved in, they were happy to talk about physical aspects such as where and when they wrote. People tended to have a regular time and place for writing, and they identified particular pens or preferred paper. Mark always did any writing he needed to do in his bedroom directly after tea; Cath always got up early in the morning to write any letters. Val did her writing directly after breakfast or at night; Lynne wrote in the afternoons.

In terms of the attitudes, awareness and values behind people's activities, and the definitions and social meanings of literacy for them, these were all people who had earlier identified problems with reading and writing. They all saw reading and writing as of value to them and their children and they turned to education as a means of changing their practices, although, interestingly, they did not regard themselves as the 'people with problems' reported in the media (see Aside 9.4); those were other people, not themselves. An earlier article describes some of the many ways in which writing was imbued with meaning for these people (Barton and Padmore 1991: 71–4).

There was a great deal of variety in how people engaged with writing. People kept diaries at particular phases in their lives: Lesley had written a diary for a year after the birth of her child; some had kept diaries as children, including Andrea's childhood diary which had been a fictitious record of day-to-day life at a stables, an example we will return to later. Similarly with letter writing: people exchanged letters with friends or relatives when they were away from Lancaster for a period of time.

From this information it is hard to make generalisations about the overall amount of writing which people did, but we do know that three of the twenty chose to sit down and write something every day. What also struck us at this point was the range of different writing activities which we encountered and the ways in which everyone seemed to have their own practices, something specific about the ways in which they used writing: Andrea, going through a difficult period with her partner, was communicating with him almost exclusively through messages left around the house; Julie was copying out bits of published poetry to put in her love letters; Paul was hiding written jokes around the house for his partner. We should remember that these are people who found some aspect of reading and writing difficult; on the other hand since they were attending college, they were also people for whom reading and writing had some importance in their lives and for whom these were salient activities.

Following on from this part of the research we moved out into the community, as we described in Chapter 4, knocking on doors and interviewing people in their homes. We began complementing the interview data with detailed observation of home practices and the broader context of community life. With this broader perspective we can return to this data. The idea of three common uses of writing in the home – to maintain the household, for communication and for personal writing – still seems valid. However, we now see that writing to maintain the household relates to the broader social practice of organising one's life. Writing as communication is part of more general personal communication. Personal writing relates to private leisure and also to documenting one's life. From our broader study we have also identified the further categories of sense making and of social participation. These are all pursued in later chapters. In the present chapter we will go on to discuss the diversity of reading as well as writing and to consider other literacy practices in the home.

Everyday reading

Turning to the broader study of literacy in Springside, our first attempt at exploring reading in the home produced a list of activities such as reading newspapers, keeping diaries, receiving letters, dealing with the junk mail. All of these activities involve reading in some way. However, we wanted to move beyond simple listing, to focusing on the underlying significance and characteristics of different sorts of reading, and examining how literacy is related to social activities and to the multiple motivations which people have.

There appeared to be two distinct sorts of activities. The first is where reading is the main and recognised goal of the activity; the second is where reading is a means to another end which is more salient than the literacy itself. As an example of the first group, there is a common and strong sense of reading when someone is reading a book or reading a newspaper. In activities of this kind, reading is completely integral to the activity, and where if asked *what are you doing?* a person might well answer *reading.* This type of reading is often connected with leisure and is a quiet personal activity. Many people referred to novels and had their particular favourite books, authors or genres. They had a strong sense of particular genres, mentioning wartime fiction, fantasy, sci-fi, adventure, crime, the occult, television serials, historical romance. People mentioned *Mills and Boon* as a type of book, and also *Catherine Cookson sort of books* – she was the most commonly mentioned author. Other authors mentioned included James Herriott and Stephen King. Lynne referred to the category of *serious books* which she had tried reading and had failed. She preferred *real stories* by authors like Catherine Cookson: *it's relaxing and you can escape.* This sort of absorption of being lost in a book (discussed more by Nell 1988) was reported by many people. Terry would sit and read a book completely in an afternoon, and others talked of not being able to put a book down until they had finished it. However, it was not just novels which absorbed people. Helen read a range of novels but also wanted books about real people, meaning factual reports of real-life incidents, such as coping with illness, and she would read these for leisure. This connects with our earlier more detailed example of Harry and his interest in books about the Second World War.

A range of factual books was reported as being read seriously, on topics as broad as cookery, gardening, witchcraft, astronomy, martial arts, shooting, climbing, animals and wildlife. People had read biographies, including ones of Rommel and Churchill. Patrick said that with any new hobby he got interested in he would always read up on it. Much of this was for leisure, but it also spilled over into work. Although not following a course, Patrick, a fitness instructor, read books on weight-training; similarly, Terry reported reading books on nursing to help with his work. Some of this book reading could be described as functional reading for particular purposes, such as several people reporting reading medical books in order to understand a child's symptoms of illness, or Shirley reading books on dyslexia. Another example of this was Terry going through books in the library to find evidence to back up an argument with someone at work that the Duke of Lancaster is in fact the Queen. In these cases people seem to read just parts of books, purposefully searching for what they need. Often this more functional reading was from magazines or instruction booklets.

People reported reading a wide range of newspapers, local and national, as well as a broad array of magazines, from glossy commercial ones to locally produced church magazines or special interest newsletters. We asked about newspaper reading and buying in our door-to-door survey and from this discovered the importance of local newspapers in people's lives (see Aside 9.1). In later interviews people often talked about their newspaper reading habits and gave their views about different newspapers or journalism in general. Some people, like Patrick and Shirley, were extremely critical of newspapers and expressed clear preferences for the more speedy and reliable coverage of television news. Others expressed contradictory or ambivalent views about newspapers – for instance, they would describe regularly reading the *Sun*, but acknowledge with laughter that it is a scurrilous paper and that they did not read it for news. In other words people were aware of the public view of the papers they read and distanced themselves from their own behaviour.

Another striking feature of the accounts of newspaper reading was the frequency with which people shared each other's newspapers, picking papers up where they happened to be or regularly reading a paper taken by another family member or someone at work. It is quite acceptable etiquette, for example on a train, to ask to read someone else's paper, but this is not true for books. This cultural habit of sharing newspapers is reflected in the national statistics, where there are quite separate figures from census returns on the readership of newspapers and circulation figures compiled from the number of sales of papers. When people bought their own paper, they commonly said they bought it for a particular part, such as the crossword or the sports section. They only read parts of the paper and often ignored whole sections. Kress and van Leeuwen (1996) talk of people following 'reading paths' through newspapers and we have many examples in our data of people describing the regular routes they took in their reading.

Aside 9.1   National figures on newspaper readership

Each weekday people in Britain read more than twenty million newspapers, including regional morning and evening papers; this is higher than in most other countries. People purchase eight million copies of weekly papers; another forty million free papers are published every week. Taking 1990 as a starting-point, the best-selling daily newspapers were the *Sun* (10.2 million readers), followed by the *Mirror* (8.7 million), *Mail* (4.2 million), *Express* (3.9 million), *Star* (2.8 million), *Telegraph* (2.5 million); *Today* (1.7 million); *Guardian* (1.3 million); *Independent* (1.1 million) and *Times* (1.2 million). In 1990 two-thirds of the population claimed to read a daily newspaper, with slightly more men than women and the highest readership in the 45 to 64 age group. Within any month 93 per cent of the population see a national newspaper. Since 1990 the sales of national newspapers have been declining. Readership of free newspapers is on the rise while weeklies are 'declining.

The age structure of the readership varies from paper to paper: readership of the *Sun*, for example, declines markedly with age from a high in the 15 to 24 age group, whereas the *Express* and the *Telegraph* have older readerships and the *Mirror* has a similar percentage of readers across all age groups. In relation to other media, figures suggest that, although television is the more trusted news source for most adults, people spend more *time* per day with newspapers; and that the function of newspapers is changing from being the primary source of news to more of an entertainment function.

Sources: Saatchi and Saatchi 1990; Central Statistical Office 1992; Gunter *et al.* 1994.

A distinct form of reading, but where reading is still integral to the activity, is reading aloud to someone else. Many people reported reading to their children. In many cases this was voluntary reading to pre-school children, part of general child-centred activities; in other cases it was in response to requests from school and was part of a school-initiated activity where parents were asked to read to their children and to record that they had done it. Other reading aloud was between adults. Lesley reported that her husband regularly read books to her. There were other reports of couples reading to each other and this seemed an intimate part of their relationships. Keith's family would read stories aloud to each other at Christmas, sitting round the fire and passing the book around from person to person. They also read together on holidays. The books read together included ghost stories, myths and long poems. In a group interview, another person, Lynne, recalled her family reading whole books together, taking turns to read a chapter out loud and then passing the book round. She was surprised to discover that other people in the group had not experienced this.

Another form of reading to other people which was commonly reported is when someone would read out a short item, usually from the newspaper or magazine they were reading, to whoever was present in the living room. Often this was reported emotively: the reading aloud was to make a point, the reader being either strongly in favour or strongly against what they were reading, as Harry and Ted were when reading the newspaper letters to one another; or it was thought of as funny or ridiculous, as with Shirley reading out from someone's autobiography.

As with the writing data, many people reported a time and a place for reading. It was incorporated into the regular rhythms of home life. Helen, devoted to reading, would regularly go to bed early in order to read; Lynne read under the hairdrier and in the toilet; Brenda read in the bath. These practices relate to public and private spaces within the home. Several people read novels only when on holiday. There were also phases in people's lives when they did particular sorts of reading: Helen had only become interested in reading in the past three years since the birth of her daughter as she didn't go out as often as she had done before. She also talked of *the book I'm reading at the moment*, reflecting the common phenomenon of people having a book they were currently relating to.

Whether it is a newspaper, a novel or a gardening book, there are many ways of reading, or engaging with the text. These vary from the totally absorbing phenomenon of being lost in a book to the other extreme of just passing the time, glancing at the paper while waiting for a friend, and maybe not being able to recall anything about the content if asked. Lynne used this contrast, saying that her husband bought a newspaper every day and read it through, while she glanced at it in the evenings if she had time. A slightly different dimension is the degree of purposefulness in the reading. Some reading is done with the express purpose of finding something out, what time the bus leaves or when the form has to be returned to school, whilst other reading is more generalised. Much reading is casual, accidental, circumstantial, in contrast to sustained purposeful reading. Reading to pass the time was often undertaken when other activities were not possible, such as in doctors' waiting rooms, travelling or when waiting at home for a friend to arrive.

In her ethnographic interview study of women magazine readers, both male and female, Joke Hermes (1995) emphasises the importance of distinguishing between fans and ordinary audiences. Ordinary audiences may be much less engaged and purposeful in their reading or viewing. In her study she was seeking to uncover the 'meaningfulness' of these popular media to their general readers and she was initially thrown by the fact that the readers themselves had little to say about the magazines, claiming that their main virtues were that they were relaxing, easy to put down, culturally insignificant and 'blend in easily with other obligations, duties and activities of daily routines' (Hermes 1995: 144). There are parallels between this casual reading and much television and radio use, as described by Anne Gray (1992). Such practices run counter to much cultural studies research which assumes that popular culture is always deeply meaningful to people.

To explain how magazines are used, Hermes also makes use of the social psychological concept of *interpretative repertoires* (see Potter and Weatherall (1987: 149), who define such repertoires as 'recurrently used systems of terms used for characterising and evaluating actions, events and other phenomena'). Readers bring a set of 'frames' or approaches to the act of reading. These cut across genres and are to a large extent independent of the structure or content of texts themselves. This is applicable to our own data where we were struck by the fact that a particular book might be read in various different ways on different occasions. A cookery book or a gardening book could be used as a source of information to answer a specific question. It could also be read more generally, to read up on a topic; sometimes a book might be scanned very casually, while at other times people might read in such a way that they were lost in the book, absorbed in their own fantasy worlds of food or gardens. People without gardens had gardening books; people who rarely cooked would be engrossed in a recipe book. People read these books when alone; they also shared them and read and used them collaboratively.

If in the above examples reading is integral to the activity, there was also a large number of literacy activities where reading was more incidental, and if a person was asked what they were doing they would be much less likely to say that they were reading. Checking appointments diaries and noticeboards, looking at advertisements, dealing with the mail, doing the shopping all involve reading. All writing activities inevitably also have reading associated with them. So, when paying bills, filling in forms, writing letters to friends or to school, writing a poem or sending a greetings card,

Aside 9.2   National figures on magazines and comics

Around two and a half thousand consumer magazines are published in the UK. In 1990 the most popular general magazines were the *Radio Times*, with a readership of 8.5 million; the *TV Times*, with a readership of 8.4 million; *Reader's Digest*, with 6.1 million. These are followed by *What Car*, *National Geographic* and *Exchange and Mart*. Each copy of *What Car* and *Exchange and Mart* is likely to be read by several people, and they are mainly read by men. The *Reader's Digest* tends to be read by older people. The weekly *TV Times* and *Radio Times* are each read by about one fifth of the adult population, equally across age and gender groups. In our study the *TV Times* and the *Radio Times* were read for their content and advertisements as well as for their guides to programmes – Shirley, Cliff and Rose all considered them to be *a good read*. (Sales figures are not collected for soft porn magazines. It is estimated that a total of 2.5 million copies are sold per month, making them significant contributors to the magazine market.)

Nearly a third of adults read a women's weekly magazine, and the same proportion read a women's monthly. These readers are mostly women, though around 3 per cent of men read them too. In 1990 the most popular women's magazines were *Woman's Own* (4.3 million); *Bella* (4.3 million); *Woman's Weekly* (3.1 million); *Woman* (3.0 million); *Best* (2.9 million); *Prima* (2.9 million) and *Me* (1 million). Of these, the traditional British women's magazines have a falling circulation and are being overtaken by new European-based publications such as *Bella* and *Prima* magazines, which entered the market in 1986/7.

Sources: Hermes 1995; Central Statistical Office 1992. Saatchi and Saatchi 1990; Itzin 1992; Ferguson 1983.

there is an element of reading. In all activities reading is more than the decoding of written text. Reading involves understanding design and layout, with forms and timetables. It requires making sense of the visuals integrated with texts in catalogues, advertisements, packaging and instruction manuals. It demands understanding other symbolic systems in knitting patterns, maps and bank statements. It is associated with other media and technologies besides paper, for example when there is reading to be done on television and computers; and reading is combined with speaking when explaining a document to someone, listening to a child read or taking a phone message. What we see in the home are the ways in which reading is integrated into coherent activities so that planning a holiday, assembling a new wardrobe or helping a child with homework are all activities where reading plays a role, and where it is difficult to disentangle the reading from the overall event. Reading is not just making sense of print, it is figuring out meaning in a broader semiotic context.

Values, morals and censorship

The idea of reading and of being *a reader* was imbued with values, just as the idea of writing and being *a writer* was. Generally reading was seen as a good thing, people approved of it. Several people referred to themselves, their children and other members of their families as either being readers or not being readers. A 'reader' normally meant someone who read books regularly, so that Helen, for example, said that her husband was not a reader, he read only newspapers. Shirley characterises herself as an *avid reader*, a term which Jane Mace explores in her oral history data (Mace, forthcoming). Rita said that her daughter, Hayley, was not a reader. Bob equated being a reader with being bright. Frances, in contrasting her two children, referred to one of them, Lisa, as being a good reader. In our historical data William Stout at the beginning of the eighteenth century used the phrase *good reader* when referring to a friend's daughter who could recite by heart chapters of the New Testament. Readers are often contrasted with other people who are not readers but who are *doers*, or Lynne, who referred to her sister as not being a reader but being *an outdoor girl*. Even families were classified as readers or not readers, so that Lesley said that her father's family were readers, but that her mother's family were not. Shirley also commented on differences between her family and her husband's in this respect.

In the oral history data from the beginning of the twentieth century, which is described in Aside 2.2, someone was referred to as being *a reader* in that her head was always buried in a book and she neglected the household chores. Several people, both at the beginning of this century and in our contemporary data, expressed the idea that reading was better than doing nothing, but that *real work*, that is physical work, was to be preferred (see also Mace, forthcoming). Individual people tried to control their partner's reading: Brenda did not like Jeff reading in bed, since she saw it as an anti-social activity. Lynne's husband was sometimes annoyed with her reading, saying it cut down on their time together. (Similar examples are cited by Rockhill 1987 and Horsman 1990.) Watching television or videos together, on the other hand, was seen as a social activity. Gray (1992) comments that the women she interviewed felt that reading novels was *lazy* in a way that watching television is not.

Having said that reading was a good thing, we also found that parents were happy to influence and control what their children read, including Patrick expressing concern that the things his children read were not worthwhile. There were several examples of parents' regulation of their children's reading. In resistance to this there were *secret readers*, including Janette, who reported reading her mother's hidden *True Detective* books and keeping a diary secretly as a teenager. Cliff's son carried on a secret correspondence with his girlfriend across the road who was disapproved of by his father and grandmother.

Pornography was mentioned very little in our data: Bob mentioned reading *dirty books* as a teenager, and two people talked of pornography as something they would definitely *not* read. Among her collection of second-hand books Shirley had a miniature version of *Maria Monk*, a nineteenth-century banned book which had to be read with a magnifying glass; Lesley mentioned that her children had brought home pages from a pornographic magazine they had found on the playing field. The local newsagents certainly had a top shelf of soft porn magazines for men, but, despite national statistics on sales (see Aside 9.2), we came across very little pornography. A newspaper report suggests that our experience is typical: 'Conventional market research reveals that nobody in Britain reads pornographic magazines and yet every month some 500,000 copies of the five leading market titles – Penthouse, Knave, Fiesta, Club and Hustler – surreptitiously vanish from top shelves' (*Guardian*, 13 January 1997).

Our only encounter is described in Aside 9.3. Interestingly, this was in a work context, rather than a private household, so it was already partly public. These papers were also described as *funnies*, not as obscenities. They are similar to photocopies which are passed around offices illicitly. Several items in the file had been photocopied so many times as to be virtually illegible. In terms of being vernacular, the cartoons were hand-drawn, not taken from publications. The letters and application forms listed in Aside 9.3 could be national, but details in the enlistment letter such as *If you can afford it, we would also like you to buy a tank – Vickers Defence at Barnbow are currently offering our conscripts a 0% finance deal . . .* suggest a local origin. Certainly with references to *The Gas Board* and *The Ministry of Pensions*, they seemed British in origin, and often dated. However, the distribution of these texts can be quite wide. For example, the non-school writing done by adolescents in a school in the United States studied by Miriam Camitta also included humorous texts they called 'funny things' (1993: 234), one of which is almost identical to one of the texts we found circulating in Lancaster.

Literacy difficulties in daily life

In examining the diversity of practices, it is worth focusing on the home literacy practices of people who reported some problems with reading and writing. The first series of people we interviewed were all attending the Adult College and wanted to improve their reading and writing. However, as

---

Aside 9.3   The secret file

Two of the workers in the Housing Project Office discuss whether to show Sarah something:

ANN: *Shall we show her our funnies?*
KEV: *Probably not*
ANN: (reaching for a brown folder in a drawer): *Go on with you, give her a laugh.*
KEV: *She'll have to promise not to be offended.*

Local people regularly came into the housing project office to use the photocopier. Ann, the secretary, would sometimes ask to keep copies: *Either they offer us one or we ask if we can keep one back for the collection. You never guess from looking at them – the sort who bring them in – it's an education.*
We were given copies of a selection of *the funnies*, as follows:

- a spoof typed letter of compulsory enlistment in the Gulf War
- a spoof application form to be ill from work
- a page of claimed extracts from letters received by the Gas Board, such as: *My husband is pretty handy but he says your men can do it better because of their tools*
- similar extracts from letters received by *a large insurance office in London*, such as: *I knocked over a man, he admitted it was his fault, as he had been knocked down before*
- a poem about having sex
- a story about flatulence
- a cartoon about buttocks
- cartoons involving having sex
- cartoons of penises

---

the national statistics make clear (see Aside 9.4), adults attending college are only a small proportion of the people who report difficulties with reading and writing; the majority never attend college. We were therefore expecting to come across people who had problems with some aspects of reading and writing when we randomly knocked on doors. This was borne out, and Harry and Eddie were two people we came across in the community who identified some difficulties with reading and writing as adults. In addition others mentioned specific kinds of difficulties that they or other people around them have experienced, as where Shirley got help for writing letters to official bodies, and talked about both her son and her mother as having problems with dyslexia.

A social practice account of literacy sees difficulties with reading and writing as a part of everyone's experience, and not just as a problem that resides in a particular group of outsiders without literacy. Throughout this study we have provided many examples showing that the technical skills of literacy, such as handwriting or spelling, are just one aspect of literacy practices. There are many different ways of engaging with literacy and everyone participates at one time or another in unfamiliar practices, meeting new demands which pose new challenges to existing resources and ways of doing things.

Adults who report problems with reading and writing nevertheless engage in a wide range of literacy activities. In our data we have many examples of adults with difficulties who keep diaries, maintain household accounts, write poetry, take phone messages, send letters. Adults with difficulties reading or writing are not empty people living in barren homes waiting to be saved and filled up by literacy. For the most part adults who identify problems with reading or writing are ordinary people leading ordinary lives. Usually when people identify problems, they have networks of support and know where they can turn to for support. Alternatively, since these networks are effective, problems do not arise or are not recognised. For both Harry and Eddie it was when their family relationships changed that their problems were exacerbated.

It is worth comparing Harry and Eddie. As was made clear in the earlier chapter on Harry's practices, there were several occasions when he had problems and received support from other people, such as when his son helped him write work references. In other situations, he collaborated with a friend to write letters that he would not have had the confidence to compose on his own. Nevertheless it was very clear that he was participating fully in literate activities, managing his life, pursuing leisure activities, participating socially, and even writing his life story.

When we first met him, Eddie was likewise leading an everyday life that did not appear limited by his reading and writing difficulties. He was in full-time employment, supporting his family with three children and pursuing his martial arts interests. At work he received help with any reading and writing from a fellow worker. His wife, Janette, dealt with all household demands and supported their three children's learning, though he did listen to his daughter recite her poems, acting as an audience for her literacy achievements. Eddie got help in reading his martial arts books from his sister. However, when we returned to the family a year later, Eddie and Janette's relationship had broken up and he had moved out. He found it much more difficult to cope. He had a legacy of emotional problems from his childhood experiences of education and violence which were connected with his literacy difficulties, and we discuss these later. By the end of our research with him, these emotional problems severely disrupted his life. Literacy was associated with these problems, but it was not a cause of them.

In our interviews with people in shops and information points around Lancaster we were curious to know how much awareness there is of difficulties with reading and writing. The library made provision for adults with difficulties reading and writing; the staff have been aware of national campaigns since the 1970s. They had tried various strategies to accommodate the needs of adults with difficulties. For a while they had a section in the library called Adult Literacy, but adults felt stigmatised by this. They tried just having the national adult literacy symbol, an open book, on the spine of books, but again people were put off by the sticker: *I'm not taking that out, they'll know I'm on adult literacy.* Library staff had been to literacy classes with books and details of how to become a member of the library, and tutors sometimes came into the library to get books for other people. Adult books which are easy to read are now kept on the regular shelves with no particular indication that they are simple.

Staff in shops and businesses including dentists and chemists had come across adults with difficulties. The stereotypical excuses for not being able to read something had been given to staff working in several shops: the manager of a city centre card shop reported someone asking staff to read the words in a greetings card *as I haven't got my glasses with me.* The travel agent had also experienced this but had not thought much about it. She saw it as a routine part of her job to act as a literacy broker by helping clients to find their way around brochures and fill in booking forms. This is also increasingly accepted by workers in other information and advice agencies.

Books in people's lives

There were some books in everyone's home, ranging from Lesley's, where there were very few, to Terry's, whose living room contained piles of books and who referred to having *old guide books and things in the loft,* and Shirley, who dealt in second-hand books, buying and selling them in car boot sales, and constantly exchanging them, borrowing them and lending them. People usually had a specific place for them, or rather several places. Cookery books might be in the kitchen, a pile of novels or magazines besides the bed, other magazines in the living room, the television guide next to the television, the manual for working the video in a drawer, and books in a bookcase in the living room. Other artefacts usually had their place, whether it was coupons, pencils, scrap paper such as old envelopes, or items cut out of the newspaper. Literacy practices are more than reading and writing, and books have more uses than reading and writing. They are also used for display, they are part of the furniture of the well-appointed living room and they can be evidence that children are being encouraged with their reading and writing. Cards are evidence that certain rituals, such as exchanging Christmas cards and remembering birthdays, have been performed.

162

Aside 9.4   The extent of adults' problems with reading and writing in the UK

Roughly one adult in ten has some problems with reading or writing in their everyday lives. This is true whatever methods are used to assess it. All standardised ways of measuring difficulties with reading, writing and maths have some limitations and each offers a different picture. Self-reports offer adults the chance to define and describe their own needs. Tests pre-define what will count as a difficulty, either in terms of what employers or the educational system thinks important or as a set of competencies presumed to reflect the uses of literacy in every-day life. They do not always come up with consistent findings. The kind of sample that is chosen from the overall population can strongly affect the findings. For the essentially context-bound practices of read-ing and writing, standardised measurement remains subject to the same kind of problems as the historical evidence which relies on sig-natures on marriage registers for assessing literacy levels in earlier centuries (see Aside 2.3 and Vincent 1989). Other measures used such as years of schooling or percentages passing exams are even more indirect means of estimating literacy.

Until the mid-1990s, the UK has never funded a large-scale survey of adult literacy competencies. This is in contrast to the USA, Canada and Australia (see OECD/Statistics Canada 1996). Instead, the UK has made use of existing longitudinal surveys and inserted questions about literacy into them The first such study was published in 1987 (Hamilton and Stasinopoulos) and was based on self-reported diffi-culties of young adults included in the National Child Development Survey. Thirteen per cent of 23-year-olds reported difficulties with lit-eracy or numeracy, writing and spelling being the most common, followed by numeracy and then reading. More men than women reported difficulties with literacy. This study also estimated that only one in ten of those reporting difficulties had actually received formal help from adult education or training. These findings are very similar to self-reported difficulties in later studies.

The most recent and reliable estimates are based on data from another longitudinal survey, the British Birth Cohort Study (Eckinsmyth and Bynner 1994). This study assessed people's skills at age 21 years, using a series of reading tasks based mainly on the kinds of materials used in the adult basic education WordPower certificate. This study confirms that very few school-leavers and adults can be described as illiterate, but around 13 per cent have very limited liter-acy skills (below the lowest, Foundation level of WordPower). A larger percentage of adults, around 20 per cent, have limited numeracy skills.

Other reports from the Basic Skills Agency have produced differing estimates of the extent of difficulties. For example, the BSA (1995) study sampled adults from 22 to 74 years to look for age-related patterns in basic skills. The overall estimates of difficulty were much lower in this sample as measured by tests, but were higher as measured by self-reports. Self-reports suggested that difficulties decreased with age, whilst the tests suggested a different pattern, with older people (aged 60 and over) having most difficulties and people in their thirties and forties having fewest difficulties.

The National Commission on Education (Brooks *et al.* 1995) reviewed evidence about standards in literacy and numeracy since 1948 in the UK. Their report concludes that, despite strong beliefs and anxieties about standards, there is not an effective system of monitoring educational standards throughout the UK so it is impossible to answer the question of whether they are rising or falling. From the available evidence they conclude that: 'Reading Standards among 10/11 and 15/16 year olds have changed little since 1945 apart from slight rises around 1950 and in the 1980's. Among 6 to 8 year olds, however, standards fell slightly in the late 1980's. In writing performance, there was no overall change during the 1980's.'

The issue of self-perception and literacy difficulties is a complex one, but it is relevant to understanding literacy. People in our own study who were attending adult education courses expressly to improve their reading and writing did not recognise themselves as being part of the 'problem' identified by the national statistics reported above. In the National Literacy Trust (1993) study of attitudes toward reading, most adults in the sample said that they do not consider people with reading difficulties to be stupid. However, this is contradicted by the few people reporting literacy difficulties in the survey, who said that they did feel stigmatised by others. They reported being teased and bullied at school and continued to experience this in their adult lives. Women felt more generally disadvantaged by difficulties with reading than men, perhaps a function of the fact that in general women valued reading more positively than men.

People acquired books in a variety of ways. Some books were bought new, but we had more reports of books being bought second-hand, of being passed on, of having been received as childhood prizes, of being borrowed. Helen joined book clubs to get the discounted introductory offers then cancelled as soon as the book club rules allowed. Patrick bought second-hand books from the library. People were lent books by relatives and neighbours, and Rita was lent books by a woman she cleaned for. There were also organised groups of people who swapped books with each other. People bought books for themselves and for other people. A book would be a common present for a birthday or for Christmas. Books were passed on in families, and several people referred to having books which had belonged to their parents. Lesley had inherited all her aunt's books when she moved into her house; she had kept them but had not read them.

The collections of books people had in their houses seemed to be a mixture of books they wanted and used, books they had read in the past and books they just happened to have. People had not read all the books in their houses, and did not expect to have done. Kathleen, in her sixties, had a set of Dickens books from her mother. Frances also mentioned Dickens, saying that she collected his books, but did not read them. Many people, like Terry, had some books stored away somewhere in the house, in a cupboard, or in a suitcase under the bed. Lynne kept books *in a cupboard out of sight . . . I don't like clutter. And to me books look like clutter.* People collected particular sorts of books, for example Cliff who collected Biggles books.

The range of books people had was very broad. Often there was a bible somewhere in the house, and a dictionary, some kind of map book and other practical books such as a home medical encyclopedia or a baby care guide. Some people had a selection of novels. Non-fiction books people had copies of covered a wide range of interests, including knitting, gardening, cookery, astronomy, wild-fowling, karate, witchcraft, calligraphy, particular parts of the country, such as Scotland, local history, travel books related to holidays. Often there were general books of facts, such as *The Ultimate Problem Solver* (Bremmer 1995), a thick hardback book available at the discount bookshop, a kind of modern *Enquire Within* with sections on 'Social behaviour', 'Food and drink', 'A roof over your head', 'The family', 'Law', 'Money','Health', 'Animals' and 'Organisations'.

Moving a little out of the home and into the community, the local city library was important in most people's lives. We were surprised to discover the extent of this importance (see Chapter 3). In nearly every household someone belonged to the library and actively used it. Where people did not belong to the library, some nevertheless had a link with it, so that Kathleen, for example, was not a member of the library but her neighbour Doris would regularly lend her library books. It seemed very common to get books out for other people. Only one or two people, such as Lesley and June, seemed to have no connection with the library.

Libraries offer a range of facilities other than book borrowing, and, as Greenhalgh *et al.* (1995) point out, it is an important social focus in many town centres where people combine a visit to the library for one of a range of purposes with a shopping trip or visit to other places. Several people in our study, like Harry and Rose, included a visit to the library in their weekly

Aside 9.5   Book reading and buying

Book reading has an important role in many people's lives. In a survey carried out in 1994, *Books and the Consumer*, 54 per cent of men and 62 per cent of women claimed to have read a book for interest or pleasure within the previous four weeks; in contrast, 51 and 45 per cent respectively had used a book for information or reference over the same period. Around half of adults reported currently reading a book for pleasure. Between 1989 and 1992 there was jump from 31 to 46 per cent in the proportion of people claiming to read every day or nearly every day. The average number of hours spent reading per week was 7.4 in 1992, and this figure has been very stable over the four years of the survey.

Statistics on book buying can be presented in a variety of ways: the percentage of people ever buying a book, the quantity of books bought and the market share of books bought all give a different picture of people's habits. This is also true of patterns which show, for example, that higher proportions of people in higher social classes buy, borrow and read books: if the percentages are calculated in terms of the proportion of regular readers to be found in each social group there is a much more even spread.

In 1992 80 per cent of adults over 15 years bought books, a slight upward trend from previous years. In terms of the quantity of books bought, fiction is the highest category, but its market share is declining in relation to reference books. Between 1989 and 1994 fiction sales went down, while sales of reference, cookery and puzzle books were increasing rapidly. A third of all book sales are children's books.

Buying for self and others

Only a fifth of book buyers buy for themselves alone, and nearly half of books bought are given to other people. These findings confirm impressions given by retailers in Lancaster. More people are now buying books for themselves than in the 1980s: in 1992 36 per cent of adults had bought a book for another adult and 43 per cent had bought a book for a child. More books bought by post are given as gifts.

routine around town. Janette said she often went three times a week. People with young children took them to the children's library. The facilities available in Lancaster's library include general and business reference materials; newspapers and magazines which can be read on the spot; video and music cassettes and CDs for loan; second-hand books to buy; community and

Who buys most books?

Seven per cent of adults are referred to as 'mega-buyers' – each buying more than fifty books per year and accounting for one-third of all purchases. More women than men are 'heavy buyers' (53 per cent to 47 per cent). Social differences can be found. People with children buy more, as do people in the 25 to 34 age group, those who are better educated and people in the south of the country. Nevertheless, given the widespread activity of book buying, no social groups can be ignored.

More second-hand books are bought by women, and more by people in higher socio-economic groups. Heavy buyers of new books also buy the most second-hand books: the buying of new and of second-hand books are not mutually exclusive.

The main retail sources of books are bookshops and stationery stores, such as Smiths, but bargain bookshops, newsagents, supermarkets, general department and chain stores are increasingly significant. More than one book in ten is bought by post; other sources include churches, schools, work-places, railway stations and airports. One-third of adults had been offered books through their workplace.

Types of books bought and read

Leading types of book bought are romantic fiction (with 7.5 per cent of the market share); puzzle and quiz books (6.4 per cent); crime and thrillers (5.6 per cent); but there are sixteen other genres listed with above-average market shares for the period 1989–94. Audio books are purchased by 13 per cent of adults, mainly for children. When books are adapted for screening on television or film, sales often drastically increase. For example, the 'People Taking Part' report (Department of National Heritage 1996) says that following the television screening of the novel *Middlemarch*, which drew six million viewers, there was a fivefold increase in sales of the book. In their study of children's reading habits, Hall and Coles (1996) found a clear influence from the mass media on the books children read, with one in seven having some sort of media connection, such as being a film or a television adaptation.

Sources: Book Marketing Limited 1995; Department of National Heritage 1996.

library information in the shape of leaflets that can be picked up; children's activities such as story telling; a quiet place to study or work; use of a photocopier. Staff reported that, in tems of requests for help, the subject which is most time-consuming is local history.

Our interview with the librarian confirmed the impression we had gained

---

Aside 9.6   Community literacy and national library usage

Nearly sixty per cent of the adult population have a library ticket, and about half of those with a ticket borrow books at least once a month. The typical borrower takes out three or four books at a time. In 1990 561 million books were issued by public libraries in the UK, 59 per cent for adult 'genre' fiction (including popular authors like Agatha Christie, Dick Francis and Ruth Rendell). Comparative figures for attendance at art galleries and museums show libraries to be the most popular and socially diverse form of public cultural provision.

Greenhalgh *et al.* (1995) point out how the public library is the archetypal product, and one of the most successful products, of 'enlightenment' thinking, developing from the idea of public reading rooms in the nineteenth century. Libraries are used by a wider variety of people than any other public cultural institution, including all social classes and all age groups. More than ten per cent of people who do not have a library ticket or ever buy books still visit the library occasionally to make use of the other facilities. In addition to the facilities offered in Lancaster, mentioned in the text, some places have public access computer terminals, careers advice and a meetings room.

The public library has the potential to expand its offerings through, for example, the public access to CD-Roms, the World Wide Web and

---

from the data: that many children go to the library but this interest tails off in the late teens and twenties. Many people have a renewed interest when they themselves have children and there is an increased library usage when people are older. As with other aspects of literacy there is a danger in assuming that differences according to age herald a decline in standards. Rather, people do different things at different points in their lives.

Books, newspapers, magazines and other written material are part of the resources available in people's lives and were used in multiple ways by those in our study. Resources also include physical places where people can go to read, write, discuss and get advice and information from others. The availability of people who can act as literacy brokers and as sources of information at certain times is discussed later. We also extend this theme by looking at the resources a community has in terms of its knowledge and practices, including the availability and accessibility of adult education, the library and local organisations.

Open Learning facilities. In terms of the interests of this study, therefore, it is a major access point for community literacy. It should be pointed out that numbers of book issues had been steadily falling over the 1980s, although other uses were increasing. There was an increase in spending in real terms between 1981 and 1991 of 14 per cent; overall the library network has expanded over the last fifteen years, though opening hours have been reduced, affecting access for certain groups of users.

According to a 1992 survey, 59 per cent of library users are women and 41 per cent are men. More men use the reference section and newspapers in the library, while more women go to the library to borrow books. Adults with children are more likely to borrow library books, as are those from higher socio-economic groups, those living in the south of England, those with more educational qualifications and those who are the heaviest buyers of books. Hall and Coles (1996) found that this holds for children too: those who own more books borrow more from the library. Over 70 per cent of children 10 to 14 years of age borrow from the public library, but the percentage declines with age as children shift from book to magazine reading. Roughly a third of borrowers take out all or mainly fiction books, while a further third take out all or mainly non-fiction

Sources: Book Marketing Limited 1995; Greenhalgh *et al.* 1995; Hall and Coles 1996.

10

EVERYDAY LITERACIES

(2) The patterning of practices

Having examined the range of diversity of everyday literacy practices in the last chapter, here we turn to more detailed examination of three areas: the gendering of home practices; the intertwining of literacy and numeracy practices; and the significance of multilingual experience of literacy. They are distinct topics, but in different ways each topic demonstrates ways in which practices are located in the broader patterning of social activities.

The gendering of home practices

Feminist research on women's writing has covered both women's response to and production of literature and it has emphasised the importance of writing in women's articulation and transformation of their experience – for example Olson (1980). Apart from the work of Kathleen Rockhill and Jenny Horsman, very little of this research has been concerned with gender and everyday literacy. In our data there were many opportunities to observe the gender patterning of literacy practices in the home. People asserted their identities through their literacy practices, and would often demarcate themselves, their partners and other members of their households in terms of literacy practices through statements such as *I usually read to the children* and *he buys the newspaper.*

Within the home there are many patterns of how literacy is distributed as people participate in different relationships with each other and assert different identities. There was patterning associated with position in the family, whether as children, parents, grandparents, aunts and uncles; there was patterning associated with knowledge people had acquired through their jobs; with various identities, such as being a single parent, a retired widow or a student. One powerful form of patterning is through gender, and many home literacy practices are gendered. There are different levels of looking at such patterning which our data can address: firstly we can identify and explore public narratives and stereotypes of gender and literacy; secondly we can look in our interview data for women's and men's perceptions of their roles. Thirdly, we have information from interviews and observations about what actually goes on in households day to day.

It is revealing to look at common stereotypes on gender and to compare them with the diversity of practices we found in our study. For example, we started out with a stereotype that home literacy practices are gendered in a straightforward way, with men having responsibility for official activities and women having responsibility for personal realms: to put it simply, that women write the Christmas cards and personal letters while men deal with the bills and official correspondence (see Barton 1991: 9). This division is believable because it maps on to traditional female and male roles in the home where maintaining personal relationships is women's work, while public and financial matters are men's work (see McMahon *et al.* 1994; Finch and Groves 1983; Deem 1986). However, the reality revealed in our data was more complex.

Gendered patterns in literacy activities and preferences were certainly shown by people in our study and were revealed as we asked questions about who pays bills and deals with other financial matters; who writes personal letters; who opens the post and junk mail; who reads what kinds of books; who sends greetings cards; who reads newspapers, timetables, instruction manuals and medication labels. These patterns occurred in both the leisure-oriented and more practical activities in the household. The networks people participated in were often gendered. There were many examples of people borrowing and exchanging books and magazines with people of the same sex; this included passing on reading materials and preferences to the next generation. Janette tried to persuade her daughter to read books that she has enjoyed; Harry and his son-in-law passed on war books to one another. Lesley passed on books to her sister.

More women than men reported reading novels. The novels which men and women talked about were very gendered, both the individual books mentioned and the genres which people referred to, with women typically mentioning romance, family sagas and historical fiction and men mentioning science fiction, spy thrillers, war, humour, action and non-fiction information books related to their leisure interests or work. Most of the magazines which were mentioned were also specific to men or to women, except for the widely read *TV Times* and *Radio Times*. More men referred to reading newspapers regularly and more intensely, and they were often the ones who brought papers into the home. One activity which seemed to be associated particularly with men was reading train timetables, as with Lynne's husband, Helen's son and several other examples. Rather than being buried in a novel, men could be lost in a timetable, perhaps pursuing fantasy consumption of another sort.

These preferences are familiar patterns reflected in national survey research of both adults' and children's reading (Book Marketing Limited 1995; Hall and Coles 1996). Gray (1992) also found continuities between these reading preferences and preferred genres for viewing video, television and film. She makes use of psychoanalytically based theory about the different emotional responses of men and women which might account for their differences in viewing preferences and sources of pleasure in texts, based on the different experiences and cultural knowledges that men and women bring to reading (see Gray 1992: 15–16).

In the National Literacy Trust (1993) survey, mentioned earlier, there were consistent gender differences among respondents' attitudes towards reading. Of those people who claimed not to read for pleasure, the main reason given by women was *lack of time* while more men gave reasons such as *lack of interest* or *prefer doing other things*. More men than women used the word *informative* to describe reading, whereas more women than men felt reading was *relaxing*. Men who enjoyed reading for its own sake gave reasons such as *discovering new information* while women talked of *disappearing into another world, escaping this world* and *exercising imagination*. Women said they preferred reading over television for this reason and they particularly mentioned the soothing and calming process of reading last thing at night. Findings such as these suggest that literacy has different meanings for women and for men; these are likely to be reflected in their day-to-day activities around reading and writing.

However, within the overall patterns of male and female preferences which appeared in our own data, there were also many counter-examples: June read the sports sections of the newspapers and Janette was an avid *Star Trek* fan. Neil's girlfriend read martial arts books and magazines. Hall and Coles (1996) similarly found girls' and boys' reading preferences to be very eclectic despite overall trends. The fact that much reading, especially of texts considered to be ephemeral, such as magazines, is casual and opportunistic means that both men and women browse through material that they might never intentionally choose. For example, a man might pick up a women's magazine in the doctor's surgery or a boy read his sister's *Just Seventeen*, even though he would never go out and buy a copy for himself. A woman might read a newspaper brought into the home by her husband, even though she does not buy papers.

More women than men reported reading to their children, dealing with school demands of letters to be answered and forms to be filled in, buying books for children and helping with the homework. In our data it was almost always the women who talk about writing letters of complaint, whether about consumer items or to school. In considering activities like this as distinct from leisure-related literacies, it is useful to think of them as literacy chores, not unlike other domestic chores around the house: women tend to do more of them; there is overlap between what men and women do; there is a range of exceptions and untypical arrangements; and often the divisions are resisted and re-negotiated as circumstances change. Both Rockhill (1993; 1987) and Horsman (1990) discuss the ways in which the literacy work of the household is seen as women's work and in which part of being a good mother is to be a literate mother – one who helps with home-work and who has good clerical skills. This ideology has been incorporated into many literacy programmes in developing countries and family literacy programmes in the USA and UK.

Another activity often treated as a literacy chore is sending greetings cards to friends and relatives, corresponding with family members who are away, keeping records of birthdays and anniversaries. This set of activities was strongly gendered with women doing the record-keeping and most of the sending of cards, and the disposing of them afterwards. At Christmas all family members might sit down and write Christmas cards, but it was usually the women who organised the activity and kept the records. There were examples of this being explicitly handed down through generations, for example with Lesley being given a book by her mother for recording birthdays. Women attended closely to the details of these activities, and, like June, frequently commented on the importance of the words that appear on greetings cards. Both women and men felt that men wouldn't care about the words in cards, but women valued occasions when they did: for example, Helen kept cards sent to her by her eldest son who she says *cares about the words like I do*. There was some sharing of responsibilities for personal correspondence, depending on which relatives and whether mutual friends were involved. Brenda and Jeff taped letters together for rel-atives abroad, a mixture of *rabbiting on, arguing, conversations and songs* which they enjoyed.

Women did tend to deal with the private, personal world, but there was a great deal of variation in how the public chores of literacy were divided up. Sometimes men dealt with the household finances and bills, such as in Pat's household. Sometimes women dealt with them, as in June's household. Often, there was some sort of shared responsibility, as where Bob sorted out the bills, while Frances actually paid them. Sometimes collaborative writing was involved, with one person drafting a letter and the other person finish-ing and laying it out, as Brenda and Jeff describe. Diane said she would frequently write an official letter for her husband to sign and send off as if it came from him. Two examples she mentions are a letter about their credit card PIN number, where she was not the main card user so the letter had to come from him, and writing to get a replacement driving licence for him. These are interesting examples of where the woman may be doing the lit-eracy work, but to an outsider it would appear as if the man had done it, and sometimes legal restrictions on women's public role make this the only option.

Paying the bills was a home literacy chore: who took on this chore was a complex matter relating to what was accepted as men's and women's work within the household, type of employment, daily routines and confidence with the technical aspects of literacy and numeracy. An individual may take on different responsibilities at different points: for example Sally, who was living with her brother when we interviewed her, looked after all the bills just as her mother had done throughout their childhood. However, when Sally had been married her husband had taken charge of such payments.

The above examples are concerned with households where men and women are living together. Obviously the situation is different for Rita, a single parent, Paul, who is gay and lives with his partner, and Terry, who lives alone. Cliff organises the Christmas cards himself. Harry had taken on new roles since his wife died.

To understand the complexity of literacy activities and gender, we need to look at the other factors which may account for the ways in which literacy activities are structured in the domestic sphere and which cut across the gender patterns which clearly do exist. Firstly, confidence in one's ability to do things will also determine who does what in the household, including children. For example, Janette took care of all household literacies since Eddie found reading and writing very difficult. In Eddie's parental home the situation had been the reverse since his mother had had very little education, and she was at a loss when his father died.

However, it is not always the most competent person who does the chores of writing official letters or paying the bills: even where one partner has declared difficulties with reading or writing they may still take on these chores. Neil, who was attending the adult college to improve his writing, and who considered his girlfriend to be generally *better educated* than himself, described how, in his view, she *acted thick* when it came to working out the bills, and Neil did it himself with help from her brother. Gray (1992) gives a parallel example from her study. She describes the range of explanations offered by women she interviewed as to who operates the video equipment within households. The explanations show how custom and tradition in other areas of household life structure the use of a new technology by mapping out territories of appropriate behaviour and responsibilities. Sometimes this is resisted by different household members. She notes how some women choose to maintain a 'calculated ignorance' so that they will not get dumped with the additional chore of recording programmes for other members of the household: she quotes one woman as saying 'I'm not going to try . . . once I learned to put a plug on, now there's nobody else puts a plug on in this house but me . . . so [laugh] there's method in my madness' (Gray 1992: 168).

The availability of resources is another factor in determining how activities are shared in the household, for example who owns or has access to a typewriter or a word processor for writing official versions of things or who has specialist skills in literacy or numeracy. This is often related to people's paid work, and is one of the areas where the work-place impinges on the household. For example, Jeff, who had a word processor, helped his daughter write poems and stories on it. Both Diane and her mother had typed up letters, job applications and CVs for Diane's husband in a replication in the home of the traditional female clerking role.

Household routines which determine availability of time in the home and routines determined by other aspects of life also structure who does what: for example, who opens the junk mail depends on employment schedules and who is around the house at particular times. Interaction with children also depends on these routines. Helen worked evening shifts and so was unable to read to her young daughter, leaving this to her husband. In Diane's household, although it was the father in full-time employment who appeared to be most enthusiastic about literacy, especially reading books, it was more likely to be the mother who helped with children's beginning reading from school or read the bedtime story. It was the father, however, who bought books for his children. In many of the households we studied, time was as important a resource as technical skills in literacy. Klassen's (1991) research with Latin American newcomers in Toronto describes how the women, with much less competence in English literacy than their husbands and children, still carried out the bureaucratic tasks for the household; the reason given was that they often had the time needed to wait around endlessly in the various offices and agencies that process their papers.

To the extent that men's and women's activities in the home and their networks in the neighbourhood are different, then their literacy practices will be different too. So, for example, where women do more shopping they are involved with more of the literacy practices associated with this activity. In this way, literacy practices are related to more general divisions of labour and of gender patterning in the household.

If the literacy work of the household is structured by these routines, so are the literacy practices associated with leisure activities. It is accepted (for example in Deem 1986; Finch and Groves 1983) that women and men have different patterns of leisure in the household and that these are structured by the domestic division of labour. We have already noted Hermes's (1995) observations on the way that women's magazines are valued as 'easy to put down' and 'time fillers' and Gray's (1992: 70) similar observations on the relationship for women between viewing television, reading and exhaustion at the end of the day when they want to be relaxed rather than stimulated by whatever activity they engage in.

In our interviews, gendered home practices were often explained by referring to the factors discussed above: confidence, resources, time and routines. Shirley explained that she did the personal writing for the household because she had more time, she enjoyed it and her writing was neater. Mumtaz explained that her husband pays bills since he is unemployed and has time to do it during the day, while she is in full-time work. Jeff explained how he did the final layout of letters drafted by his wife because he could use a word processor.

We also found many examples suggesting that people recognise the common stereotypes of what is held to be male and female behaviour around literacy. Just as we have noticed in people's attitudes toward tabloid newspapers, people seemed well aware of common gender stereotypes but then dismissed or laughed at these or contradicted them in explaining their own behaviour. Cliff admitted to being embarrassed at being seen in the library choosing romance books for his mother, although he does do this quite frequently, and also looks at her magazines at home. Men talk of themselves as *a typical man* and women talk about what *men do.*

In terms of what people read, it was only men, such as Harry, who directly expressed mistrust of and aversion to fiction. The dislike of fiction was artic-ulated in different ways by other men, including Patrick and Cliff, and it was not just put in terms of a preference for other genres but actively dismissed in derogatory terms. Patrick, who put a high value on reading for informa-tion, commented disapprovingly on the novels and science fiction his son and daughter were reading and he told them they would be *better off reading more about history and maths and such things.* He was also scathing about the soap operas they watched on the television, calling the programmes *shallow and hollow.* In this way, genres typically seen as *women's reading* were derided by these men. Such derision through constant jokes, or complaints about reading not being sociable, were common ways of regulating another's behaviour in the home, and women reported changing their habits as a result (see Horsman 1990; Rockhill 1993; Ang 1996: 122).

Although women were just as vocal as men about what is or is not gender-appropriate literacy behaviour, we did not find examples of women deriding what men read in the same way. In fact Harry's daughter, for example, was sympathetic in her explanation of why Harry and her own husband obses-sively read war books, saying that they needed this reading to come to terms with their own wartime experiences.

In terms of gender, our data is highly contradictory. People, both women and men, told us about their involvement in a wide and unpredictable vari-ety of literacy-related activities, then often in the same breath reiterated stereotypical ideas of what is male and female literacy. We therefore agree with Ang and Hermes (1996: 125) that, while there is a strongly hegemonic gender discourse around literacy, and the meanings of reading and writing are strongly gendered, the actual content of women's and men's literacy activities is more variable at the micro-level of everyday practice. The litera-cies that women and men take on within the household are influenced by practical considerations which may cut across gendered divisions of labour and traditional power relationships.

Home numeracy practices

We found many examples in our data where literacy was integrated into other symbolic systems, including visual systems of maps and sketching. It is useful to think in terms of there being a semiotic landscape of different symbolic systems and other resources which can be drawn upon to make meaning, as in Kress and van Leeuwen (1996). Written language is just one of these systems. People select and combine these resources in different ways on different occasions, depending partly upon the kinds of meanings they wish to invoke and to communicate. Here we explore the example of numeracy.

As we have already noted in passing, for example with June discussing her records of household finances, numeracy is a frequent and important component in the activities of daily life, especially in dealing with money and measurement. The uses we have documented include:

- gardening, cooking, making clothes, knitting
- following current affairs with charts and diagrams in the newspaper
- health, medicine, contraception, dieting; calculating doses and calorific values
- doing finances, dealing with bills and bank accounts
- using and recording phone numbers, account numbers
- recording birthdays, appointment dates and times
- house repairs, furniture, carpets, wallpaper
- astrology, divination
- leisure pursuits, such as betting, playing cards, board games, darts, dice, including keeping scores
- passing the time with number games, brain-teasers
- arranging travel with timetables, bus numbers, finding out about tickets, times and prices
- maintaining cars and bicycles
- shopping, including ordering from catalogues
- map-reading
- using household technology, such as video machines, alarm clocks.

In this disparate list the numbers are used in various ways and in combination with other literate activities and other symbol systems. The numbers serve different functions in these various activities including simple counting, measuring and calculating. Calculating might be thought the most obvious. When people talked of helping their children with maths homework they usually meant calculating, and things such as *knowing your tables* were considered important, for example by Cliff. It is worth exploring these other functions if only to point out that calculation is but one function of numbers in everyday life. We can illustrate this most clearly by returning to the example of cooking. It is similar to many of the activities listed above in combining counting, measuring, calculating and estimating. We observed Maria baking a pudding. The activity involved counting with two eggs, weights with 8 ounces of plain flour and 2 ounces of sugar; measures with a

6-inch cake tin, and volumes with a cup of milk. It also brought in calculation, as she was making double the amount described in the recipe. She measured the ingredients in different ways, and each measurement first involved estimation; she estimated how much sugar was 2 ounces and checked it by weighing. For estimating the flour, she used an old spoon, which was her mother's, and she knew that a rounded spoonful was one ounce. In this instance, she was using an estimate of volume, to arrive at the correct weight. Estimation is particularly interesting as it can be seen as an informal vernacular practice which improvises with everyday materials, in contrast to calculation which is formally taught and is a school practice (following Nunes *et al.* 1993).

People deal frequently with numbers when they are used in charts and diagrams, for example in newspapers and magazines. Another common use is as sequences in identification codes as in telephone numbers, account numbers and personal codes, PIN numbers, which have to be remembered and tapped into money machines. These codes are a different use of numbers and in many ways are an alternative modern version of the signature. Manipulating numbers for relaxation and pleasure and in order to pass the time was another frequent activity, as in the brain-teasers and games in popular magazines. While numbers are avoided by some people whenever possible, others, such as June and Rose, were fascinated by them and enjoyed working with figures.

Jean Lave lists more than eighty measuring and calculating devices for sale for home use in a general store (Lave 1988: 201–3). These include ten distinct devices for measuring temperature, each one specific to a fairly constrained context where a particular temperature range was relevant, from body temperature and cooking temperature to temperatures for fish tanks and cars. We also found such specificity in our data and provide some examples below.

Bi-numeracy

In almost every area in which numbers are used we could identify more than one system of units. In the cooking example, different recipe books on a shelf in the kitchen used very different measurements; as well as imperial and metric units, there were British and American differences. Centigrade and Fahrenheit were used for temperatures, as well as oven settings. In most areas two systems exist side-by-side today, and during people's recent lifetimes there have been official changes in the units used in Britain, most importantly a shift from the old imperial measures to the internationally more widely used metric system. Once again this is evidence of the specificity of practices in time and space: these practices are particular to Britain and to the end of the twentieth century. The situation is different in the United States and in other European countries.

As an example, in terms of units of length, many adults were brought up on imperial measurements of miles, yards, feet and inches and were taught these in school. Now many measurements are given in kilometres, metres and centimetres. Distances on road signs are in miles. Children know their height in metres, adults know it in feet and inches. Similar changes have affected measures of weight, liquid measurements, temperature and land area. In terms of money, some older people still count and evaluate value primarily in the pre-1970 system of pounds, shillings and pence (as described in Withnall 1995). When people go abroad on holiday, they commonly encounter different currencies and calculate costs. The new technology of digital clocks has changed the system of representing time, and now on a clock face the time might be represented in any of three ways: in numbers digitally, by means of minute and hour hands, and even by Roman numerals, such as IX and XI.

What is striking in our study is that for a particular domain of measurement the alternative systems of units are all used at one time or another. Sometimes one unit was used in one area of life and another in another area, so people might refer to the weather in terms of Fahrenheit, oven temperature in terms of Centigrade, body temperature in Fahrenheit, fish tank temperature in Centigrade. Often it is more complex than this. Milk delivered to the doorstep or sold in the local shop is in pint bottles; milk purchased in the supermarket is in litre and half-litre cartons. A recipe requiring milk might use either unit, or be in numbers of cups. In the pub, draught beer is sold by the pint, bottled beer is in metric units. In fact the size of the bottle or the carton is often the unit recognised by people, and this is gradually changing for many goods.

The potential complexity is compounded when different units are mixed in one context, as currently happens in many commercial transactions. For example, someone buying wood in the do-it-yourself store might buy *two metres of two-by-one* (that is, wood with a cross-section of 2 inches by 1 inch); shopping in a garden centre someone might buy a hosepipe which is described on the label as being *one hundred metres of half-inch hose pipe*. The instructions on the plant food label say *mix 10 ml to a gallon of water.* Carpet is typically sold in 4-metre and 5-metre widths but a customer might ask for a 4-yard length. Likewise, people often used imperial in the home, for example measuring up a room for a carpet or a window for curtains in feet and inches, while the shop dealt in metric, pricing material by the metre and measuring it in metres and centimetres. The example of bi-numeracy, above, is a case where commercial practices or school practices meet everyday practices. Part of Eddie's job in a textile factory involved checking cloth coming into the factory and converting any imperial measures into metric ones; the recording which was required added an unwelcome component of mental work to an otherwise physical job.

In situations where either metric units or imperial units could be used, it was our impression that younger people primarily use metric measurements and older people use imperial. This is to be expected, as schools have changed what they have taught in line with various government-imposed changes. Currently metric measurements, like dominant languages, are linked with public spheres, while the imperial measurements, like vernacular languages, are more associated with local life and with the private. Many of the changes in measurement systems have been propelled through commercial and other work-place practices, affecting practices in the home in a secondary way. We have not explored work links, such as how units used at work affect home practices, or how tradespeople often seem at ease going back and forth between units, sometimes translating the customer's imperial units into the trade's metric units.

The official changes in units are to some extent held back as old units stay in the language in various expressions, which are used in day-to-day language, so that *weather in the eighties* means (in the UK) it is hot; offering someone *a pint* is to offer them a drink in a pub, not particularly one pint of beer; Cliff talks of betting, *we don't put pounds on, we put shillings on*; a local builder, measuring a room by pacing, says, *the Good Lord may not have given me a pretty face, but I thank him for giving me a foot that's a foot in length.*

We have deliberately called this phenomenon bi-numeracy in order to indicate parallels between it and bilingualism, when people utilise two languages. To continue with this parallelism, people can be said to code-switch when they move back and forth between numerical systems, just as they do when moving between languages. As with code-switching between languages, the choices people make in any situation are dependent upon their knowledge base, as well as aspects of the activity including the contexts, the other participants and the purposes (as in Romaine 1989); thus, a person may refer to a measurement as being about two metres in some contexts and with some people and as about six feet in other contexts and with other people.

Numeracy as situated cognition

There are many other aspects of everyday maths that parallel our findings about literacy. Both are examples of situated practices tied to particular contexts. We see them as examples of situated cognition (Lave 1988; Nunes *et al.* 1993) in that practices develop around particular events. When people talked of having difficulties with numbers it is not just the maths, the calculating, which is necessarily the problem – for example in a gas bill or a telephone bill; it is also to do with the practices. This means that difficulties are often task-specific. Working out whether the bill is correct may involve handling a variety of specialised units which people have no feel for; carrying out complex calculations; and searching the bill for the necessary pieces of information to use in the calculation, much of which may be written in very small print.

Aside 10.1   Computers in the home

Three of the households we studied had a computer, Lynne's household, Jeff and Brenda's and Shirley's, although Shirley's was only a games computer. The adults we studied are part of a transitional generation in terms of new technologies. They had not come across computers in school, and as adults they were learning new ways of organising their lives, of writing, and of communicating using new technologies. Their children, on the other hand, were growing up with these technologies, learning about them in school, and accepting them as everyday and normal aspects of their lives.

In terms of using computers for writing, the adults were treating them as old technologies, using old practices with new technologies. An example of this is where Shirley handwrote items for the newsletter and later them copied them on to the computer in the Housing Action Project office, in order to be able to print out a neat copy. Children were not using home computers for homework. Some people had access to computers at work and used them for non-work activities, such as writing up notes of meetings of local groups.

Nationally, in 1990 22 per cent of households owned a home computer, with a higher percentage of households with children and larger families owning one. Different computers were used for a range of functions, including games, word processing, home budgeting and running small businesses. By 1993 the percentage of households owning a home computer had risen to 29 per cent, and it has continued to rise (Gunter *et al.* 1994).

If we view books and writing as another technology alongside video machines and computers, it is interesting that a more recent study in Lancaster of people's use of new technologies in the home found similar phenomena to some of the ones we found with books (Hughes, O'Brien and Rodden 1996). For example, as with books, people develop collections of videos from various sources, and they do not necessarily watch all of their videos. Items of old and unwanted technology, such as hi-fi systems and cassette recorders, are passed around to neighbours and friends in the same way as books and magazines are passed around. When buying hi-fi systems people rely on friends known to be local experts on hi-fis and their decision-making is complex, involving technical, aesthetic and practical concerns. Finally, as with reading and writing, computers and other new technology have to fit in to the limited space of the household, they become part of the furniture, and time for computer use competes with other activities.

Whether a change makes life easier or more difficult, one still has to master the new practices. These practices are often learned in adulthood, and, as Nunes *et al.* (1993) emphasise, many of those aquired in childhood are learned out of school. It may be that the current time is an especially complex transitional phase in terms of the number of systems of measurement in use side by side, because of the re-alignment of trading relations involved in the development of the European Community. However, there have always been historical traces carried in everyday practices, with antiquated terms which people may not relate to other measurements. An example from our data would be the use of *furlongs*, a term used now only in specific domains, such as horse racing, and understood by gamblers and jockeys. Some very ancient practices are carried through to the present day almost unchanged: for example people still do tallying, as in four slashes and a cross when keeping score or doing other quick counting.

In our study people did not feel there is any stigma attached to having problems with numeracy. Certainly there was less stigma than with reading and writing problems. As we have already pointed out, people were often described as being good with numbers, and it might be contrasted with their reading and writing. There seems to be much more acceptance that being good with numbers is an individual difference between people, whereas it is assumed that everyone should be able to read well. As one of the respondents referred to in Chapter 2 said, talking about her mother earlier this century, *She couldn't read, she couldn't write but reckon money up you couldn't beat her. You couldn't have diddled her out of a ha'penny.*

Multilingual literacies at home

Just under 10 per cent of the households in Springside are multilingual speakers. In our door-to-door survey of Springside we encountered both Polish and Gujarati speakers. In the detailed case study which followed the survey we decided to include one multilingual household, and we interviewed one woman, Mumtaz, and other members of her Gujarati-speaking family. Up to now in the discussion we have not mentioned Mumtaz very much. In this section we want to concentrate on her household, describing her everyday literacy practices, and we will follow the framework of the chapter so far, making comparison with monolingual households. It is useful to see the extent to which we can identify distinct literacy practices associated with being multilingual and with being Muslim.

Mumtaz describes herself as British with Muslim religion. She was born in India where she was brought up speaking Gujarati, and she also learned to read Arabic in the Koran. She came to England when she was aged ten, joining her father and a brother who had come two years previously. She immediately went to school in Lancaster, where she remembers having special lessons and learning English quickly. She left school at sixteen, which she now regrets. She corresponded with her fiancé in India for a year before he came over, and they were married when she was seventeen. Now, aged thirty, she has three children, two boys, Rashulla aged twelve, Mohammed, aged eleven, and a girl, Rosamina, aged ten.

Mumtaz has worked full-time as a machinist for several years in a garment factory where she has often been asked to act as an informal interpreter for other Gujarati-speaking women. Her husband has done factory work but is currently unemployed, helping out part-time in a local shop run by Mumtaz's father. Her brother works in a local factory and is also a part-time photographer; he did the photographs for June's daughter's wedding, mentioned earlier, and is often asked by people at work and in the neighbourhood to take photographs for them. Other family members live in Lancaster, Blackburn, thirty miles away, and London. There are also relatives in India. Rashulla and Mohammed go to the Catholic secondary school; Mumtaz fought hard for them to go there. She sees it as a better school than the secondary school which most other Gujarati-speaking children go to and she likes the fact that it is a religious school, albeit a Catholic one, although, as we see later, she has had disputes with the head teacher.

The family speaks both Gujarati and English in the home. She says she speaks more Gujarati with her husband and more English with the children, but there is considerable overlap. In terms of literacy, Mumtaz reads Gujarati, Arabic and English and has copies of the Koran in all three languages. They are on display together in a glass-fronted cupboard next to the fireplace. She reads the Koran every day and sometimes writes out pieces from it, in Gujarati or English, or from other religious books in order to memorise them or reflect upon them. She sometimes collects pamphlets on Islam in Blackburn, to read. These might be in Arabic or in English; often the religious books are bilingual.

She writes in English and Gujarati. She reads English national newspapers, such as the *Sun: I read every bit of it . . . oh, I don't read sports . . . I think I read everything because I want to know what's going on.* She is also an avid reader of local newspapers and magazines. She cuts out items about her children, being involved in school events, and keeps these upstairs in an envelope. Her father will pick up Indian newspapers and magazines in Blackburn, *the kind he can't get in Lancaster*, and pass them on to her. Other relatives bring Indian magazines from London and her mother-in-law sends her a monthly magazine on Islam from India; this is written in Gujarati. Friends at work also lend her papers and magazines. Mumtaz reads a wide range of books, including children's story books, and she also enjoys romantic stories in magazines.

The family corresponds regularly with relatives in India, writing about every three months. She will write part of the letter, in Gujarati, and her husband will write part. This is her main use of Gujarati, for writing. The children do not write Gujarati and sometimes they dictate things for Mumtaz to write in the letters. Although the children cannot write Gujarati, they can speak it and Mumtaz is keen to teach them to write *when they are old enough, when they are about fourteen*. The children write some letters in English, knowing that relatives in India will translate into Gujarati for grand-parents who do not know English. The family also keep up correspondence with other relatives in London, and Rosamina has also written to a former teacher who has retired and moved away from Lancaster. Mumtaz talks of preferring writing letters to phoning and in fact they do not have a phone in their house; when they need to phone they use the one in the nearby shop, or use one in a Muslim neighbour's house round the corner.

They send cards for the festival of Eid; a cousin buys the cards for Mumtaz in Blackburn, as they are not available in Lancaster. Although it was not a custom in her family in India to send Christmas cards, birthday cards or wed-ding anniversary cards, Mumtaz now does this. She started by celebrating the children's birthdays with parties and presents when they were younger *so that they wouldn't feel different from other children*. They also exchange pre-sents at Eid; Rosamina had asked her mother for a book as a present, and, although Mumtaz had agreed, there appeared to be a feeling that a book was not really an adequate present.

Mumtaz seems at ease with the reading and writing she has to do in every-day life. When she encounters difficulties, she often draws on her next-door neighbour, Maria, a white woman from Liverpool. An example of this was when Mumtaz was trying to get Rashulla into the Catholic secondary school and at first she was refused. She had to write letters to the local education authority to appeal, and she always showed the letters to Maria before send-ing them off. On another occasion when Mumtaz pulled a ligament in her arm, she got involved in a dispute between the chemist and the doctor as to who should deal with the sling she had to wear. Maria came to the doctor with Mumtaz to sort the problem out. This latter example is not strictly about literacy; rather it shows how Maria was used as a broker, or mediator, for dealing with the English-speaking bureaucratic world. When asked about help in the neighbourhood, Mumtaz mentioned specific men whom people would go to if they needed to clarify something written in English or if they needed something interpreted.

All three children belong to the local children's library, and Mumtaz takes them there regularly, usually once a week. Each child has particular interests; Mohammed is particularly interested in fish, and takes out books on different sorts of fish and fish-keeping. Mumtaz also regularly takes Rosamina to a local bookshop which has an extensive children's section. Mumtaz sits outside on a bench while Rosamina looks round the shop. Mumtaz sometimes goes to the adult library; she looks through the shelf of Gujarati books, but usually takes out English books.

In addition to the state school, all three children go to classes at the mosque after school. It is one of two mosques and is situated in a house on the other side of town. Around 4.30 in the afternoon the children are picked up at home by a minibus which collects children from across the town and they arrive back at home at around 7.30. Much of the mosque teaching is concerned with learning prayers off by heart, and here children come across another language, Urdu. Children copy out texts in Urdu, and sometimes have to write translations in English underneath the Urdu. They also have homework, mainly learning by heart, from these classes, in addition to any homework from the day schools. Consequently the children have little free time in the evenings outside of the classes: they said they are not interested in pop music and don't go to the cinema. Mumtaz reiterated that most of the learning was memorisation: *it's just our religion to learn things. When you pray you have to learn by heart so you can pray. I mean you can't pray and read it you know.* There are also exams at the mosque; these are normally oral tests. If they have to miss any classes, Mumtaz writes a note and it might be written in English or Gujarati. Most Gujarati-speaking children go to the classes, although Mumtaz's brother would not let his daughter go to the mosque as he was worried about her getting confused. Mumtaz disagreed with this: *my children are not confused, my child is learning German, French. He knows Gujarati. He knows Arabic. He knows English. And he's only thirteen, thirteen this month.*

Mumtaz's dispute with the head teacher of the Catholic secondary school concerned the mosque. When they reach puberty the boys are expected to go to the mosque earlier on Friday afternoons, but the head teacher would not allow Mohammed to have extra time off. After an exchange of letters and a face-to-face meeting, Mumtaz was very upset but she gave in, and instead Mohammed was given extra homework to do for the mosque. Mumtaz recalled how the secondary school in Lancaster which she had gone to did allow the boys to leave early on Fridays; she remembers *it was great – it was the best bit of the whole week, having fun in class without the boys.*

We can see clear examples in Mumtaz's life of the phenomena described earlier in this chapter, including a wide range of uses of literacy and the social patterning of practices, as in the networks of support she was part of. Our study in Springside has been primarily of the monolingual white English-speaking community; in another study, based in Leicester, we have looked in detail at the multilingual literacy practices in Gujarati-speaking communities – see Bhatt *et al.* (1996) – and other studies in Britain have been carried out by Mukul Saxena (Saxena 1994) and Eve Gregory and colleagues (Gregory 1996), both based in areas of London. Our multilingual data here in Lancaster may be different from the studies in the larger cities of Leicester and London, as Mumtaz and her family do not live in a predominantly Gujarati-speaking neighbourhood; rather, the neighbourhood is predominantly white and English-speaking. It is therefore worth examining similarities and differences between her practices and those of other people we interviewed in Springside, as well as comparing her practices with those reported in the studies of other Gujarati-speaking communities.

Firstly, it is noticeable that Mumtaz's networks of support include both monolingual English speakers, such as Maria next door, and other Gujarati speakers. She has contact with white neighbours; nevertheless she remains strongly part of the Gujarati Muslim community through her extended family and membership of the mosque. The Muslim community she identifies with in Lancaster is not bounded by a physical neighbourhood. It is a community of interests held together by shared religious practices. Just as there is a range of practices in the white community with different attitudes to literacy and its importance, this is also true in the Gujarati community, so that not all the parents sent their children to the mosque classes, and different people, especially across the generations, deployed their literacies in different languages in different ways.

In addition there were particular practices associated with being multilingual and with being Muslim. To some extent her written language use is related to different domains of her life. Gujarati is associated with writing to her family in India; Arabic is associated with the Koran, and Urdu is only learned in the mosque classes; English is used around town and in dealing with the children's state schooling. Nevertheless, Mumtaz uses a mixture of written languages in many domains; and some of the administration of the mosque is in English and some in Gujarati. Some religious instructional texts have a translation in English, or there may be written instructions in Urdu. She has copies of the Koran in three languages, and her children are learning about it in a fourth. It would therefore be an oversimplification to suggest that her religious literacy practices are associated with a particular language. Since some things are in Gujarati, some in English and some in Arabic, we can see her religious practices as a distinct literacy, but they are not bounded by particular languages. Her religious literacy cuts across languages. Similarly, she asserts her identity, as coming from India and having family in India, by writing in Gujarati, but her children write in English. Looking across her life and the way she talked about what is important to her in life, it appears that her religion structures her values and much of her life world; this is more important to her than the particular language it is expressed in. (Religious literacy practices have been pursued more in other published studies, such as Andrea Fishman's study of the Amish in Pennsylvania (1988; 1991) and Cushla Kapitzke's study of Seventh-day Adventists in Australia (1995).)

The different literacies in Mumtaz's life partly represent tensions and a mixing of values in forging new identities and reconciling conflicts about changing values, as in Bhatt *et al.* (1994) and Martin-Jones (1996). When reading the Koran, literacy was a serious way of being devotional, and great value was attached to these activities; when reading the newspaper, literacy was a way of passing the time. These represent two very different ways of reading. They encapsulate how Mumtaz originally described herself, as British with Muslim religion.

We can stress both the generality and the specificity of this case. In her devotional reading, links can be made to other religious people, or households, in the study, such as Tina in Chapter 13, below. Although they are participating in different religions, there are some common practices, and both Islam and Christianity can be seen as religions of the book, relying on the written word. At the same time there are specific aspects of being Muslim, and being Muslim in Britain in the 1990s, just as there are specific ways in which particular Christian religious groups relate to books and literacy. In Lancaster this includes Catholic, Anglican and Quaker ways of interacting with the written word.

11

HOME, LEARNING AND EDUCATION

Borderlands

Up to this point we have kept deliberately, yet artificially, to home literacies as if the home was an isolated domain, distinct from other domains such as work-places, educational settings and other public institutions. At first we imagined we would encounter a distinct home literacy which could be contrasted with work literacy or school literacy. To some extent this is true. There is a distinctiveness to many home literacy practices, but what is more striking is the range of different literacies which are carried out in the home, including work and school literacies which are brought home where they mingle together. Cecil Klassen in a study of bilingual literacy practices in a Canadian city refers to the home as 'the centre from which individuals venture out into other domains' (1991: 43), and this is how we came to see the home domain. People start from the home and move out through local activities such as shopping and going to the library or the doctor's surgery, to move or less complex engagements with other institutions through, for example, work or educational activities. They then bring back into the home resources, possibilities – and problems – from elsewhere, which are used, acted on, solved, enjoyed, talked over and worried about.

The distinction between the home and other domains is less clear-cut than we first imagined. James Gee refers to a borderland between home and school, with its own borderland discourse (Gee 1990: 183; 1992: 146). We see borderlands not just between home and school but also between home and work, and between home and public life. If we take the borderland between home and work, we find that people brought their work home, so that other members of the family regularly helped in tasks such as sorting and collating papers, or stuffing envelopes. Wives did book-keeping and typing for husbands; people with access to typewriters, computers and copying facilities would do small tasks for relatives, neighbours or community groups. People had trade magazines and nursing journals delivered to their homes and they read them at home. Practices crossed in both directions: people got advice on home form-filling from colleagues at work and took community-related typing into work to be done. People had systems of swapping books and magazines at work and organised Christmas clubs and other money pools in their lunch breaks. Another way in which the distinction between home life and work life was not clear-cut was that people did voluntary activities such as being a hospital visitor or the secretary of a club, which in other contexts would be paid jobs. Others were paid for activities, such as sign-writing and working in a health club, which grew out of their leisure interests.

People are moving in and out of the different domains in which they are active, occupying the borderlands between them, and by means of them negotiating and changing their lives. Nevertheless, in this process the home seems to be the core domain which the others relate to. Our conclusion is that homes are distinct places, but there is not a distinct home literacy. It is a place where different aspects of life are negotiated and fitted in with each other. In this process new, hybrid practices are sometimes produced.

In this chapter we explore the relationship between home and education, seeing this as just one of the borderlands which connect home with the wider public world. (We could examine work, commerce or other public domains in the same way.) We explore the links with both schools and colleges, and our aim here is to see these educational institutions from the point of view of the home.

The normal direction of movement in studies of home literacy is to start with school practices and then to investigate whether and in what ways these are supported in the home. Such a starting-point means that home practices are seen through the lens of school. In this study our intention has been to reverse this emphasis by identifying the full range of home literacy practices first, and not just concentrating on those which have immediate links with the educational practices of schools and colleges. Similarly, rather than starting from children and their needs, we have concentrated on adults and their practices in order to point out how powerfully adults' lives and practices structure home literacy. Inevitably, the focus on learning and education which we bring to this chapter involves more emphasis on children's literacy. However, we should begin by reiterating that adults, as well as children, learn in the home, and that people learn new literacies throughout their lives. We examine how children learn about literacy in the home domain and then shift from learning to formal education in considering the relationship between homes and other institutions, particularly schools. We discuss how children's school learning is supported in the home and examine home–school communications. We then move on to look at adults' experiences of education and finally discuss family literacy programmes which are concerned with the education of children and adults together.

Learning in the home

Home is a prime site for learning because it is where children are brought up and it is the place where personal life is regulated in the most intimate ways. Both adults and children learn in the home. Many of the literacies we observed people using or which they talked about were ones they had learned as adults. When people recalled where they had learned particular aspects of literacy, they talked of learning as adults from friends and relatives in an informal manner, or of learning at work or teaching themselves, or they *just picked it up*. There were many examples of the ways in which people face changing demands and are learning about literacy throughout their lives. This was true for both dominant and vernacular literacies.

Adults of different ages participate in quite different literacy practices, so the literacy demands on 20-year-olds, 40-year-olds and 60-year-olds can be quite different. Life changes such as leaving home, starting a family, getting a job, losing a job, retiring all bring different literacy demands, and people encounter new literacies at all points of their lives. Older adults in their sixties and seventies take on new literacies, sometimes embarking on major new literacy projects; an example of this would be Harry getting involved in researching his family tree and writing his memoirs (see also Withnall 1995). At the end of the twentieth century, part of this new learning comes from being confronted with new technologies. Our data provides real examples of *life-long learning*, as we see people of all ages from young children right through to elderly retired people confronting and dealing with new literacies in their lives. In examining these changing demands we were also struck by the fact that those with the fewest resources in society often had the greatest literacy demands imposed upon them, so that claiming benefit, for example, demands a complex configuration of reading, numeracy and form-filling, as well as background knowledge of the benefit system and how to deal with it (Hamilton and Davies 1993; Taylor 1996).

Literacy, home and school

Educational support at home

Children's learning and their education is supported in the home in preparation for and throughout their years of schooling. In the following section we present examples from our data of the variety of ways in which this is happening, adapting a framework provided by Peter Hannon (1995) and used by Jo Weinberger in a detailed study of children's home learning (Weinberger 1996). Starting from school and from teachers' interest in what is going on in the home, Hannon identifies four forms of support which parents can provide for young children learning to read at home: **Opportunities, Recognition, Interaction and Models**. Hannon's original

ORIM framework was designed to describe parental support for children's early literacy in terms which would influence teachers' thinking about how parents could contribute to the school's aims. We adapt this framework to start from home practices. We broaden it to include other adults besides parents, and use it for talking about all ages, not just young children. This framework can also be used for thinking about other learning of literacy in the home, not just school-related learning.

The examples in the previous chapter of the wide diversity of home literacy practices are instances of possible **models** which adults provide for children. We saw how reading and writing are being carried out in everyday situations, that they are integral to a wide range of activities and they serve many purposes. Children can see when adults find reading and writing useful. Conversely, where adults do not engage in particular activities, like reading novels, or where they use alternative media, such as using a telephone rather than writing personal letters, there will not be models of these literacy activities.

Where practices are gendered, the children see which literacies are associated with women and which with men. All the examples of the previous chapter are potential models for children, although it is hard to be definite about a particular practice acting as a model in a particular situation. It may well be that very young children do not know what adults are doing when, for example, they are staring at a book for a great length of time or poring over a newspaper. To children this may just be time when they are not being paid any attention. Sometimes the modelling was talked about explicitly. One example which was pointed out by one of our informants was where Patrick saw a link between his daughter Joanne's notice-board in her bedroom containing her school syllabus and the notice-board in the living room which Patrick's wife, a nurse, used for organising her work time. A powerful form of modelling which was also commented on was where adults were involved in education as students themselves and were doing associated reading and writing at home. Leslie, for example, would have homework from the Adult College and would do this homework in the front room with other people around. Lynne, on the other hand, would hide away upstairs to do her college work. There were several examples where, as far as we could tell, children saw and modelled these adult practices. Jeff, for example, was very conscious that his daughter Louise saw him using a word processor and that this encouraged her to write more. Other examples of modelling of literacy activities existed when adults brought reading and writing from work to do at home.

Opportunities for literacy activities were provided by the range of resources available to people. Many people, including grandparents, bought books such as dictionaries and encyclopedias specifically for children. A wide range of factual books like this were mentioned, including *Teach Yourself* books, *Ladybird* books and commercial work-books and tests bought in shops. These seemed to be purchased spontaneously and not on any particular advice from the schools. Sometimes such books were in the house already, especially if the parents had been to college, so Joanne used the books which her father, Patrick, had bought for college. Some children also had booklets, leaflets and quizzes related to learning to read from their Sunday School. Adults also bought magazines, pens, paper, drawing books and other accessories for children. Many parents regularly took their children to the library, making further resources available. Nevertheless, the homes varied a great deal in the numbers of books available to children. Rita had few books around. On one visit her daughter, Hayley, was writing an essay on the novel *Lord of the Flies*; she had no copy of the book to work from as she couldn't bring home the school copy and there was no copy at home. She appeared to have no resources at home to support the GCSE English course which she was pursuing.

'Resources' also means the space and even the time available for literacy activities, especially space for homework. There was normally no dedicated space for reading and writing. People tended to have a regular place where they did their homework, but it would be a place which was also used for other activities. If someone did their homework on the table in the back room, for example, they would have to clear their work away for meal-times. Children sometimes had their own bedrooms where they could do their homework, but often they shared a bedroom. The only space many children had of their own was their bed, and they often did their work lying on their beds. People also often had a regular time for reading and writing activities, because arranging that time was closely connected with when there was available space, so that homework was done in the back room before tea-time, as that was the only time that the space was available. The relative value of homework and studying against other activities became important when all these activities were competing for the same physical space. Some children never did homework, and some adults reported to us the ways in which they had avoided homework. Julie took to doing any homework in school, as her mother saw no value in what Julie called *book learning* and she said that doing homework *would be an intrusion on the home*. Other difficulties in doing homework at home are reported below.

In terms of **interaction**, children were brought into a wide range of the home literacy activities. Young children participated in literacy activities whether or not they were established readers and writers. People involved their children in the shopping, in sorting out appointments, in dealing with cards and letters, and with other home activities. Adults left written messages for children. Often non-school-validated knowledge is pursued by adults who incorporate their children into it. An example of this is Eddie, who took his four-year-old daughter along to karate classes when he became interested in martial arts: she watched his martial arts videos and looked at his magazines with him. Cliff took his daughters to comedy shows, and then wrote fan letters to the stars on behalf of the children. Other parents incorporate their children into religious literacy practices. Adults' active efforts to incorporate children into their ongoing activities have mixed results depending on the relationship between those involved and whether children feel coerced, ignored or nurtured in the process. The literacy practices valued by other family members and imposed by incorporation into family activities carry strong emotional inflections, either positive or negative.

An important form of interaction was apparent in the wide variety of shared reading with children. Most mothers and some fathers said they read to their young children. Those we interviewed who were grandparents said they read to their grandchildren. Our study is primarily of adults' practices, and we tape-recorded only a few examples of literacy events where adults were reading with children; for details of the interactions we rely largely on adults' reports of what went on when they read to children, not on direct observation. These reports and other research (such as that summarised in Barton 1994; Weinberger 1996) suggest there is a wide variety of different forms of interaction under the general name of 'reading to children', from the simple reading of a story in a book with little interaction, right through to ways of reading which lead to complex discussions between adults and children. The act of reading itself may be central; usually the activity serves multiple and complex purposes. Adults who had not read to their children, such as Rita and Kathleen, nevertheless often referred to telling their children or grandchildren oral stories; in their minds, oral story telling was clearly linked to reading to children (as it is in research on precursors to school success, such as in Wells 1985).

It is also worth emphasising that adults with reading problems still read to their children. Patrick's determined reading to his daughter in a monotone with little intonation had become a good-natured family joke. Nine of the twelve Basic Education students who have children of their own mention reading to their children or helping them with reading and writing activities associated with homework. For some this was part of a commitment that their children would get more out of school than they themselves had. This is stated by Neil talking about his son Ryan. Similarly, Cath and Julie were both determined that their children would lead very different lives from their own; books and education were seen as a means of escaping poverty and having a better life. In our data where an adult had severe problems and did not read to the children, as with Eddie, there was another adult in the household who did read to them, and Eddie himself could listen to his daughter recite poems she had written.

Reading with children also involves **recognition** and approval of children's activities. This is specially true as young children get older and go to school. There is less straightforward reading to children by adults; it shifts to becoming an activity where the adults listen to the children reading, often at the request of the school. In terms of the interaction, this listening to children is a very different activity from reading to children, and it is a schooled literacy practice. Adults experienced it as making different literacy demands upon them. Most parents said that they listened to their school-age children read. For some it was a chore imposed by school, for some it seemed to be part of the web of everyday life, and for Jeff and Brenda it was a deliberate way of helping their children. It may well be that the interaction around support for their children reading at home is a different activity from the interaction which goes on in school and may even conflict with it (as Eve Gregory (1996) graphically documents for some bilingual children).

Other forms of recognition included the ways in which adults follow their children's literacy development and recognise their achievements. People varied a great deal in terms of what they seemed to know about their children's progress. Patrick, for example, was proud that his son read all the books in the primary school. Several people, including Rita, kept stories which their children had written and cards which they had made. People talked of the problem of what to do with the drawings and early writing which young children bring home from nursery and school, and of the mini-crisis as the daily selection of drawings piles up in houses with very little space. Lynne got the idea from a neighbour of making a scrap book. Some households pinned up children's writing on the walls of the kitchen or living room. Jake was concerned not to let his children see him throwing away their work. How school reports were treated and whether or not they were kept was similarly noticed by children and remembered by adults.

It is not just school-related activities which are recognised, but parents recognise the non-school literacies. Independently of school, Emma would write stories and her mother, Janette, was always keen to read them, acting as an appreciative audience. Recognition is tied up with evaluation, and there are different ways at home and at school of evaluating whether or not a literacy activity is 'successful'. School reading and writing is usually evaluated formally, often in terms of correctness and accuracy. Tasks are often carried out in a way which makes them explicit and open to evaluation. Home literacies, on the other hand, embedded as they often are in other practical activities, are evaluated mainly in terms of whether they serve their purposes.

Recognition is also tied up with expectations. People had different interactions around reading with different children and seemed to have differing expectations of them. They referred to their children's different personalities, that they read more to one child than to another or how some children enjoyed it more than others. Lynne tried to treat her children the same and found that her younger daughters reacted completely differently to being read to than the older boy: David really liked it but the younger girls showed much less enthusiasm and, demonstrating the many functions of book-reading, *they enjoy it because I'm spending time with them, not really what I'm doing.* People also had clear views on how good or bad their children were academically and would categorise them in terms of abilities and interests. Helen identified each of her five children differently and pointed to different ways in which she interacted with them around literacy when they were young: two *just picked it up* while for two of them it was *more of a struggle*. From the child's point of view, Paul, a youngest child, felt he was treated differently from his brothers and sisters and that his parents *had given up by the time they got to me*.

Parents convey to their children attitudes about the importance they attach to school work, to literacy development and to homework. The fact that Lynne wrote a letter to the school, asking for more homework to be given to her daughter, also conveyed to Hayley a strong message about the value which Lynne attached to homework. It is not just a question of being positive or not being positive, but certain literacy practices were valued or not valued, or even censured, as mentioned earlier in Chapter 9.

Homework

Homework is one area where people talked of supporting their children. Adults helped with early reading, and this seemed to be the only area where schools had sometimes actually asked parents to participate by listening to their children read. Most parents had not been directly asked, but one or two had personally talked to the teachers about this. Usually the child came home one day with a book and the child explained to the parents what they had to do. One issue which came up repeatedly was that parents said that they were not quite sure what the school wanted them to do when listening to their children read. They were expected to do this and had even been given record cards or books to write in, but they were still not quite sure what to do. Sometimes what they were asked to do seemed pointless to them, so that Helen reported *every day you've to put the title of the book and the date and à comment which mine is normally 'well read' or 'very well read', 'cos what else can you put? I mean she never has any difficulty*.

The most common help which adults provided was with reading; the next most common subject which parents and other adults said they helped with was mathematics. Reading was most common with younger children, and mathematics with children at secondary schools. People commented on helping with sums or with understanding what was required in a question. Several people told stories of how intended help ended in an argument between parent and child. A common lament, here expressed by Helen, was *I mean I could tell him the answer but that wasn't good enough, you had to know how you got the answer*. Adults had different ways of doing the maths and this did not help the children. Cath recalled hiding her homework because her father's attempted help would lead to rows and tears; he would be frustrated by his inability to understand the homework *'cos the teaching was different* and he would end up shouting at her for being stupid.

More broadly, Dick expressed a similar frustration with his daughter's homework, saying there was no comparison between the work he had done at school and the work she now brought home; she was learning subjects he never studied and the ones he did study were being approached in ways which he barely recognised. Sally argued that *kids nowadays are much more advanced and are expected to do much more than when I was a kid.* She left school nine years ago and felt there is a lot more pressure on children now. She talked about how teaching methods in schools are changing all the time and that, since parents attempt to teach in the way they were taught, the children end up confused. She felt there is pressure on parents to take over some of the teaching. In the past *it was more or less left up to your teachers to learn you, and parents maybe to help you with your homework, but not teach it.*

A range of other help was provided across the subjects, and more generally with essays or projects. Here, in contrast to the examples above, literacy is a secondary aspect of the homework, not its main focus. But the literacy activities generated by a history, geography or science project are important and often complex. There was a richness in the different ways of helping, and we have only a few examples (see Ormerod and Ivanic (1997) for more on the support given at home with children's project work). With projects, adults suggested books and ideas. Keith phoned round other friends to get information for his daughter's history project. Often the help was general help with how to get organised or how to approach a question. For many adults there came a point as children got older where they found their children's homework difficult and the help became less direct. A change seemed to take place during the second year of the secondary schools, Year 8, where some adults seemed more distant from the homework. They could give general support or tell children to do their homework or revise for an exam, but often they did not get any more involved and did not directly answer detailed questions.

As we see from these examples, participating in and learning about literacy is important not only at the age of five years. Households are significant places for learning from infancy right up through the school years. The teen years are of special significance, and in our study parents were involved in the homework projects of their teenage children, as well as providing support for younger children learning to read. Issues of teenage literacies are no less important than those concerning children in the infants class, but it appears that, even though the tasks themselves are more demanding, parents are given even less guidance on how to help at this stage. A common concern which parents had was that they did not know what was expected of them by the school. Is helping children a good thing to do or will it be frowned upon by the school? There was an ambivalence that maybe it was *cheating,* a word used by several people, to be helping children with homework, as Lynne discusses in Aside 11.1, or that a small amount of help is all right but at some point it becomes unfair. Even the practice of reading to children, now commonly expected by schools, was new to many people and was treated with a similar ambivalence. Terry reported that his grandfather used to read to him and his brother; however, this was seen as cheating by the parents who wanted the children to read the books by themselves.

Helping with reading or with broader homework tasks was the occasion when some people realised they themselves had problems with literacy, or confronted them with their own educational limitations. In this way, asking parents to help their children is not straightforward but may have repercussions on adults' self-esteem and relationships within the family.

Other support

The above forms of support are distinct from deliberate teaching, whether school-related or not. Several people reported deliberately teaching their children. We had an example earlier with Harry getting his son to ring particular words like 'the' or 'and' in the newspaper. In Chapter 8 Cliff described how he wrote out times tables for his son, and tape-recorded them so that he could listen to them on his Walkman. Diane labelled items around the living room for her child. Lynne's mother would write out lists of the words which her daughter found difficult to read. This deliberate teaching was not always successful. The strategies people used seemed to be a combination of ones they had themselves learned at school, vernacular ones they had learned at home, and ones they had themselves invented. They drew on their own experiences of what had helped them to remember things, and also upon stereotypes of how teachers act and their images of school practices. There appeared to be stereotypes of how learning takes place and they applied these to their children's learning and to their own learning. In talking about deliberate strategies people revealed aspects of their theories of learning. Kathleen', and others, for example, had a strong belief in the value of repetition: *you learn by repetition*. Cliff felt that successful learning had to be pleasurable.

Finally we should reiterate that support for learning came from a variety of people, and was in a variety of directions. Support for children did not come just from their mothers. We have already mentioned the fact that several people talked of relatives or neighbours who had been guiding lights for them in their learning. Children of all ages were supported in different ways, not just pre-school children and children in the early stages of learning to read in schools. There were also many examples of adults supporting each other in their learning.

Support did not work just in one direction. There were several examples of young children helping their parents and taking on some of the literacy chores of the home: these included programming the video recorder, making sense of the letters sent home from school, being responsible for map-reading on car journeys and taking charge of the new home computer. Examples were particularly clear in Mumtaz's multilingual home where different people knew different languages and the children were often better at understanding written English. But this phenomenon was much broader than this. A good proportion revolved around new technologies, and others came from school learning. Older children helped younger ones in systematic ways. Grown-up children also commonly helped their elderly parents. Several adults, including Harry and Cliff, talked of learning from the school activities of their children or their grandchildren, especially from the homework. In fact children can also provide models, opportunities, resources and recognition to their parents and grandparents: for example, June got the idea of using a CB radio from her daughter and also the information about how to set up her own equipment.

In people's memories of childhood, there was a strong belief in vernacular learning and the importance of the home in this, that there were some things which were best learned at home. These beliefs recognise the differences in the amount and quality of dialogue with adults at home and at school, with more extended dialogue at home, different power relations between children and parents, children and teachers; and more real life modelling in home where adults are using literacy for their own purposes. Lynne remembered learning to sew, including using sewing patterns, at home, learning from her mother:

> *I learned lots of things off my mother. We used to sit and do things together for hours. All the people I know who can sew learned off their mothers. Only those who can't do it properly learned off school. You only make one thing in a year and that's not enough to do it properly. I learned all those things, sewing, knitting, lace, embroidery off my mother.*

This quote encapsulates several important points about general home learning: the intensity of tuition which is possible; the frequency of repetition and practice; and the in-context support.

Relations with education

Everyone had stories about their schooling, which they told us without being prompted, and adults frequently drew upon their own experiences of schooling when discussing their children's schooling. Their own experiences provided a framework for talking about their hopes and concerns about their children. Often the schools they went to in Lancaster were the same ones now available to their own children. The complex feelings which adults often expressed about their experiences in passing or failing the eleven-plus exam for the grammar schools coloured the way they talked about how their own children fitted into the complex system of Lancaster's secondary schools. Visiting their children's school and talking to the teachers in the same rooms they had sat in twenty years previously brought up difficult feelings.

Parents constantly emphasised how school choice was very important for them. Lancaster's complex historically and politically induced muddle of two single-sex grammar schools, along with different Catholic and Anglican schools, made for some difficult decisions. It was common for children in one family to be all going to different schools. It appeared to be fairly common for children to change primary school or secondary school partway through their school lives, at the parents' initiative. At the same time, different children appeared to have very different experiences of the same school. Some parents from beyond Lancaster were desperate to get their children into Lancaster's schools; at the same time other parents within the city were sending their children twenty miles by bus every day to schools in a different county.

The two grammar schools were often referred to; they impinged on everyone's lives because either people had gone there, or they had not gone there, and both situations were significant. Frequently one child in the family would be at the Grammar School and others not. Some of the people we talked to had gone to the Grammar School themselves, sometimes liking it, sometimes not. Harry said that he had passed the exam in the 1930s but that his family could not afford the uniform. Kathleen had to leave school at fourteen because her brother was at the Grammar School and her parents could not afford keeping both of the children at school. Helen had gone to the girls' Grammar School but had not enjoyed the experience; like one or two other people she appeared not to do very well academically at the school, and she felt the school had been quite hostile to children like her. People seemed genuinely proud of their children who were at the Grammar School and felt that they had an opportunity which they should take advantage of, but, again, parents whose children were not doing very well there were more critical of the school. Patrick's son did not pass the exam for the Grammar School, and Patrick felt this demotivated him. Patrick was convinced that places tended to be allocated to lecturers' children.

Later, when Patrick wanted his daughter to go to a particular primary school, he made great efforts to get what he thought was best for her. He wrote letters to the educational authority, and to the local MP, and was successful. Children are normally assigned to a particular school but parents receive a letter from the local education authority telling them that they have a right to appeal against the decision. In fact several people mentioned writing letters to ensure that their children got into particular schools, including another Basic Education student, Bob. Writing a letter of appeal to get a child into a school was reported as one of the rare official letters which people recall writing. Leslie, for instance, said that writing a letter of appeal for her daughter to get into a specific secondary school was only the second official letter she had ever written, and, as we described in the last chapter, Mumtaz enlisted the help of her neighbour for this specialist literacy task.

When our interviewees talked about their own childhood experiences and discussed their children, very often particular anecdotes were recalled. We refer to these vivid memories as rehearsed stories, containing particular incidents which had come to symbolise how they felt about the highly charged topic of schooling. Lynne had graphic accounts of feeling humiliated in class, one anecdote being about other children laughing at her and another about a teacher who ridiculed her. These memories stayed with her throughout adult life. Kathleen recalled being told at a parents' evening that her son was a *plodder* and *would only be an ordinary workman*. She felt incensed but did not say anything to the teacher as she was concerned that the teacher would *take it out on the child*. Overall she was very happy with her children's schooling but this one incident was still a vivid one for her.

Many of the themes of this chapter are represented in the quotation from Lynne in Aside 11.1. She is concerned to support her daughter's homework, she helps her with her writing. She distinguishes between maths and other subjects. She discusses how far to support her daughter and has a theory, which she articulates, about how children learn. In discussing her daughter's homework, she refers to her own schooling. She also has a clear view in terms of reading development on what is the school's responsibility and what is her own responsibility.

Home–school communication

There are many different forms of communication between the home and the school. Oral and written messages are sent back and forth, carried by young children. Some letters are sent by mail. There is some phone communication. General meetings for parents are sometimes held at the school. Sometimes parents have individual appointments and, for parents of younger children, there is some casual contact at the beginning and end of the day when parents are being left or picked up.

Most children who live in the city and who go to school in the city walk to school or are brought by car. When they are young, for the first two or three years of school, many are accompanied by adults; most often mothers but also fathers, other relatives, especially grandparents, neighbours with children or older siblings. At the primary schools we looked at there was a definite place, usually the door of the school, which was the dividing line between home and school. The parents did not normally venture beyond the door unless they had an appointment or a particular enquiry; here they said goodbye to their children in the mornings and welcomed them in the

Aside 11.1   Helping with the homework

My daughter came home from school yesterday and she said, 'My teacher hasn't read my poem yet Mum.' And I said, 'Oh well, she'll get round to it'. I said, 'But if there's any queries,' I says, 'Just tell her I did help you'. She says, 'Well, all my friends said that's not fair. I'm cheating.' She said, 'But I said to them, Well how am I meant to learn new vocabulary unless somebody's going to teach me and, you know, tell me what it means.'

. . . The teacher hasn't seen it yet. And I said, 'Well, if your teacher does say anything, just state that you started this poem off yourself and I've just helped you a bit where you've got stuck.' And she's quite happy to do that. 'Cos as I said to her, I said, 'It's only like you go home and maybe you're stuck with a maths problem. They'll think nothing of the mums or dads helping with that.' But they seemed to think that because it was with writing, that she was cheating. And even my husband said that. 'Cos once my daughter said, 'I've got to design a pamphlet Mum. What can I put on it?' She really didn't know where to start. So I sort of just drew her a sketch. And I do realise that I'd given her her idea and she'd just to sort of draw it. But I would sooner have done that with her than her sit there and think, 'I can't do it' and just stop there. So although the idea was mine, she did all the drawing, the colouring and so on.

I mean I can remember just getting this . . . I mean I still have it now. Just this sort of block. 'Oh I'm expected to do something. I can't do it.'

Whereas if I can just sort of help 'em along a little bit. But their friends seem to have this attitude, 'Well once you come to do it, you won't be able to do it 'cos your mum's helped you.' But I'm hoping that somewhere along, they'll take over themselves. It may work it may not. I don't know. But I am helping them, that's something.

I also said it's only the same as going . . . like you'd got maybe something to do on geography or history. Your mum doesn't know. Your dad doesn't know. You go and get a book that can give you the information. The information's been given to you. I mean okay you may have had to look up in the index to see where you've got to look and so on. But it's still been given to you.

Talking about a parents' evening: *This French teacher then says to me, she says 'But there are books you can get on spelling. You could teach her.' And one or two of the other teachers, like the maths teacher for instance, I felt they were putting all the responsibility on me to have to teach her and I said 'I'm only too willing to help her but I'm not a teacher.' I said, 'That's what I expect her to get from school.'*

evenings. Some teachers came out in the afternoons to talk to parents and there was usually a teacher on duty. Children might be carrying work they had done that day in school, or a reading book to be read at home, or a note home from the school. Once or twice a term there would be an individual written report on the child's progress.

At the same time, an equally important source of information was the fact that parents talked to each other, when picking up their children and at other times. As an off-shoot of our project, Susan Benton interviewed parents who were waiting at the gates after school for young children at two primary schools in Lancaster. She built up an impression of the communication between home and school by comparing what parents and teachers said about it (Benton 1994). Young children were the official carriers of information, bringing oral messages or written notes home, but it was clear that they were unreliable communicators. Notes were not handed on until a few days later. Oral messages were forgotten, became garbled, or the force of them changed, so that *You can wear a tracksuit,* for example, becomes *You must buy a tracksuit.*

It was apparent that that the informal networks of parents talking to each other were as important as, or more important than, the formal links of meetings, appointments and notes home. Parents would get information from each other or verify what they had been told by their own children. Crucially, the teachers were not part of these networks (except perhaps in Shirley's case), and inevitably the networks sometimes perpetuated stereotypes, myths and half-truths about school life. Interestingly, there were two groups of parents with separate networks which Benton identified at the two schools she studied: local working-class people and more middle-class parents, often not from Lancaster originally. Both groups thought that the other group had better communication with the school and greater access to the teachers.

Parents said that they did not have as much information about the school world as they wanted; in particular, they would have liked to know more about how their children were faring. Teachers, for their part, over-worked and tired at the end of the day, did not see how they could give any more time to parents. School saw communication with parents as something to be dealt with primarily by means of written notes telling parents about activities going on at the school and by reports on individual children's progress. Teachers made more contact only if there was something wrong in the child's progress.

In our study we found wide variation in the extent to which parents had communication links with the school. Several, such as Leslie, had minimal communication, not normally going to events at the school and not talking to the teachers. At the other extreme Shirley and Brenda were both in regular communication with the teachers, had a good idea how their children were getting on and felt they could easily talk to the teachers if they needed to. As parents they were themselves involved in school activities. Shirley's networks extended from the personal to the semi-official to the extent that, as reported earlier, she sought the head teacher's advice on writing a letter. In between the two extremes most parents had some communication with teachers but wanted more. It is also important to point out that people stressed that often their seeming lack of interest in school activities was because they themselves were busy, sometimes working in the evenings, like Helen, and not having time for meetings.

Where children fell behind in their progress at school and needed special help, the procedures that the schools went through raised particular problems for parents. Diane felt powerless when her disabled son was assessed for a special school; she thought the tests he was given were not relevant to her son's abilities and ignored her own knowledge of him as a parent. Often new and unfamiliar areas of knowledge are confronted. In Aside 11.2 Eddie describes his own and his mother's reaction to his primary school's decision to send him to a special school across the town after he was put back into the first grade having missed schooling through *nicking off* and through illness. She assumed that 'special school' meant educationally good; she had no idea that it meant a school for children with learning difficulties.

Aside 11.2   Nicking off

Well what I used to do is, if they got a bit, you know, got a bit so they was going to find out, I used to stop at home, say, Oh I don't feel so well, you know. Then me mam used to send a letter saying, 'Eddie was sick', such and such a day . . . and she'd put one down and I'd alter it to make it look more, go on and on . . . She didn't know I was off all the time, you know. She just thought I was only off for one day. But first day I started school I was off, off the next day, you know, I started at St Peter's. I got beat up first day I started, fighting over toys and . . . slapped this lad round the head. Next day I was off school again. That's probably where it started originally . . . I found out I could stop off then. I could get away with being sick, or tell lies.

I dropped back that much, you know, that, I couldn't catch up. And they sent me to this Daisy Ash School, and, you know, from there that was it. Finished me off. 'Cause after you've been in a place like that, you know, the names you get called, and, you daren't say where you went . . . They told us that it was such a good school and you get such an education and all that, you know. Me mam knew it was a special school, but she thought it was a really good special school, like a high education school. You know, it's frightening, I was cringing like that . . . I'm scared stiff of anybody at work finding out about it.

One aspect of day-to-day communicating with school which many adults said was difficult was writing letters to school. A letter of explanation from a parent was expected if the child was going to miss school or had been ill, or wanted to be excused from a games lesson, or for many other minor variations in the child's schedule. As one adult pointed out, parents are not actually told that they have to do this but everyone knows that they have to. A whole cluster of difficulties with the act of writing letters to school was reported. Lynne was worried about getting the spelling right and what the letter might reveal about her; Kathleen was more concerned with content and did not want to be seen as complaining. Jake was unsure about the genre expected in addressing teachers about children missing classes: *you're never sure if you're asking them or telling them.* Everyone who talked about writing letters to school expressed some hesitation about it. Concerns were not just expressed by adults with literacy difficulties: everyone finds writing to schools difficult. This general concern reinforces something about writing difficulties: that everyone has such difficulties in some circumstances and that often difficulties are to do with relationships between reader and writer and with clarity of purpose in writing.

Links with college

The above comments apply generally across our study, and unless it was relevant we have not made an effort to separate the adults who were attending Basic Education courses at the local college from the people in the rest of our data. As we discussed above, the adults with problems reading and writing still learned at home and still supported their children's education. In many ways their experiences were not that different from anyone else's. There were also not great differences in this between the adults with difficulties who were attending college and the adults with difficulties who were not attending college.

A variety of factors had prompted people to go back to college to develop their reading and writing. Even for those who made it back into college, the experience was not a wholly comfortable or easy one, and in the experiences they describe we can see some of the issues that might be insuperable barriers for other people.

This was particularly true when people ventured outside of Basic Education to other college courses. For example, Lesley, talking about a creative writing class at the college, describes a number of incidents where she felt singled out and patronised by other students as being the only one having a working-class background: *I thought here's me trotting off to college and the neighbours thinking I must be stuck up. And I get inside and the students – the Open College types – must take one look at me and think . . . look at that yobbo. Pathetic. It put me in my place. For the first few weeks I never read out my stuff.* She felt intimidated by the other students' apparent confidence and was very aware of the difference between the culture of the Basic Education groups where she felt part of *a real good crowd*. She discovered that other people saw Basic Education as only for a certain kind of person:

> *This one women said her maths was shocking so I said how I was going to the basic maths and thought I was getting on okay, and I suggested she might try it and then she sort of turned her nose up. I felt a bit put down. I mean, she'd been asking me about it and congratulating me on going, if you like. Then when I asked her if she'd give it a try she got up on her high horse. It was really a case of one law for the rich and another for . . . That's what it looked like to me anyway . . . I can't say I feel comfortable in that class. I'm the only one who's really working-class.*

Often it was strong support from someone else at home that was instrumental in getting the person to attend college and to stay there: a partner, as in Bob's case, or another family member, her sister, in Lynne's case. It was a relationship with a university student which gave Rita the confidence to go to classes. Reasons to do with their children's developing literacy and progress through school were also commonly cited. Leslie particularly mentioned a difficulty with notes from school. Bob talked of being made redundant and then realising his difficulties when he started to take an interest in his daughter's schooling. In fact, people usually gave multiple reasons for going to college. The complexity of this can be seen in Lynne's situation. Her sister went to college and another mum in the playground finally persuaded her to go; Lynne gave helping her children with their school work as the main reason for going, but there were also reasons to do with encountering difficulties at work. Lynne read essays to her husband; this had been fine at first, but now sometimes led to arguments and he did not always agree with what she said. As already mentioned, she also felt other tensions, so that she hid herself away upstairs to do her homework, and thus her writing interfered with her time with her husband.

However, people did not rely solely on formal education. In general the Adult College was little mentioned, and it played a minor role in the lives of other people we interviewed. One or two people had gone there for evening classes in languages or tried an Open College course in psychology or study skills. The more formal further education college was known locally as the *college of knowledge* and was mentioned for specific training, such as shorthand, typing and hairdressing. As we have seen, people like Harry learned to read and write as adults, but never considered going to college for help. Patrick, who eventually did go to college, says that he realised when he left school that he could not read properly. He taught himself to read by choosing a book which interested him, a book on astronomy, and going through it word by word, as he describes in Aside 11.3. He also had an explanation for why he didn't learn to read at school.

Aside 11.3   Teaching myself to read

When I left school I couldn't read. I somehow missed out so I decided when I left school I'd have to get it together, and so I taught myself, one word at a time. If I had a subject I was deeply interested in, I thought, I'm interested enough so that should be the spur. And I picked astronomy, which is very hard, so eventually I got through the book and learnt quite a bit along the way. It must have been twelve months at it before I got proficient. When I was alone, which wasn't too often, having two brothers, I'd sit down and have a go . . . I wasn't too bad at writing actually, but the reading was just like looking at a brick wall. I probably missed the basics out as I used to go shopping twice a week. There was a few of us . . . You missed the basics maybe in most of the subjects, so when you came back, you hadn't a clue what they were talking about, really. I used to get a note twice a week off me mother to go shopping. I had to stay off school that day, and go shopping twice a week.

Family literacy

One approach which attempts to link up home and school is family literacy. This is used to describe particular education programmes which offer adults opportunities to improve their own reading and writing while helping with their children's learning. We have written elsewhere about the relationship between family literacy programmes and home literacy practices (Barton 1996).

In many ways these are exciting developments, offering many possibilities to rethink some fundamental aspects of education. These initiatives give the opportunity to reassess home–school links and to rethink the role of community in education. Schools get the opportunity to involve parents; adult literacy programmes get the opportunity to act upon a need sometimes expressed by students of helping their children's learning. Bringing together the British tradition of non-formal adult literacy provision and conventional school provision provides the opportunity for a productive confrontation between distinct philosophies of education. Family literacy provides the possibility of new educational practices which need not be constrained by traditions of formal schooling. This is leading to some innovative programmes in Britain.

However, for this to be a productive exchange it is essential to examine the concepts of family literacy most critically and not to accept unchallenged narrow versions of what is possible. Within family literacy educational initiatives there is often not equal representation of home literacy and school literacy. School literacy is a dominant literacy, supported by powerful institutions and infiltrating other domains, including the home. As Street and Street argue (1991), some versions of family literacy turn out to be an invasion of school and its practices into the home. While family literacy programmes and the concerns of teachers often focus on reading to children, our research suggests that it is important to look beyond book reading, since children are observing and participating in a wide range of literacy activities in the home.

In the media, and in government publicity, the most common image associated with family literacy is that of a mother helping her young children learn to read. It is a narrow and politically charged concept of family literacy (as discussed in Barton 1996; Taylor 1997). It is important to support broader notions of what literacy can mean and to deconstruct the rhetoric of blame surrounding the term in much media discussion. The idea of family literacy has been incorporated into a discourse of blame. The media narrative on children and reading (see Chapter 1) contains a rhetoric of falling standards which blames teachers. Family literacy adds to this narrative a strand of blaming families – particularly mothers – for children's lack of progress in school. In this case, the term *family literacy* is part of a deficit model which concentrates on what children and families lack, rather than examining their strengths. It also fails to acknowledge the complexity of women's literacy lives, which certainly cannot be defined solely in terms of their relationships with their children's education. There is a danger that the way in which family literacy programmes are conceptualised and promoted can actually lead to a lack of tolerance of difference and of the diversity of local realities in terms of culture and languages.

The contribution which studies like ours can make to these debates is to provide a detailed view of what actually goes on in the home in terms of literacy. As we have shown, the home is a distinct domain of life, distinct from school; home is a place where literacy means different things, where the purposes, values, the roles people take may differ from formal schooling. Certainly, in our data, studying the home reveals a richer view of literacy than that which is often portrayed or assumed by schools. Family literacy needs to move beyond the stereotypes, and beyond the definitions of literacy offered by schools.

12

THE WEB OF LITERACIES IN LOCAL ORGANISATIONS

Local groups and organisations

One aspect of literacy use in everyday life which was apparent in our data is the prevalence of people's participation in self-organised local groups and the role of literacy in structuring these. Whilst our original focus was on individuals and their practices, this participation has enabled us to shift our attention to the role of literacy in groups. We have already seen that people make use of many kinds of informal networks among family and friends and in their contacts with official organisations, for example in dealing with schools. Beyond such informal networks are organisations which people join voluntarily outside of their work life, united by some common interest or cause. These local organisations and community groups in some ways act as a bridge between informal networks and official organisations: they often rely on personal contacts, but frequently they are also public and legal entities with a committee of responsible officers.

Looking through the data, we found that all the people we interviewed belonged to or were connected in some way to at least one local organisation. 'A significant proportion had been officers for organisations. To give some examples, Harry had been secretary of the local men's club and Helen's husband, Malcolm, was now the secretary. Like several other people, Harry also had an allotment at the top of the hill and belonged to the Allotment Association. Shirley edited the newsletter of the residents' association. She belonged to the local branch of the Dyslexia Association, and became fund-raiser for it. She had also been active in her children's school parent–teachers association. Eddie went to a local karate club. Helen was a street representative for the residents' association and had helped out with the local Brownie (girl scouts) pack. Jeff was in a writers' group and active in the chess club. Janice went walking with the local fell walking club, partly because her sister-in-law had been secretary and her brother-in-law treasurer.

The aim of this chapter is to document the role of literacy in such local organisations and community groups examining how they structure and are structured by literacy practices, how literacy is used alongside oral and other organisational resources to achieve collective goals and to deal with problems identified within local communities. Normally, for example, the written word has a significant role in maintaining these organisations, in communicating and record-keeping. A range of texts is utilised in these activities, including minutes, newsletters, correspondence and accounts.

We first say something about the different sorts of groups which people belong to, and the number of such groups. Then we provide a specific example, that of the Allotment Association. We investigate two literacy events, one a precisely time-bounded and regular one, the annual general meeting, and the other an unexpected sequence of events over a period of time, a campaign to defend the allotments against the loss of land for house building. We then compare the experience of the Allotment Association with the Housing Action Project, which has a different relationship to the local community. Using these examples, we discuss the range of literacies in local organisations, and how people participate in them and acquire the appropriate literacies. Finally, we draw together this data and use it both in this and the following chapters to elaborate a theory of literacy as communal resource rather than individual skill.

We have identified a wide range of local groups which exist in Lancaster: clubs, societies, leagues, organisations, associations, committees, campaigns, fellowships, guilds and circles. They are concerned with animals, sport, religion, music, politics, hobbies, health, support, opposition and much more. These groups vary from informal neighbourhood baby-sitting circles to formal branches of national organisations. To give a flavour of the range of groups, we provide a brief list in Aside 12.1.

In a short time we identified over three hundred local groups, and the number continued to rise. We began from a short list of community organisations in a local newspaper, and gradually added groups referred to by the people we interviewed or mentioned in the local papers. This was only scratching the surface, as even after five years each week's newspaper brought information about more groups. There were Lancaster-wide groups not included in our list; there are also many smaller, more informal groups, often belonging to just one area of Lancaster, which would never reach the newspaper. We believe the actual number of such organisations within this medium-sized town to be well over a thousand.

A precise number is not possible because of the fuzzy nature of the category of local group. At one end local groups fuse into official organisations and national organisations which have a local branch; at the other end there are informal groupings which are not actual organisations, such as people who play music together, or drink together regularly. Estimating the number is important however, in that it stresses the maybe surprisingly high number of groups; our estimates agree with the work on voluntary organisations of Konrad Elsdon and colleagues, who from their survey of organisations in over thirty towns claim that there are at least one million

---

Aside 12.1   Some local groups in Lancaster

Archaeological Society
Beekeepers Association
Campaign for Nuclear Disarmament
Disabled Motorists Club
Embroiderers Guild
Family History and Heraldry Society
Guide Dogs for the Blind Association
Hard of Hearing Club
Irish Traditional Music Association
Junior Chess Club
King's Own Royal Border Regiment Association
Ladies Darts and Dominoes League
Machine Knitting Club
Northern Foreign Birds Association
Oxfam Group
People Opposed to Noxious Gases (PONG)
Quiz League
Rambling and Fell-Walking Club
St Paul's Scotforth Over Sixties Club
Townswomen's Guild
UFO Network
Vale of Lune Harriers
Writers Workshop Group
Yorkshire Terrier Rescue Association
Zen Group (Buddhist Meditation)

---

voluntary organisations in the UK and that at least a quarter of the adult population is currently involved with managing or running such groups (Elsdon *et al.* 1995). In a study examining learning in voluntary organisations in north-west England, Percy (1988) found an inner city, a town and a rural area to have a different number of groups and different types of groups. Another study estimates that two-thirds of adults participate in sports (Department of National Heritage 1996). A survey of amateur arts and crafts in the UK (Hutchison and Feist 1991) similarly finds high levels of participation in music, dance, visual arts and film societies, and crafts. In her study of musical activity in Milton Keynes, Ruth Finnegan describes a variety of activity ranging from teenage rock bands in local pubs to local orchestras and choirs (Finnegan 1989); this mirrors our observations in Lancaster.

There are various ways of categorising groups. Our largest category was specific leisure interests, such as the Archaeological Society or the Irish

Traditional Music Association. Several were concerned with animals, such as the Yorkshire Terrier Rescue Association and the Horses and Ponies Protection Association. This category included sports, gardening and other practical interests, music groups, theatre groups. In these groups people had a specific specialist interest they wished to pursue. Some were educational or cultural in intent, and included reading groups and writers' groups. Some were for children, such as the Junior Chess Club.

Many other groups were concerned with care, often for the elderly, such as St Paul's Scotforth Over Sixties Club, or for people with specific illnesses and diseases, such as the Alzheimer's Disease Society. Several were self-help, such as the Disabled Motorists Club and the Hard of Hearing Club. Often these were medical groups, or they might be straightforward self-help like locally organised baby-sitting groups. Other groups can be regarded as general associations, some being primarily for women, such as the Townswomen's Guild, and others for men, such as the local Rotary groups.

Another category is that of campaigning groups, some of which were small, local and short-term, such as People Opposed to Noxious Gases (PONG). Other campaigning groups were branches of national or international organisations, such as the Campaign for Nuclear Disarmament (CND), which have changing participation over time. At its height in the mid-1980s the CND organised large marches though the city. In 1995 it still had nearly four hundred paid-up members receiving a regular newsletter, but only four members came to the 1995 annual general meeting, where they kept to formalities such as approving the minutes of the previous meeting. Like Elsdon, we found that a general classification of the groups is difficult, as groups can be often be fitted simultaneously into several categories: the Guide Dogs for the Blind Association, for instance, is concerned with care, with animals and probably with campaigning. Likewise, the Friends of the Grand Theatre includes theatre audiences, amateur actors and people interested in the historic building.

Groups vary as to their intended life-span, some being more temporary than others. At one extreme are the one-off fund-raisers or protests, such as the poll-tax march organised by Janice, the hairdresser on Springside, which may need very little in the way of formal organisation or structure (see Aside 7.1). Others are longer-term campaigns or organising committees for projects or events with a limited time horizon, for example the yearly Lancaster Carnival. They also vary in size: many have around twenty members; a few have several hundred.

We have limited our study to groups which treat the Lancaster area as an entity; we have only included national organisations which have a local group with its own local structure, such as the Lancaster branch of the Campaign for Real Ale. We have excluded organisations for particular professions such as dentists and teachers and trade unions. We have not been systematic in searching out clubs associated with sports, nor with churches.

There are associations covering particular sports, such as tennis, football or golf, and these often co-ordinate the activities of several smaller local clubs. Similarly with churches – there was a range of associations and there were often clubs within clubs, while the churches themselves also belonged to larger national groupings. Commercial organisations, such as the club June wanted to join to buy porcelain plates, or book clubs which other people belonged to are also not included. Nor have the informal networks of selling to friends and neighbours been included, whether it is bags of organic vegetables which people subscribe to every week, or the catalogues where people take orders from neighbours, as Rose and Shirley, for example, did, or locally organised football pools with neighbourhood reps. They can perhaps be contrasted with the even more informal buying of salmon or trout from someone in the pub, or bags of potatoes from a seller going door-to-door, which are done with little recourse to written record-keeping.

Many groups have a quasi-legal status, as in the Allotment Association, which is the formal body required by the council as a mechanism for collecting rent and administering the plots of land used by individual gardeners. Most of the time this legal status is not relevant to the members, but, as we see later in this chapter, every so often it becomes crucial in safeguarding the interests of members and allowing them to carry on their activities in a local context of legal and financial change. This quasi-official background is also true of the Housing Action Project in Springside, which was in many ways an official organisation. Others such as the first anti-poll-tax march were started locally and were truly vernacular in origins. After all these exclusions and qualifications, we still have, we assume, over a thousand local organisations in Lancaster where people join together because they share a common purpose, carrying out leisure interests, caring for themselves and for others, and acting in the social world.

From examining our data we can see that there is a web of literacy in local organisations. They often have notices, advertisements; they hold meetings with written agendas and minutes; they have forms for membership, for accounts or for funding; they produce newsletters and magazines, officers communicate by letter with members, with outside agencies and with the broader public; and many of their activities call upon literacy. Some have complex literacies associated with funding. Even the ubiquitous jumble sale and raffle involve some literacies. Looking at the networks represented by these groups reveals multiple notions of community in terms of both locality and interests. Each organisation creates a world of its own and there is a sense in which they are all communities (see for example, John Swales's discussion (1990) of a stamp collectors' club, the Hong Kong Study Circle, as a discourse community). Such informal groups have rarely been studied from the point of view of literacy practices. We return to the general uses of literacy in groups but first we describe some specific examples in detail.

The Allotment Association

We use the Allotment Association in Springside as an example of an organisation. Allotments may need some explanation, especially to the non-British reader. The need for explanation underlines how the practices which we describe are culturally situated. Allotments are communal gardens. Many were set up during the Second World War to encourage people to grow their own produce and to 'dig for victory'. The provision of allotments is a legal obligation of councils, and they can normally be found on the edges of towns and cities throughout Britain. After a decline in the 1950s there was a revival of interest in the 1960s and 1970s, with often long waiting lists to get a plot. More recently they have come under threat as councils have been forced to shed responsibilities and look for ways of making money. Allotments, like school playing fields, have become viewed as prime building land within the confines of towns and cities, despite the unmeasured contribution they make to the household economy. (For more details on allotments, see Crouch and Ward 1988.)

Allotments are particularly important in Lancaster, including Springside, where most houses have small back yards but no gardens. There are around thirteen allotment sites in Lancaster containing a total of over five hundred plots, mostly on the edges of the town. The site in Springside has around fifty plots; each is 72 feet by 36 feet; some people have half a plot, some have two or even three plots. A person might have the same plot for twenty or thirty years. Some are family ventures, with different generations involved, but traditionally most have been tended by older local working-class men. This is gradually changing towards a broader social mix, including unemployed people, younger couples and women. Each site has its distinct atmosphere and traditions, with what appears to be a haphazard vernacular architecture of sheds and greenhouses, often made of old window frames and reused timber, with water butts made from blue plastic chemical drums.

Of the range of organisations we came across, the Allotment Association is an interesting one to choose as an example because one does not immediately think of the allotment as a particularly literate environment, nor expect to see a lot of literacy on an allotment. There may be a notice or two at the entrance, a hand-written request to pay rents by the end of the month or to conserve water, or formal *Wilful damage* notices. After paying the rent, plot-holders get a receipt, maybe from a pre-printed book of receipts bought in town. If we looked in someone's shed on their allotment we might find seed packets with instructions on the back, chemicals with warnings, plant labels or someone's diary recording what, when and where they had planted things. There is a notice on the gate at the entrance saying *Private,* but apart from these examples there is very little literacy apparent in the environment. Gardeners become members of the association by virtue of having an allotment, whether or not they are aware of the fact, and several people did not know the actual name of the Allotment Association. There is no membership form; the only bureaucracy people experience may be the receipt for the annual rent. Other information, such as when and where committee meetings take place, is communicated by word of mouth or by notices displayed near the entrance to the site; these, by 1996, were no longer handwritten but decorative word-processed versions. Most allotment holders see their membership in purely practical terms: it is the means of access to a garden. There is a sense of community, in that a great deal of exchanging help and expertise takes place between gardeners, but much of this is outside of the formal organisation of the association.

Literacy in social participation: the annual general meeting

We attended a literacy event in a neighbouring allotment site. The annual general meeting of the Allotment Association was held in Alan's greenhouse. Around fifteen people were standing in a rough semicircle; only Jim, the treasurer, was sitting. Alan, the secretary, had a square cardboard box full of documents next to him, and he rummaged through it once in the course of the meeting. Effectively, the documents in this box are the association's archive, crucial in case of dispute, but quite casually stored in a cardboard box. It contained minute books; the secretary's log books; loose sheets of handwritten minutes; copies of leases going back to 1952; a variety of site plans; copies of rent collecting lists; letters to and from the County and City Councils and the Water Board; government circulars, such as information on Chrysanthemum White Rust disease; letters to and from tenants, prospective tenants, members of the committee; and copies of lists of rules of the association.

Alan, the secretary, relied on a sheaf of handwritten notes to deliver his detailed secretary's report, covering issues such as vandalism and thefts of produce, locks and security, and problems with untidy allotment holders. There was some formality; Alan addressed the group as *gentlemen*, although three of the fifteen people present were women. Sometimes he spoke freely, sometimes he read from his notes. Arthur, the chair, held a handwritten sheet with the agenda on it. He steered the meeting through the agenda and kept control of the meeting. No one seemed to be taking notes, but the three officers made reference to the minutes of previous meetings. Jim held a bank statement and a small piece of paper with a few figures on it for the treasurer's report. All the way through these reports there was discussion and comment, for example on the cost of water and how to keep water usage down.

Most discussion and decision-making came in the third part of the meeting, AOB (Any Other Business). There were several items, all brought up by the officers. The first item concerned lowering the rent for a garage on the allotment; this was agreed, but, again, no records seemed to be being made of decisions. The second point was a request from Jim to change the date for collecting rent: reference was made to the rule book and the need to change a rule; Jim didn't have a copy, but Alan produced one from his box. He held it up in the air, a small folded cardboard booklet like a trade union card. After some confusion, the appropriate rule was found and a possible amendment discussed. There were various proposals about how to inform the membership of the changed date, such as circulating an amended rule book to everyone, but no actual decision was made. After discussion of setting a new and slightly higher rent for the next year, agreement was sought by a show of hands.

The meeting had the air of attention to formalities and procedures. An agenda was followed and there was a hierarchy of who talked when, and how much weight was given to people's contributions. Nevertheless, everyone participated, for example in the consensus-reaching talk about setting the new level of the rent. The chair and secretary moved the discussion along and brought each point to some sort of conclusion. There were waves of formal and informal talk.

Meetings literacies

This short description of the annual general meeting, summarised from our participant observer's notes, is useful for illustrating several points about literacy in groups, and we use it to explore what is involved in meetings literacies. These literacies are an important component for the everyday running of many organisations, as in the annual general meeting of the Allotment Association. Firstly, a comment on the physical setting. The Allotment Association met on Alan's allotment. Meeting spaces are important for local groups, and they are not always easy to find: typical venues are back rooms of pubs, church halls and community centres. Many local groups have to improvise in this as in other aspects of their activities.

In the example described above, people knew how to act in the meeting; they knew how to talk appropriately. The time was divided into items and controlled by means of an agenda. Literacy was to some extent used as a prop by the chair, secretary and treasurer to structure the interaction, when they referred to the agenda or to the bank statements and the water bill. There is evidence in the meeting of the ritual aspects of literacy. This is apparent in the agenda and how it was utilised. However, people did not always respect this structure in the ways they participated: the chair took charge of timing but people did not particularly address the chair when talking; people all talked together, they made jokes. There were certain sorts of talk and these could be analysed in detail using discourse analysis. However, here our purpose in examining meetings literacies is to analyse the social practices, starting with how the texts were actually used: what people did with them and why and the values that these actions reveal. Firstly we can list the wide range of texts that were physically present at the meeting. These texts of the meeting included: the minutes of the previous meeting; the cardboard box containing the records of the association; handwritten notes of the secretary's report, the agenda and the accounts; a bank statement; and the rule book.

Meetings literacies are characterised by the interweaving of oral and literate; by examining this event we can see the complexity of this relationship. There was **talk around texts**, physically and in a literal sense, where one person was reading from a bank statement, and the group of people standing in a circle around the statement were discussing it. In addition there were several further texts which were not visible or present but which were referred to; here there was **talk about texts**, a term used by Moss (1996). These texts, such as the letter, a standard letter from the secretary warning tenants that they would have to quit if they did not tidy up their plot within one month, had taken on a life of their own and were a reasonable subject for discussion. Other texts which were talked about included the water bill; various letters which had been received; the waiting list; the notice of rents due at the entrance gate; the deeds.

Meetings involve specialist literacies such as constructing agendas, minute-taking, following the language of the rule book and constitution. The officers such as the secretary or treasurer are called upon to use these specialist discourses, and identifying them enables us to focus more closely on what work the written word is doing in this context and compare it with some of the themes already mentioned in relation to the more private sphere of the home. The minutes were not taken at this meeting but written up from memory afterwards (although in other Allotment Association meetings rough notes were taken). There was joint decision-making on the spot; all the men present seemed willing to speak in the meeting, reflecting a strong oral tradition and close personal networks among allotment holders. The minority of women present were less at ease.

In Chapter 1 we referred to the work which literacy can do in an activity, and the social meanings it takes on. There are examples in the meeting of literacy being used as evidence. For instance, the treasurer held up the bank statement, inviting members to examine it. Likewise, members could look in the box if they wanted to. In the meeting we can also see literacy *as record,* with examples of minutes, legal records, deeds and bank statements being referred to. We have many examples here of literacy as imposed on the group by the council, by banks, by the state, by the legal system. Banks need officers and demand that two officers be signatories. Officers of the association have legal responsibility for the association's affairs and have to sign documents and respond to official letters. This has important implications for them as individuals. These requirements came up during the meeting, and since most members had very hazy knowledge of the law they became the subject of discussion and dispute. A final point is that, partly because of the legal and financial context in which literacies are embedded, they can be used, or felt to be used, as a threat, as in the letter to allotment holders with untidy plots. A letter to the association from the Council may also be seen to embody a threat, as we see in the next section.

Literacy in social action: the allotments fight

Meetings of the Allotment Association are regular repeated events with a standard format. The annual meeting fits into the rhythm of monthly committee meetings which are held on the first Sunday of every month at ten in the morning in Alan's greenhouse. However, there are other contrasting types of event which the Allotment Association is involved with: the unexpected events which confront a group of this kind. One such set of events took place during our study of the local community when the Council tried to sell off land which included the allotments to a developer for building housing. The Allotment Association organised to resist this threat, and they were partly successful. Initially people did not know how to react when they heard about this threat but they formed an action committee involving not

Figure 12.1   Object Now

217

just the officials of the Allotment Association but other gardeners and residents in the neighbourhood, each bringing different knowledge and expertise. Letters were written, meetings were held, research was carried out; newsletters were produced and circulated, officials were lobbied.

As well as observing and attending meetings, we interviewed a range of people who described this unfolding process from their perspective and the ways community resources of people and places were harnessed for this common aim. We tracked the set of events which followed the announcement of the Council's intention to sell the land, in particular what role different literacies played in this process. We describe here the strategies and resources that local people brought to bear on this issue and discuss some of the implications of these for supporting literacy practices in communities.

This is only one example of the issues which arose during our study, and several other disputes were about land, concerning issues of ownership, access or use. Other broader issues included traffic problems, pollution, disputes about taxes and schooling issues. The points which arise from this example are common to the processes involved in all these cases. We present this example as a case study offering a framework for analysing events where a local community mobilises and organisations are formed. There are five stages to our analysis, which parallel the action taken by those involved in the dispute:

- analysing the problem
- tracking the sequence of events
- identifying the strategies used to solve the problem
- identifying the resources used
- identifying the texts involved in these practices

Analysing the problem

The allotments were on land leased from the County Council, who owned it. The Council was in financial crisis and wanted to sell the 7-acre site, used partly as public open space and partly as allotments, to a developer who would build houses on it. The land had once been designated for building a primary school, but plans had changed; the land was now deemed to be surplus to requirements and, as such, the Council was required by central government to sell it. This meant that the gardeners would lose their plots and the locality would lose a significant area of open space – in a neighbourhood of densely packed housing. The problem was recognised first of all by the allotment holders who would lose their plots, but it affected everyone in the local area because it would mean a loss of communally owned open space.

In order to act on this issue, local people needed a range of information, which had to be assembled and then shared with interested people. They needed to know what had happened so far and who was affected by this issue, in this case both allotment holders and other residents for different but overlapping reasons. They had to ascertain what the legal situation was, including the status of the land in question, who has the right to make and oppose decisions, what general rights residents and allotment holders have. They needed to understand what the possible solutions were, who makes decisions in the local and regional administration, and how these decisions are made. In this case the situation was complicated by the duties and rights of the different layers of the administration: for example the County can override the City in certain financial matters and can grant themselves planning permission even if the City objects.

Tracking the sequence of events

Our sources of data included photographs; documents such as maps and letters; interviews with local residents, members of the Action Committee, the director of the Housing Action Project, a local councillor and allotment holders; field notes of meetings; and local newspaper reports. Rumours about development began when early in July 1990 some allotment holders noticed someone digging holes in the green area adjoining the allotment site. Then a representative of Lancashire County Council Property Services visited the secretary of the Allotment Association to explain the plans, and this was followed up by an official letter to the Allotment Association on 18 July giving allotment holders formal notice to quit by January 1991. This is a short time in gardening, as many activities have an annual cycle. The chair of the Allotment Association, although pessimistic himself about being able to influence the decision, showed the letter to Beth, a student trainee solicitor and allotment holder who lives in Springside; he also talked to a number of other interested people about the problem.

A variety of individual initiatives resulted from this. Beth offered to write to the County Council on behalf of allotment holders to express concern. Other people wrote letters and there was much informal talking and gathering of ideas. Celia, another allotment holder, wrote to the MP and sent round a petition to allotment holders on her own initiative. A general meeting was held in the church hall on 15 August, organised by the chair of the Allotment Association, at which an action committee was formed, and plans for the proposed development circulated and discussed. The chair had lobbied some individuals beforehand to volunteer themselves for the committee. As well as Beth, Celia and other allotment holders, the committee included Isabel, a resident who had been involved in a car parking campaign previously, and Jeff Brown, who offered to word process and copy letters. He kept minutes of meetings, went to a legal surgery in town and organised other volunteers, for example with the street distribution of the newsletter. At the meeting people discussed possible strategies: petitioning, letter writing, persuasion of individuals, press campaign. A decision was made not to use a petition.

The Action Committee held weekly meetings, sometimes at the Project office, sometimes in people's houses. A collectively written newsletter was produced and 1,400 copies were distributed, encouraging people to write to named people and offering them ideas for what to write. Meetings were held between the action committee and city and county councillors at which the compromise plan was put forward. A compromise was offered by the Council and put to the Allotment Association at a meeting on 18 September: half the land was to be sold for housing; the rest would be covenanted to the city for open space, and the allotments would remain. No decision was taken, as there was some opposition to accepting the compromise. At a regular residents' association in October there was still some opposition to the compromise plan. A short time later the compromise was accepted by the Action Committee and formally notified to the Council. Our interest here is in the role of literacy in this community action. It has been analysed in terms of the strategies and resources used to solve the problem. Texts have been separated out, as one particular kind of resource. The strategies, resources and texts are summarised in Aside 12.2.

Campaigning literacies

Close observation of this sequence of events adds to our understanding of the literacy practices of the allotment holders. There are some similarities to the meetings literacies described in the previous section: for example, they drew upon both oral and written participation. Different configurations of practices were effective and appropriate for particular purposes, and in the meetings people discussed how to get the right balance, for example whether a petition was a useful strategy, whether standard or individualised letters were best to send to the Council. Both individual and collaborative activities were involved. Because this was a new situation making unfamiliar demands on people, there was more discussion and negotiation of process and strategy than in the routine annual general meeting. The meetings that were called were central in the action to save the allotments. People had to search out and draw upon a range of different funds of community knowledge such as the history of the dispute and previous similar ones; legal rights and official structures; knowledge of local networks including who has responsibility for making decisions and can influence outcomes; experience of other local campaigns and organisations, formal and informal.

We became more aware through this example that Springside is not a homogeneous community: conflicts and tensions rose to the surface. There were various interest groups involved – allotment holders, councillors and other residents. Another source of tension was that both long-time residents

Aside 12.2   Strategies, resources and texts: elements of literacy practices

The strategies used to solve the problem

This is what people did:

> *gather and distribute information in the local community*
> *mobilise local people*
> *petition among allotment holders*
> *hold general meetings to agree on what to do*
> *form an action committee to implement decisions and to negotiate on behalf of the community*
> *hold letter-writing campaign to influential people*
> *start press campaign in local radio and newspapers*
> *influence local officials by oral persuasion*

The resources used

These included material objects, skills, knowledge, time and ideas, money, meetings and space:

> *legal literacy knowledge of trainee solicitor*
> *use of word processor, photocopier*
> *local library*
> *accounting skills*
> *money raised by fund-raising*
> *local contacts in the Council*
> *skills in dealing with the media*
> *skills of persuasion and argumentation*
> *organising skills – offering structure and being able to work with others*
> *design skills – combining words and graphics on signs, posters etc.*

The textual resources involved in these practices

The following texts were used:

> *letters of various kinds, including official*
> *maps (for understanding the compromise plan)*
> *historical records of the Allotment Association (to see how land use and tenure changed over time) and more general history of allotments*
> *legal documents*
> *newspaper articles*
> *petition*
> *newsletter to the local community*
> *posters*
> *press release*

and recent incomers were involved in meetings, with different ideas about how to solve the problem and what would count as a resolution. People with different personalities and resources contributed in different ways, some more visibly than others. This raises many issues about who gets to play the key roles in collective action, who gets the credit for doing so and how this happens.

The Housing Action Project and the residents' association

Having described the roles that literacy plays in one local voluntary organisation in Springside, we turn to the Housing Action Project, and to the residents' association which the project workers established in Springside. As mentioned earlier, the Housing Action Project was the first local organisation visible to us when we started our fieldwork in Springside. The project workers were helpful in making contact with residents and publicising our research; and over time we collected a range of information about the Housing Action Project employees, the daily routines of the office, residents' association meetings and newsletters, as well as documents such as local press coverage, leaflets and other materials given out by the Housing Action Project to residents or available in the office. We have information from all of our case study households about how people regarded the project and the contact they had with it. Some people involved in the case studies spent a great deal of time in this office, and many people wandered in for leaflets or advice, or to use the photocopier. We tracked the events that led to the Housing Action Project being closed at the beginning of 1991 and people's views about that.

It became clear that, far from being a local initiative generated by residents in the neighbourhood, the Housing Action Project occupied a complex position between central and local government, and between local business interests and the residents of Springside. In terms of the range of community organisations discussed in this chapter it fell at the official end, being funded and heavily orchestrated by central and local government interests. Its very hybridity as an organisation was very much part of national government policy at the time. The idea of encouraging community involvement, through setting up residents' associations, for example, as an addition to the advice and grant-giving functions of the Housing Action Project was part of the national policy, although the evaluation report suggests that this element of the work was low-priority and variable in its success (Leather and Mackintosh 1990: 77). Geoff, the project manager in Springside, was committed to the community involvement aspect of his work and he encouraged residents to participate, even though no one in the locality had initially been consulted or properly informed about what the project would be doing in the neighbourhood.

With this in mind it is interesting to assess how far the Housing Action Project did embed itself into Springside. Because it was an organisation initiated from outside the area, and employing workers who, although local, did not live in Springside, it is relevant to ask how far and in what ways residents themselves engaged with the organisation or ignored it. In the limited space we have here we therefore concentrate on the variety of ways in which the Housing Action Project and its literacy practices impinged on the lives of people in the neighbourhood, and their reactions to it.

Some Springside residents, such as Shirley, became closely and actively involved with the Housing Action Project and the residents' association. For many other people their awareness of it and engagement with it was very distant and almost entirely passive. The residents' newsletter and the Housing Action Project official paper were both delivered to every household in Springside. This was a minimum level of involvement, or rather incorporation, which residents could escape from only by throwing it away. To some residents the project's offer of free house improvements seemed little different from the double-glazing and time-share offers and other seeming prizes which regularly arrive in the junk mail, and are sometimes puzzled over by people such as Cliff and Mumtaz. The publicity that the project gave out was a mixture of friendly, locally produced material and nationally produced glossy information booklets which were bizarrely inappropriate to the terraced streets of Springside – showing pictures of Tudor-beamed detached homes, with garden conservatories and smart patios.

People had different formal relations with the Housing Action Project: some were employed by it; local builders contracted their services to it; and some local residents received a home improvement grant from it. As we have noted earlier, the administrative boundaries of the housing action area cut across the natural geographical boundaries of Springside, so that only 180 out of the 660 households were eligible for enveloping. Because this was perceived by residents to be unfair, 250 people signed the petition initiated by Shirley to the local Council demanding that they extend the enveloping scheme.

Many residents used the advice and information liaison service offered by the Project, including addressing complaints to it. Almost all contacts were face-to-face in the office, which was set up to be informal and welcoming like a community centre. Other enquiries were by telephone; letters were rarely received. The national evaluation report records the Lancaster project as having above average enquiries at around forty each month. Some people dropped in regularly to it for social chats and many used the photocopier in the office, providing petty cash for the social side of office life. Office staff reported frequent requests to copy things such as insurance certificates and tax documents. Other people brought in personal papers such as poems and handwritten letters, jokes and pictures (as in Aside 9.3). Others wanted copies of posters and knitting patterns. Requests came from people of all ages including schoolchildren and students.

Monthly meetings of the residents' association were attended by a small proportion of Springside residents, to the evident disappointment of the manager, Geoff. Some people actively contributed by speaking, whilst others remained quiet. The first two meetings had a turnout of around fifty people. Subsequent ones varied between fourteen and thirty people. Shirley, Helen and Jeff from our case studies were regular attenders. June, Mumtaz and Cliff had been to occasional meetings. Mumtaz had been to meetings with her friend Maria, but said she got bored with them, and preferred to keep in touch by talking to her neighbours, including Shirley, and dealing with any problems directly with the building contractors. Some residents got involved in administrative jobs, such as delivering newsletters, becoming street representatives and helping to organise events; some also joined in the social activities and network that were organised through the residents' association. This pattern of involvement was again partly dependent on Shirley's friendship networks and powers of persuasion. Helen was one of those who reluctantly took on the job of representative for her street.

Few people used the residents' association as a resource for other social action in the neighbourhood, even though Shirley encouraged them to do so. The allotment action group was the most dramatic example of this during the period of our research. Other issues such as traffic, play space and neighbourhood watch appeared on meeting agendas but did not succeed in mobilising residents behind them. Neither did Janice enlist the help of the residents' association in her poll-tax protest, even though the poll tax was a widespread local concern.

It can be seen from this description that the textual evidence of how Shirley shifted identities within her newsletter editorials, as described in detail in Chapter 6, reflected real tensions and ambiguities within the residents' association itself, between its role as an informal social group and its more formal functions as a representative body supported by the Housing Action Project. People related to it in a variety of ways. Shirley was at one end of a spectrum of involvement, trying to pull others alongside her. In comparison, other residents' involvements and interests were much more sporadic and individually motivated.

Literacies in groups

What can we learn from these examples about the kinds of literacies involved in getting things done in groups, including the range of texts and the ways in which they are used in specific events? What work does literacy do in groups? What activities does it sustain? And what are the connections between these activities in informal groups, formal bureaucratic structures and democratic participation?

Firstly, we must reiterate that, in all the examples we have discussed, literacy fits in with other resources and practices available to groups. Any situation offers a choice about the ways in which oral and written practices may be used. Sometimes an oral invitation or face-to-face persuasion is appropriate. At other times only a written communication has the right kind of authority to produce the response that is needed. Often, combining them proves more effective than either one alone. These choices have to be carefully weighed up, and, in the case of the allotments fight where a new situation arose, people were uncertain about what to do and considerable time was spent in meetings discussing the value of different strategies. In routine contexts such choices are less likely to be discussed since traditions have already been established.

We can begin to identify some generic literacies involved in groups. One set of these involves *record-keeping,* both for internal group purposes of practical administration, as in minutes, financial records, membership lists, constitutions, and also to meet external legal and bureaucratic requirements, demanded, for example, by banks. In a way which will be quite familiar now, a given record may serve multiple purposes. For example, the written record often takes on a new significance when a dispute arises and where the main focus becomes one of protecting the group's interests, rather than maintaining or expanding existing activities. These records are fledgling bureaucracies, creating another 'world on paper' (Olson 1994). They can lead to specialised functions for officers and fixed procedures used to regulate members' behaviour, as well as to maintain and facilitate group activities. Over time they also become a historical resource for new members and officers, and a guide to how things are done in the particular organisation.

Literacies are involved in within-group communication, including circulating information via newsletters and notice-boards, canvassing opinion and getting others actively involved by means of petitions and questionnaires. A number of community organisations have newsletters; examples delivered through the door in Springside include a local evangelical church, the parent–teacher associations of various schools, the organic gardeners' group, the Civic Society and the local Labour Party. Other groups, such as the Allotment Association and many sports groups, have active committee structures but no regular newsletters: communication is achieved largely by notices and through word of mouth.

Literacy is also heavily involved in a group's communication with the outside world, including a range of official bodies, political representatives, businesses, local media and individual members of the public. Written texts in the shape of letters, forms, funding applications, advertisements and press releases are both received and produced. Correspondence with official bodies can have legal, financial and regulatory aspects; interpreting these to the membership and making access to them possible can be an important part of the officers' jobs. Some official organisations, including the Housing Action Project, also have advice or outreach workers attached to them. People acting as mediators or literacy brokers in this way are particularly important in multilingual settings (see Sayers 1992; Baynham 1993). The other side of this relationship is advocating on behalf of the group to the outside world, putting over the views and perspective of the membership and protecting their rights, as in the allotment campaign.

Texts in groups

When participating in groups, people handle a wide variety of written documents, producing them, displaying and circulating them, collecting and interpreting them, and using them to solve practical problems. We did not set out to look at newsletters, petitions, letters, posters and other documents from informal community groups, but they have emerged from our data as a common and established form of vernacular literacy practice in the local community. Our research strategy has led us to discover these texts which have not been attended to by other researchers. They are of value in their own right and worthy of more attention.

In Chapter 6 we described some of the practices surrounding the production of the residents' association newsletter. As we saw in that example, the content, style and production process of minutes and informal newsletters is not fixed by outside conventions but is fluid, creative and personal, reinvented by each group. People bring their own personal concerns and histories as writers and communicators to bear on this new task, including previous experience of writing letters or reports, and of addressing meetings. They draw on models from other groups and past traditions either identified by more experienced members of the group or brought in from elsewhere by new members. As an example of this, the incoming secretary of the' Allotment Association was given a collection of documents by the chair and told to read through them to get a sense of the past history of the organisation. Shirley had earlier helped produce the newsletter at her child's school, offering her a model for her editorial work.

We would expect some convergence to develop from this process of modelling and constant reinvention, and traces of the past will be detectable in present practice. People also make use of discourses learned in other areas of their lives, leading to intertextuality in the documents produced: Shirley drew on oral strategies, popular media and humour, and incorporated elements of telephone discourse, personal letters, advertising and official announcements, depending on the content of her editorials.

People also draw upon knowledge they have acquired at work to carry out the roles of secretary and treasurer. A particularly useful aspect of employment-related knowledge is a trade union background, with its close links to parliamentary democratic practice and traditions of training people in such skills as negotiation. One older man referred to being *brought up on Citrine*, a reference to a standard trade union book on the conduct of meetings (Citrine 1952). There are other organisations which train people to be officers such as chair, secretary and treasurer, as in one of the ladies' speaking clubs in Lancaster. Other resources which may be used include self-help books available in city-centre bookshops and occasional adult education courses.

Such styles and choices are not learned formally as part of the educational system (except where school societies and sports clubs offer a model of participation in community activities). Rather, they evolve through the process of participation and are improvised as practical responses to new situations. In this way, there are links with the activities described in the next chapter as becoming expert. There is also a strong oral tradition in all the associations we have looked at in the ways in which such expertise is handed on. This is important for people taking on new literacies and new forms of participation in groups. It is also important where new groups are formed, as shown in the allotment fight example.

This research has been able only to touch the surface of activities in local organisations as one part of our concern with everyday literacies. It raises questions about the range and variety of written texts produced by local groups, the ways they are produced and used, and the barriers which people experience to becoming involved with such activities. In future research it would be worth investigating the extent to which these texts are idiosyncratic to their editors and writers, the range of different newsletter genres, the degree of variation that exists in minute-taking and record-keeping systems and the characteristics of the kinds of collaborative production observed in this study.

Democratic participation

As documented throughout this book, people in Springside differ widely in their formal and informal networks, in their knowledge of how to get access to official representatives and in their confidence in literacy and in communication more generally. In part, this is to do with an individual's position in the community (for example Kevin being a Project employee), the resources they control (as with Jeff having a word processor), and the constraints they live within (as with Helen's evening shift work preventing her getting to meetings).

Not all attempts to get things done in groups are successful. Despite Shirley's know-how and networking with the Council, the petition she organised was not successful in extending the enveloping scheme. The allotment holders' limited success in negotiating with the Council can be contrasted with Cliff's lone battle with the Council against the traffic calming measures; he wrote many letters to individual officers, but to no effect. Janice successfully organised a march protesting about the poll tax but could not sustain it. She had strong informal networks but very little experience of dealing with official agencies or formal organisations; she did not know what to do after her initial action, even though organisations existed which she could have linked with, notably the anti-poll-tax union. She was soon dissuaded from following up her action by both the police and her husband.

These examples illustrate that there is a diversity of ways in which people try to get things done in their locality and in which they make use of literacy in groups. Individual people contribute different parts of it. Some participate by simply being present at meetings, whilst others contribute through talk or actions. The level of participation is greater for those who take on official roles on committees. People do this according to their interests, confidence, resources and expertise, as was the case with the allotment action committee. However, there are also issues about the existing power relationships which may consistently marginalise some people. There is evidence, for example, that, while women participate more in community activities, men predominate in the formal committee hierarchies of such organisations (Central Statistical Office 1993). Bea Campbell (1993) suggests that women develop and prefer open networks which are fluid and informal, whereas men's networks tend to be more closed in terms of membership and formal organisation. Gender patterns such as this, which are rooted in the different cultural experiences, constraints and resources available to men and women, have repercussions in community groups, and may lead to tension and under-representation in decision-making. Deem, Brehony and Heath (1995), for example, have documented the composition of volunteer school governing bodies, studying their decision-making processes, committee structures and communication patterns, and demonstrating how these reproduce gender and cultural inequalities.

The activities described in this chapter are fundamental for understanding the nature of local democratic participation and the role of literacy in this. Many local organisations exist largely outside government influence and statutory control and are largely unsupported by the state. They draw on material resources available in the community. Where such resources are scarce, local organisations are vulnerable. In terms of learning and sustaining the activities, they are improvised, invented and learned in the community and passed down through word of mouth and modelled traditions. There is little in formal education to prepare people for the roles they take on, for instance, or for working together in groups to solve disputes.

The relationship between literacy and local participation and democracy is more complicated than has been typically assumed, for example in the discourses of international campaigns. Literacy has a role in democratic practice, yet literacy practices are not necessarily democratic in their own right. Neither can they, on their own, promote democracy. In terms of participation in formal political structures, people do not have to be literate to have an opinion, or to vote, or to take decisions, but the bureaucracy of the modern state depends upon a literate apparatus to record the vote, to count the vote and to control the voting. As Stevens (1988: 43) argues, in many ways civil society demands, assumes and requires literacy: Anglo-American law, political thought and economic behaviour are premised on the idea of contract and informed consent. Where people do not have the literacies society expects of them, this causes problems both for individuals and for the social institutions which require it.

Simplistic notions of the relation of literacy and democracy constitute a long-standing literacy myth related to the great divide theory (see Graff 1979; Barton 1994). Detailed ethnographic observation reveals ways in which literacy can both support and subvert democratic endeavours: literacy is used in different ways, both to open up activities and to control them. This is mapped out in specific practices, as we have seen here in the annual general meeting of the Allotments Association. The record-keeping and the minutes ensure a democratic accountability, both to the people at the meeting and to the larger membership of the organisation. Everyone had the right to speak and to vote. However, it was not literacy in itself which was democratic; it was the practices. Where the practices are not democratic, literacy can equally well be used to impede participation. In other aspects of the allotment meeting, literacy was controlled, offering only a veneer of democracy: people could not actually ask to see the bank statement which was proffered, without appearing to be rude. Similarly, they could not rummage about in the box of records of the association within the expectations of the meeting. The only copy of the minutes was held by the secretary and not read out. Meetings can be democratic only if people have the resources, including information, to participate. Bureaucratic and technical literacies can be a formidable obstacle to democratic participation for many people, and it takes an effort to break down these exclusionary aspects of literacy, whether by bureaucratic organisations themselves, or by the community groups which inadvertently develop procedures that restrict the participation of people with limited education. In the local residents' association, local participation was grafted on to an organisation which had been set up without the consultation or informed consent of the residents and which ultimately they did not control.

This returns us to issues of governance. In their democratic endeavours many local organisations can be contrasted with the Housing Action Project, which had no real roots in local democracy. In a term used by Konrad Elsdon, this was really a 'Gongo', a Government-Organised Non-Government Organisation (Elsdon *et al.* 1995: 150). There is a need to examine the non-accountability of the many official and quasi-official organisations which now impinge on people's local lives. Literacy in its administrative, bureaucratic forms without accountability can be limiting, alienating and stifling. In this example it was also unsustainable, in that the residents' association collapsed soon after the demise of the Housing Project. Dealing with literacy defined by an organisation for its own purposes is very different from the processes of democratic literacy described in other examples here, where people have competence in and retain control over the record-keeping, publicity and decision-making processes involved in running an organisation.

The examples given in this chapter demonstrate the validity of regarding literacy as a communal resource, rather than simply a set of skills located in individuals. The community had resources for resisting the land developers, in the form of time to research the issue, funds of knowledge, contacts in local government, physical resources like computers and access to photocopiers, space for meetings, skills to produce posters, advertisements. However, no individual had all these resources, and it was in combination that they were effective. The local community of Springside did not have the resources to sustain the opposition to the poll tax, nor to deal with the courts, although the community of Lancaster at large, networked with national organisations, did have such resources.

What has been described in this chapter is culturally specific, drawing on traditions of volunteerism and reciprocity in local relations. These local groups underpin political participation at the local level and were important in Shirley's entering into a more formal role as a local councillor. As Finnegan (1989) has shown, the network of informal, community resources and the participation that support these activities underpin the emergence of experts and specialist professionals in the case of music. Similarly, Hutchison and Feist (1991) argue the importance of local amateur groups associated with arts and crafts in supporting professional activity. This is also likely to be true for sporting activities. As well as contributing to leisure and quality of life in a neighbourhood, therefore, the web of literacies in local organisations has much broader significance.

13

BECOMING EXPERT
Literacy and sense making

Introduction

While literacy is used for collective goals as described in the previous chapter, it is also a resource that people, both as individuals and as members of groups, can draw on to make sense of events in their own lives. This has been a strong emergent theme in our data. Sense making is motivated by the search for meaning and problem solving, either in a short-term, instrumental way or in a longer-term exploration of patterns in life-events of a broader, more philosophical kind. We found this theme expressed in our data in a number of quite different ways. Literacies are used to solve the practical problems which arise unpredictably in everyday life. They are used as a transformative tool to promote or to cope with personal change. Literacies are used to satisfy people's desires for information and explanation; to pursue leisure interests and enthusiasms; as a means of gaining control over their environment; and to create or maintain a sense of time and place. In this chapter we identify some of these different forms of sense making in people's lives. We then bring them together in a discussion of the vernacular knowledge which people are drawing upon and extending as they develop local expertise.

Becoming expert

Solving problems

Several people used reading and writing when confronted with major problems in their lives. Many of the people we interviewed had experienced situations in their day-to-day life that had launched them into a new area of learning in which they mustered all the resources they could find, including literacy. In this section we will describe the range of everyday problems that people confronted with the help of literacy. They have in common that they are to do with encounters with social institutions, and we will mention in turn medicine, the law, the state and commerce and the educational system.

Firstly there were a number of examples related to ill-health where people became expert in the treatment and understanding of particular ailments. Our case study of Cliff in Chapter 8 provides a complex example of this, related to his migraine and hearing problems. We have other examples relating to cancer, back problems and brain tumours. Some are personal examples from the adults we have talked to. Others are stories about serious health problems suffered by their children or other relatives, and which whole families have become concerned with. Such incidents are part of the currency of everyday conversations in the hairdresser's, the chemist's shop, work-places, at kitchen tables and on street corners.

The expertise people develop in relation to illness can be extensive and has many dimensions: knowledge about how to recognise symptoms, the effects of medication and other therapies, medical and institutional procedures, specialisms of medical personnel, medical vocabulary, procedure and rules for obtaining sickness benefit and compensation. All the means discussed elsewhere in this book are applied to learning about medical conditions: consulting other people, reading books and newsletters, borrowed or bought, deciphering official information, filling in forms and writing letters. When people are involved in particularly serious or prolonged illnesses they may go on to become involved in self-help groups or in counselling others. At first they use such groups for information and support; later they shift to providing the information and support or helping in other ways. One couple were involved in counselling people with cancer, and a woman whose son had died now belonged to a group *Compassionate Friends*. This is an area where the knowledge seems very specific, is often technically complex. People investigate such areas only when a problem impinges on their lives and they move rapidly from a position of having very little knowledge or background to one where they become experts.

Another common group of practical problems are legal problems and encounters with the police, courts and insurance companies. A variety of legal problems arise for individuals, and sometimes more general issues affect large groups of people, as happened when many people in Lancaster who did not pay their poll tax in 1990 faced summonses to the local court for the first time in their lives. Much information and advice was passed on informally about how to deal with the forms and how people could defend themselves from prosecution; Janice described this happening in her hairdressing salon. Extensive photocopied sheets entitled 'Guidelines for Court' were circulated by members of the Anti-Poll-Tax League in a kind of do-it-yourself legal defence kit; this collective activity was a mixture of information and advice-giving and mobilising opposition to the tax, supplemented by public meetings and demonstrations. Similar activities were going on around the country, and the literacies involved in these oppositional and self-educational tactics provide a striking counterpoint to the official forms, explanatory leaflets and letters coming from the Council offices during the same period. In the dispute over the allotment land described in the previous chapter people also acted together to pool resources and developed new kinds of expertise, and we have observed similar processes occurring in other disputes over land ownership and use.

During the research one person, Joanna, had her house broken into just after she had moved in and many different things were stolen. She described to us the time-consuming paperwork and procedures in graphic detail. She had to make an inventory of what had been stolen, make a police report, and fill in the insurance company forms. To assemble the documents needed as evidence of insurance claims she had to find receipts and other financial details; this was especially a problem for second-hand items and gifts. Many of these practices were new to her. This paperwork had to be carried out in response to events which were anxiety-provoking and involved emotional trauma. Not surprisingly, such activities are often experienced as a strain, especially where, as in the insurance claim or benefit claim, aspects of the private and unregulated realm of the personal and home sphere are submitted to public scrutiny and documentation. She did not want to do this and she did not become a general expert in this area, but she gained enough procedural knowledge to be a useful resource for other people in the future. Such knowledge may already reside in the community, so that Brenda, who was a clerical worker and had at one time worked in an insurance office, had helped people with insurance claims. She is a good example of the fact that part of the networks of support people have for solving these practical problems involves using any work-related expertise that people have.

Anita Wilson in her research in Lancaster with prisoners has documented a number of examples where inmates work from their cells to challenge court procedures or to protect themselves from unjust or irregular legal practices. In mastering the information they need for such self-protection, literacy plays a key role, especially in interpreting and writing official letters, consulting books and tracking down documents which they have a right to access (Wilson 1994: 1996). We have collected several dramatic examples of this from national newspapers, including the case of Kevin Callan, a 37-year-old man who had been jailed for the murder of a 3-year-old child. In setting out to prove his innocence he had to challenge both the medical world and the legal world. He did this from within prison. He had left school without educational qualifications and is quoted as saying:

> I wasn't exactly an academic. But I had plenty of time on my hands and used a medical dictionary . . . Within a couple of months I'd got about a dozen books on the go. One title led to another and I just kept asking the library to order more. I read the same books over and over again, upside down and back to front and even dreamt about them.
>
> (Guardian, 7 April 1995)

He also began writing letters to medical and legal experts about what he had discovered about the neuropathology relevant to his case. His research eventually led to his acquittal and the discrediting of the pathologist who had been a key witness in his trial.

Another common group of problems which people confront and have to solve are employment-related problems. These include searching for and applying for jobs, dealing with official bureaucracy when registering as unemployed, claiming welfare benefit entitlements or tax refunds; and setting up small businesses. Cliff, for example, was claiming Disability Benefit, Mumtaz's husband was unemployed; Janice established her own hairdressing business. Although we did not concentrate on this kind of literacy in the current study, in other research in the north-west we have looked in detail at one of these domains, that of job search among long-term unemployed adults (see Davies 1994; Hamilton and Davies 1993). This project looked at the barriers faced by long-term unemployed people as they looked for jobs, and as they negotiated the complexities of the employment services with their increasing systems of monitoring job applications and insisting on attendance at courses to 'help' people back to work.

This project vividly revealed how people were forced to become expert, not perhaps at finding jobs but certainly in negotiating the demands of the employment service and maintaining their benefits under rapidly changing regimes of bureaucratic rules. As well as making use of more formal sources of advice, claimants and their friends and family shared this knowledge and supported each other in filling in forms and attending difficult interviews. Particular people were known as being knowledgeable about this area. In terms of literacy difficulties, employment services staff often identify the lack of basic literacy skills of claimants as a barrier to getting jobs. Claimants themselves were much less likely to agree with this and to identify lack of jobs or discrimination on grounds of age, health or ethnicity as the main barriers. They saw the employment service demands as creating unnecessary paperwork, which was often experienced as threatening because of its legal status and its mismatch with claimants' own goals. As an example of this, people regarded the requirement to write and show evidence of speculative letters of application as a futile strategy for obtaining a job, since many of them relied more on personal contact and word of mouth for news of job vacancies. They learned how to do this because they were required to, but they did not connect up the activity with actually getting a job.

A fourth area where people confronted problems concerned parenting and problems associated with their children especially around schooling. There were a number of accounts in our data of people's encounters with schools, where as parents they were acting on behalf of their children and dealing with systems which they found quite mystifying and opaque. Their efforts to obtain resources for their children were often frustrating and consumed a great deal of their time and energy. We have already seen in

Chapter 6 how Shirley managed to speed up the statementing process for her son, who had been diagnosed as dyslexic. Shirley's story illustrates her confident use of many different kinds of resources, not exclusively literacy, and effective use of personal contacts to get an understanding of how the system she had to deal with worked. We have also had the examples of Mumtaz and of Patrick learning how to deal with the system of allocating children to schools. Patrick did not know how to appeal against his son's treatment. However, by the time his younger daughter came to start at primary school, he was well aware of what to do and successfully advocated on her behalf: *I got my way. I thought, 'it'll never happen again, not to me'.*

One telling thing about many of these experiences is that they involved dealing with or confronting professional experts and specialised systems of knowledge which people have to define themselves and their own knowledge and purposes in relation to. They do not know the literacy practices of these discourse communities. These practices often involve writing and responding to a series of formal letters, and dealing with official documentation. People do not know whom to write to. They need to know not just how to phrase or interpret the letters but something about the structure of the organisation the letters will circulate within, who needs to get copies, where to apply pressure and what kind of support they are entitled to. Forms present particular difficulties, each one raising different problems. As we have shown, these are not easy things to do, even for someone with confidence and resolve. Shirley succeeded with the help of a head teacher. It took Cliff a long time to challenge his doctor. Diane, Patrick and Mumtaz described frustrating and stubborn struggles to get what they perceived to be their rights for their children's education, and in all these cases they were only partially successful in their efforts. What these different sorts of problems have in common is that they demonstrate that anyone can become confronted by crisis or an intractable problem that gives them, overnight, the occasion and motivation to become an expert.

Personal change

Reading and writing are used by some people in our study for understanding the self and the world, for exploring identity and working ideas out when change is in process. We have seen in Shirley's editorials for the residents' association newsletter how writing can signal shifting identities and allegiances. This public form of writing at a time when Shirley was beginning to move into the more formal world of local politics was an important part of the process of change she was going through.

Diary-keeping and other kinds of personal writing seem to be particularly affected by times of personal stress and change. We found examples both of people starting to write and of people being unable to write during such times. Tina wrote a diary only when she was depressed: *If I'm feeling particularly low or whatever, or if I'm feeling in a turmoil, I'll jot something down, you know, questions and things like that. And then just screw them up and throw them away so nobody can see them.* Another person, Dick, used writing to cope with changes in his life, involving illness, unemployment and separation, and he kept a diary for twelve months: *It was putting in a diary, putting on paper what I couldn't say; it was a good idea . . . but it drained me . . . it was mainly private thoughts.* It was the first time since leaving school that that he had written anything except applications for jobs. On the other hand, Rita had the opposite reaction to the role of writing and personal problems: *You can't read and write when you are going through a bad time.* When her husband left her and her mother died, she felt she was *living on her nerves* and she never picked up a book or a pen.

At the time we interviewed her, Tina was just in the process of becoming converted to radical evangelical Christianity; it was filling a void in her life which she had recognised for a long time. This had put her into personal turmoil, especially as her grandparents, to whom she was very close, were devout Catholics and she was becoming an active Protestant: *I'm just in a constant battle at the moment between God and the world . . . I think about God constantly.* Although in the past she had enjoyed reading fiction and women's magazines, she had now narrowed her reading down to the Bible and religious books and pamphlets which a friend from work passed on to her. Even junk mail, which she would have once looked through, she now threw away without looking at, because it was a distraction from reading the Bible.

INTERVIEWER: *And do you read stories now? Do you read fiction?*

TINA: *No. The only book I'm really interested in reading is the Bible. That's the only one that means anything.*

INTERVIEWER: *That's because it's taken over your life at the moment, is it?*

TINA: *Mm, yeah. Well for ever I hope . . . My friend is always lending me books . . . the girl I work with. She lends me a lot of little booklets that she gets to do with being a born-again Christian . . . Billy Graham* [and various others].

INTERVIEWER: *So a book like that . . . would you read that right through or would you . . . ?*

TINA: *I'd read it right through. And it wouldn't take me very long because once I start reading it and I'm interested, I just can't put a book down.*

Tina's use of religious texts as transformative can be contrasted with Mumtaz's reading: her devotional reading was to sustain existing beliefs (as in Heath 1983), not to change her life.

The tenacity of Tina's quest for personal meaning, which was reflected in her reading habits, stands out, but it is not the only instance we found in our study. Another example of an urgent quest for meaning was Eddie's interest in becoming expert in the martial arts, as in Aside 13.1. Karate and other martial arts were mentioned by other people in our sample. Eddie was someone who finds both reading and writing difficult. He attended a special school and, in connection with this, was badly bullied by other children in the neighbourhood. This experience made him very agitated about protecting himself and his family from violence and the need to find some way of gaining control over others. His discovery of judo and, later on, other martial arts, seemed to answer this central preoccupation and quest in his life. In Eddie's case an interest in the physical skills of martial arts led him on to the literature about the associated mental and spiritual disciplines. His enthusiasm also led him to introduce his children, including his four-year-old daughter, to karate classes. When Eddie described these interests during the interview he became the expert, explaining to the interviewer his detailed knowledge.

Adults often use education and the writing associated with it as a site of personal change. Lynne's everyday life changed in many ways when she returned to college (as described in Barton and Padmore 1991: 68–9). Education changes people, and people use education to make changes in their lives. Often reading and writing are central to these changes. We have given examples from adult Basic Education, but this is true in all areas of education. Roz Ivanic (1998) provides examples of the struggles over identity in the academic writing of mature students at university.

Accessing information

Some people appeared to have an insatiable curiosity for information and to pursue their interests by using literacy and other available media. They were hungry for information, critical and curious about the world. The motivation behind this varied and took a different form and focus depending on age, gender, confidence with literacy, available time and other resources.

We saw this in Patrick, for example, a self-taught reader who emphasised his desire for independence as a motivating force. Getting hold of information was very important to him. He was curious about the world. His interests included: science, technology, nature, travel, history, sport, the martial arts, antiques, human behaviour and religious beliefs. He was a very active person: on top of a full-time job as a manual worker, he was also a part-time physical training instructor, and he enjoyed clay pigeon shooting and cycling, as well as following other sports. Over the years he had pursued a number of different sporting interests and read up about them, in books and magazines, as he went along.

Patrick used reading, observation, watching television, his own experience and discussion with friends to develop his interests and expand his knowledge. When he got an interest he would use every method he could think of to find out more about it. If he knew someone who had personal knowledge and experience of a subject, a local expert on shooting for example, he

---

Aside 13.1 Martial arts

INTERVIEWER: . . . *I don't know how you pronounce that, what's that?*

EDDIE: *Tao.*

INTERVIEWER: *'The Tao of Long Life'. 'The Chinese art of Chang-Ling'.*

EDDIE: *The Chinese is best. The Japanese copied everything. This is . . .*

INTERVIEWER: . . . *the 'I-Ching'.*

EDDIE: *This is mathematical, that's why I can't . . . I haven't done that, me sister done them.*

INTERVIEWER: *Your sister's interested in this sort of stuff too?*

EDDIE: *Oh no, no, I've talked to her. 'Cause I'm obsessive about it I give her the book. She said 'I don't really want it' and all that, but she started trying to follow it. It's supposed to be your future . . . What I read I can understand. It's like there's complementary forces, you know, I can understand that, but, it's the figures, you see, all this lot . . . all these lines and all that, I can't follow that . . . mathematical equations.*

INTERVIEWER: *And is she mathematical, your sister?*

EDDIE: *Yeah, well she's trying to start her own business up. You see, it tells you, hexagrams . . . I'm really interested in that.*

INTERVIEWER: *Where did you get hold of those books?*

EDDIE: *Well it's just local shops, Waterstone's.*

INTERVIEWER: *And, what, do you go and get them? Or do you . . . ?*

JAN: *Well, we go down together, and if we haven't got the money, he'll write it down and I'll go and get it later on.*

INTERVIEWER: *'Yin and Yang'.*

---

would pick their brains. He seemed to value particularly the knowledge gained through personal contacts. Reading was just one way of getting hold of information – and reading is not always reliable. Patrick saw himself as a critical reader and, like Shirley, said he didn't bother with newspapers because he doesn't trust them. He saw them as an unreliable source of information and got his news and other information from television. He described himself as an active viewer, watching things which made him think and which taught him something. He enjoyed documentaries and followed programmes on wildlife, science and technology. He had a good memory: *I find that being able to read now and the television . . . watching the right programmes . . . I soak it up like a sponge.*

People pursue hobbies and interests, becoming knowledgeable about areas such as birds, plants, heraldry, embroidery. These may be lifelong interests, or people may pass through them to different interests. Children as well as adults may get involved with serial enthusiasms, interests which they pursue intensely for a while and which then become less important. We

EDDIE: *That's the main one, that's the main one I'm interested in, 'Yin and Yang'.*

INTERVIEWER: *'Fighters, the martial arts magazine'; 'World Ju-jitsu'.*

EDDIE: *Ju-jitsu. I know, I mean I can look at a tape, or movie on telly, and tell you what style it is, but, nobody else can at work, even the people that's doing it. I can, I can tell if it's taikwondo, which is Korean, or kung fu . . . I can't tell the styles with kung fu, there's too many of them. Or shotokan, karate . . . ju-jitsu, aikido . . .*

INTERVIEWER: *How did this interest start? I mean, I can see how these things, the I-Ching, Yin and Yang, this came out of . . .*

EDDIE: *Well, that's coming higher, that's going past martial arts.*

INTERVIEWER: *Yeah, but how did you first get interested in the martial arts?*

EDDIE: *Well I don't know, it's getting smacked in the mouth and you want to block it and things like that, you know . . . this lad picked on me and beat us up . . . And he did the Irish Whip . . .*

INTERVIEWER: *And what's the Irish whip?*

EDDIE: *Well, you get hold of the arm, and you bring it round, and then you bring it back, and bring it round again.*

INTERVIEWER: *So like a windmill movement, yeah.*

EDDIE: *But your arm only goes so far, and you bring it back and it locks it. And it, it locks it that way, and whips it, Irish whip, and it, brings the whole body right round. And he dropped this lad on the floor, waited till he got up, and then he, showed me again how to do it. I said, 'Well, what is it, what is it?' He says, 'Judo.' I said, 'Learn me that then.' So he dropped me on the floor, you know, but that was the first thing I saw was judo. I used to practise on me brother . . . I think that's why he doesn't like me.*

saw this, for example, in Mumtaz's son and his enthusiasm for tropical fish. As well as getting books from the library and watching videos, he would read the same battered magazines repeatedly, memorising their contents and claiming to get new information from them each time. Some people were content with their interests and hobbies, such as having a pet or a car. Others felt they had to know everything about their chosen interest, and to be constantly finding more out about it.

For some people, acquiring facts seems to be an end and a pleasure in itself, not linked to an outside interest; people referred to playing popular games like *Trivial Pursuit,* and watching television programmes like *Mastermind.* Quiz leagues have been common in pubs locally for years, before *Trivial Pursuit* made them a national pastime. Every Monday team captains come to a pub in the city centre to collect sealed envelopes containing this week's questions. Then, half an hour later, teams throughout the city in nearly every pub compete with each other over a pint of beer. League tables of results are published in the local paper on Fridays, alongside football results and darts results. Such games depend on knowledge of facts obtained from books, newspapers and television. This cult of the fact largely figured as entertainment in our data, but it has a more serious side as a demonstration of cultural insiderness and knowledgeability. This was represented in some of the books of facts people had in their homes. 'Knowledge as facts' represents one popular view of what knowledge is, and it is somewhat akin to the idea of 'cultural literacy' promoted by Hirsch (1988).

Comments by people such as Rita and Cliff show a degree of wonderment at the gaps in educated people's knowledge; this parallels researchers' and teachers' incredulity that many adults cannot read a bus timetable or spell words such as 'occurrence'. Rita was amazed that one of the people whose house she cleaned, a lecturer at the university, did not know how to fill in a pools form. Cliff had a number of stories about the stupidity of academics:

CLIFF: *I once went on a Quiz League and . . . there was a Professor on and they asked him 'What's sold in crans?' He said, 'Cranberries'. Now, can you believe that from somebody from University? Do you know what they sell in crans?*
INTERVIEWER: *No.*
CLIFF: *Fish. Straw baskets aren't they . . . that they put fish in. And they said 'cranberries'. And this is supposed to be somebody with intelligence. I thought, 'Well, there's a chance for me somewhere'.*

For some people, part of the motivation in the pursuit of information seems to be to keep control over and organise their environment: these were people like Harry's son who had copies of train and bus timetables and was turned to by others for travel information. Another example was the daily record Cliff kept of the temperature. Related to this is the person such as June, who keeps up with the news and who is tuned to radio and television news throughout the day, as well as reading morning and evening papers.

Creating a sense of time and place

Another group of activities we recorded during this study relate to asserting or creating identity, either as an individual or as a member of some grouping. The motivation for engaging in this kind of literacy practice may vary across the lifespan and certainly across cultural and personal circumstances. We mention here a few examples we came across. Harry had been researching both his family history in the north-west of England and also local history about Lancaster. Beginning to write his life history was also a way of asserting a sense of time and place. Other people were using diary writing for similar purposes. Several people, including June, Terry and Mumtaz, documented their lives through photographs and were keen to show them to visitors, going through them and explaining them. People mentioned family records which had been passed on to them and which they had kept;

these included birth, death and marriage certificates, memorial cards, family bibles, newspaper cuttings, membership cards of clubs, a birthday book, cycling diaries, an army discharge certificate.

The death of a relative is one occasion which may bring to light records not known about before, scraps of information that may not have been orally passed on. In Jake's family different members of the family had each charted separate branches of the family tree and they swapped information. Sometimes one member of a family will write an autobiographical account: Maria's aunt wrote a long piece about the life of her parents for Maria's mother who had grown up after the family had been scattered because of the death of her own mother. This was passed on to Maria when her own mother died.

People's interest in documenting their lives very often extended beyond their own life, and was part of a process of situating themselves within the wider context of family, cultural group, nation and even world history. In the case of minority cultural groups, or those who have been displaced, this can recreate a sense of identity. (See Horovitz's study of Jewish memorial books for an example of this (1995) and the example given by Weinstein-Shr (1993) among Hmong refugees in the United States.)

The activities of personal and family record-keeping merge and can cover diaries of various sorts, family bibles, family trees, autobiography and accounts of local history. Mumtaz had displayed on the walls of her front room a mixture of cultural artefacts from Britain and from Gujarat, some secular and some religious. To investigate the past, people make use of the wide variety of public documents and archives which exist, including school registers, church and registry office records, the Lloyds register for ships, customs registers, wills and census returns. Such public records are, however, selective of certain kinds of officially recognised activities and achievements. Other, vernacular archives exist, kept by individuals, in private houses. Many groups, organisations and sports clubs had a sense of history and kept written records of their activities over time; the Dukes Playhouse, for instance, had an honorary archivist. These interests in creating a sense of time and place link in with the widespread activities of community publishing groups (Mace 1995; O'Rourke 1994), oral history and reminiscence work with older people (Duffin 1990) and local history adult education courses and publications. As one participant in a family history course commented: *It was to me a moving feeling to open a musty church register and view the signature, sometimes with only an 'x' as a mark, of my ancestors.*

Vernacular knowledge

There are a number of implications from these observations about how people use literacy to make sense of the world. In all these areas people are engaging with literate worlds. This is particularly true when people confront problems with the social institutions of medicine, the law, education and government bureaucracy. These are social institutions which function through particular kinds of literate activity: to interact with these institutions and to have access to the knowledge they control, people use literacy. Also, in making sense of their lives and in changing their lives we have seen how the literate world of books and records is often of central importance. Often people are entering new worlds of literacy and engaging in unfamiliar literacy practices. Again, when using education to make changes in their lives, people are entering a world mediated by literacy in specific ways.

In making sense of the world, people both draw upon and create areas of local knowledge or *vernacular knowledge*. In Lancaster the areas of vernacular knowledge which we have identified include home economics and budgeting, repair and maintenance, child care and health, gardening, cooking, pets and animal care, and family and local history. Some people had also developed knowledge of legal and medical topics. These are just some of the areas of vernacular knowledge in existence. When people know about a specialised area, it is probably important to distinguish between different kinds of local knowledge. Some people have procedural knowledge of a topic, in that they know how to do something in a straightforward way; or they may have a more complex relation to the knowledge which enables them to explain, pass on, question and reflect upon the knowledge. (See Antaki 1988; Wynn 1992; Myers 1996). Much of this knowledge has significant local dimensions to it, in that it is specific to this locality. Gardening knowledge, for example, is inherently local, dependent as it is on local climate and soil conditions. General knowledge about education is tempered by specific knowledge about the schools and colleges of Lancaster. Medical knowledge about illness contains beliefs about local conditions, down to such details as the efficacy of specific medical specialists in the area. In the next chapter we demonstrate how this local knowledge is an important component of vernacular practices.

In his research with Mexican-American households in the United States, Luis Moll (1994) refers to 'funds of knowledge' in communities which parallel what we have called here vernacular knowledge. Funds of knowledge are the practical exchanges and responses to needs for information and resources shared across families, between siblings, neighbours, friends. Our areas of vernacular knowledge can be compared with those which Moll identifies, although he uses some different terms. Moll found funds of knowledge in areas such as agriculture, economics, construction, religion, arts and repair. Others have referred to 'popular knowledge'.

Local expertise

In the examples of this chapter we have seen some of the ways in which people draw upon and extend their areas of vernacular knowledge and how some people become experts through their sense making activities. Everyone appeared to have their specialised areas of knowledge, although they may have different relationships to that knowledge. As a result of their activities and the information they acquire, some people become known in their family or neighbourhood as experts in certain areas and others go to them for advice and to get problems solved. We have repeatedly come across these examples of local expertise. We have observed them, people have talked about them and, sometimes, people have lapsed into expert mode when talking to us, changing the dynamics of the interactions by giving lengthy explanations of a topic to the interviewer, scattered with technical terms and details, as in Eddie's description of martial arts in Aside 13.1. There were also examples of this from Shirley, Cliff, June and others.

These examples illustrate also the importance of informal learning strategies and the support that is available from other people in the community. In local expertise the knowledge is situated, and the learning is situated. This is articulated most clearly in Chaiklin and Lave (1993), and we agree with them in not distinguishing learning and ordinary participation in human activities. Learning is possible in all activities and it becomes defined as changing participation in activities and participating in new activities. To paraphrase their view on learning and its relation to activities (Chaiklin and Lave 1993: 5–6): situated activity involves changes in knowledge and action and these changes are central to what we mean by learning; participating in activities is engaging in learning; learning is effectively people's changing participation in culturally designed settings of life, or, as we prefer to call them, events. (See also Percy (1988) on the different forms of formal and informal learning which take place in voluntary groups.)

Across all these examples we have seen how expertise is uneven and it is developed in relation to real-life contingencies. The strength of motivation, the imperatives for learning are so strong that people tackle very complex materials'and draw on all the resources available. The unevenness of the spread of expertise on any topic means that there are great differences in individuals' knowledge. Combined with the fact that people do not attempt just what is thought of as appropriate to their so-called level of literacy, this makes it difficult to talk in terms of levels or to measure adults' literacy in a generalised way.

Local expertise and professional knowledge

The observations about the nature of literacy practices and becoming expert link into current social theory, where Giddens (1991), Smith (1988) and others have argued that the institutionalisation of knowledge and the specialisation of expertise through professional communities is a key feature of modern societies, and one which helps form a sense of identity. This applies to areas such as medical, educational and legal knowledge. Parenting is a good example of the conflict between traditional and professional knowledge. It is often a conflict between oral and literate traditions, but we would argue that it is more complex than that: local expertise today involves integrating oral forms of knowledge with written forms, along with other complex ways of knowing.

What counts as useful and valid knowledge and expertise in the local area may be subject to different criteria from what counts in the professional or academic realm. This brings us back to the issue of what is culturally validated and privileged knowledge and what is not. The professionalisation of expertise is enshrined and reinforced in the education system. This happens in several ways: through the institutional separation of school and college from the community, 'the closed doors' of the classroom referred to by Jo Weinberger (1996: 110); through separating the roles of teachers from those of parents or mentors; and, in particular, through the elevation of book-based knowledge as a kind of disembodied received wisdom which has to be absorbed by the student. This has not always been the case, as Johnson (1983) has pointed out: in the eighteenth and nineteenth centuries before compulsory education for children, there was much less separation of education from the rest of everyday activity. Adults and children learned alongside one another; printed information circulated in pubs and coffee houses and reading rooms and was informally shared, often read out loud.

People making sense of the world will also try to use resources that challenge the normal rules of the social regulation of texts, using texts which they would normally not think of being for them, for example when consulting the medical books or legal documents which are normally seen only by a professional. In an extension of the terms used by De Certeau (1984), this can be seen as a kind of trespassing into other discourse communities and poaching or appropriating texts for their own use. Complex material is used even by people who have considerable difficulties with literacy. An example of this was Eddie studying martial arts and Eastern philosophies. Like everyone, people with difficulties reading and writing may be dealing with unfamiliar literacies, and they learn about the literacies at the same time as they obtain the content they need.

Many people in our study were ambivalent about professional experts, deferring to them through lack of confidence, but privately sceptical about their knowledge and skills. They distinguished their own expertise from the expertise of professionals. We have already seen some examples of this in the section on accessing information. In addition, Patrick commented on academics writing about Lancaster. He felt that they did not really know the places they were writing about and they remained superficial: *they've thrown me the edges . . . but where's the meat?* Harry contrasted book knowledge and practical knowledge, arguing that his son would be able to pass the fire service exams but that would not make him a good fire-fighter.

When people assert or develop themselves as experts, and especially where this involves confronting or challenging professional experts, then this is a key process in redefining and empowering the self. Patrick said, *I've found out your own ideas are just as good as anybody else's and you should do what you think is right.* There can also be a redefining of people's relationships, and home dynamics can change. This was apparent in the tensions when some women returned to work or to education. There can also be a redefining of relationships where children have areas of knowledge which is useful in the home, such as computing, or in Mumtaz's household where there was differential access to particular written and spoken languages. This relates to the concept of authorship, of literally seeing oneself as an authority. Becoming an authority, seeing oneself as capable of this and as having a valid standpoint from which to deal with others, to evaluate and challenge other authorities, is the key to becoming a critical user of literacy, to using literacy in an empowering way.

Auto-didacts

We can see links between these findings and reports from other sources of long traditions of auto-didacts, people who are in some sense self-taught and who are self-directed learners. William Stout, mentioned in Chapter 2, improved on his elementary education by *reading religious books, or history or geography, surveying or other mathematical science* whenever he had spare time. In our study Patrick is one person who would be regarded as an auto-didact, and other people were self-directed in their learning. There is a whole strand of liberal adult education that has been built around this tradition (see Hoggart 1957; Keddie 1980) and which shows how people change and grow as adults and can be further supported in these activities.

Ursula Howard (1991) uses autobiographical sources from the eighteenth and nineteenth centuries to trace these traditions of self-education. She shows how the common stereotype of the auto-didact as a lone and lonely learner is far from áccurate. Whilst at some points individuals may pursue their interests in isolation, very often they join with others in mutual self-help groups or have the support of informal mentors – a phenomenon that we already mentioned. What they have in common is that they make their learning their own. There is also evidence from other studies of the frequent intentional learning that adults engage in outside of formal educational settings, either alone or in self-organised groups. Alan Tough (1979), for example, has specifically looked at projects of personal development which people may engage in over long periods of time, many of which would not be offered by formal adult education. His observations support our view that that this kind of self-motivated intentional learning is a frequent type of activity; it is not marginal or idiosyncratic to the selection of people in our study.

Even where people do successfully acquire the facts and skills to become expert in a topic area, they may still find themselves outsiders to the discourse community of educated people. James Gee argues that a person may know a great deal about a subject but may not be accepted as a member of that discourse community if they do not display

> the right type of talk, writing, values, attitudes and behaviours . . . 'Auto-didacts' are precisely people who, while often extremely knowledgeable, trained themselves and thus were trained outside a process of group practice and socialisation. They are almost never accepted as 'insiders;' 'members of the club' . . . Our Western focus on individualism makes us constantly forget the importance of having been properly socialised.
>
> (Gee 1992: 115)

There are degrees to which people are self-directed learners. Some people are auto-didacts or self-directed learners, and this is a central part of their approach to life; for others it is less important. Nevertheless, everyone contributes to and relates to areas of vernacular knowledge. However, we should not romanticise the issues surrounding the process of becoming expert. It is still true that people cannot always get access to the information they need; that certain kinds of knowledge are hard to pick up casually or without specialised support or resources and people can be misinformed or half-informed, either knowingly or unknowingly. Support which is offered may be insecure, untrustworthy and inexpert itself, as in Hamilton and Davies (1993); Ziegahn (1991). Some people do not learn systematically in situations of practical need, especially where they are confused, are put in a deliberately powerless position, and are struggling with the stresses induced by limited time, money or physical health, as in Taylor (1996). For these reasons there will always be a role for professional scribes, advisers, advocates and mediators. Likewise, access to information and other resources is important, including information about how the council and schooling system works, and processes of appealing against government decisions, as well as the availability of physical resources such as word processors and photocopiers.

Vernacular knowledge is valid in its own right. It starts from its own purposes, and addresses its own problems. It is with this local knowledge that people interact with official knowledge and institutions. Self-organised groups of auto-didacts, or local experts, though, can make positive use of this process of socialisation and offer the possibility of developing alternative discourse communities to the professional experts. These can eventually become powerful sources of authority in their own right, like, in Lancaster, a women's health group and the dyslexia group. Similarly, as we have seen earlier, ordinary people form themselves into groups to confront legal and bureaucratic organisations, such as the group formed by local residents to protect their allotments and the one which purchased their gardens from the railway company. These then strengthen the base of vernacular knowledge which is available in the community.

14

VERNACULAR LITERACIES

Vernacular practices

In bringing together strands from the earlier chapters the concept of vernacular literacies provides a useful summary term for much of what we have uncovered. Vernacular literacy practices are essentially ones which are not regulated by the formal rules and procedures of dominant social institutions and which have their origins in everyday life. As we will see, vernacular literacies are in fact hybrid practices which draw on a range of practices from different domains. As part of summarising what people do with reading and writing in their everyday lives we will give some examples of these vernacular practices before discussing more fully what we mean by the term and before contrasting them with other practices.

In this book we have identified six areas of everyday life where reading and writing are of central importance. This set of practices develops on from lists of functions sometimes provided in earlier studies (such as Heath 1983; Taylor and Dorsey-Gaines 1988). As discussed in Chapter 1, it is hard to identify functions on the basis of particular types of text. We have found that any reading or writing activity can have multiple and overlapping significance in different people's lives. People engage differently with a given text depending on the context in which they encounter or produce it, their motivations and the cultural resources they bring to it.

The first three areas of everyday practice are ones which in a general sense we knew about when we began and which were unsurprising; in the study we have amplified them with examples and with greater detail. These areas are organising life, personal communication and private leisure. Many examples of these were given in Chapter 9. To these three areas of everyday practice we add three further ones: these are documenting life, sense making and social participation. These are practices whose significance we came to realise during the study, in the process of collecting and analysing the data. We will go through these areas one at a time. Just as our research started out from observations and interviews with individual people, we start from people's individual lives, activities and goals but move on to view these practices more broadly as part of social organisation.

(1) **Organising life.** Much day-to-day practical organisation involves literacy. People have notice-boards for details of appointments and social activities; also calendars and appointment diaries, address books and lists of phone numbers. Within the home there are places where letters, pens and scrap paper are kept. Different sorts of books are kept in different rooms, and the order on the shelf may be important, reflecting particular classification systems. People keep complex records of weekly finances; transient handwritten notes are also important for organising life, whether they are for shopping, lists of things to do or lists of people to pray for. There may be records kept of cards and letters which are sent and received, and lists of Christmas cards sent. Many of these activities are the literacy chores of everyday life. Some organisation is done by individuals for themselves, while other aspects are for the family, the household or other group. These administrative activities are elementary forms of bureaucracy, but so long as they are not part of a set of formalised institutional rules they could never become a real bureaucracy. As we discuss below, however, some of these activities, such as dealing with bills and tax returns, are responding to literacy demands for accountability from institutions outside the home, in which case people are incorporated into bureaucratic literacies.

(2) **Personal communication.** People send cards and letters to relatives and friends. All sorts of letters are sent and received and letters come in various guises: they can be for family news, to start or end relationships, to invite, to thank. They can be fan mail to pop stars, or enquiries to unknown people. They can be friendly or threatening, signed or anonymous, serious or jocular; they can be collaboratively written and read, recorded on video or audio tape or elaborately decorated. They may be especially important for people at times when they are isolated from family and friends. There are many sorts of personal communication. We include in this category the various photocopied sheets which people send to each other, some scurrilous, 'some humorous, some rude. There is a range of cards for birthdays, Christmas and anniversaries, as well as ones for occasions when someone is ill, an exam is passed or a baby is born. Some are commercial, some are individually made at home; often they are mixed, with handwritten words added to the printed message. In addition, personal communication is not just letters and cards. People leave notes of all sorts for each other, on the stairs so that they are seen when someone comes home, in the kitchen concerning shopping or meals, stuck on other people's doors, or slipped through the letter box. These may be functional, they may be expressing relationships of affection or anger. Some messages are privately circulated, others are designed to be declared and displayed publicly: within the home on the mantelpiece or wall. Outside the home, they are found around the hospital bed. In Lancaster people put up signs announcing birthdays, births and engagements publicly on the traffic roundabout. They pay to put details of births, birthdays and marriages in the local newspaper. These are some-

times humorous, as when a fiftieth birthday announcement is accompanied by a photograph of the person when they were five years old. Personal communication takes many forms and serves many purposes, and the literacies used are equally varied and wide-ranging.

(3) **Private leisure.** People read books and papers for leisure as ways of relaxing and passing the time. Some people read books and magazines every evening, some only when travelling or when on holiday. Children and adults can be *lost in a book*. Equally, they can be lost in a map, in a magazine, in the local paper or the mail order catalogue. Some of this involves fantasy consumption. People sometimes do this when they are alone; and, sometimes, in order to be alone, reading creates a way of being private in a public space. There is the idle reading of newspapers and magazines. Most of the private leisure we came across was reading, but people also wrote as a leisure activity, for themselves or for others. In particular we were surprised at the number of people who reported writing poetry as a leisure activity; it seemed a particularly accessible form of personal writing for some people. This, like other examples, fits several of these categories, as sometimes poetry was written for other people, for special occasions, and sometimes it was personal communication. Leisure pursuits are often mediated by literacy. Some leisure activities, such as being a fan, involved a range of literacy activities spanning reading and writing and incorporating other media, and as a form of personal leisure. People varied as to the extent to which they used literacy for private leisure; nevertheless, many seemingly straightforward leisure interests, such as betting, drew upon a complex range of literacies. Leisure interests vary in the intensity and enthusiasms with which they are pursued – sometimes in seemingly casual ways and at other times bordering on the obsessive, as if part of a much bigger quest for meaning or satisfaction.

If these three forms of vernacular practices were in a sense expected and predicted at the beginning of our study, there are three others which are less expected and which we derived from the data.

(4) **Documenting life.** People maintain records of their lives in many ways, through keeping documents such as birth certificates and school reports, and from cutting out reports of their lives such as weddings and sporting achievements from the local newspaper, and keeping souvenirs from holidays and festivals. Some people take photos, and have albums and scrap books. Many people make and keep recipe books, or records about car maintenance, or gardening diaries, as well as records of finances. People write diaries at various points in their lives, and then keep the diaries; they keep some letters for years, but not others; people keep old address books. Some of these documents are passed on across generations. For a few people this activity develops into writing a fully fledged autobiography. Certain people write their life histories; others intend to. This can be an example of the changing practices throughout a person's life – where people of seventy decide to write their life histories. People investigate their

family history, a topic popular enough to have its own national magazines in the newsagents. Local history courses are among the most popular of adult education courses. This aspect of vernacular literacy may be for oneself, for one's family or for a broader community.

(5) Sense making. People consciously carry out their own research. In the simplest sense this involves reading instruction booklets and guarantees for household items to see how they are used or for effecting repairs. It includes devotional reading of religious and other inspirational books, and deliberate investigations of unknown topics, such as those covered under the topic of sense making in Chapter 13. People become local experts on particular topics, whether it is an illness, their child's difficulties, or a legal grievance. There can be a tenacious imperative to learn, to find out more, to solve a problem by trespassing into areas of expertise, and tackling literacies normally reserved for others. People have to learn how to do this, and, as adults, they learn how to learn and find out where and how to get the resources they need. Less pressingly, as mentioned above, people may have interests and hobbies which they pursue; these can lead to great differences in what individuals know about. There is a wide range of difference in what people know about, and it is revealing to look across a community and to investigate the vernacular funds of knowledge which exist.

(6) Social participation. People participate in a wide range of social activities. In Chapter 12 we described the range of groups and clubs and the ways in which it seems that everyone in Springside has connections to at least one such organisation and several people are officers. Participation in groups can involve literacy in many ways. People read and contribute to notices and newsletters, participate in meetings, raffles and jumble sales, design posters. People write to local newspapers as members of associations and send in reports of activities or other local activities. There are different modes of participation; even when people are not actual members of associations they may still go to meetings, read about the activities of neighbours and friends in the local paper and display notices. As a form of social participation a minority of people can be described as *politically active* and, in fact, they describe themselves in these terms; many others, nevertheless, participate in local political activity by signing petitions, attending public meetings, writing letters and going on marches and demonstrations. A few people write graffiti in public places and deface posters, either as individuals or on behalf of groups. In this context, literacy is being used a transformative tool, to effect change. It is noteworthy that at both the demonstrations we have details of, the first anti-poll-tax march and a demonstration against the smell in one part of the town, there were people who said they had never been on demonstrations before. People may participate socially in different ways at particular points in their lives and may move in and out of being active.

In the previous three chapters we have mentioned a number of general points about literacy which emerge from discussing these activities in people's lives: that there is change throughout people's lives; that they learn throughout their lives, that people have to learn how to learn; that people engage with literacy in a variety of ways; that people become local experts about topics of importance to them; that knowledge is located in the community, within local organisations and access points for literacy such as libraries.

The six categories above were identified by starting from individuals' lives but they may also serve group functions. In identifying the domain of these activities we have moved between different terms, at times ascribing these activities to families, to households, to neighbourhoods and to communities. We found that all four of these terms were useful, they all had a role in understanding some aspects of people's literacy. Whether or not the people in a house are related, there are some functions of households which are carried out anyway. These are to do with practical household management and communication. Families were important when people talked about their informal learning of literacy and some networks of support and obligation. People used a broad notion of family; often they referred to relatives, who in some cases lived nearby, on the same street or round the corner, and in other cases who lived elsewhere in Lancaster or in nearby towns. The practice of letter writing was very important for families maintaining communication when they are separated by distance. The physical neighbourhood had some salience, where people relied on neighbours for support, and where common local issues, such as traffic problems and street lighting, were addressed. Some of these topics were initiated by local people, others by the Housing Action Project, the City Council or the police. In them local people identify a common interest but they were not the most important determinants of people's sense of social identity: they also had networks and communities of interest that stretched way beyond the boundaries of Springside. Some issues that linked people, such as the poll tax, were of common interest city-wide. The notion of community is an amorphous one, but people nevertheless identified with particular communities of interest, such as allotment associations or as parents of children attending particular schools; literacy often had a significant specialised place within these communities. The one Gujarati-speaking household in our case study, Mumtaz's, did not live in a multilingual neighbourhood but in a predominantly monolingual English-speaking neighbourhood; her immediate neighbours were local white people. Nevertheless she was part of a strong Gujarati Muslim community in Lancaster and the north-west of England.

Defining vernacular literacies

With these examples in mind we want to define what we mean by vernacular practices and identify how they are similar to and different from other practices. The vernacular literacy practices we identified are rooted in everyday experience and serve everyday purposes. They draw upon and contribute to vernacular knowledge. Often they are less valued by society and are not particularly supported, nor regulated, by external social institutions.

Firstly, vernacular literacy practices are learned informally. They have their roots in people's homes and in their upbringing. In Chapter 11 and elsewhere in the book we have given examples of people's vernacular learning. An important distinction between vernacular learning and other learning, such as that within an educational or training context, is that vernacular learning is 'learning not systematised by an outside authority'. (This is the way in which Ursula Howard (1991) describes the learning of autodidacts.) The roles of novice or learner and expert or teacher are not fixed, but shift from context to context, and there is an acceptance that people will engage in vernacular practices in different ways, sometimes supporting, sometimes requiring support from others.

Secondly, literacy learning in the home is rarely separated from use; rather, learning and use are integrated in everyday activities and where literacy remains an implicit part of the activity. This can be contrasted, as we saw in Chapter 11, with many school practices, where learning is separated from use, divided up into subject areas, disciplines and specialisms, and where knowledge is often made explicit, is reflected upon, and is open to evaluation. There are also other senses in which home literacy practices are integrated: in home literacy events, written and spoken language are often integrated (in the ways in which Shirley Brice Heath has demonstrated in her work, 1983); different media are integrated; literacy is integrated with other symbolic systems, such as numeracy, and visuals; and different topics and activities can occur together.

Where specialisms do develop in everyday contexts they are different from the formal academic disciplines, reflecting the logic of practical application. As we have mentioned above, the six areas of vernacular literacy practices we have identified are not hard and fast categories: vernacular literacies are as diverse as social practices are. They are hybrid in origin. They overlap, and often it is clear that a particular activity belongs in two or more categories. In addition, people may have a mixture of motives for taking part in a given literacy activity. Preparing the residents' association newsletter, for instance, can be social, it can be leisure and it can be sense making.

In these ways, vernacular literacy practices can be contrasted with other, dominant literacy practices. Dominant literacies are those associated with formal organisations, such as those of education, law, religion and the workplace. To the extent that we can group these dominant practices together, they are more formalised than vernacular practices and they are given high value, legally and culturally. They are more standardised and defined in terms of the formal purposes of the institution, rather than in terms of the multiple and shifting purposes of individual citizens and their communities. In dominant literacies there are experts and teachers through whom access to knowledge is controlled.

Self-generated, voluntary and creative?

Because of their relative freedom from formal institutional control, vernacular practices are more likely to be voluntary and self-generated, rather than being imposed externally (a distinction used, for example in Ivanic and Moss (1991) and Clark and Ivanic (1997: 123–5), in discussions of purposes for writing). They may also be a source of creativity, invention and originality, and the vernacular can give rise to new practices – improvised and spontaneous – which embody different sets of values from dominant literacies.

These aspects have been noticed by Miriam Camitta in her study of the non-school writing done by adolescents in a school in the United States, which included personal notes and diaries, autographs, jokes, raps and song lyrics, chain letters, flyers to advertise social and fund-raising events. She refers to this as 'vernacular' writing and defines vernacular as 'that which is closely associated with culture which is neither elite nor institutional, which is traditional and indigenous to the diverse cultural processes of communities as distinguished from the uniform, inflexible standards of institutions' (1993: 228–9). Part of this diversity is that the vernacular gives possibilities of more voices and a range of different voices.

However, when thinking about the creativity associated with vernacular literacies, it is important to avoid the idea that there is some kind of 'natural' form of language or literacy unencumbered by social institutions. This could be an implication of Gee's notion of 'primary' discourse (1990) and also of the notion of 'self-generated' literacies. Rather than returning to such asocial formulations, it is important to stress that vernacular literacies are still subject to the social pressures of the family and other social groups and they are regulated by them. While these pressures may be less formal than the strictures of school, law or work-place, and people may often willingly accept them, institutions such as the family are powerful social institutions, and their influence can be strongly restraining to people. Pressure is exerted through the intimacies of day-to-day interactions, attitudes, humour, traditions and routines, rather than through formal procedures and legal sanctions – though these may be resorted to when other pressures fail. The notion we have already introduced of incorporation into literacy activities is especially useful here and for understanding how children and other literacy learners may engage with new literacies in specific domains and networks: at first, learners are incorporated into the practices of others (see also Reder 1994; Hannon 1995).

Literacy in networks

One of the ways in which social institutions work is by means of the networks they sustain, and we have located literacy practices in people's networks of support throughout the book. Much of people's reading and writing involved other people and was located in reciprocal networks of exchange. Many of these were personal networks of friends, neighbours and family around Springside and Lancaster. Everyone we talked to had such personal networks of support and advice that they could draw on and contribute to, though they were more extensive for some people than for others. We found that people participate in networks in a variety of ways, however, as Chapter 12 has particularly shown, taking on more or less active and publicly visible roles in them. Sometimes people experience these networks as constraining and oppressive rather than supportive. Networks also have limitations: they may break up as a result of people falling out with each other or moving away, and they may not provide expertise in the ways that are needed at a particular time. A further point is that changes in people's networks of support can result in changes in the support people have for literacy activities. Loss of networks can cause problems. Personal networks are important when people want to make changes in their lives, and networks can both support and constrain such changes.

Whilst everyone is forced into contact with official bodies, whether paying the poll tax, for instance, or dealing with the medical or educational systems, people in this study varied a great deal as to whether they had networks which extended into these more public arenas. In fact personal networks have a particular importance when people confront the official worlds. We found great variation in whether people chose to deal with the challenges posed by their interactions with these official agencies as individuals or collectively.

We have also seen a range of activities which cannot be adequately described as either self-generated or imposed and which call for an extension of this simple dichotomy. Helping other people, for example, a common form of literacy practice, involves reciprocity and obligations which are not imposed. Doing things for other people, or on behalf of others, is a way of being collaborative that is often closely tied into people's sense of identity and self-worth among family, friends and neighbours, as Janet Finch and Jennifer Mason (1993) have pointed out in their study of how responsibilities are negotiated between members of extended families. Finch and Mason make use of the notion of commitments which individuals take on in relation to other members of their family (and, we would argue, this can also apply to friendship and neighbourhood networks). They found that while gender and kinship hierarchies play their role in expectations about the commitments people take on, the process of negotiating them involves many other factors and is not prescribed or imposed in a rigid way. Our data similarly suggests that, in addition to the categories of self-generated and imposed literacies, we need a notion of 'negotiated literacies', which are not necessarily reciprocal but are integral to the social relationships people develop in their local lives. They are closely connected with feelings of identity and self-worth within a significant community; participating in these relationships can be a practical way of expressing solidarity and common purpose within that community. They sometimes involve struggles with bureaucracy or opposition to other outside bodies, and the mutual help offered by welfare claimants is a good example of this.

In summary, we have confirmed the importance of networks in people's lives and we can also sketch out some of their complexities. Reciprocal networks of support are widespread, but the links between people are not always positive. Networks can also act as constraints, within both personal networks and the semi-institutional ones which people participate in associated with work, school and official bureaucracies. Often these are experienced as having elements of imposition and compulsion.

What's under the table? Secrets, silence and privacy

In many ways vernacular literacies have a low cultural value, although we have argued that they are creative and generative of new culture and often underpin and support the development of more valued literacies. They are often downgraded and not valued by schools. They are often actively disapproved of, and they can be contrasted with other officially sanctioned literacies which are seen as rational, and of high cultural value. In this, they are similar to much literacy associated with popular mass media of television, film and video, which come under the 'disapproved of' category. Mass media literacies may not be hidden or secret but, rather, they are ignored culturally and given low status compared with other art and literature, even though these literacies are influential and valued in people's lives, and are widely circulated and discussed.

We have seen that vernacular practices are frequently less valued by society and are not particularly supported or approved of by educational and other dominant institutions. They are more loosely regulated by official institutions. They are more common in private spheres than in public spheres. Often they are humorous, playful, disrespectful, sometimes deliberately oppositional. They are entwined in people's emotional lives in very obvious ways, as we saw in the discussion of fans, earlier. All literacies have an emotional dimension to them but this is down-played and denied within many formal literacies. Despite this, the most formal, 'rational' piece of paperwork, such as a business contract, an insurance claim or an exam result, can evoke and be handled with extreme emotion.

This leads to another cluster of concepts which may illuminate some aspects of vernacular literacies: that they are in some ways informal, secret and private – either pushed to be so by those in authority or withheld by people. We saw this in a simple way in the forms of reading and writing which people did not regard as *real* reading or *real* writing. Often, as we have seen, reading magazines or newspapers was not counted as reading. Filling in forms or sending cards did not count as writing. Other practices we came across were hidden in some ways. These included vernacular practices which were personal and private, where reading or writing were ways of being alone and private, ways of creating personal space. There were also secret notes and letters of love, abuse, criticism and subversion. 'Under the table', to use Janet Maybin's (1996) phrase, we also found comics, horoscopes, fanzines, scurrilous jokes, pornography. And, as we have pointed out already, while some private spheres were shared with us, we were not offered access to all people's private practices. These findings link in with work by Gemma Moss (1996) on children's informal literacies and uses of television texts and Sue Rogers's (1994) and Miriam Camitta's (1993) work on the informal literacies of teenage school girls. Perry Gilmore (1986) adds another dimension to this discussion when she discusses *sub-rosa* (secret) literacy. She defines this as literacy which is 'owned and demonstrated in peer contexts' where students defined by school as failing can be seen to be using complex literacies. In some of these hidden areas, then, people may be very competent, even if they would not appear so in terms of dominant literacies.

Dominant and vernacular literacies in the home

Although we have set limits on our research, a study of local literacies has to include the ways in which dominant literacies impinge on local lives. This happens in various ways, including the range of bills people have to pay, the demands of schooling, medical encounters and legal activities. In the home there can be a range of practices from other domains, including religion; among these are particular ways of reading books; bureaucratic government practices, such as those associated with choosing schools, claiming benefits, filling in the electoral register; commercial practices, such as dealing with advertisements, shopping and junk mail; and work practices of many sorts. The range of official encounters people have varies a great deal. As we have pointed out elsewhere, there is often a great deal of complex imposed literacy associated with dealing with the state, whether one is elderly, ill, unemployed, poor or a combination of these. Often those who are least able to cope have the most literacy demands of this sort placed upon them. The example of bi-numeracy, discussed in Chapter 10, is a case where commercial practices or school practices meet everyday practices in unavoidable ways.

We have found it useful in this discussion to contrast dominant and vernacular practices, but the divide is not clear-cut. Some of the documenting of life, for example, which we have classified as a vernacular literacy, is required by outside agencies such as for making tax returns or claiming benefits, where people have to keep records of their activities. This involves participation in dominant literacy practices, and people are incorporated into these bureaucratic practices by means of legal and financial penalties. Similarly, sense making and social participation can involve participation in dominant practices, though often in the sense of trespassing across the social boundaries of appropriate reading and writing.

The example we gave in Chapter 1, of making and keeping of recipes for cooking, is an area which is part vernacular and part institutional, with recipe books and magazines, catering courses in colleges and cookery demonstrations on television. Nevertheless, people have their own practices around making and keeping recipes, and often they create individual and personal texts which may be passed on across generations.

Another way in which dominant and vernacular practices overlap is that there can be a distinction between the text and the intentions of the producer, on the one hand, and what people actually do, their vernacular practices, on the other hand. There may be official texts, like a letter from the Council, or commercial texts, like a newspaper or a catalogue. The texts are official, but what people do with them, the practices themselves, can be vernacular. People develop their own practices around these texts. Vernacular practices can therefore be responses to imposed literacies. Some vernacular responses to official literacy demands disrupt the intentions of those demands, either functionally or creatively, to serve people's own purposes; and sometimes they are intentionally oppositional to and subversive of dominant practices. Graffiti would be an example of this, especially where it is used to challenge official public messages. What is interesting here is how people make literacies their own, turning dominant literacies to their own use, by constant incorporation and transformation of dominant practices.

The texts of everyday life

The main focus of this book has been on literacy practices and events, on exploring cultural ways of using written texts. In our analysis of the data generated by our research study, literacy practices remain central and we examine how written texts fit into the practices of people's lives, rather than the other way round. The texts themselves have taken a subsidiary place within our analysis, and in this way we have deliberately redressed an imbalance that we perceive in the literature about reading and writing. Nevertheless, in the course of this study of practices we have encountered and collected a range of vernacular texts which are highly interesting in their own right. These are the texts of everyday life, the texts of personal life, generated in the course of everyday activities; often these are created by people and circulated locally.

There is a wide range of very different texts within the areas of social practice we have identified. Organising life can involve notes, notices, diaries, address books. Social participation can bring in notices, newsletters, minutes. A particular literacy event can utilise a range of texts ranging from informal transient handwritten notes through to official published public documents. Having identified particular groups of texts, we then find that they contain great diversity. Diaries, as we have seen, can include a mixture of genres, including fantasy, poetry and record-keeping; they serve many different purposes for the writers.

This is a distinctive constellation of texts which are not usually studied by the analysts of discourse. They are not educational texts, not mass media texts, and not the published texts that emanate from and reflect dominant institutions and discourses. Because they are not defined and constrained by such dominant discourses, the texts of everyday life can be more fluid, inventive and hybrid in their discourse characteristics. They provide rich ground for pursuing many of the theoretical issues that we have highlighted in this book: the nature of informal learning; the variety and invention of literacy genres; notions of domain and purpose; the social relationships that constitute literacy practices; questions of identity and how these are negotiated within the text.

Some of the texts we have identified in our study are vernacular texts, others are not. Often a text is part commercial, as in bought address books, or pre-written greetings cards. Some of the ways in which commercial practices have supported the development of a text may not be obvious. Letter writing, for example, has been supported and shaped by the postal service since the nineteenth century, as has sending Christmas cards, holiday postcards, birthday cards, and valentine cards (see Vincent 1989: 32–52); and these practices, along with using the telephone, are now intermittently supported by direct television advertising. For commercial reasons there is currently a battle over our vernacular communication practices.

It is tempting to assume that vernacular texts are always local and indigenous, but we have a number of examples of them turning up simultaneously in different places, circulating in similar ways to jokes and urban myths. We saw in Chapter 6 how Shirley's newsletter editorials drew on a variety of different discourses, and it is likely that examining other newsletters from community groups would reveal both differences and overlaps with Shirley's. Vernacular literacies also have a complex relationship with the rhetoric of popular media such as television and newspapers, which both draw upon and influence vernacular forms.

In summary, while the research described in this book has started from a study of everyday practices and events, we believe there is much to be gained from bringing together the study of literacy practices and the study of texts, and viewing texts as part of practices. The example of Shirley editing the residents' association newsletter illustrates the potential richness of data that is generated by a strategy of identifying significant texts from a study of practices and moving between the analysis of texts and practices in a cyclical way to develop an understanding of contemporary literacies. In this way we believe that researchers in literacy studies can provide a distinctive contribution to the study of written texts.

Vernacular practices in a time of change

Although we have made generalisations about literacy in the previous sections, we are still referring to practices in one place at one point in time. What counts as a vernacular or a dominant literacy, and the relationships between the two, varies at different times and places. A number of changes were apparent even during the period of this study, the 1990s. Many are changes which reflect national or international forces, and we saw traces of their impact in the local area of Lancaster. The media narrative on literacy outlined in Chapter 1 assumes that literacy demands are changing in that they are constantly increasing. While this may be true in some general, long-term sense, a detailed examination suggests that this analysis is too simplistic. It is undoubtedly true that literacy practices are not static, and constantly having to deal with change brings its own complexity. However, any specific change is located in broader social practices; this results in contradictory trends, whereby some activities become more difficult while others are simplified.

Deliberate policy initiatives and the development of new technologies have led to frequent changes in the dominant practices of commercial and government organisations. For example, in Britain the language of telephone bills and electricity bills has become simpler in the 1990s and they have been rewritten in 'plain English'. Nevertheless this has not necessarily made them simpler to understand. The bills follow the logic and demands of corporations. The units measured have become more complex, the billing periods are often different from the periods described in the bills, and in other ways the layout and information provided have become more complex. At the same time, other changes may have made the bills easier to deal with. For example, they may have become easier to pay, with an encouragement to use direct debit facilities, so that in fact the consumer needs to do nothing in order to pay the bill. This system, however, demands that people have bank accounts and monitor their payments efficiently. Many people have traditionally paid using cash, and these people are affected by changes in the places where bills can be paid in person: some showrooms have closed down in the city centre, while some bills can now be paid at local post offices. These changes in the social practices of businesses all affect how people deal with their household bills. Our overall impression is that bills are now more difficult to understand, but easier to pay!

A physical aspect of changes in the consumer environment has been a shift in the kinds of shops in the centre of Lancaster. Several shops have moved, closed, or expanded; the market has been relocated within a large new shopping mall. There are more temporary shops, including cheap bookshops selling a wide range of books including dictionaries, factual books, gardening, cookery, children's books, art, popular and classical novels; these are sold alongside cheap stationery, videos and classic favourite

CDs. Another change during the period of the study is that stationery, such as paper and pens, has become a fashion accessory for young people, with new city centre stationery shops, selling fashionable pencil cases and school bags, and a range of brightly coloured paper. The range of greetings cards has also expanded, and card shops sell other accessories for birthdays and anniversaries to appeal to many ages. There has been a shift from there being one local computer shop to four or five, including branches of nationally advertised chains.

Books have become a different sort of commodity, now available in supermarkets and in a range of bargain shops, and given away on offer with confectionery. There are more titles published than ever before, and one change has been a move to cheaper, more dispensable books, such as novels or extracts from longer books costing less than a pound. There appears to be more purchasing of books by mail. In the library, books have had to make room for videos and CDs. Magazines are increasingly tied in with other media and are often sold with 'free' CDs or even videos.

Some of the changes apparent in the 1990s are related to the spread of new technologies and the increasing number of homes with computers. We referred to this earlier, in Chapter 10. Institutions have changed their practices through introducing new technologies and people have had to respond to these changes – by using automatic bank tellers or computerised library catalogues, for example. Although many of the developments around computing were not aimed at everyday literacies but for more specialised working practices, people have turned them to their own uses. One publicly visible difference which has resulted from the coming of computers in the home has been changes in the way people have produced newsletters, advertisements and flyers for clubs and associations.

The new technological knowledge associated with computers, telephones and video recorders can change relationships within families, since people acquire this knowledge at different rates. Children often develop expertise which their parents do not have. Children's funds of technological knowledge can threaten teachers too, especially as such knowledge, unlike some other areas of vernacular knowledge, is valued by schools. This threat is greater where teachers themselves may not have this expertise (Stevenson 1997). The phenomenon of children possessing knowledge which is of value to families is also apparent in bilingual homes where children sometimes know more English, or have greater familiarity with everyday practices, than their parents. This is probably true wherever families are dislocated and where children have greater access to education than their parents. Nevertheless, the changing relationships within families caused by technological disparities is particularly apparent in the late twentieth century.

Several changes in practices seem to follow a similar pattern. These are changes which involve a shift where consumers or citizens have to do more of the literacy work, using it to regulate their own behaviour. An example of this is car parking in the centre of town, where the person parking has to do the work, in buying the ticket and marking it with the time of arrival and other details. Another example is the coming of self-assessment in taxation, where people have to keep more records, and they face penalties if forms are not submitted in time; or where unemployed people have to provide written records, such as lists of application letters sent off, to demonstrate that they are actively seeking work. Other changes which increase the burdens of written language on people include the fact that the test which has to be passed to get a driving licence now contains a compulsory written section. Also, in the time we are considering, the one-year passport, purchased over the counter in the main post office, was abolished, so anyone planning a holiday abroad has to fill in a long complex form, which has to be sent off, with the fee, in order to get a full ten-year passport. Alongside these changes has been a growth in mediators who, for a fee, will check people's tax forms or passport applications.

Increased literacy demands have also affected social participation in local groups. The closure of the Springside Housing Action Project in 1991 when government funding was withdrawn is an example of something happening more generally throughout the public sector. Like many other initiatives, it had been a short-term, experimental project, dependent on continual renewal of funds through a bidding process to local and central government. Support for such activities is now haphazard and unpredictable, with groups bidding against one another for resources. Even long-term established communal resources, such as libraries, are having to compete for ever scarcer public funds. Many sorts of funding now demand complex applications and, to be successful, organisations need someone who knows how to fill in the forms. Such a process places new literacy demands on the officers of such organisations and it is not clear how this expertise is to be acquired. With declining trade union membership, opportunities for training to participate in meetings as officers of associations is now available to fewer people. On the other hand, we noticed that in 1995 the Adult College was advertising a course for officers of associations.

Looking more broadly at social change, we agree with Fairclough (1992, chapter 7) and Giddens (1991) that there is greater regulation and surveillance of social practices, especially in terms of the encroachment of the professional into the private realm of the family. This is apparent in shifting literacy practices, for instance in the practices surrounding children's emergent reading, where there is more state intervention in children's pre-school lives. Even during the period of our study there have been moves to increase the regulation of literacy practices in households as family literacy programmes are promoted by the government, along with suggestions about what parents should do to improve their children's reading and writing, and certificated courses are developed for parents themselves. This regulation is generally rooted not in an appreciation of vernacular practices but in the views of schools and policy makers about the kind of support that families should provide their children with. Many areas are becoming more influenced by institutional and commercial pressures, and the personal and vernacular is being eroded.

Changes in the relation of home and school are part of broader shifts which are happening in attitudes to schooling and education. There appears to be greater media and political attention paid to education in the mid-1990s as it becomes one of the main focuses for policy debate between political parties. In relation to vernacular literacies, our impression is that while schools may have the potential to introduce children to a wider variety of voices than that experienced in the home, the spread of the National Curriculum is reducing the variety of literacies in the classroom. Education is disputed territory in the 1990s and part of this is the range of variation of voices permitted (see Hamilton 1996).

The changes described here are in some ways eroding the literacy practices which bind communities together, and making older practices obsolescent. In other ways they present opportunities to re-shape and strengthen the power of literacy in community life. New demands keep literacy practices constantly on the move for people organising and controlling their everyday lives. This results in changes in a complex balance of relationships involving resources, expertise and needs for support. In this study we have captured one moment in this period of change.

15

AFTERWORD

This book has been concerned with making sense of literacy within one community. In one way this study is complete in itself: it celebrates the uniqueness of individual relationships to literacy, documented in a specific time and place. A specific description is of value in its own right, and we hope that our readers have been drawn into the lives of people such as Shirley and Cliff, just as we have been, and have been left with a richer view of the kaleidoscope of literacies in everyday life.

In carrying out the study we have seen the value of researching a culture we know already and which we are in many ways part of. To the extent that we are insiders we are confirming what we know already, approaching the research with a certain theory of literacy and adding nuance and detail. We are also adding examples and substantiating things we felt were true, which we knew from experience or which we knew from our reading of previous studies. For example, the study has shown the ways in which new practices are built out of old, in individual people's lives and in historical traditions; the extent and quality of personal networks in people's lives; the role of literacies in the lives of people who find reading or writing difficult, and the fact that there are many kinds of interdependencies, some which are reciprocal and supportive while others are felt as negative or unequally based.

However, there were also areas of literacy practice which we had not pieced together before and which the data enabled us to see more clearly. An example of this is the way in which Shirley moved from being a private individual to being a public figure as a local politician, and how writing had played a part in this change. Another example is that we could see the ways in which people are learning new literacies throughout their lives and are incorporating new technologies into their everyday activities. The gulf between the perceptions of parents and the perceptions of teachers impressed itself upon us, and, more generally, the gulf that often exists between institutions and people's lives, and between media images and people's lives.

Thirdly, there were aspects which were unexpected and which surprised us, and, even if we had read about them in passing, we had not fully appreciated their significance in terms of literacy. Some were specific details, such as the importance of local libraries in people's lives, or the importance and difficulty of school choice to people. More generally, we had not realised the extent of local organisations and the range of literacy practices they support and demand; nor had we understood the variation and spread in knowledge throughout the community. We were also struck by how institutions such as the church or adult education are extremely important to some people, while they are completely unimportant and distant for many other people. The amount of change in people's lives was also surprising. It can be understood, partly because in six years people find themselves six years older and doing different things, and partly because in these six years there have been significant social and technological changes which have affected, and are continuing to affect, people's literacy practices.

In terms of theory, we have elaborated the notions of networks and of vernacular literacies. We have extended the notions of literacy events and literacy practices and clarified the relationship between them. Similarly, we have identified ways in which texts are part of practices. We have argued that print literacies can be understood within the same framework as other media in the home. Dimensions in which aspects of literacy are often discussed such as fact and fiction, and self-generated and imposed, have been elaborated.

Research always feels like unfinished business. Life continues in Lancaster, and one can always point to directions for further exploration, or identify alternative paths one might have taken. Even working with the data we have, there is a great deal more which could be said about literacy in this particular community. However, our intention has always been to say something beyond this community. The special value of research is the insights it can generate which go beyond the particular which it deals with, to extend out from the study and relate the local and the global.

As discussed in Chapter 4, it is important to be clear about the sorts of generalisation which are possible from a local ethnography. We do not want to assert that identical practices can be found in other communities. The detailed literacy practices of Lancaster, England will be different from those in Lancaster, Pennsylvania or Lancaster, California. Nevertheless, our study provides a set of questions to ask of these other communities and identifies significant dimensions of social organisation which will affect the literacy practices in different places. The theoretical concepts, such as networks of support, or the distinction between dominant and vernacular practices, can be applied to other situations and to any domain, including work-places, schools, prisons, hospitals. These concepts offer anchor points for discerning common patterns under changing conditions, for tracing literacy practices across time and space.

We hope that the approach we have described will prompt other studies which complement and extend what we have done. For example, such studies could examine in more detail the social institutions, both formal and informal, which people are part of. More detailed critical ethnographies are needed of dominant institutional literacies, such as in work-places, legal and other bureaucratic agencies; how these are perceived and learned; and how people are incorporated into them. More could be done on vernacular learning, with more understanding of vernacular reading and writing, and further exploration of different ways of reading and engaging with particular literacy practices. Studies could examine further the relation of print literacies to other media.

Looking at different situations reveals not just different practices but communities held together in very different ways, where the roots of the practices can be very different: in one community social practices may be structured strongly by religious belief; in another they may be structured more pervasively by work relationships. What is meant by community varies by time and by place. If we look we find communities defined in very different ways, with distinct practices, but which can be recognised and understood within a similar theoretical frame, such as the one we have offered in this book. Taken together, such studies can offer a powerful challenge to dominant and simplifying discourses of literacy, and support the recognition of multiple literacies within educational and social policy.

Appendices

Appendix 1

PEOPLE INTERVIEWED IN THE LITERACY IN THE COMMUNITY PROJECT

Springside case study data

People living in Springside. Several interviews were carried out with each person and additional data were collected. People's names are pseudonyms (see Aside 4.3); ages, occupations and living situations are all as at the time of their first interview.

E1. Shirley Bowker, in her early thirties, lives with husband Jack and two sons at primary school; currently unemployed, she has had a variety of jobs including bar work, aerobics instructor, working in a printer's. Secretary of residents' association. Special themes for later interviews: home–school relations; Housing Action Project. Additional data: Met at residents' association meetings; she collected letters from school; we have newsletters she has written. Participated in Collaborative phase a year later.

E2. Eddie and Janette Wilcox. Eddie late thirties, Janette early thirties, three children. Eddie factory worker, Janette unemployed. Special themes for later interviews: interviewed separately and together. Eddie: work, life and his own difficulties at school; martial arts. Janette: networks, family life. Eddie participated in Collaborative phase a year later after their relationship had broken up.

E3. Cliff Holt, in his mid-fifties, on invalidity benefit. Close relationship with half-sister, Rose. Has grown-up children. Special themes for later interviews: medical conditions, betting. Some joint interviews with Rose. Participated in Collaborative phase. Additional data: They both kept literacy diaries.

E4. Mumtaz Patel, aged thirty, three children, factory machinist. Born in India and came to Lancaster as young child. Special themes for later interviews: religion, work, extended families. Additional data: visit to nursery school.

E5. Terry Patterson, in his late twenties, single, lives alone, psychiatric nurse. Special themes for later interviews: work, networks.

E6. Harry Graham, in his mid-sixties, has a grown-up son and daughter and has grandchildren, retired fire-fighter. Special themes for later interviews: interview with friend Ted, the war. Additional data: visit to library and to café; collected junk mail. Participated in Collaborative phase.

E7. Kathleen Jenkins, in her sixties, three children and grandchildren, retired, twice widowed, lives alone. Special themes for later interviews: networks; grandchildren

E8. Brenda and Jeff Brown, in their thirties, one primary school child. Jeff does voluntary work, Brenda clerical work. Special themes for later interviews: some joint interviews, allotments, home–school relations. Additional data: recording reading with daughter.

E9. June Marsh, mid-forties, four grown-up children, one still at home, works on market stall. Special themes for later interviews: CB radios. Participated in Collaborative phase.

E10. Helen Renfrew, late forties, five children, part-time cleaner. Special themes for later interviews: maps and networks.

E11. Diane Maude, around thirty, two children, unemployed. Special themes for later interviews: house roles, children and literacy.

E12. Tina Benson, mid-twenties, two children at primary school, works in old people's home as care assistant. Special themes for later interviews: literacy and religion.

Survey data

Sixty-five people contacted by means of door-to-door survey in Springside. This work is summarised in Aside 3.3.

Other Springside interviews

D14. Manager of Housing Action Project, initial interview
D15. Eileen Blamire, local councillor
D21. Janice Andrews, local hairdresser, started anti-poll-tax demonstration; two interviews
D22. Three interviews with Housing Action Project staff
D24. Trainee solicitor living in Springside
E13. Edna Worthington, long-term resident
E14. Ida Mason, long-term resident
Also several allotment holders

Lancaster city interviews

Using real names: see Aside 4.3

D1. Vicar, St. Thomas's Church
D2. Manager, City Books
D3. District Librarian
D4. Mrs Croxall, Founder of local branch of Dyslexia Association
D5. Manager, W. H. Smiths
D6. Manager, Waterstone's book shop
D7. Manager, Paper Book Back shop, bookshop
D8. Lancaster City Council Information Booth, Bus Station
D9. Hugh Jones, Federation of Sub-Postmasters
D10. Postmaster of Ingham, another neighbourhood
D11. Long-time member of a Quiz League team
D12. Manager, Viewfield books, stamps and gifts shop
D13. Manager, Papertree card shop
D17. Tourist Information
D18. Editor, *Off the Beat* magazine
D19. Meriel Lobley, Adult Basic Education co-ordinator, Adult College
D20. Owner of Victoria College, a small private college in the centre of the city
D23. P. Jones, Employment Training
D25. Andrew White, Curator of Lancaster City Museum
D26. Owner, Atticus Books.
D27. Manager, McCormack's Bookshop
D28. Owner, market book stall
D29. Manager, Lunn Poly Travel Agents
D30. Manager, Boots the Chemist
D31. Sharon Dexter, Citizen's Advice Bureau

Adult College data

People's names are pseudonyms; ages, occupations and living situations are all as at the time of their first interview.

B1. Cath, aged forty-seven years, separated, two grown-up children, lives alone, works part-time, in a dairy; at time of interview was attending Workers' Education Association (WEA) women's group; reads broadly and writes for pleasure but asks for help with forms.

B2. *Roger,* thirty-two, single, lives with parents; unemployed; has attended Basic Education classes since 1981; some difficulties with spelling and punctuation; recently started writing for pleasure at home; avoids reading.

B3. *Julie,* forty-five, separated, two grown-up children and one grandchild; lives alone, unemployed, attending WEA women's group at time of interview; reads broadly and writes for pleasure; sometimes turns to children for advice.

B4. *Ray*, thirty-three, single, lives alone, works part-time as a cleaner and has attended Basic Education classes for a number of years; he likes support when writing unless copying but is more confident about reading.

B5. *Lesley*, thirty-four, lives with partner and three primary school age children; works part-time as a cleaner/child minder; has attended Basic Education classes for two years; enjoys writing but dislikes reading. Participated in Collaborative phase.

B6. *Val*, forty-two, single, lives with elderly relative, unemployed at time of interview but doing voluntary work for the church; has attended Basic Education classes for two years; reads quite broadly and quite enjoys writing.

B7. *Lynne*, thirty-four, lives with husband and three children, works part-time (cooks, cleans, and serves in fast-food shop); attends Basic Education classes; enjoys both reading and writing. Participated in Collaborative phase.

B8. *Mark*, twenty, single, lives with parents, works in a printer's; has attended Basic Education for two years, now about to go to art college; dislikes writing because he has difficulty spelling but has just started to enjoy novels.

B9. *Duncan*, twenty-four, lives with parents (at time of interview), single, unemployed; attends Basic Education classes; some general writing difficulties but enjoys computer work and medical books; went to a special school.

B10. *Liz*, thirty-nine, lives with partner, two grown-up children; unemployed at time of interview and attending Basic Education classes; reads newspapers and novels but has some real problems with writing.

B11. *Sally*, twenty-five, separated, lives with brother; unemployed and attending Basic Education classes, some writing difficulties but reads widely; came to college to take mind off physical condition – rheumatoid arthritis.

B12. *Rita*, thirty-seven, separated, lives with teenage daughter, part-time cleaner/caretaker, attends Basic Education classes; some writing difficulties but reads novels occasionally; came to classes for social reasons. Participated in Collaborative phase.

B13. *Pat*, forty-four, lives with his partner and child by previous marriage; full-time manual worker; has attended Basic Education classes in the past; taught himself to read after leaving school, now reads broadly but avoids writing. Participated in Collaborative phase.

B14. *Neil*, twenty-six, lives with partner and primary school child; full-time supermarket worker; attends Basic Education classes; can read but has real difficulties writing.

B15. *Dick*, around forty, separated, one child; lives in room in another family's house, unemployed due to physical ailment; having been a Basic Education student, now attends Open College classes; reads broadly and has enjoyed writing.

B16. Ruth, thirty-six, lives with partner and three children; unemployed and attends Basic Education classes as a step to other classes; wants to become a nurse; writes for pleasure every day, has some writing difficulties.

B17. Paul, twenty-five, gay, lives with partner, has attended Basic Education classes for several years; took access courses and is now on a degree course; reads widely and enjoys writing 'short pieces' for pleasure.

B18. Bob, thirty-six, lives with partner and two children; full-time builder, has attended Basic Education classes in the past and has real difficulties with reading and writing but doesn't worry about them. Participated in Collaborative phase.

B19. Frances, thirty-five, lives with partner, Bob, and two children; full-time clerical worker, has attended Basic Education classes in the past; no obvious problems but doesn't read much; enjoyed creative writing at college. (Interviewed with Bob.)

B20. Andrea, thirty-two, lives with partner and one child at primary school; unemployed at present, attends Basic Education classes; can type, enjoys reading, and loves writing; talks of herself as a compulsive writer.

Other informants

People living in other areas of Lancaster.

C3. Catrin
C4. Maria
C5. Jake
C6. Keith
C7. Sue
C8. Joanna

The Collaborative ethnography data

Ten respondents followed up one year after the case studies and two years after the Adult College interviews.

Collab. 1 = *E6. Harry Graham*
Collab. 2 = *B12. Rita*
Collab. 3 = *E1. Shirley Bowker*
Collab. 4 = *E2. Eddie Wilcox*
Collab. 5 = *E3. Cliff Holt*
Collab. 6 = *B18. Bob*
Collab. 7 = *B5. Lesley*
Collab. 8 = *B7. Lynne*
Collab. 9 = *B13. Pat*
Collab. 10 = *E9. June Marsh*

Appendix 2

TOPICS COVERED IN THE LITERACY IN THE COMMUNITY INTERVIEW

These are the topics covered in the standard interview. For the Lancaster city interviews a specific set of questions was written for each separate interview. Interviews of case study people started with these topics and in later interviews moved on to further topics.

LITERACY PRACTICES
Reading matter
Reading processes
Writing practices
Writing processes
Record-keeping
Public and private

ACCESS
Borrowing and owning
Use of libraries
Acquiring reading materials

VALUES
Attitudes
Value of ownership
Morality
Censorship
Religion

ROLES
Asymmetry of roles

NETWORKS
Networks of support

CONTEXTS
Other forms of information exchange

HISTORICAL BASIS
Reading and writing life history
Childhood

Appendix 3

METAPHORS FOR THE RESEARCH PROCESS

We want to bring into our account the different ways in which the people we interviewed made sense of the research process. In a straightforward way people were voluntarily participating in a research project, freely and generously giving their time and sharing their lives. At the same time they were making sense of the activity and using it for their own purposes. Silverman (1993) discusses the different contexts in life where people experience the kind of activities used in this research – such as interviews, hearing one's own words recorded or seeing them transcribed, giving a summary account of oneself, receiving feedback about how others see you. He suggests that people try to situate the research among these other familiar contexts, using them to frame and make sense of what is going on.

The people we were working with had experienced many different contexts which they could draw on to make sense of different aspects of the research process. For example, some had heard their own recorded voices in making taped letters to correspondents abroad; they had described their own experiences in personal letters, diaries and CVs; they had been interviewed by the unemployment services, employers, doctors or counsellors and watched talk shows and news interviews on television; they had read biographies and autobiographies; some had proof-read letters and other items that they had written for public newsletters or newspapers; at least one person had taken part in a research study before.

In some cases people specifically mentioned these activities as being *like* the experience of the research, and they used these activities as analogies to explain their understandings to the interviewer. We have identified a number of ways in which people used the research process. (Further details are given in Hamilton 1998.) As we developed relationships and discussed them in the research team, a number of metaphors emerged that seemed to capture the ways in which people interacted with the researcher and made sense of the research process in our project. They came partly from the topic, partly from the research methods we used and partly from the context shared between researcher and participants. Frequently, there were elements of more than one kind of interaction in a given relationship.

Research as fortune telling

It was common amongst the adults we interviewed to view the research process as imposing order or pattern on their lives rather than as simply reflecting self-evident truths about themselves that they could correct, or facts that could be misrepresented. The analogy Cliff uses, of the researcher as fortune teller, casting horoscopes, captures the way in which people received our writing about them as revelatory rather than as being correct or incorrect. When asked if he recognised himself from our descriptions, Cliff replied:

> *Yeah, I think so. If somebody had given me this and said 'What do you think of this?', you know, I would have probably said to myself, 'If this had been in the form of a horoscope or something . . .' I would have said, 'By Jove, that nearly fits in to the way I am' . . . I don't know whether sometimes you can read into things that you think ought to be there, you know. Like horoscopes, you know, you can go, 'Oh, that is me'. But it's because it's how you want it to be or what I don't know. But yeah. It's quite good is this.*

June also expresses this feeling of recognising a new light on herself in much the same away that someone might react to having their horoscope or fortune told:

> *All the facts and everything – that's right. But when you say things like 'I deeply care about things', you know, I've never really thought about it. I mean it's made me think, 'Gosh . . . well it's right'. You know, it is right but I've never, ever thought about it [laughing].*

Having a fortune told or a horoscope read provides an interpretation of the influences and directions in life. This interpretation offers an additional perspective that can be weighed up alongside self-evaluation and other predictions of likely futures. Just as we may agree to have our fortune told by an authorised teller, deciding to take part in an interview involves a kind of surrender to another person's interpretation of our experience and a willingness to confront their representation of us.

Stranger on the train

In a number of cases the research interview appeared to serve as a place apart from everyday networks and concerns, where things could be said and stories told to a sympathetic, non-evaluative ear without immediate interpersonal consequences. We have identified this as the 'stranger on the train' approach, where people talk intimately to a person they meet by chance. Though it was never named as such by any of the people we worked with, we sometimes had an acute sense of being used in this way by interviewees. One person we interviewed told many stories of marital conflict and family problems which would have been extremely difficult to talk through with the people involved. The interviewer was uncomfortably aware of her own role as confidant and confessor, as someone who acted as a distraction from everyday worries and enabled the woman to unburden herself. This metaphor of stranger on the train also expresses the common dilemma faced by researchers about the boundaries of the research relationship, issues of closeness and distance, of public and private communication and of reciprocity which are discussed by Rudolf Egger (1994) and by many feminist researchers, such as Shulamit Reinharz (1992).

Ghost-writing

Two people made the explicit analogy with ghost-writing, where an experienced writer writes a life story on behalf of someone else. One of the people who mentioned this was Cliff, with his interest in stardom and media fame; he commented:

It's like . . . I suppose that's what people do when they have ghost-writers, you know. People write, 'Oh, I've just written my autobiography'. They've not put a word on paper. Somebody else has done it for them haven't they? Just get to do what you're doing now: get a lot of useless information and then pick through it until they've got a story and put it down.

Related to the idea of ghost-writing are many other comments about how it feels to read about oneself through someone else's words. People recognise themselves, the facts are there, but the force with which they are expressed changes. This was apparent when people saw written transcripts of words they had spoken, and when they read the interpretations we had made of the interviews. There were various reactions to this. Some people felt the researchers writing about them made them sound too serious and intelligent. Others felt their transcribed words represented them badly and showed them up as being ignorant, often when noticing colloquialisms or local dialect in the written transcripts.

Research as counselling

Elements of the counselling relationship entered into several of our interviews. In most cases possible therapeutic aspects of the research were referred to appreciatively and light-heartedly as offering welcome opportunities to reflect, and indulge in self-analysis with a view to making change happen. Some people commented explicitly on the way in which the interview process had caused them to reflect on change in their lives. Lynne comments:

It's made me sit down and analyse myself a little bit, this [laughing]. *You know, who am I? What am I? What do I want to really do? . . . After our last conversation, I went out, I thought, 'I'm going to try and be more positive'.*

It seemed that the non-judgemental and empathetic style of the interviews encouraged her to re-assess herself and to question the lack of confidence she often expressed in her own abilities. Other people made similar comments. Eddie made a direct connection between the research interviews and counselling he was receiving from the probation service and he wanted to take copies of the transcripts to his counselling sessions.

Remembering the past

Among some of the people we interviewed, reflecting on the past and making sense of it was evidently part of what the research prompted – or perhaps fitted into. A clear example of this is Harry, who had expressed worry and dislike of writing during the interviews. Harry had never done anything that could formally be called reminiscence or writing a life history. By the end of the project Harry had started writing his own wartime memoirs for publication in a newsletter. He had stopped referring to writing as a difficulty and worry and began talking about it as a pleasure.

Appendix 4

RESEARCH INTO PRACTICE

In studying literacy this book has deliberately not started out from education and other practical applications. Nevertheless, such links can be made. As we have said elsewhere:

> practice often means *education and teaching*, and we are concerned here with how new views of literacy can be applied in educational settings. This includes classrooms, which can be nursery, primary, secondary, as well as adult basic education and further and higher education. There are links to be made: Adult Basic Education students are learning to write; university students are also embarking on learning to write in new ways. Putting views of literacy into educational practice also means its role in professional development, where tutors, not just students, can address questions of the role of reading and writing in their lives.
>
> Secondly, putting into practice can mean in *policy* – the way that the future of literacy programmes is visualised and the institutional frameworks within which they operate; how governments and potential governments might think about reading and writing and act on this understanding.
>
> The third important sense of putting into practice is where it means moving out of the classroom and into *everyday life*, seeing how something affects what we do. We are concerned with how new views of literacy are put into practice in everyday life, in how people in their homes deal with their children's education, with officialdom and the legal system. This also includes a critical examination of how the media represent literacy issues.
>
> (Barton and Hamilton 1996: 16–17)

The first pedagogic point to stress is the importance of reflection, of encouraging people to take an ethnographic stance towards literacy. By this we mean enabling people, whether as teachers, students, parents, community organisers or ordinary people leading everyday lives, to reflect upon the literacy practices around them. In this appendix we suggest ways in which people can become ethnographers of their own experience (as in Heath 1983: 165) and we provide other links with education. The first section provides ideas for using this book in a direct way. The second section briefly lists some ways of encouraging students to research literacy practices, and the third section suggests a range of other links with educational practice.

Using this book

1. We have included *key quotations* which could be used as starting points for a more detailed discussion of the concepts involved in researching literacy practices. Each quotation illustrates several different aspects of literacy as a social practice. These are

Aside 5.10   Imagination and reading (Harry)
Aside 6.1   The petition (Shirley)
Aside 7.2   Doing the accounts (June)
Aside 8.4   Learning betting literacy (Cliff)
Aside 11.1   Helping with the homework (Lynn)
Aside 13.1   Martial arts (Eddie)

Other asides are also written to be self-contained and can be used in the same way.

2. An example of how to begin analysing a text is provided in Aside 6.10, **The text world of Shirley's editorials**, the analysis of the residents' association newsletter (see also Fairclough 1992).

3. The example of the fight to keep the allotments, described in Chapter 12, can be used as a case study in training workshops for literacy tutors. We have used it, asking the following questions:

(*a*) Can you identify similar problems in the communities where you work?
(*b*) How would you go about finding out what concerns people have?
(*c*) What are the similarities and differences between here and the communities you work in, in the events, the strategies used and the resources available?
(*d*) What use could this kind of analysis be in planning and resourcing a literacy programme?

Other activities

1. As a general framework we utilise the following steps in researching literacy practices:

identifying a domain
observing the visual environment
identifying and documenting literacy events, with words and pictures
identifying and analysing texts
interviewing people about practices.

2. In a course at Lancaster University entitled Literacy Studies, students are asked to explore the literacy practices of a domain of their choice. Often they just deal with one or two of the above steps. They are most imaginative in their responses, carrying out studies of literacy associated with motorway driving, rock climbing in the Lake District, working in shops and other work-places, the intricacies of scoring in cricket. One student researched betting shop literacy. He went into the betting shop and observed the range of texts and practices. Crucially he discovered that he could not learn about betting shop literacy just by entering the shop; there were no instructions, it was assumed people knew already. In the end the student resorted to looking through the waste bin to see what other people had done.

3. Photography can be particularly revealing. As an example of professional development we worked with some literacy trainers from Bangladesh. The course was in Lancaster. As part of the course we gave them disposable cameras to document literacy in the city centre. The results were very exciting, in that they took different kinds of photos from the ones we had been taking, and this led to discussions about the value of being an *insider* or and *outsider* researching a community. This group developed distinct views of reading and writing in a British city, and we could then use their photos in class discussions of how literacy is socially situated, how it belongs to a particular place, and to make comparisons with their own situations.

4. The Connect Family literacy project in Edinburgh has encouraged teachers and parents to co-research home practices and use the information to inform curricula for family literacy courses (see Keen 1995). In London Nora Hughes took Mukul Saxena's (1994) description of the literacy practices of members of the Panjabi-speaking community in Southall and used it to design a set of activities for her English classes, transforming her students into ethnographers who researched their own communities (Hughes 1992).

Other links with educational practice

1. A social practice approach to literacy argues for the importance of self-consciously researching local culture and perspectives on literacy and building this knowledge into learning programmes, using it as a basis for discussion and investigation of literacy issues with learners. This does not necessarily mean incorporating vernacular literacies into formal teaching by

directly using or modelling them in formal educational settings, since this inevitably changes their meaning. The basic issue is to acknowledge the existence of vernacular practices and to respect the vernacular, understanding that educational practices are not the only literacy practices; rather they are a particular set of practices which may complement and enhance the practices of home and community, but which are also capable of violating and devaluing them.

2. A social practice approach to literacy demonstrates the changing demands that people experience at different stages of their lives and offers convincing evidence of the need for lifelong learning systems which people can access at critical points when they need to respond to new demands. When talking about educational implications we are thinking not just about schools but much more widely about a range of institutional contexts for literacy, including community education, work-places, libraries and advice centres, all the points in the web that help sustain a culture of literacy. Additional ways that support communities and not just individuals can also be explored.

3. When we approach literacy as a set of practices embedded in everyday life we are confronted with a different logic in the way that literacies function from the way they are presented in educational settings. This embedding has several important aspects:

(a) Differences between home life and the formal school life of the classroom can have implications for literacy. In school, literacy is focused on as an object of study in that it is explicitly talked about and taught; literacy is central to many classroom activities. Using literacy for formal learning produces a distinct school literacy. At home, literacy is brought into many activities, but it is often incidental to the main purpose of the activity, which may be shopping, paying the bills or finding out local news. Literacy is used to get other things done. Everyday literacies are subservient to the goals of purposeful activities and are defined by people in terms of these activities. This raises questions about any strategy of teaching or testing autonomous and disembedded skills and argues for the importance of integrating learning about literacy with other subject areas.

(b) People's responses to printed texts are not dependent on observable features of the text alone, such as its genre; but people bring their own interpretative repertoires such that a given text may be used in many different ways, for many different purposes according to a person's motivation or ruling passion. Meaning does not reside in the text alone but in the associated practices; attention needs to be paid to why, how and by whom texts are produced and used.

(c) Literacies are embedded in social relationships that give them their meaning. Attention needs to be paid to what these social relationships are in schools, colleges, classrooms and other learning groups, and what the power dimensions of these relationships are in terms of the ability to make decisions, confer value, demonstrate expertise. The informal social networks which sustain literacies need to be drawn upon.

(*d*) Print literacy is often interchangeable with other media in achieving particular goals, such as communication, finding out information, etc. In their everyday lives people move unconsciously between media, and many people do not privilege literacy, but evaluate its worth in relation to available alternatives. This supports notions of teaching literacy in the context of other media and exploring the ways in which these other media are structured and their meanings in people's lives. In general, a social approach de-emphasises the differences between speech, writing and other, non-verbal means of expression. It supports not only critical language awareness but also critical awareness of other semiotic systems and the possibilities for their use.

We see an important contribution of this book as being to enable people within and beyond education to appreciate the variety and creativity of everyday literacy practices, to encourage others to go beyond this research in questioning received wisdom about literacy, in finding out more about practices in other settings and in devising educational responses to these growing understandings. We need to find ways of developing reflective partnerships which can mediate between homes, communities, schools and adult education programmes and to help learners, both children and adults, develop a sense of their own expertise and authorship, to take control of available literacies and put them to work to benefit themselves and their communities.

BIBLIOGRAPHY

Alasuutari, P. (1995) *Researching Culture: Qualitative Method and Cultural Studies*, London: Sage.

Ang, I. (1996) *Living Room Wars: Rethinking Media Audiences for a Post Modern World*, London: Routledge.

Ang, I. and Hermes, J. (1996) 'Gender and/in media consumption', in I. Ang, *Living Room Wars: Rethinking Media Audiences for a Post Modern World*, London: Routledge.

Antaki, C. (ed.) (1988) *Analysing Everyday Explanation: A Casebook of Methods*, London: Sage.

Atkinson, P. (1990) *The Ethnographic Imagination: Textual Constructions of Reality*, London: Routledge.

Bakhtin, M. (1953/86) *Speech Genres and Other Late Essays*, ed. C. Emerson and M. Holquist, trans. V. W. McGee, Austin, TX: University of Texas Press.

Barton, D. (1988) 'Exploring the historical basis of contemporary literacy', *Q: Newsletter of the Laboratory of Comparative Human Cognition*, 3: 70–6.

Barton, D. (1991) 'The social nature of writing', in D. Barton and R. Ivanic (eds) *Writing in the Community*, London: Sage.

Barton, D. (1994) *Literacy: An Introduction to the Ecology of Written Language*, Oxford: Blackwell.

Barton, D. (1996) 'Family literacy programmes and home literacy practices', in D. Baker, J. Clay and C. Fox (eds) *Challenging Ways of Knowing: In English, Mathematics and Science*, London: Falmer Press.

Barton, D. and Hamilton, M. (1992a) *Literacy in the Community*, Final Report to ESRC, project no. R00023 1419.

Barton. D. and Hamilton, M. (1992b) *Collaborative Ethnography*, Final Report to ESRC, project no. R00023 3440.

Barton, D. and Hamilton, M. (1996) 'Putting the new literacy studies into practice', in S. Fitzpatrick and J. Mace (eds) *Lifelong Literacies: Papers from the 1996 Conference*, Manchester: Gatehouse Books.

Barton, D. and Ivanic, R. (eds) (1991) *Writing in the Community*, London: Sage.

Barton, D. and Padmore, S. (1991) 'Roles, networks and values in everyday writing', in D. Barton and R. Ivanic (eds) *Writing in the Community*, London: Sage.

Barton, D., Hamilton, M., Ivanic, R., Ormerod, F., Padmore, S., Pardoe, S. and Rimmershaw, R. (1993) 'Photographing literacy practices', *Changing English*, 1, 1: 27–140.

Baynham, M. (1993) 'Code switching and mode switching: community interpreters and mediators of literacy', in B. Street (ed.) *Cross-cultural Approaches to Literacy*, Cambridge: Cambridge University Press.

Benton, S. (1994) 'Networks of communication between home and school', in M. Hamilton, D. Barton and R. Ivanic (eds) *Worlds of Literacy*, Clevedon, Avon: Multilingual Matters.

Besnier, N. (1993) 'Literacy and feelings: the encoding of affect in Nukulaelae letters', in B. Street (ed.) *Cross-cultural Approaches to Literacy*, Cambridge: Cambridge University Press.

Besnier, N. (1995) *Literacy, Emotion and Authority: Reading and Writing on a Polynesian Atoll*, Cambridge: Cambridge University Press.

Bhatt, A., Barton, D. and Martin-Jones, M. (1994) *Gujarati Literacies in East Africa and Leicester: Changes in Social Identities and Multilingual Practices*, Lancaster University: Centre for Language in Social Life Working Papers no. 56.

Bhatt, A., Barton, D., Martin-Jones, M. and Saxena, M. (1996) *Multilingual Literacy Practices: Home, Community and School*, Lancaster University: Centre for Language in Social Life Working Papers no. 80.

Bloome, D., Sheridan, D. and Street, B. (1993) 'Reading Mass-Observation writing', *Mass-Observation Archive Occasional Paper no. 1*, University of Sussex Library.

Book Marketing Limited (1995) *Books and the Consumer*, London: Book Marketing Limited.

Breen, M. (1994) *Literacy in its Place: Literacy Practices in Urban and Rural Communities*, School of Language Education, Edith Cowan University.

Bremner, M. (1992) *The Ultimate Problem Solver: A Complete Encyclopedia For Your Home*, London: Hutchinson.

Brooks, G., Foxman, D. and Gorman, T. (1995) *Standards in Literacy and Numeracy: 1948–1994*, London: National Commission on Education.

Brymon, A. and Burgess, R. G. (1994) *Analysing Qualitative Data*, London: Routledge.

BSA (1995) *Writing Skills: A Survey of How Well People Can Spell and Punctuate*, London: Basic Skills Agency.

Cameron, D. (1995) *Verbal Hygiene*, London: Routledge.

Camitta, M. (1993) 'Vernacular writing: varieties of writing among Philadelphia high school students', in B. Street (ed.) *Cross-cultural Approaches to Literacy*, Cambridge: Cambridge University Press.

Campbell, B. (1993) *Goliath: Britain's Dangerous Places*, London: Methuen.

Central Statistical Office (1992) *Social Trends 22*, London: HMSO.

Central Statistical Office (1993) *Social Trends 23*, London: HMSO.

Chaiklin, S. and Lave, J. (eds) (1993) *Understanding Practice: Perspectives on Activity and Context*, Cambridge: Cambridge University Press.

Citrine, W. M. (1952) *ABC of Chairmanship*, London: NCLC Publishing.

Clark, R. and Ivanic, R. (1997) *The Politics of Writing*, London: Routledge.

Clifford, J. and Marcus, G. E. (1986) *Writing Culture: The Poetics and Politics of Ethnography*, Berkeley: University of California Press.

Cohen, L. and Manion, L. (1994) *Research Methods in Education* (4th ed.), London: Routledge.

Constantine, S. and Warde, A. (1993) 'Challenge and change in the 20th century', in A. White (ed.) *A History of Lancaster*, Keele: Keele University Press.

Crouch, D. and Ward, C. (1988) *The Allotment: Its Landscape and Culture*, London: Faber and Faber.

Crow, G. and Allan, G. (1994) *Community Life: An Introduction to Local Social Relations*, London: Harvester Wheatsheaf.

Davies, P. (1994) 'Long-term unemployment and literacy: a case study of the restart interview', in M. Hamilton *et al. Worlds of Literacy*, Clevedon, Avon: Multilingual Matters.

De Certeau, M. (1984) *The Practice of Everyday Life*, Berkeley: California University Press.

Deem, R. (1986) *All Work and No Play? The Sociology of Women and Leisure*, Buckingham: Open University Press.

Deem, R., Brehony, K. and Heath, S. (1995) *Active Citizenship and the Governing of Schools*, Buckingham: Open University Press.

Department of National Heritage (1996) *People Taking Part*, London: HMSO.

Dey, I. (1993) *Qualitative Data Analysis: A User-friendly Guide for Social Scientists*, London: Routledge.

Dubin, F. and Kuhlman, N. A. (1992) *Cross-Cultural Literacy: Global Perspectives on Reading And Writing*, Englewood Cliffs, NJ: Prentice-Hall.

Duffin, P. (1990) 'A place for personal history', *Adults Learning*, 2, 1: 17–19.

Eckinsmyth, C. and Bynner, J. (1994) *The Basic Skills of Young Adults: Some Findings from the 1970 British Cohort Study*, London: Adult Literacy and Basic Skills Unit.

Egger, R. (1994) *Biographical Research in Adult Education: Contradictions and Risks in Using Narrative Methods*, Proceedings of Life Histories and Learning Conference, University of Sussex.

Elsdon, K. T. with J. Reynolds and S. Stewart (1995) *Voluntary Organizations: Citizenship, Learning and Change*, Leicester: NIACE.

Fairclough, N. (1989) *Language and Power*, London: Longman.

Fairclough, N. (1992) *Discourse and Social Change*, Cambridge: Polity Press.

Ferguson, M. (1983) *Forever Feminine: Women's Magazines and the Cult of Femininity*, London: Heinemann.

Finch, J. and Groves, D. (eds) (1983) *A Labour of Love: Women, Work and Caring*, London: Routledge.

Finch, J. and Mason, J. (1993) *Negotiating Family Responsibilities*, London: Tavistock/Routledge.

Fingeret, A. (1983) 'Social networks: independence and adult illiterates', *Adult Education Quarterly*, 33, 3: 133–46.

Finnegan, R. (1989) *The Hidden Musicians: Music Making in an English Town*, Cambridge: Cambridge University Press.

Fishman, A. (1988) *Amish Literacy: What and How it Means*, Portsmouth, NH: Heinemann.

Fishman, A (1991) 'Because this is who we are: writing in the Amish community', in D. Barton and R. Ivanic (eds) *Writing in the Community*, London: Sage.

Foucault, M. (1972) *The Archeology of Knowledge*, London: Tavistock Publications.

Foucault, M. (1977) *Discipline and Punish: The Birth of the Prison*, London: Allen Lane.

Gee, J. (1990) *Social Linguistics and Literacies: Ideology in Discourses*, London: Falmer Press.

Gee, J. (1992) *The Social Mind: Language, Ideology and Social Practice*, New York: Bergin and Garvey.

Gee, J., Hull, G. and Lankshear, C. (1997) *The New Work Order: Behind the Language of the New Capitalism*, London: Allen and Unwin.

Geertz, C. (1983) *Local Knowledge: Further Essays in Interpretative Anthropology*, New York: Basic Books.

Giddens, A. (1984) *The Constitution of Society*, Cambridge: Polity Press.

Giddens, A. (1991) *Modernity and Self Identity: Self and Society in the Late Modern Age*, Cambridge: Polity Press.

Gilmore, P. (1986) 'Sub-rosa literacy: peers, play and ownership in literacy acquisition', in B. Schieffelin and P. Gilmore (eds) *The Acquisition of Literacy: Ethnographic Perspectives*, Norwood, NJ: Ablex.

Glaser, B. and Strauss, A. (1967) *The Discovery of Grounded Theory*, New York: Aldine Press.

Goetz, J. and LeCompte, M. (1984) *Ethnography and Qualitative Design in Educational Research*, London: Academic Press.

Goody, J. (1986) *The Logic of Writing and the Organisation of Society*, Cambridge: Cambridge University Press.

Gowen, S. G. (1992) *The Politics of Workplace Literacy: A Case Study*, New York: Teachers College Press.

Graff, H. J. (1979) *The Literacy Myth: Literacy and Social Structure in the 19th Century City*, New York: Academic Press.

Gray, A. (1992) *Video Playtime: The Gendering of a Leisure Technology*, London: Routledge.

Green, J. and Bloome, D. (1996) 'Ethnography and ethnographers of and in education: a situated perspective', in J. Flood, S. Heath and D. Lapp (eds) *A Handbook for Literacy Educators: Research on Teaching the Communicative and Visual Arts*, New York: Macmillan.

Greenhalgh, L. and Worpole, K. with C. Landry (1995) *Libraries in a World of Cultural Change*, London: UCL Press.

Gregory, E. (1996) *Making Sense of a New World: Learning to Read in a Second Language*, London: Paul Chapman.

Gunter, B., Sancho-Aldridge, J. and Winstone, P. (1994) *Television: The Public's View*, London: John Libbey.

Haines, C. M. C. (1981) *Libraries and Newsrooms in Lancaster Prior to the Adoption of the Public Libraries Act, in 1892, and a Brief Survey of the Development of Public Library Services, from 1893–1974*, unpublished manuscript for Diploma in Library and Information Studies, King's College, London.

Hall, C. and Coles, M. (1996) *The Children's Reading Choices Project, Final Report*, University of Nottingham.

Hamilton, M. (1996) 'Keeping alive alternative visions', in J.-P. Hautecoeur (ed.) *Alpha 97: Basic Education and Institutional Environments*, Hamburg: Unesco Institute for Education.

Hamilton, M. (1998) 'Histories and horoscopes: the ethnographer as fortune teller', *Anthropology and Education Quarterly*, 29, 2.

Hamilton, M. and Davies, P. (1993) 'Literacy and long-term unemployment: options for adult guidance, support and training', *The British Journal of Education and Work*, 6, 2: 5–19.

Hamilton, M. and Stasinopoulos, M. (1987) *Literacy, Numeracy and Adults: Evidence from the National Child Development Study*, London: Adult Literacy and Basic Skills Unit.

Hamilton, M., Barton, D. and Ivanic, R. (eds) (1994) *Worlds of Literacy*, Clevedon, Avon: Multilingual Matters.

Hammersley, M. (1990) *Reading Ethnographic Research: A Critical Guide*, London: Longman.

Hannon, P. (1995) *Literacy, Home and School: Research and Practice in Teaching Literacy with Parents*, London: Falmer.

Harding, S. (1987) *Feminism and Methodology: Social Science Issues*, Bloomington, IN: Indiana University Press.

Heath, S. (1983) *Ways with Words: Language, Life and Work in Communities and Classrooms*, Cambridge: Cambridge University Press.

Heath, S. (1995) 'Ethnography in communities: learning the everyday life of America's subordinate youth', in J. Banks and C. McGee Banks (eds) *Handbook of Research on Multicultural Education*, New York: Simon and Schuster Macmillan.

Hermes, J. (1995) *Reading Women's Magazines: An Analysis of Everyday Media Use*, Cambridge: Polity Press.

Herrington, M. (1995) 'Dyslexia: old dilemmas and new policies', *RaPAL Bulletin*, 27: 3–9.

Hirsch, E. D. (1988) *Cultural Literacy: What Every American Needs to Know*, New York: Vintage.

Hoggart, R. (1957) *The Uses of Literacy: Aspects of Working-Class Life*, London: Chatto.

Horovitz (1995) Unpublished Ph.D. dissertation on Jewish Memorial Books.

Horsman, J. (1990) *Something on my Mind Besides the Everyday*, Toronto: Women's Press.

Horsman, J. (1994) 'The problem of illiteracy and the promise of literacy', in M. Hamilton, D. Barton and R. Ivanic (eds) *Worlds of Literacy*, Clevedon, Avon: Multilingual Matters.

Howard, U. (1991) 'Self, education and writing in nineteenth-century English communities', in D. Barton and R. Ivanic (eds) *Writing in the Community*, London: Sage.

Hughes, J., O'Brien, J. and Rodden, T. (1996) *The Intelligent Home Project*, CSCW, Lancaster University.

Hughes, N. (1992) *Now Everywhere is English: An Exploration of Language and Literacy in Everyday Life Carried Out with Adult Learners in East London*, unpublished Diploma dissertation, Goldsmiths' College, University of London.

Hutchison, R. and Feist, A. (1991) *Amateur Arts in the UK*, London: Policy Studies Institute.

Itzin, C. (1992) *Pornography: Women, Violence and Civil Liberties*, Oxford: Oxford University Press.

Ivanic, R. (1998) *Writing and Identity*, Amsterdam: John Benjamins.

Ivanic, R. and Hamilton, M. (1990) 'Literacy beyond school', in D. Wray (ed.) *Emerging Partnerships: Current Research in Language and Literacy*, Clevedon, Avon: Multilingual Matters.

Ivanic, R. and Moss, W. (1991) 'Bringing community writing practices into education', in D. Barton and R. Ivanic (eds) *Writing in the Community*, London: Sage.

Jenson, J. (1992) 'Fandom as pathology: the consequences of characterization', in L. A. Lewis (ed.) *The Adoring: Fan Culture and Popular Music*, London: Routledge.

Jenkins, H. (1992) *Textual Poachers: Television Fans and Participatory Culture*, London: Routledge.

Johnson, R. (1983) 'Really useful knowledge: radical education and working class culture 1790–1848', in M. Tight (ed.) *Educational Opportunities for Adults*, London: Routledge/Open University Press.

Kapitzke, C. (1995) *Literacy and Religion: The Textual Politics and Practice of Seventh-day Adventism*, Amsterdam: John Benjamins.

Keddie, N. (1980) 'Adult education: an ideology of individualism', in J. L. Thompson, (ed.) *Adult Education for a Change*, London: Hutchinson.

Keen, J. (1995) 'Family literacy in Lothian: Connect community learning programme with and for parents', *RaPAL Bulletin*, 28/9: 22–30.

Kincheloe, J. and McLaren, P. (1994) 'Rethinking critical theory and qualitative research', in N. Denzin and Y. S. Lincoln (eds) *Handbook of Qualitative Research*, London: Sage.

Klassen, C. (1991) 'Bilingual written language use by low-education Latin American newcomers', in D. Barton and R. Ivanic (eds) *Writing in the Community*, London: Sage

Kress, G. and Hodge, R. (1988) *Social Semiotics*, Cambridge: Polity Press.

Kress, G. and van Leeuwen, T. (1996) *Reading Images: The Grammar of Visual Design*, London: Routledge.

LaTour, B. (1993) *We Have Never Been Modern*, Hemel Hempstead: Harvester Wheatsheaf.

Lave, J. (1988) *Cognition in Practice*, Cambridge: Cambridge University Press.

Lave, J. and Wenger, E. (1991) *Situated Learning: Legitimate Peripheral Participation*, Cambridge: Cambridge University Press.

Leather, P. and Mackintosh, S. (1990) *Monitoring Assisted Agency Services, Pt 1: Home Improvement Agencies: An Evaluation of Performance*, London: HMSO.

Lemke, J. (1995) *Textual Politics: Discourse and Social Dynamics*, London: Taylor and Francis.

Lewis, L. A. (ed.) (1992) *The Adoring Audience: Fan Culture and Popular Media*, London: Routledge.

Lull, J. (ed.) (1988) *World Families Watch Television*, London: Sage.

Mace, J. (1992a) *Talking About Literacy*, London: Routledge

Mace, J. (1992b) 'Television and metaphors of literacy', *Studies in the Education of Adults*, 24, 2: 162–75.

Mace, J. (1998) *Playing with Time: Mothers and the Meanings of Literacy*, London: UCL Press. ,

Mace, J. (ed.) (1995) *Literacy, Language and Community Publishing: Essays in Adult Education*, Clevedon, Avon: Multilingual Matters.

McMahon, M., Roach, D., Karach, A. and van Dijk, F. (1994) 'Women and literacy for change', in M. Hamilton *et al.* (eds) *Worlds of Literacy*, Clevedon, Avon: Multilingual Matters.

Marshall, J. D. (ed.) (1967) *The Autobiography of William Stout of Lancaster 1665–1752*, Manchester: Manchester University Press.

Martin-Jones, M. (1996) *Enterprising Women: Multilingual Literacies in the Construction of New Identities*, Lancaster University: Centre for Language in Social Life Working Paper no. 69.

Mason, J. (1996) *Qualitative Researching*, London: Sage.

Maybin, J. (1996) Presentation at *Texts and Practices Seminar*, Lancaster University, July.

Maybin, J. (1997) *Children's Voices: The Contribution of Informal Language Practices to the Negotiation of Knowledge and Identity amongst 10–12 Year Old School Pupils*, Ph.D. Dissertation, Open University.

Moll, L. (1994) 'Mediating knowledge between homes and classrooms', in D. Keller-Cohen (ed.) *Literacy: Interdisciplinary Conversations*, Creshill, NJ: Hampton Press.

Morley, D. (1992) *Television, Audiences and Cultural Studies*, London: Routledge.

Moss, B. J. (1994) *Literacy Across Communities*, Creshill, NJ: Hampton Press.

Moss, G. (1996) *Negotiated Literacies*, Ph.D. Dissertation, Open University.

Myers, G. (1996) 'Out of the laboratory and down to the bay', *Written Communication* 13: 5–43.

National Literacy Trust (1993) *Omnibus Survey*, London.

Nell, V. (1988) *Lost in a Book: The Psychology of Reading for Pleasure*, New Haven, CT: Yale University Press.

Nunes, T., Schliemann, A. and Carraher, D. (1993) *Street Mathematics and School Mathematics*, Cambridge: Cambridge University Press.

OECD/Statistics Canada (1996) *Literacy, Economy and Society*, Ottawa: OECD.

Ormerod, F. and Ivanic, R. (1997) 'Texts in practices: interpreting the physical characteristics of text', Paper presented at conference *Situated Literacies*, Lancaster.

O'Rourke, R. (1994) *Written on the Margins: Creative Writing and Adult Education in Cleveland*, Deptartment of Adult Continuing Education, University of Leeds.

Olson, D. (1994) *The World on Paper*, Cambridge: Cambridge Univesity Press.

Olson, T. (1980) *Silences*, London: Virago.

Padmore, S. (1992) Presentation at *Why People Write*, literacy symposium, Lancaster University, December 1992.

Percy, K. A. (1988) *Learning in Voluntary Organisations*, Leicester: Unit for the Development of Continuing Education, Leicester University.

Pikulski, J. J. (1996) 'The International Reading Association and "learning disabilities": an update', *Reading Today*, 14, 3: 34.

Policy Studies Institute (1993) *Cultural Trends no. 17*, London: PSI.

Potter, J. and Weatherall, M. (1987) *Discourse and Social Psychology: Beyond Attitudes and Behaviour*, London: Sage.

Prinsloo, M. and Breier, M. (1996) *The Social Uses of Literacy: Theory and Practice in Contemporary South Africa*, Amsterdam: John Benjamins.

Radway, J. (1987) *Reading the Romance*, London: Verso.

Reder, S. (1987) 'Comparative aspects of functional literacy development: three ethnic American communities', in D. Wagner (ed.) *The Future of Literacy in a Changing World*, Oxford: Pergamon Press.

Reder, S. (1994) 'Practice-engagement theory: a sociocultural approach to literacy across languages and cultures', in B. Ferdman, R.-M. Weber and A. G. Ramirez (eds) *Literacy Across Languages and Cultures*, New York: State University of New York Press.

Reder, S. and Wikelund, K. R. (1993) 'Literacy development and ethnicity: an Alaskan example', in B. Street (ed.) *Cross-cultural Approaches to Literacy*, Cambridge: Cambridge University Press.

Reinharz, S. (1992) *Feminist Methods in Social Research*, Oxford: Oxford University Press.

Roberts, E. (1984) *A Woman's Place: An Oral History of Working Class Women, 1890–1940*, Oxford: Blackwell.

Roberts, E. (1995) *Women and Families: An Oral History, 1940–1970*, Oxford: Blackwell.

Rockhill, K. (1987) 'Literacy as threat/desire: longing to be somebody', in J. S. Gaskill and A. T. McLaren (eds) *Women and Education: A Canadian Perspective*, Calgary: Deselig.

Rockhill, K. (1993) 'Gender, language and the politics of literacy', in B. Street (ed.) *Cross-cultural Approaches to Literacy*, Cambridge: Cambridge University Press.

Rogers, S. (1994) *Literacy Practices in English and Gujarati: Four Bilingual Teenagers in Leicester*, MA Dissertation, Lancaster University.

Romaine, S. (1989) *Bilingualism*, Oxford: Blackwell.

Saatchi and Saatchi (1990) *UK Media Yearbook*, London: Saatchi and Saatchi.

Sanjek, R. (1990) *Field Notes: The Making of Anthropology*, Ithaca, NY: Cornell University Press.

Saxena, M. (1991) *The Changing Role of Minority Literacies in Britain: A Case Study of Panjabis in Southall*, Lancaster University: Centre for Language in Social Life Working Paper no. 28.

Saxena, M. (1994) 'Literacies among Panjabis in Southall', in M. Hamilton *et al.* (eds) *Worlds of Literacy*, Clevedon, Avon: Multilingual Matters.

Sayers, P. (1992) 'Making it work – communications skills training at a black housing association', in N. Fairclough (ed.) *Critical Language Awareness*, London: Longman.

Schieffelin, B. and Gilmore, P. (eds) (1986) *The Acquisition of Literacy: Ethnographic Perspectives*, Norwood, NJ: Ablex.

Scribner, S. (1984) 'Studying working intelligence', in B. Rogoff and J. Lave (eds) *Everyday Cognition: Its Development in Social Context*, Cambridge, MA: Harvard University Press.

Scribner, S. and Cole, M. (1981) *The Psychology of Literacy*, Cambridge, MA: Harvard University Press.

Silverman, D. (1993) *Interpreting Qualitative Data*, London: Sage.

Silverstone, R., Hirsch, E. and Morley, D. (1994) 'Information and communication technologies and the moral economy of the household', in R. Silverstone and E. Hirsch (eds) *Consuming Technologies*, London: Routledge.

Smith, D. (1988) *The Everyday World as Problematic: A Feminist Sociology*, Buckingham: Open University Press.

Smith, D. (1993) *Texts, Facts and Femininity*, London: Routledge.

Solsken, J, W. (1993) *Literacy, Gender and Work in Families and at School*, Norwood, NJ: Ablex.

Spradley, J. P. (1979) *The Ethnographic Interview*, New York: Holt, Rinehart and Winston.

Stephens, W. B. (1987) *Education, Literacy and Society, 1830–70*, Manchester: Manchester University Press.

Stevens, E. W. (1988) *Literacy, Law and Social Order*, DeKalb, IL: Northern Illinois University Press.

Stevenson, J. (1997) *Information and Communications Technology in UK Schools: An Independent Inquiry March 1997*, London: The Independent ICT in School Commission.

Street, B. (1984) *Literacy in Theory and Practice*, Cambridge: Cambridge University Press.

Street, B. (ed.) (1993) *Cross-cultural Approaches to Literacy*, Cambridge: Cambridge University Press.

Street, J. C. and Street, B. (1991) 'The schooling of literacy', in D. Barton and R. Ivanic (eds) *Writing in the Community*, London: Sage.

Swales, J. (1990) *Genre Analysis: English in Academic and Research Settings*, Cambridge: Cambridge University Press.

Taylor, D. (1983) *Family Literacy*, London: Heinemann Educational.

Taylor, D. (1996) *Toxic Literacies: Exposing the Injustics of Bureaucratic Texts*, Portsmouth, NH: Heinemann.

Taylor, D. (ed.) (1997) *Many Families, Many Literacies: An International Declaration of Principles*, Portsmouth, NH: Heinemann.

Taylor, D. and Dorsey-Gaines, C. (1988) *Growing Up Literate: Learning from Inner-city Families*, London: Heinemann.

Tough, A. (1979) *The Adults Learning Projects* (2nd ed.) Toronto: OISE.

Vincent, D. (1989) *Literacy and Popular Culture: England 1750–1914*, Cambridge: Cambridge University Press.

Wagner, D. A. (1993) *Literacy, Culture and Development: Becoming Literate in Morocco*, Cambridge: Cambridge University Press.

Weinberger, J. (1996) *Literacy Goes to School: The Parents' Role in Young Children's Literacy Learning*, London: Paul Chapman.

Weinstein-Shr, G. (1993) 'Literacy and social process: a community in transition', in B. Street (ed.) *Cross-cultural Approaches to Literacy*, Cambridge: Cambridge University Press.

Wells, G. (1985) 'Preschool literacy-related activities and success in school', in D. Olson, N. Torrance and A. Hildyard (eds), *Literacy, Language and Learning: The Nature and Consequences of Reading and Writing*, Cambridge: Cambridge University Press.

White, A. (ed.) (1993) *A History of Lancaster*, Keele: Keele University Press.

Williams, R. (1976) *Keywords: A Vocabulary of Culture and Society*, London: Croom Helm.

Wilson, A. (1994) *Reading, Writing and Rhetoric: A Case for Non-literacy in Closed Institutions*, MA Dissertation, Department of Linguistics, Lancaster University.

Wilson, A. (1996) '"Speak up, I can't write what you're reading": the place of literacy in the prison community', *Journal of Correctional Education*, 47, 2: 94–100.

Winstanley, M. (1993) 'The town transformed, 1815–1914' in A. White (ed.) *A History of Lancaster 1193–1993*, Keele: Ryburn Publishing, Keele University Press.

Withnall, A. (1995) *Older Adults' Needs and Usage of Numerical Skills in Everyday Life*, Department of Continuing Education, Lancaster University.

Wynn, B. (1992) 'Misunderstood misunderstanding: social identities and public uptake of science', *Public Understanding of Science*, 1: 281–304.

Young, P. and Tyre, C. (1983) *Dyslexia or Illiteracy? Recognising the Right to Read*, Milton Keynes: Open University Press.

Ziegahn, L. (1991) 'Beyond reciprocity: exchange around literacy in Adult Basic Education', *Adult Basic Education*, 1, 2: 79–97.

INDEX OF INFORMANTS

In alphabetical order of first name

INDEX

up almost in a single movement, knowing even before she turned it over that it bore the small red cross on it.

Feverishly she ripped open the envelope. Her heart thumping heavily, she pulled out the single sheet of limp recycled note-paper and unfolded it swiftly, hardly daring to breathe, hardly daring to let her eyes scan what it had to say. It took only the first two lines to send a sensation of debility spreading through her limbs so that she had to clutch at the newel post to keep her from falling. The waiting was at an end. At last they knew.

Tears she had kept unshed all this time started to flow and she didn't try to prevent them as she sank down on the stairs and, all alone in the house, gave herself up to weeping, the letter crumpled in her hand. Slowly, though, she gathered her thoughts. She must let Leonard know. Her hand automatically reached for the telephone on the hall stand, she dialled the operator, gave her the number of Leonard's shop and waited. It seemed to take forever before his receiver was lifted, but she felt too drained to think in the interval. Her brain seemed quite dead. She actually gave a small start as Leonard's voice sounded close to her ear.

'Hello? Ward's Electrical Shop.'

'Leonard! We've heard. We've heard from the International Red Cross – a letter – this morning. Leonard – they've found him. He's a prisoner of war. That's all they know. But, Leonard, he's alive. Our Matthew's alive.'

There was a second or two's silence, then his voice came, trembling, just as hers had. 'I'm coming home. I'm closing up and coming home.'

'But your customers. You can't . . .' It sounded quite inane. News of Matthew traced and she was worrying about customers?

'Sod the customers!' He never swore in her hearing. She wouldn't have it. But today she forgave him.

Chapter 20

The rain had ceased. The flood within the railway cutting had subsided and with it part of the earth wall which must now be shored up. The guards, tempers uncertain at the best of times and now made more vile by the appalling conditions which they and prisoners alike were compelled to share, were calling for more speed. Anxious to return to their dry quarters and some warm food, they backed their demands with stick and stone aimed at any prisoner who flagged at his task.

The cutting rang to their demented yells, to the screech of steel being dragged from antiquated lorries, the clang of hammers on the metal spikes securing the rails in place while the sickly glow of carbide lamps gleamed on the glistening shoulders of those who toiled into the night.

To Matthew's fevered mind the whole thing resembled scenes from Dante's *Inferno* as on hands and knees he groped in the yellow mud for the bolts of the fishplate that would join together the two rails placed there.

His last meal of cold boiled rice diluted by monsoon rain had been eaten at mid-morning, eight hours ago. He would not eat again until their overseer, the shoko, called a halt to measure the day's quota of work sometime just before midnight. His brain felt it was bursting from the most recent attack of malaria; he dared not dwell on how he would get through the remaining hours, but get through them he must.

Evading the prospect, he found himself turning his thoughts inward – a sort of mental escapism he'd long ago learned – a way of withdrawing into the depths of his own brain as into a dark little world secluded from all this misery outside. Slowly a wonderful phenomenon would occur, though it was only imagination. Inside his head there would appear a bright disc and within the disc he'd visualise Susan's face, smiling, gentle as she reached out to him. The clamour around him would recede and he would seem to float on a tiny island of peace, remote from the violence and hunger that made up the world he now existed in. A figment of a feverish mind, perhaps. What did it matter? It sustained him, and with a fanaticism born of sheer desperation he clung to that wavering disc with an insane – because one could become insane in this place – but obdurate conviction that while he could conjure up that disc of light inside his head, he would survive.

He had never dreamed he would, that day of his being taken prisoner. Hands raised, his pockets being rifled, he'd protested at Susan's photo being torn into pieces, had taken a step forward. One of his captors had sprung at him, bayonet whipping round. It was then he'd thought his life over, but the bayonet just scored his outstretched forearm.

The captives, bound together by their own belts in twos, had been pushed and prodded along jungle tracks with the noise of the river, which had meant safety, receding; they had finally been incarcerated in a small bamboo enclosure, full of Indian and British soldiers, which became filthier as the days passed with no latrines and a constant scramble for water. His arm had swollen to twice its normal size from the shallow bayonet wound bound by a piece of his own shirt.

Rangoon fell a week later. He had joined a lengthening column of POWs, taken back across the Sittang River, by then spanned by a hasty bridge flung up by the Japanese, past shattered metal and unburied bodies and into the city.

The poison from his festering wound had spread and he remembered little of the trek across the Irrawaddy Plain beneath a burning sun, but it was then that the strange disc-like brilliance with Susan's image inside it began to fill his head. Bob, who had been with him, and still was, had said that he was holding whole conversations with her. But he'd been convinced then as now of the telepathic origins of that bright light. Susan's thoughts were encouraging him, spanning the thousands of miles between them.

It had been Bob Howlett who'd practically carried him into the Rangoon jail from that seventy-mile trek, who had badgered him into putting one foot before the other, holding him up, telling him not to give up, that he had Susan and a baby to get home to; Bob who had fed him with tiny morsels of watery rice and bits of fruit as he lay desperately ill.

Now it was Bob who lay desperately ill with dysentery, so pernicious that Matthew feared he would lose him. So many friends had been parted, they had been fortunate staying together this long. If Bob died, there'd be no panacea of shared comradeship, nights spent in their rotting tent talking quietly of their hopes of what they were going to do when they got back home, their wives, their memories of happier days. If Bob died, he'd be totally alone.

With the wall shored up and this particular group of railway workers at last clear of the cutting, a whistle blasted; work ceased abruptly while the shoko went forward to inspect the quota completed. Silence fell, broken only by the dripping of rainwater from sodden vegetation, the drowned earth sucking and bubbling, the laborious breathing of the men, a cough or two, the idle clink of a metal tool and the sigh of the sick, their mates waiting to help them back to the huddle of tents they called home.

With the shoko signalling permission, each man lined up for his mess-tin of cold rice doled out from an old oil drum positioned under a strip of leaking tarpaulin, afterwards to slither their way along a morass of a path to their tents and sleep. But first there was water from the river to be boiled, to cook the edible lizard he'd caught and killed that morning. Anything caught was supposed to go into the common pot, but he meant to cook it himself and feed the broth to Bob, who would have done the same for him.

Armed with a bent and battered petrol can, he made his way from the tent designed to hold three Japanese schoolboys comfortably but now used by eight men, and headed a quarter of a mile down the slippery path to the stagnant backwater of the river. It had to be the backwater. The torrent of the main river could wash away a man, especially one in a weakened condition. Men were already there scooping up the cloudy liquid, a perfect breeding ground for disease. The last to arrive, Matthew sank down on a decaying log to wait for the pool to clear, his head buzzing from his malaria. He watched each man depart with a full container, slipping, sliding, shambling back up the greasy track, all the spring of youth gone out of their step. Sitting here, he too felt like an old man, trying to summon the will just to raise himself up and fill up his can with the cloudy water.

Holding the petrol can below the surface to fill, he stared across the river into the darkness of the jungle. The roar of the river was deafening. A slow, lethargic thought came. What was the point of it all, squatting here, a half-naked, emaciated travesty of a man, shaken by fever, tongue raw from pellagra that made every mouthful of what food he got an agony? Would he drag on for a few more months in this hopeless corner of the world, or somewhere like it further along this growing railway, lost, forgotten, to succumb and be buried under a bamboo cross, one among all the countless other bamboo crosses that lined the route?

'God! Why in Christ's name did you do this to me? Why in Christ's name won't you help us?'

The roar of the river bore away the insane cry. The buzzing night-jungle swallowed it whole. There was no one to hear, just some unseen monkeys disturbed by the strange man-cry, replying with a distant demented howling while the incessant chirruping of myriads of insects in this primeval tangle of sodden vegetation continued uninterrupted.

There was a reply – voiceless in his own head, the memory of a smile, Susan hovering in his head across thousands of miles of sea and desert and mountain and jungle, waiting for him. He couldn't let her down. He couldn't let Bob down, sitting here nursing his own misery while Bob hovered at the edge of death. Rationality returned. The can was full and he had jobs to do.

It was heaven to close the door, to curl up in one of the old armchairs in the partitioned-off part of her room upstairs, to be alone.

Emma was a wonderful and supportive friend, but her chatter could get a bit much sometimes. With Mattie being looked after downstairs by a willing Emma, who adored girls, she could relax with the latest paperback romance, identifying with the beautiful heroine in the embrace of the dark handsome hero, who in her imagination was Matthew, until it was Mattie's bedtime.

But all the imagination in the world could never compensate for the real thing. She and Edie spent most Saturday nights being whirled around a dance floor by Uniformed worthies, one of them invariably whispering a certain invitation in her ear. It was a source of pride to her that she resisted, loyal still to her married state. But sometimes she envied Edie leaving with a partner's arm around her waist. 'You be orlright goin' 'ome without me?'

She'd nod and watch her leave then go and sit at the side of the hall knowing that the next partner – there always was one – asking her to go for a walk with him, the question heavy with innuendo, would get a short answer. But oh, how she envied Edie.

Once, hurrying to catch her bus home, she'd passed a couple hidden in a dark doorway. In the blackout she would have missed them but for a girlish giggle she recognised as Edie's. She heard the deep drawl of a GI and knew that tomorrow Edie would be displaying a fancy bar of toilet soap, or a bar of chocolate or a pair of nylons, perhaps even, with a brash flourish, bring out a packet of US government-issue contraceptives to shock her friend.

'It's safe as 'ouses, Sue, an' what 'arm are yer doing, keepin' the poor things 'appy, far away from 'ome, making yerself feel better in the bargain?'

But she couldn't do that. What if she did fall by accident? How would she ever face Matthew's parents? Yet it had been so long since a man's hand had touched her, really touched her. Her whole body ached at the thought of it. It was now August. August 1943, seven months since she'd heard Matthew had been made a prisoner of war; almost two years since she had last seen him; at times she couldn't remember his face unless she looked at a photo of him first; Mattie's first birthday had come and gone two weeks ago and he had never seen her. She often thought nowadays of herself and Mattie, never herself, Matthew and Mattie.

'I wish I had your courage,' she said to Edie on the Monday morning, knowing Edie had throughly enjoyed her Saturday night by evidence of yet another handful of Hershey bars and a pair of nylons.

Edie ran the gauzy stockings through her fingers. 'Can't get these in this country,' she tempted.

It wasn't the gifts American boys could dish out that made Susan squirm at Edie's efforts to tempt but the thought of someone's arms around her. It was a terrible thought and made her want to cry. Her first joy at the news of Matthew having been traced had long since dwindled. She had been allowed to send him a message if that was what it could be called. Fifteen words on a form, all the Japanese permitted. Whether Matthew received it who was to say? There had been no reply. It felt for all the world as though her message had been written to a ghost. She had never dared voice those sentiments to his mother, who had sent off her own forlorn fifteen words of encouragement and love that day. She would have been appalled. How much more appalled would she be were she to know how his wife yearned for the feel of a man's hand fondling her even though it wasn't her husband's. No, she couldn't.

All very well for Edie in the arms of some frustrated warrior far from home. Edie had changed a lot this year, voiced a different slant on her husband these days.

'Two years away – and God knows 'ow many more years. I mean, the man's stuck out in the Falklands. When're they goin' ter give 'im leave from there? Meanwhile I could go barmy waiting fer 'im ter come 'ome and make love.'

'But don't you feel some loyalty to him?' Susan asked and received a sceptical chuckle as Edie sorted out men's small from men's large, ready for despatching.

''Ow do I know 'e's not 'aving it off with some Falklands floozie? I do know 'e 'ad a rovin' eye, even when I first married 'im. It didn't matter then, I was there to keep my eye on 'im. But now, miles away. Why shouldn't I 'ave a bit of pleasure too? You must feel the need too, Sue? Keepin' yerself like a nun – it ain't natural. What the ole man don't know won't 'urt 'im. You ain't gonna confess all when 'e comes marchin' 'home, are yer? Fer God's sake, Sue, you'll be a physical wreck by the time 'e does if yer don't let off a bit of steam now and again.'

Frustration had its own way of dealing with things. Alone in her room, her senses keened from reading cheap romances about larger-than-life heroines and handsome forceful heroes, she would furtively turn the key of her door, quietly so no one would hear it. Secure behind the lock, she would slip out of her clothes and survey herself before the mirror, run her hands slowly, slowly, over her body, gently following the curve of her small breasts, still firm; over her flat stomach that child-bearing had not marred at all. Closing her eyes she would imagine her fingers to be those of Matthew, tenderly exploring, growing urgent until her disquietened senses shrieked for relief. Then, throbbing from the lack of fulfilment she would fling herself on to her bed to squirm and weep in self-torment. How tempting it would be at these moments to follow Edie's example, to find herself someone to fondle her, fulfil this emptiness inside her – surely more honest than this pathetic self-pleasure that was no pleasure at all and left only misery in its wake.

'I wish I knew if Matthew was all right,' she confided in Emma. 'It could be years before I ever know. I'm so lonely.'

'At least yer've got Mattie,' Emma said, busily darning one of her Geoffrey's socks. He'd gone away for a day or two as usual.

'You have her most of the time these days,' Susan said.

Emma looked up sharply. 'It's you wot asked me ter look after 'er. You goin' ter work an' all. I'm not keepin' 'er away from yer.'

'I know. I didn't mean anything.' She was glad of Emma's help. She wasn't cut out to be a mother, she didn't think, driven to distraction when Mattie got herself into a temper, shrieking at the top of her voice. A child's shriek could be like a hot iron searing right through a person's eardrum. Smacking only made things worse. Many times Susan had been forced out of sheer frustration to resort to a smack on her legs, finally having to rush her down to Emma to pacify her. Emma was a natural mother. At times Susan felt quite envious of her.

'I'm just a bit down, I suppose,' she excused herself now. 'I hope she don't play you up too much.'

'Good Lord, no. She's a real dear. 'Cos, the only fing is we 'ave ter put everyfink up out of 'er reach now she's 'oisting 'erself up on 'er feet. Got 'er little 'ands inter everyfink. Real explorin' character she is. Quick. An' if she don't get wot she wants, gets a real tantrum on 'er. Strong-minded. It's good. She probably takes after 'er dad. You're more of a pliable person, you are. She don't look as if she's gonna be. She ain't gonna be moved from wot she wants in life.'

'Sounds like she takes after Matthew's mother. Nothing can move her either.' She didn't say it in bitterness, just stated what was the truth. Mrs Ward had never deviated from the certainty that Matthew would come home, even though her poor little message hadn't been answered; had not deviated from continually telling Susan that she must be strong and pray for him to come home and not to give way to 'any temptation that may come along'. Such instructions made Susan shudder. What did the woman know of the feelings she harboured? Probably nothing. She was merely wise to such things, being older and having seen and learned more, for all her primness.

'I miss Matthew so much,' she said in an effort to evade thoughts of those temptations Mrs Ward hinted at with more emphasis than Susan cared to acknowledge. 'I know Geoffrey's not in the forces but he's away a lot too. Don't you miss *him*?'

'Miss 'im!' Emma put away the sock she had darned and picked up another, studying the dangerously thin place on the heel that next week would become a hole. 'I'm glad to see the back of him sometimes.'

Shocked, Susan stared at her. 'You don't mean that.'

'Yes, I do.' Emma gave a good-tempered chuckle. 'So will you when he's bin home fer a few years. Most wives do. Not nasty-like. But it's nice ter 'ave 'em out of the way occasionally and get on wiv yer own fings. Before 'e 'ad this job of 'is, it was, "Wot yer goin' out fer? 'Ow long'll yer be? I don't feel like goin' ter the pictures ternight." So I couldn't go either, could I? Not on me own an' leave 'im 'ere on 'is own. Married people don't do that. An' when yer spend all day mendin' 'is socks an 'ironing 'is shirts, an' bringin' up 'is kids, an' gettin' 'is breakfasts and dinners, an' makin' 'is sandwiches, an' bein' woken up out of a deep sleep because 'e wants a bit of the other . . . well, yer've had enough, ain't yer, an' yer want a bit of time to yerself. Miss 'im? I think this job 'e's got 'as bin a godsend. I know 'e's safe, not overseas somewhere in the fick of it all. But Geoff's the limit sometimes – expecting me ter be runnin' after 'im. The least sneeze and I'm 'is nursemaid. Men!'

Her darning needle flew fast but without ill will. 'Babies, most of 'em. I expect they're brave enough amongst themselves, but get near their wives an' they're little babies, straight they are. I'm a bloomin' muvver to Geoff.'

She stopped to tap the hand of her youngest trying to fish into her workbasket for the glass marbles that always got in there. 'Yer'll prick yer fingers, yer silly little bugger! I'll get 'em out for yer after I've done this. Jus' wait!' She directed another laugh towards Susan watching. 'Even at that age. You 'ave ter fink for 'em. Mind, I don't mind Geoff wantin' his rights. I'd love ter 'ave a little daughter, just like your'n, it's just 'im waking me up out of a sleep fer it . . .' Another tolerant laugh. 'My mum use ter say, "Before yer married yer could feel yer could eat it. After yer married, yer wish you 'ad!" '

'I hope I never feel like that,' Susan said fervently.

'You will, luv. You will. Anyway I've got my little remedy – just tell 'im I'm out of bounds fer a week. I've told 'im, if 'e wants more'n I can give 'im, 'e can find it wiv a bit of skirt on 'is travels.'

She glanced up at the domed clock on the mantelshelf and sighed, ignoring Susan's look of horror as she put the rest of her husband's socks back into the workbasket to finish off later. 'Come on, you kids, time fer bed. Yer've got school in the mornin'.' Mattie, just a baby, had been put to bed ages ago. Emma's edict was met with a howl from the younger two, because Malcolm was still out playing.

'It's still light, Mum.'

'This time of year, it's always light. It's still eight o'clock and time fer bed.'

'Malc's not bin called in yet.'

''E will be. Soon as you two are up them stairs. Come on now.' She threw Susan an amused backward glance as she ushered them from the room in front of her. 'I was only jokin', Sue. My Geoff'd never go off wiv anuvver woman. 'E knows only too well where 'is bread is buttered, don' you worry.'

In the flimsy bamboo and attap construction they called the hospital, Matthew eased his way between the low platforms of sick men, some still as death, some tossing and turning in delirium, some bloated by beri-beri or calling for a pan as they strained to the flux of dysentery, or waited to have tropical leg ulcers attended to.

Bob lay at the far end, a cadaverous figure whose hair had mostly fallen out to leave just a few dry tufts. His dull eyes glowed in the depths of their sockets and his lips parted in a grin at Matthew's approach.

'Hi.' He was unable to say more.

'Hi,' Matthew returned. 'How goes it?'

The thin shoulders hitched a fraction. 'Fine,' croaked the voice.

Kneeling beside him, Matthew recounted the day's news as he gave him a drink and then the soup he'd concocted from rice and a tiny bit of dried fish, but Bob turned away after the first mouthful, appetite destroyed.

'Cream of asparagus,' Matthew made the pathetic joke, 'straight from Harrods.'

But Bob's body had doubled up in pain, and Matthew held the panshaped piece of tin beneath his pal as the bowels evacuated the black blood-stained fluid. He felt helpless. How Bob had stayed alive for so long was beyond him. Sheer will-power sustained him and nothing else, for he no longer ate.

There were no drugs and food was his only chance. But rice alone was not food enough. For his friend, Matthew stole, but not well. Bob had always been better at it than he, his cheerful slant on life serving him well in the face of the anger of their conquerors if caught. Even for them food was not all that forthcoming and understandably they were apt to become overwrought by light-fingered prisoners purloining the tiniest portion of what small comforts they did receive. But stealing was a necessary part of survival. Bartering what inedibles he stole called for patience, and again Bob's stolid approach to life had allowed him to stand the strain of it and the disappointment that often followed. Wily villagers knew they had the edge on British POWs with half a mind on prowling guards. The Nippon cigarettes or stolen truck spares they'd risked their lives for would reap a couple of tiny eggs or a pomelo or two or a scrap of dried fish. But beggars couldn't be choosers.

The watery dawn coming up, Matthew turned his face towards camp with a lighter heart than usual. Under his loincloth hung half a tiny chicken, a bit high but edible. It made him walk oddly but the gait of anyone with a raw scrotum was easily ignored. Once the chicken was made into a soup, Bob must surely find the appetite to take a few mouthfuls.

The night shift had been unusually short. Yamagata, their shoko, had miscalculated the quota and his pleasure at their apparently superhuman efforts to reach the target he'd set showed on his round face, his tone almost pleasant as he'd called out *'Yoroshii,'* which meant things were good. Or men finish.

With the railway growing apace it was a long march back to camp. By the time they reached it, Yamagata would have eaten and been in the arms of Morpheus. It was a surprise then to see him coming back to meet them, his short arms flailing like stubby windmill sails, his face animated. He had obviously discovered his error in judging his quota and intended putting it to rights; no doubt he'd been hauled over the coals himself for the mistake. But instead of marching the men back to the railway, he took them down another narrow path into the jungle to arrive at another camp.

It was empty. It didn't take long to discover why. Every one of the native labourers there was dead. Ordered to burn every corpse, a strong suspicion grew that they were disposing of cholera victims and Matthew thought that no Japanese could ever have seen men work faster. Two hours later they were marching back to their own camp, a very sober, thoughtful bunch. But worse was to come. In their absence three British POWs had died of something also strongly resembling cholera.

Matthew felt his flesh creep, seeing the Japanese running about making ready to flee before it struck them also. He noticed too that the guards with his column had disappeared. Nothing would prevent a man escaping except the jungle itself; thousands of square miles of rainforest; a mapless terrain where he would climb and slither endlessly; inedible plant life, poisonous insects, evil water; he would go round in circles until he died. No iron bars could have made a better prison.

In a steady rain that had again begun, the camp was a nucleus of panic, the sick being transported from the hospital on makeshift stretchers to be unceremoniously dumped on the bare, wet ground. Catching the panic, Matthew grabbed the arm of one of the helpers.

'I'm looking for Bob Howlett.'

The man looked put out. With over a hundred sick to get out of this place at the double, who the hell remembered one man's name? 'Go and ask the bloody MO.'

'Where's the MO?'

The orderly shrugged free of his grip. 'Listen chum. We've got just five minutes to get these poor buggers out before them bastards set fire to the hospital. They're bleedin' terrified. If you can't help us, sod off!'

He had jerked a thumb towards three guards, no doubt ordered by their CO to stand their ground, which they would, more frightened of his wrath than cholera. Two had set up a machine gun, obviously meant for any protesters as the third stood by with several cans of kerosene. Their faces, full of terror, were the colour of putty.

'There's blokes gonna die being moved like this. But they ain't gonna burn. Now leave us alone if you ain't gonna help.'

Matthew found the MO inside the hospital frantically supervising the exodus. 'Bob Howlett,' he enquired urgently. 'Lantern-jawed chap. Has dysentery.'

The distinguishing feature had made an impression. The MO paused in his work, his expression one of commiseration. 'Were you the mate who used to feed and wash him?'

There was no need for the man to say more. Matthew felt numbed.

'When?' he whispered.

'Buried him last night.' The statement was almost callous. The MO had expended his compassion in this direction. Now he must return his attention to the living.

'Where was he buried?' Matthew persisted.

'Cemetery.' The soldier with the kerosene can was coming forward, approaching cautiously as though the dread killer might pounce out on him.

'Where in the cemetery?'

'I don't know where!' The MO pushed past, pointing to his helpers. 'You, over there with that one. Quick now!' His shout was one of exasperation. Two British officers, identifiable by the tattered shirts they still retained, were arguing with the soldier.

'Wait – please – wait.'

But he pushed them aside, shaking his head. *'Iie! Dame desu! Kirai! Hayaku!'* He was demanding they move out of his way. Those with the machine gun had grown tense. Defeated, the officers fell back. The can at arm's length splashed against the hut. Numbed by his own grief, Matthew watched a lighted match thrown into the place, heard the fuel ignite with a soft roar. Flames met rain-soaked material, hissed, spluttered, hesitated. A pall of yellow smoke rolled the length of the hut. Men running in and out, bearing their occupied stretchers, coughed in the smoke, shouting, getting in each other's way. More fuel was splashed on, another match struck. A growl rose up from the rescuers, but the Japanese had the machine gun and were trigger-happy.

Conquering the wet bamboo and palm-leaf roof, the flames leapt, and still the rescuers ran in and out, the sick draped over their shoulders, men, hardly able to stand, clambering over the open sides of the hospital.

His own personal loss dulling his senses, Matthew ran with the others, blindly helping the last of the sick to safety until the heat finally forced him to retreat. With the flames crackling behind him he went towards the cemetery at the far end of the camp where a tangle of jungle prevented any further intrusion. There he stood gazing at the rows of bamboo crosses, each tilted in the sodden mud, each bearing a pathetic attempt to inscribe the name of whoever lay beneath.

It was very still here. Just the sound of pattering rain on the soft earth and the distant cries of those still helping with the rescue and the red glow from the burning hospital flickering on the drunken crosses in the monsoon-dulled morning like something in a weird dream.

Which cross belonged to Bob? Was he yet to have a cross? So many crosses. So many. From some of them a fine rivulet of mud was trickling. By the end of the monsoon many of the markers would be horizontal. As the camp moved on, following the railway, the jungle would return, cover them with vines and roots and fungus, all signs of them obliterated as though they had never been. By that time he and others would be far away, perhaps themselves beneath the mud under a rough bamboo cross out there in this senseless tangle. All were living on borrowed time. All a man could hope for was a mate to hold his hand so he would not die alone.

But Bob had died alone. The man who'd been his friend from almost the beginning of their Army service, who had carried him for two days on the march to Rangoon, who had bathed him so many times when he had been sick and helpless, had been denied the privilege of a companion to ease his last moments. Amid other dying men he had gone unnoticed, alone.

The thought of that loneliness constricted Matthew's throat muscles. He should have been with him, should have been there to put an inscription on his pitiful bamboo cross, to honour Bob's burial with his presence.

Without strength Matthew let his knees buckle, sank down in the mud which, disturbed by his light weight on it,

offered up a fulsome stink. And as he had failed to comfort
his dying friend, so there was no comfort for him – only
the rain mingled with salt dribbling down his cheeks; only
the empty silence of the lonely graves, the intermittent
calling of the wild things of the rainforest, and, faintly, the
shouts of men trying vainly to help each other.

Chapter 21

'I really enjoy these moments of peace and quiet.'

Geoffrey Crawley lounged in one of the sagging arm-chairs in the living half of Susan's partitioned room. 'Between you, me and the gatepost,' he continued, 'Emma's jolliness can go right through one sometimes.'

'She's a very nice person,' Susan defended, handing him the cup of tea she'd made on the small gas ring she seldom used except when he came up here to escape the constant din of wife and kids downstairs.

'Oh, don't get me wrong.' He took an appreciative sip of the tea. 'I'd be the first to challenge anyone who says anything against her. Salt of the earth – Emma. But sometimes . . .'

Susan smiled. He seemed to like her as an audience, to get off his chest the little things that bothered him or to regale her with little anecdotes of his travels which Emma, managing three growing boys and a house, had no time to listen to and had probably heard before. At first it had been a little embarrassing, him coming up here. What if Emma got the wrong idea?

She'd said as much to Emma who had promptly viewed the whole thing with amusement. 'Keeps 'im out of my way while I'm gettin' dinner. S'long as yer don't mind 'im. If yer don't want 'im up there, just send 'im packin' back down 'ere. Yer don't 'ave ter put up wiv 'im. Need yer own privacy sometimes, I expect. Just turn 'im out when yer've 'ad enough.'

But she didn't want to turn him out. It was nice having a man's company all to herself. He made good conversation but his was quiet where Emma's could be so noisy. He brought her little things, sweets he'd got from under the counter, most of them for his children and for Emma and even Mattie, but a few for her. Lately he'd been giving her more and more little presents: a pair of nylons; a length of parachute silk from which she made herself a couple of slips; a lipstick on her birthday – Max Factor – not easy to come by. The ends of previous ones were melted down and poured in to one container to make them go further. Emma didn't wear lipstick since having the boys. 'He knows what I look like,' she'd said when Susan had offered her a touch of hers. ''E'd 'ave a fit, me dolled up. Think I'd got meself some other bloke.'

Susan accepted them all gratefully. At least she didn't have to go with some GI like Edie to get them. On her first Christmas with the Crawleys – she'd refused to spend it with her in-laws – he had brought home a tiny wooden doll for Mattie. At Easter a real chocolate egg, not a cardboard one. On her first birthday a pink dress, and on Susan's birthday, lace hankies. Where he got these things from she never asked; she was just flattered by the attention. And ever since her birthday he'd come up to sit in her armchair and chat for an hour or so, whatever

Sunday afternoon he was home. It had become almost a habit.

Christmas came round again, and again she refused to spend any of it with Mr and Mrs Ward, nor, to be fair, with her own family. They were too much of a journey away and the house remained crowded with her grandparents still there, their home still uninhabitable. She sent them a card though, one of those postcard things that now took the place of the fancy pre-war ones.

But Mrs Ward was as put out as she'd been the previous year. 'We never see Matilda unless we come to you. Surely one Christmas with us.'

Susan had remained silent, sullen, but she had her way. Here was fun, she could be herself with an easygoing family. The thought of spending it with the Wards, the long silences, the brooding atmosphere she always sensed there, though it was probably of her own making, made her cringe. She turned from the knowledge that there would be just three people at the Wards' house this Christmas, Mr and Mrs Ward and Louise, home on leave, and they would sit and mourn the absence of their son through the whole festive season. She wanted none of it.

On Christmas Eve came an uproar from below, exactly as last year, when Geoffrey arrived home with presents. As before she remained in her room, not wishing to intrude. But soon footsteps echoed up the stairs and she heard a light tapping on her door.

Opening it she saw Geoff standing there, face flushed from the many whiskies and gins offered by various customers and reps who could still get hold of it. Swaying slightly he held out a large square brown paper parcel with a smaller one on top.

'Happy Christmas!' he burst out, thrusting the packages at her, and, too excited to wait for her to open them when the time came, announced in a slurred voice: 'Dolls house f'r Mattie. Cardboard I'm 'fraid. The small one's f'r you, pair o' gloves.'

Susan felt her face flush with pleasure. 'Geoff, you shouldn't have.'

'Part o'th' family, hey?'

Even tipsy, he spoke much better than Emma. A Cockney twang could still be discerned there but Susan supposed that his work called for better speech. He was the exact opposite of Emma in every way; she bonny, sloppy, talkative, animated, her hair fair and frizzy; he slim, neat and quiet, brown hair slicked back by brilliantine. He was something like eighteen years older than Susan – Emma said he was nearing forty though she hadn't said how near – but he looked younger than that. Although shorter, he resembled Matthew in some way, but was more sleek and not so dark-haired and his eyes looked an indeterminate shade of blue where Matthew's had been brown. (She had used the past tense when that thought had come to her, though it had gone unnoticed.) But Geoff was here, and she had begun to notice him a lot. Not only was he nice to look at but he smelled nice, from lotions she supposed he picked up on his travels.

'I've got everyone something,' he was saying, still swaying in the doorway. As she stood back to let him in, he plonked the packages on a chair.

'I've got something for everyone too,' she said. They were already wrapped and waiting, in brown paper. Christmas wrapping had become a thing of the past. 'Wooden toys for the boys,' she announced. 'Someone I know makes them out of old furniture.' It was a man who worked next door to where she worked. 'I've got a brooch for Emma.' That too was made from wood with a picture painted on it by the same man, making quite a trade out of it, it seemed.

'And this is for you.' She handed him the tiny package.

'What is it?'

'I'm not saying. Wait 'til you open it.'

He giggled. 'I've told you what I got you. Tell me what you've got me.'

'It isn't much.' They were cuff-links, not expensive.

'Ah, th' best things always come in li'l packages?' He was regarding her closely and she felt he was referring to her personally. She felt herself blush.

'Don't be silly.'

'No.' He swayed towards her. 'I mean it.' His breath smelled sweetly of whisky, not at all unpleasant. Leaning forward, he laid a kiss on her cheek. Suddenly all the loneliness she'd been pretending wasn't there whenever Edie regaled her with what she'd been up to the evening before welled up inside her. She lifted both arms and put them around his neck and at the obvious invitation, his lips settled on hers.

Susan felt herself trembling with all the longing that had lain inside her, and she realised that he too harboured a certain loneliness, though why he should, with Emma there for him, she couldn't understand. But at the moment she didn't want to understand. Her whole being was crying out for comfort. For a second, her thoughts flew wildly to the bed behind the partition. Her heart seemed to be pounding through her entire body, her blood throbbing to its thumping. Then suddenly he released her.

'God, I must be more stoned than I thought. God, Sue, I'm sorry.'

How could she cry out, 'Don't go'? How could she make herself look cheaper than she must already look? She stood watching him back away towards the door. It was all she could do. What her expression was like she didn't know, but she hoped it wasn't imploring. He was still apologising, clutching the present she had given him. This would be the end of their moments together up here in this room. She'd driven him away by her own stupid actions and now she'd have no one. There was a dull ache where the throbbing had been while he stood teetering in the doorway, apologies still on his lips.

'If you knew, Sue, what I was thinking just now, you'd throw me out,' he said, and it was then that she found her voice.

'Geoffrey, don't go.'

She waited. Then very slowly he closed the door and came back into the room.

She had got through her finals, she was a State Registered Nurse at last. Jenny telephoned her mother, then armed with a four-hour pass went out to celebrate in a local pub with the others of her group who had passed.

'What d'you plan to do now?' asked mousy-haired Molly Fergusson who'd become her best friend. Everyone was asking the same question of each other.

Sipping her third Sanderman's sherry, Jenny thought about that one. The idea of applying for the QAIMNS/R made itself felt again. This time she would apply. Mumsy would be distressed, but she needed some of that freedom she had always dreamed about, which even becoming a nurse had not as yet fulfilled. It meant she could be sent abroad; she couldn't help it but somehow the idea identified her with Matthew, silly fool that she was. When would she ever grow up?

She knew of course that he was a prisoner of war. Susan walking out on his parents as she had, knowing how things stood, had to her mind been a terrible thing to do. Now she lived with some rough family off Mile End Road rather than the nice home into which she had been so generously accepted. Susan must have been off her head. But it was none of her business. She had to get on with her own life. And how often had she told herself that as soon as Matthew came into mind? As he came to mind now, so she pushed the thought away and told Molly of her plans.

'Watch it,' Molly said ominously. 'They could send you anywhere.'

But she was adamant now. It was what she wanted, to be sent anywhere. It was what had happened to Matthew. And she was thinking of him again. All these years and she still thought of him.

Quickly she stopped thinking of him. Even so, she applied, and soon found herself saying goodbye to all the friends she'd made at the London Whitechapel, except for Molly who having readily told her to watch it, had decided to go with her. It felt good to have someone, not exactly to hold her hand, but to be a support in a corner, to be in the same boat with. Paddling one's own canoe could be all very well, but a lonely business, and Molly had become a good friend. It would have been hard to say goodbye to her.

'I feel a bit guilty leaving here at a time like this,' Jenny confided. Air raids had begun again, this time more concentrated, the bombs heavier and more destructive. Dispirited Londoners who'd thought they'd seen the end of the Blitz called it the little Blitz; almost as many victims were being brought into the London as before. The second front was still being talked about, but this time everyone knew it would come soon. Guilty feelings or not, she was determined nothing should stop her now, visions of being sent overseas filling her mind.

'Adventure at last,' she said, shrugging off feelings of guilt.

'Aye, adventure at last,' Molly Fergusson agreed.

Conditions overseas could be uncomfortable, Jenny was told at her interview. She didn't mind. She could be sent anywhere. She didn't mind. A medical was followed by a lengthy shopping list, with her expected to pay for the items it contained.

'We'll be out of pocket a whole month at least,' she grumbled. 'I never considered us needing these things.'

They were items that very few of the nursing recruits had considered: folding camp bed and bedroll; a collapsible canvas bath, wash bowl and bucket; gumboots; portable paraffin stove. Even the uniform, grey suit and greatcoat with scarlet facings, a change of grey shirts and ties, hat, a change of grey cotton dresses, cape trimmed with scarlet, a lawn veil, had to be bought. Her mother generously sent her a bit of money to help out along with her laments at her daughter no longer coming home most evenings – not coming home at all. She was in the forces, it hadn't properly registered until now. She'd be called sister. Nursing Officer J. Ross number T/348509. And she and Molly were to be sent off to a military hospital somewhere in England. So much for going abroad.

In fact they ended up in Essex, at a large manor called Hamdon Hall, now a military hospital in a village of the same name – far from being hundreds of miles from home, she could have cycled there!

New Year's Eve, like Christmas, had been wonderful, the house filled to overflowing with all the Crawley family: friends, relatives, mostly women and children or men too old to have been called up, a sprinkling of uniforms of those who had been lucky enough to be home on short leave. The New Year seen in, the party had lasted until around one in the morning, until slowly growing stale and dwindling as one after another relatives yawned, remembered their own homes, minds on a cup of cocoa and bed. Now they had all gone. All were living close by and did not need to stay the night.

In the now-quiet kitchen surrounded by the debris of the party while Emma said goodnight to the last of them at the door, loath to see them go, when she would have to come back and face the clearing up, yapping away with them in the silence of the freezing early hours of 1944, Geoffrey gave Susan a long, searching look.

'Fancy a nightcap? There's some whisky left, or a drop of port.'

She shook her head. 'I think I've had enough.'

She started to leave but he took hold of her hand. 'Look, Sue, I'm sorry about the other day.'

She wanted to say, '*I'm* not,' but she wasn't even sure about that. It had been so wonderful, then afterwards so wretched knowing what she'd done, and then she had wanted it to happen all over again. She ended up saying, rather stupidly, 'Emma must have wondered why you was so long delivering the Christmas presents.'

'Probably reckoned I was just chatting,' he mused. He moved nearer to her. 'Are you sorry about what happened?'

It was a direct question, one she couldn't answer except to give a small shrug, her eyes lowered. Taking her silence for collusion, he drew her gently to him. 'I love you, Sue.'

His breath smelled of alcohol. She held herself stiff in his embrace. Any moment Emma would be back in, her goodnights said. Fear made her body grow even more tense. 'You don't,' she whispered. 'You had too much to drink that day. You've had too much to drink tonight. We mustn't . . .'

He put a hand gently over her mouth. 'I love you. I can't remember when it started. All those times I sat in your room I could hardly keep from taking hold of you and kissing you and telling you how I felt. But you gave me no encouragement – no sign. I knew how you felt about your husband so I didn't dare . . . I wouldn't muck you about, Sue. You're too nice for that. But that day, when you asked me not to go, knowing by then how I felt . . .'

He let his words drift off, his hand falling away from her mouth. In his arms she felt limp. 'But I don't love you,' she managed to say. She had to be honest with him. But what was honesty? What was truth? 'I was lonely.'

The strength went out of his clasp on her, his tone took on a touch of harsh disappointment, bitterness. 'And I came in handy.'

'No.' She heard Emma call out a last goodnight, the night air making her call sound flat and far away. She would stand watching her guests until they disappeared into Mile End Road, a woman so full of demonstrative affection that she couldn't bear to let those she was fond of fade from sight until forced to by the intervention of something like a street corner. There were a few more minutes left before she came back indoors. Meanwhile Susan gabbled what she needed to say to Geoffrey.

'That's the trouble, all I could think about was you, you near me and the wonderful feeling it gave me. I should've thought about my husband, but I didn't. He's like a dream – something that never really happened.'

'Then why hold me off?' He too was talking fast, knowing his wife would be back any moment.

'Because,' she said, 'I don't know how I feel – if I was trying to put you in his place . . . Geoffrey, I could let you love me, easy as anything. But I must have time to think.' Any minute now Emma would be back indoors. Susan pulled free of the hand still holding her wrist. 'You must leave me alone, Geoffrey. And don't come upstairs to see me any more, please.'

The street door scraped to and closed with a tortured grating thud. The wood had swollen in the damp winter weather. Susan fled to the kitchen door and stumbled past Emma coming along the unlit passage.

'You all right, Sue?' came the startled voice.

'Just want the lav,' she mumbled, making for the stairs. 'Think I'll go straight to bed.'

'It's all that beer – makes yer run. Wanna nightcap? Tea? Cocoa?'

'No thanks.'

Reaching her door she stumbled into her room. Closing the door she leaned against it. Her body felt like an empty sack as she let herself slide to the floor to give herself over to weeping, ceasing only when Mattie stirred in her cot, dreaming, giving a small whimper.

For three months they hadn't moved from where they had been quartered. In huts erected in the grounds of Hamdon Hall, in the depths of January and February and March, they looked forward earnestly to the warmer spring weather. With the second front still being talked about, they treated cuts and bruises on men returning from training manoeuvres, saw to fingers squashed in lorry bonnets, dosed sore throats, winter colds, caught colds themselves and dosed each other.

'Fun, don't ye think?' Molly said, her nose red and sore from the constant application of unforgiving hankies.

Jenny chuckled and wiped her own tender nose. Molly was a tonic. Always jolly, always looking on the bright side, a girl to turn every soldier's eye. She was tall, like Jenny herself, but whip-thin, and looked as though the smallest breeze would knock her sideways. Like all women with such figures she looked wonderful in her smart grey and scarlet uniform, whereas Jenny saw herself as doing her uniform no justice whatsoever despite the appreciative remarks of the soldiers about the colour of her hair and the lovely grey-green of her eyes. She took it with a pinch of salt. They'd pay compliments to any nurse in uniform attending their trivial medical complaints.

So their lives continued, spring sunshine lifting the spirits as they went on occasion to the local pictures in nearby Chelmsford, attended the village fête at Easter, went to the community hall dance that had once only catered for a sprinkling of villagers but now was crammed with a variety of uniforms, hospital staff, and patients. Molly hardly ever danced with the same man twice; she went into town on the arm of every Tom, Dick and Harry. Jenny did the same but somehow could never allow herself to get close to any one man, so she supposed she too lingered on every Tom, Dick and Harry's arm and it was an ever-changing foursome that marched off into Chelmsford for an evening at the pictures or a better-class dance at the town hall.

The next two months passed like a dream, surrounded by the gentle warmth of the Essex countryside, by contentment, comradeship, and all the while learning ever more of the skills and requirements of her chosen career. At last she was forgetting to think about Matthew. This was a different life, her old life and all its sense of confinement and commitment left far behind. As for the yearning to go overseas, although the QAs were an overseas division of nursing, it seemed this was where they would remain for the duration of the war.

Things, however, were to change. Towards the end of May the whole unit of QAs upped stakes and moved to outside Deal in Kent to meet a mounting stockpile of ammunition, military vehicles and chaos. They got fitted out with sloppy dungaree-like garments, heavy boots, webbing, respirator and haversack, raincape-cum-groundsheet and all the other paraphernalia that was designed to hang around the frame of military personnel.

Miles from anywhere, for the last weeks of May life assumed a state of utter immobility beyond the vast camp site with its growing mass of men and military machinery. The first week of June began wet and windy, the wind at times whipping to gale force, making life under canvas more than miserable.

Emerging from the prefabricated canteen that first Tuesday in June to a newly washed morning after the gales of the previous few days, Jenny became aware of a low and steady distant roar that made every girl look up, wonderingly. Within seconds the distant roar was filling the air.

'Christ! Look at that!' Molly's voice had to screech over the growing racket.

As though being raised on a vast curtain, a cloud of dark shapes had begun to loom over the tree-tops from the west. Bearing down on the awed, open-mouthed watchers below – the whole hospital had turned out to see what the thunderous noise was all about, the building itself being shaken by the weight of it – wave after wave of planes began to pass overhead. Each bomber towed a glider, Halifaxes, Lancasters, Blenheims, the huge Flying Fortresses, moving almost wingtip to wingtip in steady purposeful majesty, deceptively slow, forming a virtual ceiling above the upturned faces.

'It's the second front,' shrieked Molly, the deafening roar practically carrying her voice away. 'It's started. At last!'

But with the last waves of planes receding into the distance, silence descending strangely upon ears still ringing from the earlier noise, Jenny and Molly looked at each other, as did all the women of their unit.

'We'll probably be following them soon,' Molly said, serious for once.

Chapter 22

Obeying her wishes, Geoffrey hadn't visited her room again. Downstairs he was polite to her as though nothing had ever occurred between them. Weeks stretched to months; for Susan it was a most miserable time. The colder he seemed towards her, the warmer he appeared to become towards his family, playing with his boys far more than she was sure he once did whenever he was home. He was good with Mattie too, bouncing her on his knee until she chuckled fit to burst, but not one warm glance did he cast towards herself. She ached for him to give her just one look that said he too remembered Christmas Eve in her room and yearned to repeat it.

Even Emma noticed. 'You done somefink ter upset Geoff?' she asked. When Susan raised her shoulders sullenly without offering any explanation one way or the other, he laughed, assuring Emma he was being a perfect gentleman to their tenant, the innuendo not escaping Susan who wanted to burst into tears and tell him that if anything he was behaving perfectly rotten to her.

She even contemplated giving up her rooms and moving on, but how could she explain why to a bewildered and hurt Emma? Not only that, the courage she had possessed on that one single escapade when she'd left the Wards now evaded her; she couldn't repeat that, not with a twenty-month-old child in tow with all its attendant toiletries, nappies, clothing. And she'd never find herself another place like this with such wonderful people. She gritted her teeth and forced herself to stick out Geoffrey's horrid attitude, knowing it had really been of her own making.

He had even managed to avoid her during the little Blitz when they'd all huddled in the Morrison shelter in the tiny cluttered basement, the air raids less regular but as devastating as the real Blitz three years before – incredible to think the war had gone on so long.

In April they also had ceased as abruptly as the first Blitz, leaving the big cities in a period of quiet, Hitler foiled again. For Susan, terrified as she had been of a direct hit, the debatable closeness of Geoffrey, who continued virtually to ignore her, was taken away. A month had gone by since then and this weekend was only the second time Geoffrey had come home, she and he, as usual, avoiding each other like the plague.

After putting Mattie to bed, she had stayed up in her room, sick of looking at his averted face as he played with his sons. She'd been up here some time and when a gentle knock came on her door she guessed it was Emma wondering why she hadn't come downstairs again. Emma worried that way. She opened the door ready with an excuse, to find Geoffrey standing there. He looked apologetic.

'I'm sorry, I had to come up. Emma's been asking why

I never come up here now. I thought I'd better make it look good – just for half an hour. Do you mind?'

'No,' she answered woodenly and stood back for him to enter.

'I could go if you want.' But he was already sitting in the armchair. She stood near hers, not sure whether to sit down or not and make this seem like the cosy little times that once had been.

'Do you want me to make you a cup of tea?'

'No, I shan't stay long. Fact is, after the boys went to bed, Emma went next door to Mrs Fulham for a chat. She'll be in there about an hour, if I know her.'

'Oh,' her voice sounded flat, neutral. Suddenly he was out of his chair.

'Sue, I can't go on like this. I'm in a state. I can't work, I can't think, I can't think of anything but you. Sue, I'm so bloody unhappy.'

She wanted to say that he looked happy enough to her, but she said nothing. Her heart was racing. This was what she had wanted to hear all those months, and now her heart was going like a steam hammer and her mind was in confusion and she could find nothing to say. The fact was, she had no need to say anything. He was saying it all for her, still in the same place where he had stood up from the chair, as though his feet were nailed to the floor, his pale blue eyes trained on her.

'I really do love you, Sue. I'm not a man of any special talent. I don't know what to say on these occasions. All I know is what I feel for you. I've tried to conquer it, as you'd asked me to.'

'I never . . .' But he was rushing on.

'I *know* it's wrong. I'm a married man, but I've never felt for anyone the way I feel about you. I *know* you said you love your husband, that you were just lonely when I . . . when we . . . I'm married. You're married. But we can't help these things happening.'

'Geoffrey.' She tried to stop the flow of pitiful clichés, but he did not hear her.

'I know you love me – the way you look at me. Sue, darling, if you feel anything for me you can't possibly feel the same for – well, anyone else. Do you still feel anything for . . . anyone else?' She knew who he meant, loath to say the name.

'I – don't know,' she stammered.

'You do feel something for me?'

'I – Geoffrey, I don't know.'

'You must know. If I didn't matter to you, you wouldn't go around looking so downcast. I know you love me. You do, don't you?'

She allowed a glum nod, a half-nod really, but enough for him. He came forward and his arms were about her, the sweetness of his breath flowing across her face, she in turn clinging to him, needing this reality.

She couldn't remember reaching her bed, but she would never not remember the delicious, the overwhelming joy of being made love to, all the more wonderful for the mad snatched affair it was, filled with need and with tension and with fear of time overtaking them. She had never felt so fulfilled as when he came inside her, she rising up to meet him.

Afterwards she didn't feel at all ashamed as she had that first time. Lying in Geoffrey's arms, luxuriating in the contentment that flowed over her, she found herself drawing a veil over the man she had once adored, found herself forming a mental note to put his photo away from its place on the bedside table. What could be gained by staring at the flat, lifeless image of a smiling man that a scrap of paper proclaimed was her husband? How did she know where he was and if he still existed? Nothing was ever heard of those whom the Japanese had captured. They stubbornly recognised no conventional rules of war, were said to be fanatical about dying for their emperor and to see captives of war as unworthy of respect. Fearful tales had come out of the Far East of massacres and terrible deeds done by them. How was she to know what might have happened to Matthew?

In Geoffrey's arms, seeing her vigilance as a waste of effort, she blocked out everything else but the hope that this would be the beginning of a long summer of ecstasy, perhaps a lifetime. Only later when he left, dressed and dapper as always as his wife came in through the front door to get his evening cup of cocoa, did she give some thought to what they'd done and what they intended to go on doing. With Emma suspecting nothing. But one day she would, or would have to be told. And then . . .

A shudder passed over Susan at the misery that awaited Emma, and she felt suddenly sick.

The doorbell, of course, didn't work. It had never worked. Lilian would have liked it to work so that she could have kept her thumb on it indefinitely, displaying her anger until the door was eventually opened. Instead she must use the door knocker which wasn't the same thing for she'd be disturbed by the noise as would the neighbours, whereas a bell upset only those on the other side of the door.

It was Mrs Crawley who answered, but that didn't matter. Lilian's wrath was directed as much to her as to Susan. She'd promised she'd make herself responsible for the girl and she had let the side down.

Susan's letter had completely taken her breath away, shocked her to the very core. Unabashed it was, no matter how shamefacedly worded, the grammar and spelling, bad as ever, adding to the ill grace of it.

. . . I've got to tell you sometime. I feel I've got to be honest, because Emma Crawley's walked out on Mr Crawley as him and me are living together you might say. It all just hapened. We couldn't help ourselfs, and now I've found out I'm pregnant. So I thought it was best to tell you the truth. I know it sounds bad, but it wasn't intended to be like that. It just what happened. I don't expect you'll forgive me and I know you'll say I should wait for Matthew but I could just be waiting in vane? But now there's Mattie to think of. Mr Crawley don't like her around now Emma's not here to give eye to her. He askd me if I'd ask you if you'd like to have her for a wile, being her grandparents . . .

She'd crumpled the letter up and thrown it from her half-read, only to retrieve and re-read it, still with disbelief. How anyone could be so shameless, so brazen? And to choose now of all times to write such things, three years almost to the day Matthew had gone away, had kissed his wife – his *loyal* wife – goodbye to march off into captivity. *Three years!* How could anyone be so faithless? She couldn't wait, could she?

Her mind again seething with the contents of that letter, Lilian had begun to wonder if there was anyone at home. Her knocking was taking so long to be answered. As if there wasn't enough to put up with, she continued to wait for news of Matthew that never came, clinging desperately to the belief that one day she'd hear, that one day, when the war drew to an end, he'd come home.

But this war was on their doorstep yet again in the shape of the doodlebug. Just as the news of Allied advances had everyone reading the papers as though following the football results, excited by it all, there had come the spluttering-engine roar of those V2s, like black crosses spouting blowlamp fire in their wake. From D Day and throughout June, July and August they had laboured across the sky. All warily watched their course as they cut out, soughing on ominously, the watchers unsure whether to duck or not. When they finally came plunging to earth they demolished homes in huge explosions that fanned out flying glass and debris, killing scores of people, for no one knew where they'd fall. Sometimes a hundred would come over in a day, several at once so no one knew where to look or run. The old air-raid shelters proved of no help;

cowering in them would have halted all normal life, they chewed up a body's nerves. Several had fallen near to her, too near for comfort, and people had again left London in droves.

Yet, as though none of this mattered, Susan had had the audacity to carry on an affair with her landlady's husband, heedless of his wife who'd befriended the girl, of her own husband who was a prisoner of war. She was thinking only of herself, her needs, her pleasures.

Lilian's first thought had been to seek out Leonard and show him the letter. On Saturday the shop stayed open until five thirty, but she had eventually decided against going there and demeaning herself by telling him such news in front of goggle-eyed customers. She had to deal with this herself. Making up her mind in a fit of anger, she had got herself ready and now, half an hour later, was waiting for someone to answer her knock.

But she had not been prepared for it to be Mrs Crawley herself. Even so, she collected herself, fluttering the letter in the woman's face. 'This arrived from my daughter-in-law an hour ago. She gave me to believe you'd left. I hardly expected to find you here, circumstances being what they are.'

Mrs Crawley's face was bleak. No longer the amiable woman, she regarded Lilian with a steady pride in her eyes. 'It's still my 'ome, Mrs Ward. I just come back fer a few fings wot's mine.'

'I see.' For a moment she was stumped. 'Is my daughter-in-law here?'

'Upstairs.'

'Is he . . .'

'Wiv 'er? Yes. 'E's wiv 'er.'

Again she was caught by the simple truth spoken so directly, without inflection. 'I need to see her,' was all she could find to say.

Without a word Mrs Crawley stepped aside, allowing her to enter. Her face lifted briefly towards the top of the stairs, indicating for Lilian to go up. She too said nothing, but nodded her head in Mrs Crawley's direction as she passed, noticing a battered suitcase in the hall with a hat balanced on top.

Mounting the stairs, there was no sound behind her but she had the feeling that the woman hadn't watched her go, and reaching the door to the room where Susan resided, she heard the front door close quietly and knew that Mrs Crawley had let herself out.

For the first time she felt fear. What would she find on the other side of that door? It took all her reserve of courage to rap on it with her knuckles. Then she remembered the letter, how she'd felt reading it, and her rap became firm.

'I couldn't tell you before. You were at work.' Leonard was visibly upset by her going off like that without a word to him.

'You should have allowed me to be there, Lilian. I'd have been able to lessen the impact rather than you having to deal with it alone.'

'I managed well enough.'

She had managed, facing up to the situation that had confronted her on stepping inside Susan's rooms, seeing the state the girl had allowed it to get into. And that poor little mite, Matilda; she could have cried for her.

Entering, she'd been met by the sight of Geoffrey Crawley. In white shirt, brown trousers, plain brown tie and sleeveless pullover, he presented quite an elegant figure until one noticed the pale stubble on his chin. The man hadn't shaved that morning. Lilian knew immediately that her entrance had been heard downstairs. There must have been an unholy rush to dress, making it seem as though they had been up for hours.

Eyes sharpened by the sight of that stubble saw more telltale things: through the open door in the partition wall, a glimpse of an unmade bed and this at eleven thirty in the morning; clothes left on the floor; breakfast cups unwashed. The two must have been idling around the place in a state of undress. The knowledge brought bile into her throat as she swallowed fastidiously. Worst of all, Matilda, who was standing up in her cot, the covers twisted into a heap, was still in nightclothes, her dark curling hair dishevelled, her little face unwashed and still sticky from a piece of bread and jam that now adhered to the cot rail. She'd been crying, no doubt for attention that wasn't forthcoming as these two indulged in each other – evidence of her distress was visible in the mucus drying around her nose. Lilian had never seen the child in such a mess. Usually Mattie looked quite presentable at other times when she had visited, but now she knew that had been Emma Crawley's doing, never the mother's. And there had stood Susan in a clean dress and hastily applied lipstick, though her long hair had not been combed quickly enough, for Lilian had seen one or two tangles that had been missed because of this couple's vile goings-on earlier this morning.

It was then she had found her voice. With the letter held at arm's length to the girl, she demanded what was the meaning of it. 'Are you saying that this . . . animal has got you pregnant?' she'd asked, quite illogically, for had it not been written there in black and white?

Crawley had stepped forward, full of indignation. 'I say, hold on.'

Lilian had recalled her words all the way home and recalled them now with a mixture of pride in her own self-control – her ability to find the right words about which she was now justly satisfied – and of controlled anger which now struck her as totally correct in the circumstances. 'Yes, animal. That can be the only word to describe the sort of person who leads a young woman with a child away from her true path, loyalty to a husband who is not here to fight for her. I call it despicable. It is nothing less. That you, who have so far kept yourself out of the forces by your job while young men are fighting and dying for you, can find it in yourself to break up my son's marriage, is a despicable act. A different story, I can vouch, if he were here. Then a coward like you would run with your tail between your legs. You are a coward, a traitor, a parasite. And you,' she had turned on the trembling girl, her daughter-in-law, 'you are a harlot. I'd rather see my son dead than take you back!'

That had been a mistake. She shouldn't have said that. On reflection it seemed she was condemning her own son.

That was when she had nearly broken down. To combat her weakness, she had gone into the other room to stand over Matilda, the other two following at a distance.

Looking down on the child, averting her eyes from knickers, bras, stockings and men's pants that draped every chairback, she'd been revolted by the musty odour that rose up to meet her from the cot itself, an offensive effluvium of urine, long-unbathed skin and unwashed bedclothes. She'd half expected disorder but not this abomination. The cot, like the bed, must have been crawled in and out of for weeks without any change of linen, and looking at Crawley with his fresh-looking skin and his attention to dress, it was unbelievable he would put up with such squalor as met her eyes. There had been another smell too in that room. A faint reek that she could not at first place. Susan and her abominable lover had been crawling all over each other night after night, filling the room with the reek of their coition. One word had escaped her as she lifted the child, who must have witnessed this copulation time after time, out of her cot: 'Slut!' And again, enlarging on the word: 'You disgusting slut!'

In a smouldering fury she had commanded Matilda to be washed and dressed, a process that had involved a great deal of perseverance to control the miniature tempest at the unaccustomed washing. Susan had told her this was how Mattie always was and that it was easier not to bother and upset her, a likely excuse for laziness. Finally, Lilian had borne the child home with her, as Susan had asked.

It still escaped her how the child's mother had stood by and watched her being taken away without one word

of protest. The last she had seen of Susan, as she bore
Matilda down the stairs and out of the house, was her
standing there leaning slightly against Crawley, his arm
protectively about her, a declaration if ever there was one
of her intention never to go back to her husband when he
finally came home. Lilian was still certain of that.

She now cuddled her granddaughter to her. After a
proper bath, her hair now brushed to a dark sheen, the
little body still convulsed with the occasional sob from
screaming at such mishandling. One would think she'd
never seen water in her life, which must almost be true,
sad to say, and Lilian again felt hatred build up against the
mother.

'You should have seen those rooms,' she said to
Leonard. 'She was never like that when she lived here. I
took her always for a clean girl, clean-living. You could
have knocked me over with a feather. And her cries when
Matthew left, I'd never have believed she could turn so far
the other way.'

'Well, she's here now,' he soothed, his arms opening
for Matilda to come to him, which she did readily, to lie
against her grandfather, thumb in mouth, dark eyes slewed
round towards the grandma who had so handled her.
'She'll be with us until Susan wants her back.'

To which Lilian huffed, 'We'll see about that.' And
smiling at the child, added, 'One day, you'll thank
Grandma. When Daddy comes home.'

As the year drew to its close, that he would come home she
was more than certain. And soon. Of that too she had no

doubts, the news being what it was, all good. This year of 1944 marked a turning point if ever there was one; despite buzz-bombs, despite frightening V2s that had come after – in June alone Rome was captured and the landings in Normandy took place, but much more heartening, for her at least, was the defeat of the Japanese invasion of India. For her it was a light at the end of the tunnel. A few more months and they'd be defeated entirely and Matthew would come marching home. In the face of that thought, all other victories had paled, even when Paris was liberated in August, then Brussels. And then on the twentieth of October had come the most wonderful news of all, of the Americans' re-landing in the Philippines. Not long now before she saw her son again. Then another heartache would begin when he learned that the wife he loved so much had been and still was unfaithful. At least they had his child here. A beautiful two-and-a-half-year-old to be introduced to him, to call him Daddy, compensation for the loss he did not yet know of. Lilian's heart almost broke for him at what faced him on his return.

Meanwhile it was a new half-forgotten world she and Leonard had entered, taking Matilda into their home. They'd scarcely remembered what it was like to bring up an energetic young child. Louise had been quiet, doing all that was asked of her, never resorting to tantrums, when hurt, running to her parents for it to be kissed better in the stubborn knowledge that all would be well. She could be quite self-willed when the fancy took her, but Lilian had always managed her.

Even Matthew, who had been the harder of the two to

bring up, a rebel always wanting to kick over the traces, going into a corner to nurse his hurts, brazening out hurt pride with abrasive flamboyance – even with him she had managed. Until, that is, he'd gone against her advice to go for a commission, instead joining up as a mere private. She still felt he had done it just to spite her, though why, she had never been sure, she with only his well-being at heart. And look where his action had got him.

But all the good and bad in her two children had become a distant memory as they'd grown away from her. Louise was now an independent young woman, hardly ever coming home when on leave and, so her letters said, going out with a young Canadian by the name of Ken Turnbull from Winnipeg. They planned to go steady and, reading between the lines, she was hoping to go back with him to Canada after the war. With Matthew a prisoner far away, Lilian prayed daily, if God were willing, that he would come home, but she knew he would probably be a changed man.

Yes, her memories of bringing up a child had dimmed considerably. Matilda, however, altered all that. Invading her grandparents' stagnant lives, she hounded them, small as she was. Being a demanding child, rather like her mother, but charming with it, she made her grandmother's head spin and sometimes ache with her liveliness. With no idea how to stay neat and clean, her clothing coupons never went far enough, and to keep her prettily dressed, Lilian dragged out her old sewing machine, cutting down her own dresses, unravelling old cardigans and often sacrificing her and Leonard's own coupons. But there were rewards, seeing a child they'd brought home looking and smelling like some workhouse waif transformed into the pretty little thing she was. And so like Matthew that it hurt.

It had pained them at first hearing Matilda's plaintive cries of 'Mummy, Mummy'. She said little else, for she was terribly behind with her talking, not yet chattering as a child that age should. It passed, as she was too young to sustain a memory, but Lilian took care not to take her to see her mother and awaken the child's renewed distress. Susan seemed not to mind.

There was never a word from her unless Lilian made it her business to seek her out.

'Aren't you interested in how your daughter is getting along?'

Susan, displaying sullenness at her insistence in coming, had merely shrugged. 'I know where she is if I want her.'

Come Christmas, heavy with her bastard, off-handed and rude to her mother-in-law, Susan had apparently made up her mind that she had been right about Matthew. Now certain she was a widow, she treated Lilian as an interfering old busybody who no longer had any jurisdiction over her actions. Lilian, keeping to her rigid faith, fostered hatred of the weak-willed girl for it.

The International Red Cross, with so much on their plate, were still working hard tracing prisoners of war, and had said that they'd made contact in certain quarters and the name Matthew Ward had been on a list which the Japanese had reluctantly released just prior to Christmas. It could have been any Matthew Ward, the name was not an uncommon one, but Lilian saw it as too much of a coincidence for it not to be her son. His wife had no such weight of faith, continuing to prefer her life with the abominable Geoffrey Crawley. Her and Matthew's child was slowly becoming Lilian's whole life, a straw to cling to, someone to take the place of her son in the unlikely event of his never coming home. But that thought she put from her.

Chapter 23

Sister Ross moved briskly across a quadrangle of the Shaftesbury military hospital.

Hard to believe the war was over at last. Having only just returned to England, she'd missed the VE celebrations here, and could only hear about it from her mother and from the nurses here.

From her mother she had gleaned all sorts of news, amazingly detailed for one supposed to be reserved, unless of course Jenny's absence had brought her out at last. She heard how Matthew's wife was living with the husband of her erstwhile landlady. Jenny wasn't a bit surprised by that, only sad. Sad for Matthew who would learn of it when eventually he came home, soon, because the war in the Far East couldn't last much longer for all the tenacity of the Japanese in refusing to surrender to superior forces, their allies in Germany allies no longer. He would discover that while he had been sweating it out in Japanese hands, his wife had been enjoying the comfort of another man's arms.

Jenny learned too that his parents had charge of his child, were bringing her up admirably; that his wife had had a baby by her lover, a boy; that she had nothing now to do with Matthew's parents, considering herself wholly a widow. The war had passed her by.

As she walked on, Jenny thought back over her own war, over all that had happened to her after landing in Normandy. Having crossed the Channel in a full gale that seemed at the time to have been waiting just for them, making the whole unit, herself included, seasick, they'd moved forward with the advancing Allies, tending the wounded as they were brought in. Some were injured so grievously it had taken all her resolve not to show revulsion or pity before the sights that greeted her lest she undermine the brave face the wounded had put on. She marvelled at the resolve of most of them not to be done down by their ghastly, disfiguring wounds before their comrades.

She had seen foreign towns and cities, Bayeux, Caen completely in ruins from Allied bombardment, Rouen which had been let off relatively lightly as the troops went through. The gunfire always ahead of them, their trucks had rumbled along in the wake of the advance, bucking and pitching over the shell craters they'd left. And always the grey-faced wounded, the air filled with their moans, the hospital tents packed with hardly room enough for stretcher-bearers, medics, and nurses to go about their business, usually all under a continuous relentless barrage.

She had learned swear words she had never before known existed. She'd also learned a smattering of German as, success following success, German prisoners began being brought in, wounded prisoners in as much need of attention as Allied wounded. The QAs tended them all.

She'd seen Paris and had been entranced by its beauty,

and finally, with the guns falling silent, she had been posted to a town called Rotenburg, not far from Bremen, to a small hospital to help nurse the pitiful victims of Sandbostel, a concentration camp in the north of the country. After all she had seen of the wounded and dying, that place had provided the sights she most wanted to erase from a heart still apt to sink with sickening regularity at the slightest recollection.

Finally home, leave, and transfer here, caring for servicemen who had contracted tuberculosis, mostly ex-prisoners of war, victims of conditions they'd been compelled to live under. She had seen a little of the world. In time she'd return to civilian nursing. But she would never forget.

Shovelling sawdust into sacks wasn't pleasant at most times. Now, as with most things in Japanese hands, the extractors had long ago fallen apart and no longer sucked away the fine dust. Despite strips of sacking tied over nose and mouth, it got into the lungs to be hawked up later in thick yellow phlegm.

The officers complained regularly. The gaol commandant, Major Tanaka, listened sympathetically and did nothing, just as he did nothing about the diabolical bullying by his men, especially one known as Valentino from his handsome narrow face and the dramatic way he swivelled his eyes.

Having felt the weight of his bullying, Matthew trudged back through the gates of Rangoon gaol at sunset in a black mood. Loading sacks on to a barge, one had slipped, spilling sawdust everywhere. Valentino had pounced, wielding his bamboo stick like a samurai warrior, ending up by booting him headlong into the water, strutting off to leave his victim to be fished out by his workmates.

Showering briefly under the Heath Robinson contraption built by the POWs which the Japs allowed to be turned on for just half an hour each evening, subsequently causing long disappointed queues, Matthew worked to take his mind off his treatment, thinking instead of Susan. She no longer floated in his mind as during the days of the railway. He'd come through it, just, though he still suffered malaria from time to time. Almost callously, he had fought to put behind him thoughts of comrades who had died on the way. He had survived. He was determined to continue to survive, and to this end, he put behind him too today's thrashing, and thought only of Susan, of going home to take up their lives together, when all this would become a thing of the past.

In the midst of thinking that as he soaped himself with the tiniest sliver he'd been handed by an officer – told not to overdo it as others had to use it too – the name Jenny flashed into his mind and for a second he saw her quite clearly through the thin curtain of dripping water: her flaming hair, her wide smile, her well-formed features.

Strange though, he thought a lot of Jenny Ross; she came into his mind at the oddest of moments, like now. Mostly it was to recall that ardent kiss she'd given him in the street, right out in the open, all that time ago. Typical of her to do a thing like that. Never seemed to get it right.

Matthew lifted his face up to the drips falling from the makeshift shower head, a perforated canvas bag being spasmodically filled by a pipe from a tank someone in turn kept refilling as long as the water would last.

Her kiss had been a fleeting thing, leaving him to smile reflectively at the lingering sensation it had brought, one that had stirred him enough to make him want to write to her, perhaps further the relationship she had begun. But then his unit had been transferred to Birmingham and he'd met Susan. From then on *she* had taken up all his thoughts.

Strange he should think of Jenny Ross now, and with a small pang of sadness to go with it that he'd let her down. Where was she now? Was she still a nurse or had she married someone, was she raising a family? Without warning an empty place took up residence inside him, a sudden longing for things to be again as they had once been, carefree, safe, full of fun. He could see them all now. And Jenny, she had been a stunner, hadn't she? Just that she hadn't been his type. But a stunner just the same. He should have told her so. He regretted that now. Pity she hadn't had as much confidence in her looks as some men had in them – that Dennis Cox – he'd been smitten by her but hadn't the nerve to tell her. Someone had said Cox had been killed. Well, lots of blokes had been killed. Women too. Serving abroad, nurses being sent overseas, their ships sunk. Perhaps Jenny had been one of them. He wouldn't know, would he? Not here. A stab of panic gripped him then sank away, leaving a sort of empty grief that had no substance because it was unfounded, all in his mind. He had begun to fall in love with Jenny at one time, he was sure, but then he'd met Susan . . .

'F'Chrissake, y' doughy Pom – get a bloody move on,

bloody mooning about. Y'r thirty seconds was up bloody ages ago.'

Shot back to the present, Matthew slipped hastily out from the dribbling shower to receive a basinful of ripe epithets from the Aussie waiting to take his place.

'Keep your hair on,' Matthew growled irritably as the man named Phil shouldered roughly past him. Phil glared at him but Matthew's mind was now taken up with more immediate interests, even above thoughts of Susan and Jenny, as he walked away still dripping wet. So were his ragged shorts, with his time under the shower too brief for them to be taken off. They would dry as he dried. His thoughts now were on what news there might be, if any, over the grapevine.

Hidden beneath the dirt floor of a low wooden lean-to, once a tool shed belonging to the saw mill, then a makeshift latrine but now just a haven for flies and maggots, was a radio, constructed by some boffin or other. With a look-out squatting idly against the sagging rotting walls, certain chosen men – not himself, thank God, for it was an execution if the Japs ever discovered it – would take it in turns, a couple at a time, to squeeze under the floor of the lean-to, lying flat, and follow the crackling news of Allied invasion in Europe, American successes in the Pacific or how many tons of bombs B-29s had dropped on Japanese-held territory, very little of it accurate, being mainly from Japanese sources rather than Allied.

But the news they most sought was lacking – the Fourteenth Army's penetration into Assam and northern Burma five months ago had gone silent, and along with it any speculation of an early release from captivity.

He turned as an angry snort was heard directly behind him, Phil having caught him up after his own thirty seconds had been apparently cut short by two seconds owing to Matthew's delay in getting out as promptly as was required. Phil, a dismal-faced individual who shared the next cell to his with a dozen other Australians, was in a bad mood and obviously wanted to make it plain to the miscreant. Giving him little time to finish his complaint, Matthew turned on him. His own temper was none too good, his shoulders smarting still from Valentino's cane.

'Why don't you put a fucking sock in it?'

The Australian looked hurt. He wasn't a brave man, at least not rash in the face of the other's baleful glare that threatened a punch on the nose.

'Don't bloody take it out on me because yu've had a bloody blue with some lousy bloody Nip.'

Crisis over, Matthew continued walking in the direction of the three steaming oil drums from which wafted a bland aroma of saltless boiled rice.

'I'm not taking it out on you.' A fit of sawdust-laden coughing prevented him saying any more and gave Phil possession of the argument.

'We've all got bludgers t'put up with. Ain't no sense antagonising 'em, is there?'

Harry Hope, who shared Matthew's cell, once a short, naturally chubby man, but now from whose skeletal back, ribs and hips protruded, unhealthy skin hung fleshless like thin grey rows of pelmets, caught the two up, his brief shower over as well. The last of it dripped off his ridged skin like raindrops off a gutter. His voice was soft, with a West Country accent. 'Stay off our Matt's back, old son. He's been a mite touchy all day.'

'Too right, he's touchy.' But Harry ignored the man as he surveyed Matthew's shoulders.

'It do look bloody zore.'

'It is bloody sore.'

'You need to keep that covered. Got a shirt?'

'Flogged it last week for a bag of bran.'

Rice bran, discarded during milling as fit only for animal feed, was a precious commodity, rich in vitamin B, and coveted because it helped avert beri-beri and other deficiency diseases. It was consequently hard to come by. Matthew's haul had amounted to under a quarter of a pound, for which he considered himself fortunate all the same.

'I've got a shirt you can borrow until you've healed a bit.'

Giving Matthew no time to thank him, shirts too being precious commodities, Harry made off towards the queue forming behind drums of steaming rice, their supper, leaving Matthew to stare after him until the small dry cough caught him again and he followed after Harry.

Leaning down from his rickety bunk Harry surveyed him lying directly below. He'd been disturbed by his cough. All those in the cell were disturbed by it. ''Bout time you saw the quack on that, Matt, old son. Don't like the zound of that. Zounds loik a touch o' TB ter me. Don't loik your colour either.'

Matthew raised his eyes to the head hanging upside-down. 'You really know how to cheer up a bloke, don't you?'

'Only an opinion, Matt, only an opinion. But if it be TB I don' wanna catch it.'

From the next cell, divided only by open bars, came Phil's monotone drawl. 'Not as it makes any difference. All gotta go sometime, so what's it matter, hundred years from now, if yuh died at nineteen or ninety? Tryin' to live a long life – you're just a bloody gnat on an elephant's arse. Fifty years after they shove yuh under, forgotten, what's it matter if you lived at all?'

Angered, fighting another cough, Matthew turned away from the would-be philosopher. 'You're just a miserable bugger. You might not have anyone to go home to, but I've a wife and a baby waiting for me.'

On that score, senses heightened to the possibility of tuberculosis, next evening after work found him outside the TB outbuilding transfixed by the sight of those within its open door, chests sunken, eyes unnaturally bright, cheeks with that peculiar transparent flush, as his were.

An orderly, just finishing ministering to a frail stick of what three years ago had been a strong young man, now having to be fed sips of watery rice gruel from a tin cup, looked up at Matthew.

'Looking for someone, chum?'

Feeling suddenly fraudulent, Matthew shook his head; he watched the man gently ease his patient down on the platform that served for a bed and with a piece of khaki rag wipe the residue of gruel from the man's lips. The tenderness of the action touched Matthew more than anything had done in a long time. This man with his gentle hands, these men quietly heroic in their suffering, they humbled him. This endless stream of sufferers, crippled by tropical ulcers, blinded by vitamin deficiency, swollen with beri-beri and withered by dysentery, so many struck down by all the diseases the tropics could throw at them; many died without fuss lest they undermine the will of others to struggle on. None had distinguished themselves in battle but they were heroes just the same in their silent acceptance of death. And here he was shivering in fear of his own miserable life as though he were someone special, as if he were the only man who yearned to make it home to wife and child.

The orderly had stood up and was coming towards him. 'Can ah help ye, laddie?' The soft Scots accent emphasised the hush of this place. He gnawed at his lip. He had no right to waste this man's time.

'It's nothing,' he blurted.

The man was looking at him with the eye of the experienced. 'Ye think ye're tubercular then. Hold on a minute.' Drawing Matthew into the outbuilding with him, he began fishing into a box nearby, drawing out a stetho-scope, home-made from rubber tubing and the handles of a metal filing cabinet he'd probably come across at some time. 'Let's have a listen.'

Submitting himself to the examination Matthew breathed, coughed, uttered thirty-three when told to. The stethoscope was put slowly away. When the man looked back at him, his smile was fixed, too reassuring by far.

'Ye was reet to come here. But it's no' too bad. In a cool dry climate, why, it cud be cured in three months, Ah'd say.'

But the look on the man's face told its story. In a cool dry climate with good food and rest, of course recovery would be certain. Here, in this humid heat, watery rice for fare, working without respite, it was a death sentence as surely as if he stood before a firing squad.

These three years he had stared at death. Now it had arrived. He nodded casually at the advice to take it easy. 'At least I know where I stand,' he murmured and received a short nod. As he left, an insane notion went through his head. Why wait for death? Why not go out in a blaze of glory, a heroic act of sabotage, take a few of those sons of Nippon with him? But he knew he would do no such thing. Like those who had gone before him, like Bob Howlett, he would await his time, quietly, patiently, reluctant to make a fuss, and carrying Susan's image in his head, would silently say goodbye to her and hope to find courage and a small semblance of dignity when his time came.

'Ain't no good, the bloody thing's had it.'

He and another man named Derek gazed down at the now silent wireless that had crackled itself to its death. From now on they could receive no news of the outside world, no heartening snippets about Germany herself being overrun by the Allies.

'No chance getting hold of another valve?' It was a valve that had gone. It might as well have been the whole set for all that could be done.

Derek shook his head viciously. 'Just when something good came over. Something about the Fourteenth Army fighting around Mandalay. Mandalay's only just up country. Didn't you hear it?'

The sound had been so faint, Matthew hadn't heard. Within days, however, rumours were going around. And the Japs were looking decidedly jumpy. Perhaps Derek had heard right. But everyone had grown concerned by their captors' attitude. If rumours were correct and their liberators not far away, what would the Japs do?

'Don't look too good,' Harry said. 'They're sayin' if the Fourteenth Army do make it to Rangoon, the Japs'll start usin' us for sandbags.'

'If that's the case,' Matthew said grimly, 'I'd sooner be shot running than being a shield for some . . .'

The rest of his words were drowned in a fit of coughing from which Harry moved hastily away. But it didn't matter. He now had hope to cling to and his spirits lifted of their own accord.

May, the monsoon yet to begin, the weather still as sweet as any tropical climate allowed, Matthew came awake from a sleep already disturbed by the bouts of sweating peculiar to his condition and a wonderful dream about Susan to a hand shaking his shoulders. Phil was standing over him, all his worldly goods draped about his waist like tarnished charms on an old bracelet. Above it all the normally doleful hatchet face looked grim.

'Sorry t' disturb your sleep, Matt. But us lot 're movin' on.'

The Japs had been growing more and more jittery of late, even their interest in forcing their prisoners to work all hours dropping off. The air was still full of rumours, all of which the prisoners believed purely because they needed to feel that soon they must be released by the fabled oncoming Fourteenth Army. Now all the rumours suddenly took substance as Phil went on.

'They say your blokes're just up the road. Nips're movin' out. Taking all us *healthy* buggers with 'em. To Moulmein ready for shipment to Japan. You cripples are stayin' behind.'

It was meant to be witty but the grin was one of sick disappointment. From the courtyard, came the bellow of the retreating Japanese assembling their 'fit' prisoners.

'S'long then, sport. Take care of y'self. Yuh gonna make it y'know. Bet y'shirt on it.' The grin widened determinedly, the first time Matthew ever remembered Phil smiling without it being a sneer. 'Send yuh a postcard from Sydney one day.'

Going to the now wide-open door of his wing of cells Matthew watched the long gangling figure, deprived of freedom that was nearly his, shoulders hunched in despondency, go off to join the men assembled. He'd never liked Phil all that much but now it felt he was saying farewell to a comrade in a chain of comrades to whom he'd said farewell, one way or another. He should have been feeling elated by the news he'd been given. Instead he felt he wanted to cry. In fact, he was looking at this gangling bundle of misery through a mist and one of his cheeks was being dampened by a thin rivulet.

He forgave himself the tears; TB made a man over-emotional. But in his way, Phil had been close to him, perhaps by his very dolefulness. Watching him go, Matthew thought of all those he'd known, some closer than others: little Taffy Thomas, the endearingly libidinous Welshman blown apart in the retreat to the Sittang River; Bob Howlett, the gentle man who had succoured him on that long march to Rangoon, himself dying alone; another, Colin Pardoe, a religious man of simple faith who had dragged him back to sanity after Bob's ignominious death – where he was now God only knew, might even be sitting at His feet right now for all Matthew could tell what had happened to him. There had been others, and Harry Hope was still here, but one by one they had all gone. Now he felt only utter loneliness as Phil, the man of misery, turned and waved for the last time.

Dawn broke grey and heavy, announcing the coming monsoon season. The sick awoke to find the prison gates standing open, the guardhouse deserted – a faintly bewildering experience after so long close-confined.

Matthew and a few others wandered through them just to savour the sensation of this new freedom. They found a note in English nailed to one of the gateposts: YOU ARE FREE TO MOVE AS YOU WISH. FOOD AND MEDICAL SUPPLIES HAVE BEEN LEFT FOR YOU. THE BRITISH WILL SOON BE HERE, YOU MAY WAIT FOR THEM OR GO TO MEET THEM AS YOU CHOOSE.

Thus, as the British had fled Rangoon three years earlier, so the Japanese, who'd scorned them for their cowardice, had likewise fled before the conquerors. The wheel had turned full circle. Slowly. But it had turned. He was going home, home to Susan. How she must have wept over him, worried herself silly over his well-being, how lonely she must have been.

And himself? The years spent struggling to survive yet seeing death at every turn waiting to pick him up, were over. Death had been waiting for him to thumb a lift from all the misery and degradation that had almost sucked him down into its depths. Thank God he had resisted that dark presence, even through the worst of times. It was over. It hardly seemed true that soon he'd be going home, picking up the threads of his life.

He felt all in, very near to tears at the enormity of this moment as he stood in the emerging sunlight with all the others waiting for their liberators to appear down that road. When they did he would show them that his head had not been bowed, that his spirit had remained strong, had endured. He would throw them a cheeky wave, perhaps even chuck up a smart salute, and not show the true emotions that were ruling inside him. His throat ached from the effort.

All the good intentions. When the first well-clad, sturdy, full-cheeked soldier came marching up to the gaol gates, he could only stand there staring at the health of the man, who smiled at him with such pity in his expression that Matthew found himself stumbling towards him. And as the soldier held out a hand to him, he laid his emaciated arms about the man's neck and sobbed.

Chapter 24

Matilda was not an easy child. Lilian, with recollections of her own, had been taken by surprise. Her little hands were in everything. She was so quick, and it was all her grandmother could do to run after her, those sturdy little legs going like pistons as she found her feet.

It had taken a while to find them, left as she had been in her cot for days on end where she could come to no harm, Susan had said, from the stairs which she could have fallen down, the gas ring from which she could have pulled a kettle of water over herself, the sharp corners in the room. Excuses. Children came to know these dangers by having an alert parent watching them. No, the real reason was that vile man Crawley who didn't want a child that wasn't his hanging around.

Emma Crawley had taken their boys with her to stay with her sister in Valance Road a couple of streets away so that the boys hadn't had to change schools or anything. And of course, in the quieter house, the cries of Susan's baby to be given more freedom had disrupted his enjoyment with his mistress when he was home.

Let free in her grandmother's large airy house, the child found her feet. Five months later and still she was wearing out her indulgent grandparents.

'She's as energetic and high-spirited as Matthew was,' she said to Leonard one night, once the child finally fell asleep after lying wide-awake and bored in the drawn-out daylight of long May evenings, taking up time they would have preferred to have to themselves.

Leonard looked up from his *Evening Star.* 'We should have known what we were taking on. Do you regret it, Lilian?'

'No, I don't,' she answered emphatically, picking up the embroidery she was doing on a dress for Matilda – when she had the time. 'All I dream is for her father to come home and see the pretty little daughter he has. That's worth all the trials and tribulations we've undergone in taking Matilda on.'

She fell silent, bending her head to the rosebud she was fashioning on the front of the cotton garment. It had been a cream skirt of hers. Now it was a dress, needing just this sprinkling of rosebuds to lift its plain colour. Leonard went back to reading his paper.

A quietness descended on them both; it brought thoughts drifting through Lilian's mind as she worked. The war in Europe was over, Hitler dead by suicide. He had deserved a far worse death. Mussolini too was dead, his body afterwards hung by its feet from a lamppost by a mob, those he'd once ruled as dictator, his face kicked in. Lilian shuddered. That should have happened to Hitler too. The ghastly pictures in the papers revealed the horror of those terrible concentration camps. And poor President Roosevelt, a natural death, but a sad, sad loss.

Now there was peace, but not everywhere. The newspapers, when they weren't reporting about the Nuremberg
Trials, now concentrated on the Far East and what the
Japanese regime was really like. A statement made in
January by Anthony Eden in the House of Commons had
described the fearful treatment of prisoners by the Japanese,
and later, a Japanese prison ship transporting prisoners of
war to Japan, had been sunk. The state of the surviving
captives showed them to be in the most appalling state.

What then of Matthew? He could easily have been on
that ship, one of those who had not survived. No news,
never any news. The war in Europe was over, but they
might still find that their son had died perhaps a year ago
or more.

Holding her baby in her arms, Susan went to answer
the knock on the door. She was not really concerned who
stood there, except that whoever it was had interrupted her
quiet afternoon nap. Trevor, a good baby, unlike Mattie,
slept in the afternoon, allowing her to do likewise until
Geoff came home. Since the war had finished he'd applied
for a transfer nearer home to be with her more, and now
worked at a Gas Board office in London. Wonderful. She
saw him every night. Well, almost, because some evenings
he went round to see his sons. She hated those evenings.

Casually she opened the door, then gasped. Mr and Mrs
Ward stood there with Mattie between them, Mrs Ward
holding the child's hand in her usual iron grip. Mattie,
now nearly three years old, looked happy, her small face
animated at seeing the mother she seldom saw these days,
but the look on the faces of her grandparents suggested

they had received bad news. Susan's mind flew to Mattie
with a stab of dismay. Had they brought her back? What
the hell was she going to do with her? She had Trevor now.
How could she deal with two children?

'What's the matter?' she blurted, hitching Trevor to a
less weighty position in her arms. 'What's she done?' She
had to have done something awful for them to look like
this. Not angry; strange, strained.

'It isn't Matilda,' Mrs Ward began, but Mr Ward cut in.

'We've had news of Matthew,' he said.

Another stab of dismay. If they'd had news that he was
dead, she'd be sorry, thinking back to that glorious time
they had spent together making love on Beacon Hill, then
their wedding day and the little love nest he had found.
She saw again the cramped little room with the sunshine
coming through the window lighting everything golden.
The cosy silence they had shared, the way he had so
masterfully commanded her to make love to him, laughing;
the love they had made. They had been such wonderful
days, but so brief. So long ago. A blur, a photograph, a
faded photograph.

And what if the news was that he was alive . . . She
tightened her lips, all the complications it would entail
filling her head. Did she love him after all this time? She
tried in those few seconds to feel what she once had for
him. But it wasn't there, only fond memories that could
have been those of someone other than her, someone not
her any more, totally different.

And what of Geoffrey? She recalled those twinges of
excitement when Matthew had talked of the trust made for

him, enough to buy a house, live comfortably. His father
of course had a shop, so there was money there too. But
Geoff had a house, here. She felt comfortable in it. She
could imagine the home Matthew would make for them.
His mother would constantly be popping in, criticising this
wasn't right and that wasn't right, looking askance at her
for not keeping the place spick and span and sparkling.
She almost shuddered at the thought, knew immediately,
staring from one to the other of his parents, that if he was
alive she'd still have to choose Geoffrey, comfortable,
dependable Geoffrey, who treated her like a goddess, and
no one to interfere in what they said or did.

She became aware that Mr Ward was saying something
to her which she hadn't caught and had to beg his pardon
to ask what it was he'd said.

He looked irritated. 'I said . . . Look, Susan, may we
come in. I can't stand here on the doorstep explaining
news as important as this.'

Automatically she stepped back, allowing them inside.
She'd had fish and chips for dinner (she'd get Geoff's
tonight when he came home) and the smell of it hung in
the house – she knew it did by the offended twitch of Mrs
Ward's nose, though she said nothing.

They followed her into the still-cavernous front room,
no longer with the old blackout frames stuck in the corner.
Letting the two sit on the huge sofa, she positioned herself
on one of the upright chairs, laying Trevor in one of the
armchairs where he wouldn't roll off while Mattie went
exploring the room.

'I'm sorry I wasn't quite listening when you were

speaking,' she said looking at Mr Ward, but it was his wife who reacted with a disapproving sniff.

'I would have thought you'd at least be attentive seeing that it concerns your husband.'

Mr Ward raised a mollifying hand. 'I said, Susan, that we'd had good news of our son, your husband. He's still your husband, Susan.'

'Yes, I know.' It sounded fatuous, but he'd said it with such distaste for what she supposed he saw as her carrying-on behind Matthew's back. What did he know of how she felt? No one could turn love on and off like a blessed tap.

'Our news,' he continued, 'if it's worth anything to you now, is that Matthew has been released.'

Susan stared. 'But the war out there's not over yet.'

'You *may* have read,' put in Mrs Ward, her tone intimating that Susan's reading power was limited to say the least, 'that the Fourteenth Army recaptured Burma some weeks ago.' Even so excitement rang in her voice. 'They found Matthew there.'

Responding more to her own churning of feelings than the news itself, Susan wasn't sure how to react. To give herself time to analyse how she felt about all this, she merely said, 'Oh.'

Mrs Ward's eyebrows shot up into her forehead, her controlled joy smothered instantly by exasperation. 'Aren't you going to enquire how he is? Aren't you interested?'

'I'm glad he's safe,' Susan offered automatically, taking it that was what she was expected to say. Uppermost in her mind, however, now she'd had time to sort out her reactions, were the complications this news brought. She saw a line of legal wrangles, divorce courts, three years at least being fettered to a man she'd all but forgotten, never again to feel at ease with her Geoffrey without her husband's mother breathing down her neck. She would be marked as the guilty party. She was the guilty party, true, but how can anyone turn aside natural feelings, the way she felt about Geoffrey? A tiny place in her mind cried, why couldn't he have died, a voice she brushed aside the instant it spoke, shuddering that she could even harbour such an evil thought. She wouldn't wish that on Matthew, on anyone, for a million pounds.

In the nurses' home Jenny opened her mother's letter. The hospital overlooking the Blackmoor Vale had a timeless charm; with its smooth grey stone over which this hot, sunny June day seemed to slide like treacle left the interior cool, placid and airy. The windows stood wide open to the fresh breezes essential for those with half a chance of recovery; tuberculosis was a known killer, fresh air, rest, good food were all they could hope for. There was talk of some drug called streptomycin; the press had called it a miracle cure, promising to make TB a thing of the past, but it was still in its experimental stage. The papers hadn't referred to it again, the headlines bowing out to more important political news. The first peacetime general election was set for the fifth of July. Small things like reporting work on a wonder drug took second place. What a glory if it could be used on the patients she cared for. It was heartbreaking to see those glowing-faced young men, the deceptive transparent bloom a cruel symptom of the disease, slip away. Heartbreaking when they died so young, having come through all the perils of war. It was only when Jenny opened her mother's letter, the usual two closely written pages relaying all the home gossip, that the disease suddenly became a personal thing. Halfway down the letter, her eyes paused over the next words:

. . . You remember Matthew Ward, don't you? He was a prisoner of war and they lost trace of him. Well, they've heard from him at last.

Jenny's heart leapt inside her chest, continuing with a thumping of joy and anticipation as she skipped the observations on how it couldn't have been jolly for them, everyone celebrating VE Day, the other war still going on.

Matthew's parents had no idea he was in Rangoon. He could have been anywhere. It must have been absolutely marvellous, our boys recapturing Burma like that. Mrs Ward's been telling the whole street about it. He's in hospital in Ceylon. They think he's got TB. Isn't that dreadful, after coming through all he's been through . . .

There was more about the bits she'd found out about Matthew's wife. And a part that made Jenny go suddenly cold with anger. Hearing of his release, the girl had written to him telling him about the man she was living with.

What an awful thing to do. Some people can be so
cruel. How he must feel I just don't know. How could
anyone do such a thing? She should at least have
waited until he came home, I would have thought.
But I gather she doesn't have much sense, or so Mrs
Ward once said, a long time ago now. But . . .

Jenny lifted her eyes from the page of neat, tight little
writing, her head a hotchpotch of thoughts, silent prayers
touching her lips in a gush of thanks for his safety, of
pleading for his health, of joy, of hope for him to be sent
back to England very soon and for her to see him again,
and the opportunity for her to be at his side should he need
someone, anyone.

Quickly she scanned the rest of her mother's letter but
there was nothing more about Matthew. He just constituted
a passing bit of information among all the other snippets
her mother had written, the letter closing with a hope that
Jenny could be allowed a holiday soon so she could get
home.

I don't know why you want to work so far away. The
war is over and there are adequate hospitals around
here. But if you must work with TB patients, and I
hope to God you don't catch it, tuberculosis is so
infectious but I expect you're immune by now, we've
one just the other side of the park where you first
went to get a job, do you remember? You could find
a place there . . .

Yes, she could. But not yet. First she'd set about making enquiries about Matthew, find out where they would send him once in England. A lot of the boys from that area came here after landing, because it was convenient from Southampton. If she could ask the right people.

Whether her efforts had anything to do with it, there was no way of finding out; a few replies came from different quarters saying it would be looked into in due course but no one could give any promises. Her case, she suspected, was put aside, for the months had gone by and she'd heard no more.

Two weeks earlier the dropping of the atomic bombs on Hiroshima and Nagasaki had brought about Japan's capitulation. Great Britain celebrated VJ Day but, less energetically than VE Day, having done it all once. Her mother's letters no longer mentioned Matthew or his family. Jenny made her way across to the TB wing, under a clearing September dawn which promised to become a fine day after twelve hours of rain, to relieve Staff Nurse Merriman from night duty.

Merriman leaned back on her chair, flexing her stiff shoulder muscles, and yawned widely.

'Ooh-ahh . . . What's it like outside?'

'Beautiful. It's going to be a fine day. What sort of night has it been?'

'Pretty quiet,' came the answer. Merriman was already gathering up her bits and pieces. 'Corporal Douglas haemorrhaged and got a bit panicky. Otherwise all quiet.'

The wards were coming alive. Strident voices of nurses

were urging patients not to fall back to sleep after having been aroused at five thirty with tea and wash basins. The clang of bedpans resounded from the sluice, and the corridors echoed to the rattle of crockery-laden trolleys bringing the breakfasts. A nurse going off duty hurried in to deposit an admission file on the desk, gave the incoming sister a brief smile, grabbed her cape off the peg behind the door and departed.

'Oh yes,' said Merriman, pushing the notes across to Jenny. 'I meant to tell you, Admission phoned a few moments ago. He's probably on his way up now. Everything's ready for him, so there's nothing to do.'

Jenny laughed. 'Thanks.'

She took the cup of tea handed to her by a skinny first-year nurse who surveyed Merriman with tired, hopeful eyes.

'Is it all right for me to go off now, please, Staff?'

Merriman was in an authoritative mood, still in charge for the while. 'If you've left the sluices clean, yes.'

'Thank you, Miss Merriman.'

'And charted the temperatures?'

'Yes, Miss Merriman.'

'Is the kitchen tidy?'

The girl nodded vigorously. 'Can Harvey go as well, Miss Merriman?'

'If she has finished everything.'

'Oh, she has. Thank you, Miss Merriman.'

As the girl's flat heels clicked urgently away along the corridor to be joined by Harvey's, Merriman sighed and stood up. 'Time I was off too. I need my bed. And I want to wash my hair.' She made a stack of her notes on the desk, laying the admission file on top. 'There, over to you.'

The day staff were coming in, chattering. Jenny heard Staff Nurse Reid's sharp tones reminding them who and where they were. The chattering ceased abruptly. Jenny reached for the admission folder as Reid burst in, her voice querulous.

'You'd think this was a four-ale bar, not a hospital. To hear those girls, you'd never guess there were sick people here.'

Jenny's gaze was fixed on the now-open folder. She hadn't heard what Reid was saying. Reid leaned over her shoulder to see. 'Oh, no, not an admission this early in the morning. I'll take it.'

The file was snatched up from under Jenny's eyes. 'Why can't they come at a convenient time? And we've a probationer coming on the ward today. All our time will be taken up telling her what to do.'

A porter popped his head around the door, his attitude full of self-importance. 'Where d'yuh want this one?'

'I'll deal with it,' Reid said briskly and clutching the folder waved the porter on, leaving Jenny staring into space. After all those letters she had written, all those enquiries, entreaties. They had paid off. Unbelievable. Quite unbelievable. If she hadn't been on duty she'd have burst into tears.

At first she thought she must have been mistaken, misread the file in that short time before Reid had snatched it so imperiously from under her hand. For a moment it was impossible to associate this patient with the man she had once known, the young man full of laughter and abrasive wit, the khaki-clad soldier she last remembered, so certain of where he was going, carrying himself with all the zest of life.

This man, propped up with pillows, bore no resemblance to that one. Her practised eye already noted that he did not yet have the high colour that went with his disease, which hadn't yet secured such a hard grip on him as it had done on others. It was possible that with care and attention he'd overcome it. But of the man himself? The eyes, deep in their sockets, looked out not on a sunny ward but back in time to an existence that had all but destroyed him as it had so many thousands whose lives he had shared. Everyone now knew of the Burma Railway, the prison ships, the conditions of men incarcerated in jails throughout the Far East, the ghastly massacre of men and women in hospitals as they lay sick and wounded. Some, if not all of that, men like this one must have seen, struggling single-minded to survive. Here was such a man. It glowed from his eyes and Jenny shuddered.

It was only after a moment or so that a slight movement of his head touched her as singularly familiar, at first vague but growing stronger so that all at once she wondered why she hadn't been able to recognise him instantly. Gaunt, cheeks still sunken from years of starvation, eyes that dwelled on the past, it was nevertheless Matthew.

As she spoke his name he looked at her, in those few short seconds his regard blank as hers had been: puzzled, uncertain, trying to pinpoint a memory. A spark of recognition lit up his dark eyes, coupled with disbelief.

'Jenny?'

She tried to laugh. 'Jenny Ross. Sister J. Ross, Q.A.I.M.S.'

It was a poor joke and she felt immediately ashamed, seeing the smile trying to reach his eyes, ridden as they were by dark ghosts. Her own eyes filled with sudden tears she tried hard to keep from showing. The last thing a man wanted was what would appear as a superficial show of sympathy, the giver with no idea what it had been like for him.

Instead, she said simply, 'I'm glad to see you, Matthew.'

'Oh, Jenny.' With a cry from the heart, that bond they'd once known formed itself anew, the way it had done when the promise stretching before them had been bright upon a horizon they hadn't then known concealed the shadows of what was to come. It hadn't been a bond of love then, and now it was more a renewing of a friendship that had flourished briefly only to be interrupted by circumstance. But now he was here, she'd nurse him back to health and for her, for the time being, it was enough.

Thank God the disease was proving less advanced than she'd first feared. Despite the conditions under which he'd lived these last three years he'd retained a strong enough constitution to fight it in its early stages.

For that at least, Jenny offered up prayers of thanks. If only his state of mind showed as much promise. He'd sit in the hospital grounds, wrapped up with a coat against the stiff, health-giving breezes from the Blackmoor Vale which patients were expected to endure daily, staring ahead, seldom glancing around him as people normally do. If she approached him, he'd tense, his gaze averted. Asked how he was – a nurse's question after all – his reply would come back in a monotone. He offered no conversation, no observation of his own, leaving her to maybe lift the wrist, feel the pulse, play the nurse's role. Should she try to further her concern for him she'd inevitably be fobbed off with a terse reply that nothing was the matter and why should there be?

At these times Jenny would feel a blaze of anger against Susan Ward, for it could only be she who was the cause of such anguish. Of course some of his attitude stemmed from what he'd endured as a prisoner of war. But with a loyal woman at his side he'd have surmounted it in time. His wilful, selfish wife had let him down – if her mother had been right, and no reason why she shouldn't be. Susan's letter to him had revealed her adultery while he'd been away and helpless to do anything about it. After all he'd been through, to come home and hear something like that! Worse, he never spoke about it and Jenny felt powerless to alter the situation. Even as she came up to him now, she knew there would be no help she could give him.

To think she'd offered the girl friendship. Had she known what she was like, she'd have had nothing to do with her. Reaching Matthew's side, she found herself hating Susan as she'd never hated anyone in her life before.

As Jenny had anticipated, he did not look up at her as she too let her gaze wander to the trees on the horizon, their billowing of full-leafed heads darkened by distance against the sky with its small lamb-clouds marching in procession across the azure expanse. Matthew had said nothing and she tried not to see herself as an intrusion as he continued to ignore her, his hands curled into tight fists against the arm supports of the hospital Bath chair in which he sat. Yet she couldn't walk away, not with the torment she could see in the tightness around his mouth, the fine brows drawn together, the eyes seeing nothing but what must be seething inside his head.

Unbidden, she sank down on the small bench beside him. This time she didn't go through the motions of taking his wrist ineffectually to feel the pulse. He would know it as only a ruse. Nor did she speak. Making smalltalk would only reap a sarcastic response and send her away hating herself for having stupidly intruded. The time spun itself out, slowly, the silence between them heightening the faint hum of traffic on the road, the musical trill of a nearby thrush, the soft twitter of a myriad other birds in the grounds, the distant intermittent conversation of people further off, enlarging the silence between them as though they sat within a vacuum. When he did speak, low as his voice was, Jenny's nerves jangled sharply although her body itself did not move.

'I'm trapped here,' was all he said. She remained silent, encouraged for a hopeful moment or two, but he didn't appear to want to say anything more, and her hopefulness died.

She reached out and laid a hand on his clenched one, letting it lie there. He didn't draw away as she had half expected. The fist remained there, unmoving beneath hers, the warmth of the skin penetrating hers, her nurse's enquiring mind immediately registering that he might be feverish. A little maybe, nothing to be concerned by; temperature could go up and down. It was expected, so long as it did not flare. She did note something else, that the fist began slightly to relax. He moved his head a fraction and let his gaze fall on to her consoling hand. Did it seem to be a consoling hand to him?

A nurse's voice nearby startled them both. Then the nurse and her charge moved on, the voice fading. Jenny followed their departure with her eyes, so it was a second or two before she became aware of Matthew speaking, of what he was saying, his voice halting and so low as to be hardly audible except for the sibilant sounds.

'Places like that – you need someone. Something. To cling to. In my head. She was in my head. Fever. Does weird things to you. But she *was* real. Thinking of me. Far away. Thinking of me.'

He was talking about Susan. 'But for her I'd have gone under. She kept me going. Once – a mouth full of ulcers – vitamin deficiency – couldn't eat . . .' There came a low mirthless chuckle. 'Starving, and I couldn't eat . . . She kept me going. In my head. And all the time I didn't know. Had no idea she was . . .'

He broke off this time with an intake of breath that sounded more like a sob caught in his throat.

Jenny had said nothing, letting him talk. She hadn't expected this. His need to talk had come out of nowhere, unprompted, unless it had been the way she had lain her hand on his. But she'd done that before only to have him snatch his hand away. There was no reason for her to congratulate herself, nor did she try to probe what had prompted him. She merely sat saying nothing, letting him get it all out of himself, or praying that he would.

He hadn't looked at her once. He seemed to be trying to fight the emptiness that was consuming him, but she was glad he hadn't given way to tears which she knew instinctively would have destroyed his dignity in his own mind. All she could do as he lapsed into silence was to wait and listen if he chose to say more, and if he didn't then she must let it go at that and keep her platitudes to herself. But the emptiness he nursed proved too strong for him. Startling her, he suddenly pulled his hand from under hers and she thought he was about to reject her. Instead, he took her hand and lifted it to his forehead as though in dire need of her comfort. No sound came from him, though she could feel his silent grief as a faint vibration on her arm. When again he spoke, the words were muffled by the cuff of her uniform. 'I love her, Jenny. I should hate her. But I can't.'

Jenny nodded, stifling emotions of her own. The comfort she'd thought he sought from her was merely what he would have sought from anyone. He still loved Susan.

Chapter 25

People were putting the war years behind them; forgetting was perhaps another matter. Rationing still gripped hard, so Christmas had still been frugal, but it had felt more relaxed than for six years. New Year 1946, this first full year of peace, held out fresh promise for the future.

Spring, welcomed in with open arms, saw hoardings going up around bombed areas, cranes being ferried in to shift the rubble in preparation for rebuilding. Soon, the damage covered over with new buildings, no one who hadn't been here would know there had been any. The old raw fear for one's life was giving way to all the petty concerns of peacetime – politics, nuisance neighbours, making ends meet, keeping children clean. Demobbed men, this time in orderly fashion unlike the mad release of the First World War, were going back to old jobs to demand the sort of wages enjoyed by those essential workers who'd been kept out of the forces. For some the way ahead looked rosy. For those still nursing grief, remembering loved ones never to return, it hardly glimmered.

Watching Matthew's slow progress, Jenny knew it wasn't glowing for him either. He had at last been told the whole truth about Susan by his well-meaning parents: how she'd walked out of the house while heavily pregnant, not a word of warning, not a word of thanks for all they'd done for her; how she had treated them when they'd found where she was living, was still living (they told him the address); the affair she'd had, still ongoing, with her landlady's husband, Geoffrey Crawley; Mrs Crawley finally leaving him; how distant and rude Susan had been to them when they had called on her to persuade her to go back home with them; how they had found her and this Crawley fellow living together, but how without a qualm she had let them take her daughter – Matthew's daughter – away from her, the child in a terrible neglected state, as though she had no care or love for Matilda at all; how not once from that day to this had Susan asked after her. (They brought photos of Matilda, now a bonny three-year-old, but they hadn't brought her in person, for fear of infection.)

He had listened to it all without comment, but afterwards Jenny had found him abstracted and unresponsive, his expression frozen, his lips a tight white line in his narrow, set face. Jenny had wondered if now had been the best time to tell him everything. Of course he would have had to know at some time, would have known soon enough once he went home. The drug Streptomycin was now helping to save sufferers from the old resort to surgery. Matthew had escaped the trauma of the knife, and was declared fit to go home and attend checkups at a local hospital. But how would he face going home, knowing what he did? Not only from his parents but from Susan herself. She had not once visited him or written to him, but she did that Christmas.

It was just after Christmas when Jenny came upon him asleep on his bed one cold afternoon. The windows as ever stayed open to admit draughts of vital fresh air against which patients must huddle under blankets and wool cardigans.

For a moment Jenny allowed herself the luxury, or perhaps the imposition, of watching him asleep, an intrusion upon his privacy she knew, but he looked so peaceful that she needed to take more than a brief glance at him. It was then she noted that his sleep wasn't as peaceful as it first appeared. Nothing specific, just something about the expression, even with his eyes closed, caught her attention and made her frown.

Her gaze travelled to the hand lying limp above the coverlet where she saw that his fingers, that had been curled about a sheet of notepaper, had loosened their hold. Without touching the letter she bent forward, conscious of the cruelty of her intrusion into an unsuspecting person's privacy, to read what she could see of it, a few words only. But they were enough. In fact one word had been enough: divorce. The childish handwriting was that of Susan.

Compressing her lips to stem the seething anger that rose up in her, she could only hurry away, knowing there was nothing she could do to help him. She could not know, not until he told her, and he would not do that. He would keep his pain to himself as he'd learned to do all through his three hard years of suffering while Susan, the treacherous little bitch, had been having a good time with some other man.

*

All this time, Jenny felt instinctively that her presence had been a bolster for him; she sensed that he clung to her as a friend who would hold his hand should he need it. Now he was leaving. Who would he have to hold his hand against the onslaught of Susan's infidelity? Not his mother, who meant well but who found it impossible to unbend. His father? Perhaps. What he needed was someone who loved him as she loved him. Yet what right had she to presume that her silent love, which would always be there for him although he wasn't aware of it, was what he needed?

On the day of his leaving, he took her hand, grinned up into her face and said, in the same way as he had once told her she would be one of the nicer of his memories, 'I'll miss you, Jenny. Keep in touch.'

He had needed her throughout his time here, sometimes desperately. But love? There were all kinds of love. Maybe he did feel something towards her, something deeper than just friendship, and perhaps such a relationship could grow into something more meaningful given time, but it would never be what people called being in love. And for all Susan had done to him, Jenny knew he still loved her with a desperation that pulled him apart.

So she smiled at him as he got into his parents' car, and said with cheery encouragement, 'Of course I'll keep in touch.'

Mrs Ward smiled her wintry smile at her and nodded her gratitude for all the nursing she had given Matthew, and Jenny, returning the acknowledgement, knew the woman was grateful, although her nature was unable to allow her to express how she really felt.

Mr Ward, coming round the car to take Jenny's hand, was more open and forthcoming. 'He wrote, you know, to tell us all about you. You mean more to him than I think even he realises. You've been a tower of strength to him and I don't think he'd have got this far, little as it is, but for you. I wish . . .' He paused and his eyes studied hers. 'I wish you and he . . .'

Jenny knew what he was trying to say but felt it right that he shouldn't be urged to further it. She broke in quickly. 'Matthew and I are very good friends, Mr Ward. Have always been that. He needs friends.'

'Yes, of course.' The relief that he hadn't had to say what was on his mind was apparent, that and a depth of understanding between them in the significant way he added before going back round to the driver's side of the car, 'Don't lose touch with us, Jenny.'

Watching them go, Matthew appearing wretched and somehow defeated, looking neither right nor left, not even waving to her, she thought about his father's parting words. 'Don't lose touch.' An ordinary saying, but expressed so earnestly that she knew it carried a totally different meaning to the normally light-hearted one. Yet her heart did not rise with hope. It was up to Matthew, not his father, how far their friendship progressed, and Matthew would never let go of Susan. His love for her would forever haunt him, fill his heart, and Jenny Ross would have no chance to squeeze into whatever minute portion of his heart might be left free.

Matthew's going was a signal for her to leave the QAs.

She had no more use for them, nor they for her. But it was impossible to see herself as leaving the profession. The mere idea of going back into office work after all she had experienced made her feel like a deflated balloon. She would stay a nurse to the end of her working life. She'd become a civilian nurse. Ignoring the vision of the years stretching on, while she, unmarried, dedicated herself to moving steadily up the ladder one day to become a matron, she applied for a post of nursing sister at the London Chest Hospital, and got it. That she was back near to Matthew's home and would still see him from time to time, she chose to ignore. She had come back for her mother's sake and nothing else. Except for her mother she might possibly have applied for a place elsewhere in any of the distant counties, pastures new, Matthew a closed book. This she told herself, almost convincing herself that he had nothing at all to do with her return home.

But it was good to be home again, with her mother cooking for her in the evenings, seeing the pleasure and contentment in her face. It was good to spend her days off with her, pick up where she'd left off. But that part of it wasn't quite true. The threads of that old life before the war had been well and truly cut. The friends she had known had gone their own ways: Matthew's sister Louise had married and gone to Canada; Jean Summerfield's people were still living wherever they'd gone to (she could no longer recall where it was) and Jean no doubt was married by now; Freddy and Eileen Perry, with their two children, lived in Romford, Essex – she had their address but probably wouldn't bother writing to them; Dennis Cox, poor Dennis, was dead . . . she felt sad for a young life lost, so many young lives lost. But for the war she might have ended up marrying Dennis, settled down to being the wife of a successful solicitor, perhaps with one or two children, attending social events. But there *had* been a war and it *had* altered all their lives, their once carefree, happy lives. Now this was her life and she must settle for that.

'It's nice knowing I don't have to be sent anywhere and everywhere,' she told her mother who, at last convinced that her daughter would be home almost as regularly as if she had gone back to office work, was happily setting the table for this, their first evening meal together for some considerable time. 'Though all the friends I used to know around here are all gone now.'

'There's still the church, dear. You might find someone there.'

'I think I've got a bit old for that, Mumsy.'

Her mother shrugged as they sat themselves down to the table. 'Well, I expect you'll soon make new ones, dear. Perhaps from the hospital. And there's still young Matthew Ward across the road. Now he's home again, I expect he'll be attending there for check-ups. It's the nearest place, easy for him to get to. You'll probably see him now and again.'

Blithely she prattled on this new tack, how ill he was looking, as she began on the stew she'd prepared. 'To think how he once was, poor dear.'

Jenny too remembered.

She had an old photo somewhere around the house of them all, her old friends, all of them happy and unsuspecting of what lay ahead, snapped in the act of fits of laughter. She remembered it being taken by Louise, then a girl of sixteen. Matthew had made a quip in his usual mocking manner: 'Look at her, worst photographer this side of Lower Wallop and west of Katmandu!' Coming unexpectedly, it had them all falling about so that the snap was slightly blurred. It still lay in her dressing-table drawer. He'd been so debonair then, and now looked so thin and ill and haunted.

'His mother looks worried lately,' her mother was saying, chewing on a piece of the precious still-rationed scrag end of lamb. 'For him I suppose, him and his so-called wife. I think I said something about it in one of my letters to you, that they were more or less separated? She really let him down while he was away, poor boy, a prisoner of the Japanese, and nothing he could do about her so far away. His mother looks after their little girl now, you know. That's a comfort to him at least.'

Jenny nodded obligingly as she ate. She had never divulged her secret feelings to her mother, to anyone. She vowed to find an excuse to pop across the road at some time or other and see how he was.

It was with some surprise one bright Sunday afternoon to be welcomed in by his mother on her first tentative visit. Much of what she had always considered the woman's frigid mien melted at the sight of her.

'Of course, my dear, come in,' she said readily. And then, her voice dropping to a whisper, 'He certainly needs someone else's company than just ours. It's hard for him, going nowhere, doing so little. He sits in the garden doing nothing. It was suggested he go to Southend sanatorium for a while. Sea air. Good for his chest. But he won't go. It's a good job we have the park nearby, the air's fresher here than most places in London. Mr Ward thought we should move to the country for his health, but Matthew got himself into such a state about it, we've dropped the idea. He's in the garden.'

All this she relayed as she conducted Jenny along the bright, neat hallway and through the spotless kitchen to where Matthew was sitting in a deckchair on a narrow paved patio which the sun at its summer height could just about touch for a couple of hours.

His head was bent over a photograph but as he looked up at her emerging from the house with his mother he quickly slipped it out of sight between himself and the deckchair fabric, but not before Jenny glimpsed the glossy black and white image of a young woman. That and his reaction to her coming upon him could only mean it was of his wife.

Jenny pretended she hadn't noticed. 'Hope you don't mind me popping in. I just wanted to see how you were.'

He was trying to smile. Watching the effort it was obvious he'd been tormented by the now-hidden photo. Now he must look at this visitor as though nothing had happened, and Jenny felt the weight of guilt at her intrusion, wishing she hadn't so blithely taken it into her head to come over here. His mother having gone back into the house, leaving them to it, she could hardly depart the second she had arrived. Best to brazen it out and make an exit as soon as decently possible.

'See you're taking advantage of the sunshine,' she said brightly. He nodded and she gazed about the long, narrow garden for some inspiration. 'This garden's bigger than ours, but then, your house is larger too. These are nice houses. I see your dad's already taken out the old air-raid shelter. I think ours will stay there permanently if we're not careful, though I suppose in time we'll get a man to take it out for us and grass it over.'

She was talking rubbish, anything to fill the threatening silence.

He was saying nothing. She wondered if he was even listening. What was he thinking? It was hard to tell and she was beginning to feel a virtual idiot standing here talking nonsense about gardens and air-raid shelters.

She stopped, regarding him. What had she come here for? To cheer him up? To give him a pep talk? To pry? All she wanted to do now was say, 'Nice to see you again, Matthew – goodbye,' but she merely stood looking at him, desperately probing her mind for something to say. What else? Glad you are looking better? But he wasn't looking better. He was looking . . . not ill; he had filled out a little from that first time she'd seen him brought into the hospital. No, not exactly ill, but drawn, pulled down, despondency oozing from him because he saw no hope of any future for himself. And didn't she know why? Of course she did, and prayed to be able to put it right for him, without becoming an interfering nuisance. He wouldn't welcome her interference. His pain was private and it was obvious he intended to keep it that way.

So it took her by storm when he said, as though to himself, 'It's her photo. I was looking at her photo.'

She could have said, 'Were you?' and nearly did, but that would have been crass, false innocence. She had seen him, and he knew she had. She could have said, 'Whose photo?' but she knew whose it was, and he knew that of her as well. So she stood silent.

'There's nothing I can do,' he said in the same flat tone.

Now was the time to say something. 'What can I do?' she said simply.

He turned his eyes to her, dark with the grief that was eating him. 'I don't know.' He wasn't telling her to mind her own business, that there was nothing she could do, just that he didn't know.

'If there is anything I can do, Matthew. If you need me. I'll be here.'

She spoke few words now, not that earlier inane chatter. Words that had some meaning, she hoped. She saw relief flow into his eyes, saw him incline his head in a small gesture of acceptance and she knew they would talk again and little by little he would release into her keeping all the suppressed grief and rage and hopelessness that was within him and perhaps in this way she would lighten the burden that at this moment seemed unbearable.

Even now he was on the verge of saying something. She waited while he contemplated what he needed to say. He, who had once been unstoppable with ready quips and digs and careless laughter, must force himself to look at every word, each drowned in a mire of unspeakable memories, having to be wrung from him, and now with an added reluctance after what had been done to him by one who he had thought had stood by him.

'Jenny . . .' he said at last. 'Jenny . . . I have to see her. I've got to talk to her. Somehow. If I could see her . . . There's no one, no one who'll help. They say I . . . I mustn't . . .'

Now he halted altogether, but she knew what he was trying to say. His parents' well-meaning efforts to defend him against the wife who'd caused him such hurt had resulted only in antagonising him more. They were too close in their shared grief to be of any good to him. But could she do any better?

Now wasn't the time to broach it. The least said at this moment . . .

There was movement in the house, the sound of voices, one of them high, childish. Matthew brightened immediately as a small figure came out in a rush. Jenny turned to see a small girl of around three-and-a-half pull up sharp at the sight of her, a stranger, while Jenny, relief surging over her at this timely interruption, smiled down at her. 'Hello.'

Mrs Ward stood behind her granddaughter. 'Matilda, say hello to daddy and Miss Ross.' Jenny caught the coupling of her and Matthew's names, as though she'd have liked to see them as such.

Shyly, Matilda stood her ground, her head dropping as she surveyed Jenny from under a generous dark fringe of hair. She was a beautiful child, softly rounded, sweet-faced, her eyes cornflower-blue, the rest of her hair cascading down behind her small shoulders.

Jenny glanced at Matthew. He was regarding his daughter, his eyes suddenly tender, a faraway look in them. Was he thinking of Susan? Did his daughter look like her?

She turned back to the child. 'And where have you been?' she asked.

No reply was forthcoming and the little rose-red lips began to pout in childish self-consciousness. But her grandfather, who appeared in the doorway, went to her rescue.

'We've been out, haven't we?' he said in an indulgent voice. 'We've been to Epping Forest. I came by some extra petrol so I took her out for the day. Matthew's mother stayed here for Matthew's sake. He didn't want to come along.'

'Not much point, was there?' Matthew's remark was sharp, but his father chose to ignore it, turning his attention to the child, bending towards her encouragingly.

'And what did we see in the woods? We saw squirrels, didn't we?'

'Squiddles,' repeated Matilda, picking up the spirit of it.

'And what else? What else did we see?'

'Squiddles.'

'And? Tell daddy what you saw. And . . . what flies in the air?'

At last she was in full command, embarrassment forgotten. 'We seed some birds and squiddles and . . .' She broke off to twist round to consult her grandfather who mouthed something at her, she in turn working at it. 'Pheasints!' she cried in triumph. 'And lots of sheeps.'

'That's really nice,' Jenny offered, bending down to be rewarded by the girl coming forward to put a small soft hand in hers. 'She's lovely.' Jenny turned to Matthew but his eyes had grown hard, not looking at any of them, so she turned hastily back to his parents, who nodded their wholehearted concurrence.

'She is,' Mrs Ward said, a little sadly. 'And very well behaved.'

'Yes.' More a sound from Matthew than a word, it was weighted with bitter incrimination leaving Jenny wondering if it had been directed at his mother, who would have insisted on good behaviour even from a three-year-old, or at his wife, whom this child obviously took after. Not a bit of Matthew could be seen in her.

'At least in that,' his mother turned on him, 'she takes after you, thank the Lord. And she has your colour hair, and . . .'

'So Susan's hair isn't dark?' he shot back at her, almost viciously. 'She takes after her in everything. *Her* eyes, *her* stature. And who does she take after for tantrums? There's only one. Well-behaved, yes, sometimes, but there are times when even you can't control her. If that's not Susan I don't know what is. Why don't you bloody well admit to it?'

'Oh, Matthew,' his mother's exasperated voice rang out. 'Why can't you put that woman out of your mind? Why must you always bring her up?'

'Because I still love her. You can't see that. All you can see is your own damned righteousness. She was alone. She had no one. I wasn't there. I should have been. Instead I

was . . . I was . . . Christ, if you'd only see how it must've
been for her. So she's done the dirty on me, found someone
else. But you're not helping make it any bloody easier for
me.'

Jenny got to her feet awkwardly, an outsider witnessing
family dissension. This was a side to Matthew she had
never seen. Even all that time ago when he had spoken
against his mother's efforts to encourage him to go for a
commission at the beginning of the war, it had not been
this acrimonious, his hatred of people trying to help, the
world itself. It wasn't what he was saying but the way the
words were being spat out with such vehemence that was
so frightening.

Matilda was looking from one to the other, her pretty
face animated with anguish, nearing tears. On impulse,
Jenny gathered her to her with one arm around her and the
child came readily, huddling against her.

Matthew had got out of his deckchair to stand glaring
at his mother, and without thinking Jenny found her voice,
directing it at him.

'You're frightening your daughter, Matthew.' It amazed
her how calm her voice sounded and he shot an enraged
glance at her, instantly modifying it as their eyes met. He
took a deep breath, a shuddering sigh, and his posture
sagged a little.

'I'm sorry, Jenny, that you should hear all this.' His
whole mien seemed to diminish and, appalled, Jenny let
go her hold on Matilda and went towards him. He must
not be diminished.

'Oh, my dear. Don't. It's not your fault. I started it.'

Of course she hadn't, but it felt like it. He was breathing hard. He began coughing, small, sharp little coughs. He looked all in, had worn down what energy he had; the disease still lurked in him. She put an arm about him, supporting him while she looked at his parents.

'I think he ought to rest,' she ordered, she the nurse in charge, and they, like admonished children, moved back before her as she went with their son into the house.

Once Matthew was installed in bed in his room, she apologised as a formality to his parents for her being here, for being a disruption to their private life. She waved away their insistence that she hadn't been, but she was still in her role of nurse, advising as she saw fit.

'I think he ought to be got to a sanatorium for a while, you know. His mind must rest as well as his body, and it's not being rested here. He's too near his wife. I think he needs a few months away, in spite of what he says.'

It was gratifying to see them nod agreement, but Mrs Ward surprised her on taking her to the door by putting a hand on her arm before opening it.

'You are of course, quite right, my dear.'

Chapter 26

There wasn't a lot he could do about it. Between them all, his parents, his doctors, Jenny Ross, whom he alternately turned to for support and backed away from, he knew that if he wanted to get better he must bow to their superior judgement, submit to being packed off to the sanatorium.

He did need to get better, to be well again to claim Susan back from that bastard who'd tempted her away. Susan was easily led. It wasn't her fault. She had this thing about sick people, but once he got himself back on his feet, all that would disappear.

The sanatorium was bright, two-storeyed, with more windows than walls, and verandas positioned to catch every vestige of sunlight. The grounds had the benefit of sea air to help with the cure, and with one of the mainstays of cure being to keep up the patients' spirits, make them feel at ease with the world, the nursing staff were attentive and cheery. He too was expected to feel at ease with the world, but he wasn't. He was an inconvenience, to be put away. He had no means of getting to Susan from here, for the sanatorium was effectively a prison too. At home he might in time have evaded his mother's eagle eye, boarded a bus for Mile End Road and burst in on Susan in the hope, vain perhaps, of getting her back. Here he could only wait to be declared fit before ever being allowed to escape and be his own man to do as he pleased.

Do as he pleased! That was a laugh. It seemed all his life he'd been in captivity. Home, the Army, prison camps, hospitals; his mother, even Jenny Ross joining the ranks of his keepers. Where had all that free spirit gone he'd dreamed of in his youth? At twenty-eight he felt every bit an old man. There had been such thoughts before the war of one day leaving home to soar free as a bird. He had left, but merely to swap one form of imprisonment for another, and there was no way he would ever be free. Only with Susan had he been free, tasting a tiny morsel, enough to reveal the golden glory of it, before it had all been snatched away.

Stuck here in this place, this morning watching his parents' cautious approach like that of people about to confront a time bomb, he wondered what was the point of all the efforts to make him well while inside memories both wonderful and evil entwined in a form of torture until he could no longer tell them apart. These memories could not be shared with anyone because no one understood what it was like to love and have it snatched away, to be strong and have that snatched away, to ache for beauty and see only misery and privation and degradation and betrayal, to contrast the wife he had loved and trusted with the truth he had come home to face. Only one sure way to be free remained. This he contemplated with strange detachment as he sat watching his parents' progress along the clean, bright ward towards him, and when they had each kissed him and asked how he was, he answered with a sort of perverse wish to witness their horrified reaction, a despondent need to gain their attention.

'Tell the truth, I've just about had enough of everything. What's the point of it all? I'd be better off finishing it and being no more worry to anyone.'

His remark was ignored.

'It's time you started thinking what you're going to do about Susan.' He turned his face away from his mother's probing eyes. 'All this hoping for miracles, it's just ludicrous, Matthew. She wants a divorce and she's not particular how she gets it.'

His eyes remained averted. No point responding when she got on this track, leaping on it the moment she arrived, and Dad putting his oar in as well.

'If you think she'll ever come back now, Matthew, you're just banging your head against a brick wall, son.'

'If she did come back,' his mother's tone sounded righteously adamant, 'I for one wouldn't give her the smell of my dish rag, much less house room . . .'

But she wasn't in love with Susan. At times his chest felt as if it was being torn out. Even his father no longer took his side. Matthew felt totally alienated seeing his father nodding at every word his mother said.

'We've spoken to a solicitor, Matthew. He has written to her on our behalf advising her to get one of her own in this matter, and she's done that now.' All this had been done without once consulting him. 'They both agree that the marriage is unsalvageable. Susan is quite happy to be cited as the guilty party.' She was as eager as that? Something inside Matthew plummeted. 'Apparently this Crawley fellow has no objections to being cited as her lover. His wife is apparently thinking in terms of divorcing him anyway. Pity it all has to take so long, and meantime the solicitor is running up a nice fat fee.'

Was that all they cared about, costs? He kept his face turned away.

'It's up to you, Matthew. How much longer are you going to let things drag on? There's nothing you can do. She's made up her mind, the slut.'

Now he turned. 'Don't say that!'

'I will say that, Matthew. Because that's what she is. How can you feel anything for her after what she's done to you, you a prisoner of war, all you went through, while she enjoyed herself playing fast and loose.'

How could he, even if he wished, tell them what he'd gone through and how it had been Susan alone who had kept him going? He still believed that, fervently, still believed she *had* thought of him, willed him to live. This adultery had come later. It didn't matter what they said, there had been a time, at first, when she had willed him to live, prayed for his safe return, cried for him. If everyone would only stop interfering, he and she could come together again. He would forgive her everything. The war had done this to them, had taken all good things out of their hands. And he could, would forgive her. If only she would come back to him.

'There's nothing you can do about it, Matthew.' This from his father, his tone pleading. 'It's gone too far. Gone on too long. You've got to file for a divorce, son. There's nothing more you can do.'

What did they bloody know? He looked at each of them, his eyes ice-hard, but there were no words he could say and he turned away again. Let them get on with it. They would, no matter what he said. But once he was out of here, then they would see a different Matthew. No longer did he contemplate suicide. He'd fight for what was his – once he was strong again.

'I just feel I'm being buried here, Jenny, bit by bit.'

The words seemed to come from deep inside his soul and Jenny fancied she felt every iota of his pain as if it were her own. She counted the days to each visit, coming to see him whenever she could get time off from her work.

There had been a wild idea when he'd gone off to the sanatorium to give up her present post and follow him, but in time he would leave there and come home for good. It was always a fool's game following others around the country. They always moved on, leaving behind a void much as before. Not only that, here she was a visitor, a friend, a confidante. As a nurse she would have become an overseer, an official figure, not to be trusted. Things were better as they stood.

She sat now beside him on the veranda that caught the slanting, fast-diminishing warmth of an October sun. He was in a wickerwork easy chair, a cardigan about his shoulders, she on a hard chair that made her back seem unacceptably rigid. She would rather have been allowed to recline a little, to look more at ease. This way he had to look up at her which didn't help an easy relationship. Though mostly he stared at the tiled floor as he emptied out his heart to her.

'If I could only go to see her.' He seldom mentioned Susan by name. By this time they all knew who *her* referred to. 'I know I could sort things out. But no one agrees, they keep telling me it'll put my health in jeopardy, but that's an excuse. They don't want me to try getting her back. They hate her so I must hate her too.' He let his voice trail off and they sat on in silence for a while, then suddenly he looked up at Jenny, his eyes brightened by new hope.

'But you could go.'

'Me?' She was startled, lost for words. How could she go to his wife, trying to convey to her what was in someone else's heart? It was impossible.

He was looking at her from under his brow, his eyes slewing sideways towards her. She hurried on. 'It wouldn't be right for me to pay her a visit on your behalf. What could I say to her?'

'No one has ever bothered to talk to her,' he said bitterly. 'Except to condemn her.'

She waited. He had dropped his gaze and she could see his face working very slightly, could almost see the thoughts going through his head, the pain, the longing, the hope and the hopelessness that seethed there. And memories too, memories that would never die. All he'd suffered these past years would be with him always. But none of it, looking at him now with grief and emptiness showing on every part of his face, had scarred him as Susan had.

Jenny could foster only contempt for the girl which instinctively she knew she must smother for his sake. If she did consent to being his errand boy, she would have to be sweet and understanding to gain Susan's confidence. It smacked of an unsavoury business because subterfuge did not come easily to her. But wasn't she resorting to subterfuge at this very moment, visiting him in the guise of a friend, when her whole being cried out to touch his hand in love, to kiss his lips and be kissed in return, the way he had kissed her before he'd gone away and it had all gone cold for her when he had met Susan?

'Please, Matthew, don't ask me to do that,' she pleaded. But for his sake, for the sake of the love she had for him, if he pressed the point . . .

As well she had been looking at him or she'd have missed the hand half-raised in a small poignant gesture of defeat, of humiliated pride, an effort not to recognise that he must rely on her to do his work for him. He needed help yet felt belittled by that need. Innocently she *was* belittling him. He would not ask her again, that she knew. She knew too that their friendship was being placed in jeopardy, that he would never trust her again. She needed his trust as much as he needed hers. It was a kind of love in its way.

'I'll have to see,' she added lamely; not a promise nor a denial, neither one thing or the other, a way of avoiding the total commitment she knew she was in danger of being held to. To escape it, she got up to gather up her coat and handbag, preparing to murmur some sort of farewell, when, only halfway out of her seat, she was taken by surprise as his hand closed about her wrist.

'You will see her, Jenny? You promise.'

'I haven't . . .' The commitment was already being made for her. Blackmail, trading on the affection she had for him, the thought shot through her head. He knew, he must know, how she felt about him, and was using it. That was unkind, cruel. For a second Jenny was aghast at the anger that swept through her. But the eyes staring up into hers were filled with pleading, not craftiness, were sunken with desolation, dark with pain, and though that in itself was a form of blackmail, how could she refuse him?

Yet still she hesitated. He was asking too much of her love. And she had expected him *not* to ask again, so was now taken off guard. 'What on earth could I say to her, Matthew?'

'Just that I . . . I want her to come back to me.'

'I can't tell her things like that. If you wrote a letter, I could take it to her.'

'I've written letters.'

'This time I'd be there to hand it to her, while she reads it, tell her how you are, how you feel.'

Oh God! She had walked right into it. Hope had begun to glow in his eyes. Hope was filling him as a deep hole is filled with lifegiving soil to nurture the tree with which it is about to be planted. And it was glorious to see him come suddenly alive. How could she destroy that?

'All right, Matthew. Write to her. I'll wait.'

She sat down again, put her hat and handbag aside and watched him fish a small writing case from his locker, feverishly open it and pull out the fountain pen resting inside to write his private letter to his wife.

All the while Jenny's heart was pounding against her chest wall, partly at the prospect looming before her, partly at feeling herself being used as a sacrificial lamb, partly with the same emotion he himself suffered – love that tore at the very being but which the sufferer knew to be quite futile no matter what they did.

The feeling of being made a sacrificial lamb still lingering, she reluctantly prepared herself to visit Susan.

She made three calls that week, during break times from the London Chest Hospital, none of them successful. She received no reply to her knock and had no way to tell whether they were out or merely pretending to be. Each time it had rained, not heavily but with miserable persistence that carried all the odours of the East End with it, and after her three separate attempts, standing on the doorstep wet and fed up and growing more and more annoyed, she gave up. There was only so much one could do. Besides, it was all pointless anyway. Susan would never go back to the man she had rejected. Obviously happy with her lover, what did she want with a sick man? Which Matthew still was.

In a way it was a relief not seeing Susan, loathing the girl as she did for the way she'd behaved. But more than that, a tiny spark kept leaping into her mind that the longer Susan stayed away from Matthew, the more chance there was of his coming to terms with it. Would he one day see the futility of chasing after her and turn to someone else – herself perhaps? His friend all these years, always there for him, he was fast becoming dependent on her. Could that one day lead to love?

The thought made her laugh. Little hope of that. But a week from now she'd have to confront him with her admission of failure, see his face. She found herself putting it off and on that Saturday decided to postpone seeing him until another of her days off. Instead she'd try to see Susan one last time, have something she could tell him. But that morning it rained again . . .

It was his mother who forced her hand that very morning. It came as a shock to open the door and find his mother standing there, an umbrella above her head. Mrs Ward demeaning herself to come across in the rain to a lesser neighbour's door revealed the extent to which some of her high-necked values had taken a nose-dive since the war.

She looked almost supplicant, the weight of her son's plight making her a wholly different woman from the one who'd once lorded it over others. Her principles, however, had not slipped to the extent of agreeing to Mrs Ross's invitation to come inside.

'It's Jenny I wish to speak to,' she said, her voice as sharp as it ever was, and turning to Jenny she asked directly, 'When do you next hope to be visiting Matthew?'

'I was thinking of perhaps going this afternoon,' Jenny lied, trying hard not to sound reluctant.

'That's what I thought.' Mrs Ward compressed her lips in a manner natural to her. 'We'll be seeing him too today, as soon as Mr Ward gets the car out. You can come with us. Save your train fare. Could you be ready in, say, half an hour?'

Still some of the old Mrs Ward there. Assuming everyone would fall in with her plans came as naturally to her
as breathing. Jenny chewed on her lip. She and Mumsy
had planned on a quiet afternoon together, but it could
probably be put aside. They'd have all evening. And part
of her did want to see Matthew very much, despite her
trepidation at what she had to tell him.

'Yes, I could be.' His parents being there might soften
his reaction.

Mrs Ward inclined her head in a small gesture of
acknowledgement. 'He often asks after you, Jenny,' she
said, but broke off abruptly as though that information had
embarrassed her in some way.

This woman would never let her high standards slip
entirely no matter what the circumstances, but Jenny
had detected more than once, as she did now, a ring of
suppressed hope in Mrs Ward's voice that she might
one day see her as part of the family. A daughter-in-law
perhaps? Vain hope, that, but she smiled as Mrs Ward
added a little too briskly, 'Well, we'll pick you up in half
an hour then,' before turning and going down the steps and
back along the road to her own house.

Matthew was in the day room, it being too wet to go
outside. October, nearly at its end, already heralded a bad
winter, and the room buzzed with families and patients.
Jenny prayed he wouldn't ask her what she had achieved.

She sat by while his parents put their offerings of fruit
and a bar of Fry's chocolate from their sweet ration before
him, asked him how he was and began on all the trivialities
of their lives since last seeing him. He murmured his

thanks for the gifts, after a while turning aside from what they were telling him, his attention wandering while he muttered occasional comments in whatever seemed the appropriate place.

Several times Jenny saw his eyes come to rest on her, saw the query in their depths. She smiled weakly, knowing he would wait for a moment when they were alone. As if he had planned it, his father went out on to the veranda to smoke his pipe; his mother joined her husband, leaving Jenny to hold the fort. It was a moment she had been dreading.

The second they were out of hearing, his question came direct. 'What did she say?'

'Your wife?' She stalled, trying to remember how she'd rehearsed this moment. He said nothing, but the look in his dark eyes said, 'Who else?'

Jenny steeled herself, 'I went there several times, Matthew, but there was never any answer to my knock.'

He sat silent for a moment, then said, 'You didn't speak to her.'

'I tried. Oh, Matthew, I did try so hard.'

'I expect you did.' His tone was soft but full of condemnation. 'It was unfair of me to ask that of you.'

'No, it was right.'

He shook his head, throwing off the failure. 'I've let myself down. The only one to go and see her is me. Can't ask things like that of you. My fault, expecting too much.'

'No, Matthew. I understand how you feel.'

He looked directly at her. 'Do you?' The look made her

squirm, a look one would give one's executioner, defiant yet resigned.

'I want to.' That she'd let him down she felt keenly. 'I want to help.'

'You're putting yourself in a high place, aren't you, Jenny, thinking you can do anything for me? I could tell you all of what's inside me. I could tell you for a hundred years, you still wouldn't know.'

'I feel so useless.'

'Then how the bloody hell do you think I feel?' His voice had risen, bringing all heads turning in his direction. 'You all think you know how people like me feel. Trotting out your damned platitudes. "It's all behind you now – forget it – we'll make it better – tell you some jokes – snap you out of it. It doesn't matter that you wake up in a cold sweat, crying out for the friends who died while you stayed alive, feeling bloody guilty for surviving, feeling that you'd trodden on them to stay alive while they died. Why d'you keep crying for the girl whose picture you kept inside your head through all those years, who you thought was waiting for you to come back home, to find it was only a dream? You must get over it." Well I can't get over it. And all your bloody understanding, Jenny, isn't going to help me get over it.'

He stopped as suddenly as he'd begun. Now he stood up, staring around him at the faces turned to him in stunned silence. His parents had come back in to gaze at him in alarm. For a moment he regarded them, then with all those in the day room watching him open-mouthed in the manner of people who feel unable to pinpoint any reason for odd behaviour, he strode from the room.

No one, not even his parents, moved, but Jenny was already on her way, hurrying after him. Thus when she caught him up they were alone. Just one other person could be seen in the corridor, a porter at the far end going about his business.

Taking Matthew by the arm she swung him round to face her and pulled him to her, gathered him in her arms. He came without protest, his head turned so that his cheek rested on her shoulder, allowing his face to bury itself in the hollow of her neck.

Cradling him, she could feel his body being shaken by quiet sobs. She heard herself crooning soft, half-formed words as a mother might do to a hurt child. 'No, no, dear, no. It's all right. It's all right.' Silly words to a grown man but they afforded the comfort of understanding and shared feelings.

But he was right. How could she share what went on in his mind? Who had any idea what it had really been like for men like him, only from what papers and newsreels showed? She had seen a Nazi concentration camp after its liberation and had been horrified. But by the time accounts of the experiences of the freed emaciated British lads had reached the papers, too much coverage had been devoted to those newsreels of Nazi atrocities for much more to be given to the horrors of Japanese prison camps. The inmates had been too far away. Also they'd been British and American and Australian, men who surely hadn't succumbed to such barbaric treatment as had those Jews of the concentration camps, their

skeletal corpses piled high in ditches for the public to
see on cinema screens and the front pages of newspapers.
No one saw the thousands of crosses lying deep in the
jungle, too deep for photographers to penetrate with their
cameras. Why bother? They had the groups of smiling
if skeletal freed prisoners to snap. Brits, Yanks, Aussies,
Kiwis, with bottles of beer in their hands given them by
their rescuers, all doing thumbs-up for the cameraman
as they held each other up on matchstick legs, bony
arms around each other's necks. They were all right.
They weren't lying in obvious piles of dead. They were
coming back, all of them looking cheerful and victorious
as though they'd won a war, and no one saw the horror
that lay behind those smiles, the dead comrades who'd
forever haunt their dreams. Jenny's arms tightened about
Matthew, imagining the pain for some like him whose
wife or sweetheart hadn't waited for them.

'It's all right,' she murmured again, her face buried in
his dark hair that smelled of him, spicy, and of shampoo.
'Just let me be here for you.'

Suddenly she too was crying. 'I love you, Matthew.
You're all the world to me. You've always been all the
world to me. That's why I've never got married. I hoped
. . . I never gave up hope of you coming home. I kept it
alive because I . . .'

She realised all at once what she had been saying. His
body had grown calm and he lifted his head, his dark eyes
still shining with moisture, looking into hers. Flustered,
Jenny dropped her eyes from the gaze that seemed to bore
into her. Then she heard his voice, hoarse from grieving for

the woman that was his no longer, 'Jenny, I didn't know.'

Still looking down, she shrugged dismissively, no longer in command of herself, embarrassed by having her adoration revealed.

'It's a private thing,' she managed to say. 'It doesn't matter.'

'It does.'

He was looking down upon the crown of her still-bent head, she could feel it. 'I don't deserve you, Jenny. If only . . .'

She looked up as he broke off, but he was moving back from her, putting her from him. She took a deep, fortifying breath and gathered herself up. 'I'm sorry I let you down, Matthew. I did try hard.'

'I know.'

Footsteps hurrying along the corridor invaded the private moment. Voices broke in, at once irate and concerned. 'Matthew! What on earth's going on? What upset you? You'll do yourself no good getting so upset. Jenny, what upset him?' As though he couldn't talk for himself.

Jenny looked at him and a mutual spark passed silently between them. He was aware now of her feelings, but he had to bow to the stronger obsession that drew him, and she accepted that he felt tenderness towards her, a caring love which couldn't match that which was destroying him.

'I have to do this myself,' he said, mouthing the words so that only she heard them as his parents reached him. Wondering at the words he'd mouthed at her, she had a vision of a man walking knowingly to his doom. He would let Susan destroy him because he wanted her to and there was nothing anyone could do about it.

Chapter 27

'When do you think you'll be bringing Mattie to see me again?'

The last time he'd seen her had been August. It was now November. His daughter would be left with the woman who cleaned for his mother a couple of days a week with a few shillings extra to keep an eye on Mattie when they visited.

He'd liked to have said, 'ordain to bring her', his mother having the final say in things concerning him, even whether he saw his own daughter or not. Matthew felt bitterness run through him like a trickle of acid as his parents sat looking awkward and concerned. His mother frowned.

'It's too cold these days.'

'It's warm enough in here.' Weak as the autumn sun filtering through the conservatory roof was, it was enough to warm up the place considerably apart from a constant draught from the obligatory ever-open top set of windows. Used to so-called healthy draughts, it felt warm enough to him, but his mother had another ready excuse up her sleeve.

'During the summer, Matthew, she could play in the open, but with winter coming on, it's boring for her cooped up inside. It would be for any child her age. She'd get on the other patients' nerves. It's not fair on them or her.'

And besides, he finished in silent sarcasm, a sanatorium's no place for a child. True, it wasn't, but he missed her; missed Susan; felt rebellious.

'She's my child.' His and Susan's, so like Susan, even at four. He'd feast his eyes on her, still filled with wonder at this his daughter, a surge of love for her twisting inside him so that he wanted to hug her to him. Of course as yet he dared not. TB was catching, not so much from him now, as because all patients came here to this out-of-quarantine visiting area. Visitors were safe at arm's length, but Mattie had to be discouraged from approaching too near, for her own sake.

Not that she ever came that near to him. To her he was a stranger still, a man she had been told to call Daddy. As a child who had never known one and was still only four years old, she hadn't any real idea what a daddy was meant to be. His father she called Grandad, his mother Grandma, and she had experienced the feel of that, but him, he was Daddy in name only. How he longed to clasp her to him and show her what it meant. But if he did, she might ease away from him, his hug unfamiliar, maybe even a little alarming. And that was another reason why he did not try to embrace her.

The weak sun had disappeared without anyone seeing it go. A pale fog moving in from the estuary had begun licking cold white tongues against the glass, promising to rime the lawns outside with frost before morning. His father noticed it and looked at his watch.

'Nearly four o'clock. We best be getting along, son. You'll be coming home soon. By the New Year. They're pleased with your progress. You'll be with Mattie then, for all the hours you want.'

'Do call her Matilda, dear,' interjected his mother, but Matthew hardly heard her.

Five weeks and he'd be home, to do what he liked. And he knew exactly what he would do. But that he would save for later. Five more weeks cut off from outside contact, seeing only the other patients, their visitors, the staff, and occasionally Jenny when she could get time off from her work. He had no letters to read, except from Louise, who was married and in Canada now. There seemed little point in anyone else sending letters when they came each Sunday.

Nor did Jenny write. What would she write about? Work, her life, his health, hers? She knew better than to resort to all that rubbish. His heart lifted at the thought of her. Since that unexpected episode a few Saturdays ago he hadn't been able to get her out of his mind, the way she had folded her arms around him, drawn him to her, the way she'd whispered her love for him; seemingly it had burst out of her.

And him? Something had stirred in him, but the image of Susan had immediately made him push Jenny away. To feel anything like that for her would destroy the love he nurtured for Susan and he couldn't bear that. It felt like being caught up in the strangling tendrils of a vine but not wanting them ever to fall away. Yet other than the unlikely hope of any visit from Susan, he found himself waiting for Jenny's visits more than anyone else's. But she wasn't visiting so often as before. She had embarrassed herself too much that day. He wanted to see her to tell her she had no need to feel bad, that he understood. But when she did finally arrive, alone, the first Sunday in December, he said nothing, seeing his planned comment as a platitude, an insult to her feelings.

He was reading Louise's letter when she came in. Louise sounded full of her life in Canada, making it seem romantic and exciting. She and her husband were so much in love with each other. He was miserably comparing his wrecked marriage to her successful one, wishing she didn't have to be so full of it. She was promising to come over to see him when they could get the money together for the flight. She'd gone out there by sea, but swore she would never set sail on the sea again; she would use one of the new airlines opened up since the war. However they had started a family, 'at last', and she didn't think it the right thing to do in her condition. She would make it next year once the baby was born, if they could still afford it. 'You know how much money a baby takes.'

No, he didn't know. He hadn't been there when Mattie was a baby. He had just screwed up that letter in a fit of suppressed hate, against whom he wasn't sure, perhaps circumstances, perhaps himself, when Jenny came in. Thus he was not exactly in any receptive mood to see her.

Sensing it, Jenny sat awkward and self-conscious. 'I hear you'll be coming home soon,' she said for want of something better to say.

She had been to see him only once since her outrageous

performance in the corridor, when his parents had caught her in the act of cuddling him. Not that they mattered. Mrs Ward had appeared highly approving. But *she* had felt a fool, them seeing her holding their son, a married man, to her bosom.

'When I come home,' Jenny became aware of a mordant edge to his tone, 'I might finally be allowed to think for myself.'

'Don't you do that now?' Immediately she saw the inanity of the remark. Here, everyone thought for him, he was powerless to do what he wanted. She knew what was in his mind. Once home he would go and find Susan with no one to stop him, probably taking her daughter with him, confronting Susan with her duties as wife and mother. It would be a disaster. Jenny could see it a mile off, the selfish, spoiled, wilful bitch throwing his pleading back in his face. And where would that leave him? Didn't he realise the harm he'd be doing himself? She wanted to tell him, warn him, but it would sound presumptuous, could even wreck their friendship, certainly any hope she fostered of anything more than that. Again she squirmed at the way she had held him to her, murmured her stupid words of love. How he had looked at her then, his eyes dark and deep. Recalling it now, had his look been one of understanding and mutual affection, or merely fear and rejection?

It was the best Christmas Susan felt she had ever spent. Just her, Geoffrey and little Trevor. She wondered how Emma Crawley was. She hadn't come nigh or by since leaving. She and Geoffrey's boys were living with her sister not far away, but she might as well have been in Timbuctoo. Geoffrey never spoke about her, though now and again he would go and pay a visit for the boys' sake. It annoyed Susan a bit, but she shrank from complaining, a little superstitious that if she did, she might lose him.

From Matthew's parents there had been no sound, other than letters from their solicitor to hers. Nothing as yet was moving regarding the divorce, with Matthew playing at delaying tactics all the time. She would have gone to tell him how useless these were, that nothing would induce her to go back to him now, but her solicitor had discouraged it, urging her to leave it all in his hands. But he was taking such a bloody long time about it. Still, he was right, no point rocking the boat. Matthew was well out of the way in that sanatorium near Southend.

She didn't wish him ill, didn't hate him or loathe him. Just the illness made her shudder to think how he must be, handsome looks all gone, in their place a gaunt individual who coughed and spat blood and lay pale and vapid – she'd seen it portrayed in films, the victim wasting away, dying in the arms of a lover. She'd always hated hospitals. Even setting foot in one as a visitor made her feel sick and shaky. Having Mattie in one had been bad enough. Thank God she'd had little Trevor at home.

None of these thoughts did she impart to Geoffrey. Why spoil things? Christmas passed like a dream; they'd had a wonderful time indulging in all the goodies he'd brought home. Nineteen forty-seven waited two days off and rationing was becoming less harsh even though the winter was already proving one of the severest they'd known since the one at the beginning of the war. But settled before a bright fire whose rising heat stirred the now-dusty Christmas trimmings, Susan's whole world was lit up and life couldn't be sweeter. Matthew was just a memory, at least until the divorce came through. After the New Year the solicitors might get their silly fingers out and get things moving.

But she wouldn't think about that. She'd just think about her and Geoffrey. Little Trevor was safe asleep in bed, she and Geoffrey had the evening all to themselves. Already in a slinky black nightdress, her dressing gown open to reveal her at her best behind the lace and satin, she was beginning to feel worked up by the way he was looking at her over his glass of whisky. Both their minds were focusing on the same thing. Her insides crawled deliriously as she thought how she intended to make him really happy tonight. In fact they might not even wait to get to bed. She came over, put an enticing arm about his neck, easing herself into his lap.

He grinned at her, and, the whisky glass still in one hand, fondled her breasts with the other, easing them from their flimsy lacy covering. That he kept the glass in his hand while doing so added a certain masterful casualness, heightening her senses even more to see how far this would go before he was compelled to put down the glass. Her dressing gown fell from her shoulders, the straps of the satin nightdress also slipped from her shoulders, letting the garment slither to her waist. Geoffrey's free hand was beneath the material, fingers manipulating firmly, teasing her desire with uncontrollable force. She moaned. When would he put down that damned glass? What was she – his bondmaid to do what he liked with, arousing her until she screamed? Already urgency was rising faster than she could ever remember. She cried out to him, sobbed for him to put down the glass, for God's sake, she could take no more of this. And yet how wonderful it was – this awakening without him even entering her. What a man she had.

She was hardly aware of the glass finally being put on the sideboard, of him easing her down on the hard lino, but only of his weight on her.

From somewhere came a pounding, like iron being bashed against wood. A voice raised outside in the street came dimly to her. She heard Geoffrey swear, felt his weight ease, became suddenly aware that the street door seemed in danger of being broken down.

'What is it?' Angry, she lifted her head that a moment ago had seemed to be spinning, now completely still and filled only with disappointed anger at this untimely disruption.

The voice in the street was demanding entry, the street door rattling on its lock and hinges with a resumption of the pounding it was taking. All sorts of thoughts raced through Susan's mind. Fire? Trevor fallen out of the window? A drunk? The police – what would they want, bashing on the street door? She thought of Matthew – perhaps he was dead, her husband, and they were here, to inform her. Geoffrey was on his feet, frantically buttoning his fly. Still sitting on the floor, she was equally frantically dragging on her nightdress, gathering her dressing gown about her.

Even so, she hissed to him, full of fear of the unknown: 'Don't answer it.'

'I've got to. Someone might be in trouble.'

'It's not our business, Geoff.' But she was thinking again of little Trevor upstairs. Was he all right? And then she too was on her feet, trying to find her slippers as Geoffrey, now respectable, made for the hallway.

She heard him open the door, waited to hear a policeman's voice. What had he to tell them? What she heard made her clutch at her throat. All these many years since she had heard that voice, its deep timbre, yet she recognised it instantly. 'Where is she?' it demanded.

Though his parents didn't know it, he spent Christmas at the sanatorium at his own request. He felt in no hurry to celebrate it at home with them carping at him to do something about his marriage. But yesterday he'd been obliged to concede. He was due to leave anyway, now or in a week's time. Two days before New Year's Eve, with the sanatorium nursing staff stretched because of leave through the festive season, his parents thought it only right that he make it now and welcome in 1947 with them as a family.

'Start the New Year afresh. Let's hope that will be the last time you have to go into hospital. They said you're clear, at last, and so long as you look after yourself and don't fret, you can only look forward.'

His first night home had to have been the worst he had ever spent under this roof, lying awake in his room while his parents slept, their sleep sound and contented in the assumption that with their anxieties for him a little easier for the present, he must be at ease too. How could he be?

Letters were lying on the doormat as they'd come in from collecting him. His father had picked them up, sorted them out, selecting one above the rest to hand to him.

'Looks like it's from your wife's solicitors.'

Taking it, he'd put it in his jacket pocket, and saw his father's face draw together with concern.

'Aren't you going to open it? It could be important.'

'It can wait,' he'd told him and, parrying his mother's arguments that followed, refused to open it for them to see what Susan was asking. He already knew what she asked, the same request kept being trotted out – for him to divorce her, she would give him grounds enough, she was in love with . . . He couldn't even read the name without a burning rage compelling his fingers to screw each letter into a ball. He would give no answer to any of these letters until he saw her face to face. This statement he'd written repeatedly, but she (or her solicitor on her behalf) had not once acknowledged them. He might as well be crying into the wind.

But whatever it contained wasn't for others to cluck over, full of their damned advice. 'Divorce her, Matthew, and get it over with. She's no good to you. You wouldn't take her back after all she's done.' No, he wouldn't give them the satisfaction of raising his voice against their demands.

The letter had stayed firmly in his pocket. Finally he opened it in the privacy of his room, hating the task and what would be written there. As he had suspected it had been the usual cry. But this time a small sealed envelope had been enclosed, the flap signed across with her small uneven signature – no, not signature, just the Christian name, Susan. She didn't even deign to include her married name, which in itself provoked anger and remorse from him.

What she'd written had taken his breath away. 'I'm tired of asking. If you can't grant me a divorce, it's no skin of my nose. I'll carry on living with Geoffrey until I die wether you like it or not. What I really want to tell you once and for all is I don't ever want to set eyes on you. It would make me sick. I wasnt never cut out to be a nurse for anyone and I'm not ready to start with you. I'm sorry if I hurt you but I don't no how plane I can make it.'

Hurt him? With a seething mind he'd risen, dressed himself, fumbling in his fury and pain at her words that seemed to so encase his brain in iron that no thought could get through but the one intent of getting to her, half killing Crawley and taking whatever came from that. He'd had sense enough to creep from his room without making any noise and waking his parents up, downstairs to where his father's car keys lay on the kitchen sideboard. The car had once been given to him as a twenty-first birthday present in the happy certainty that he would have years of pleasure from it, not knowing what had awaited him. They'd kept the car, during the war years of petrol rationing, on the gravel driveway under a tarpaulin, his father cleaning and servicing it with loving regularity. This ritual silently declared the certainty that Matthew would indeed return. 'It's yours again, Matthew,' Dad had said, but until he came home and felt well enough to drive, Dad continued to use it to keep it in running order. A way of encouraging him to get fit, Matthew supposed. Well, tonight he'd be fit, if necessary.

Muffled in an overcoat, he'd driven off almost blindly in the rage that still consumed him. It was ten thirty and people were still about. Only turning into the Mile End Road from Cambridge Heath Road was his brain cooled by force as a man coming out of one of the pubs made straight across his path. The car's tyres screeched to a skidding halt, in front of the man swaying and glaring at him. 'Gerrout, y'silly sod! Watch where yer goin'. Nearly knocked me darn.'

The man had staggered on across the road, as Matthew leaned his head on the steering wheel for a moment to clear his thoughts.

Geoffrey Crawley had no notion what was in store for him. Opening the door to the frantic yelling and thumping, uttering, 'What the hell . . .' he was taken totally by surprise when a hand thrust itself against his chest with such force he was thrown back against the wall, his head connecting with solid brick with a whack that for a second sent him dizzy. He had the presence of mind at least to lunge back, enough to deny the intruder entry for a brief moment during which his attacker shouted again, 'Where is she?'

Crawley, indignant now at his home being invaded, held the man with both hands on the shoulders, countering inanely, 'Who are you? What d'you want? You can't come barging in here like this!' All of it ran together like a single sentence. The man was leaning against his efforts to hold him off.

'I said where is she?' he repeated.

'Get out of here!' Frightened, Crawley felt thin fingers begin to force him from the hold he was vainly trying to retain on the man. 'Go away! Who the bloody hell are you?'

For an answer, Matthew let go of the hands trying to prevent his entrance, reached back with his right and took a swing at his wife's lover. It grazed past the man's cheekbone, making his head connect again with the passage wall though less violently than the first time. The man let go of him to clap a palm to his abused cheek.

'Godawlmighty!' he screeched. 'I'm calling the police. Sue! Sue! Get out at the back, quick, get Mr Adams next door.'

Matthew heard her voice come plaintively, quavering with fear and perturbation, from a room down the passage. 'I can't. I'm not dressed.'

Not dressed? Visions of her and this bastard naked together a moment ago assailed him. He lunged, grabbing the coward by the throat, bearing him down the passageway with the force of the rush, taking him to the floor as Susan tried to run out from the room, screaming, finding her way blocked by two grappling men at her feet.

'Matthew! Oh, God, leave him alone. You'll kill him. Leave him alone!'

Crawley was making strange choking, rasping sounds as his hands flapped about, in turn trying to break the hold on his throat or scratch his assailant's face. The choking and rasping were becoming more pronounced, the defending hands weaker, now flopping to the floor between attempts to release the grip. The face had turned puce, the eyes were beginning to stare, bulge. At first deaf and blind to all else but wreaking revenge, Matthew became aware of that dreadful colour. Sights and sounds came leaping back into his brain, as Susan screamed and beat on his shoulders, plucking at them in an effort to tear him away. Yet he couldn't let go. His fingers seemed to have locked about that neck. Meantime, the face below him was darkening rapidly. Geoffrey's eyes were closing; his mouth was falling open but no sound came from it now except for a faint and fading hiss. The hands, which had ceased to flap, lay quite still against the floor, flung out as in a posture of crucifixion. It didn't need Susan's cry, 'You've killed him!' for his own brain to cry out, 'God, I have. I've killed him.'

Standing there, knowing he must go, yet feeling utterly incapable of moving himself, Matthew heard a small sound like a tiny rasping intake of breath. He saw one of the dead man's hands stir ever so slightly, turning over until the palm lay downward instead of limply on its back. Susan heard and saw it too.

'Geoffrey!' Her scream rang through the house. At the same time a small fretful cry came from upstairs. A child had awakened. Susan's child. Hers and this man's: the man who lay in her arms, miraculously stirring.

'Geoffrey, Geoffrey,' Susan continued to shriek. She was trying to shake him awake. He had begun breathing again in pain-racked, difficult gasps. It would take a stronger grip than that of a man still weak from his years of captivity and illness to kill a man in his prime, well fed, well paid, and at ease with his world.

Matthew moved forward instinctively. 'Susan?'

She turned on him like a tiger, blue eyes blazing. 'Get out! *Get out*! I never want to see you again. I hate you! I hate everything to do with you.'

'Susan.'

But she was crying, her head bent over the stirring, gasping Geoffrey. Her muffled words sounded full of unhappiness now. 'I did love you, Matthew. I did love you. But you weren't here.'

'That wasn't my fault.' It was a silly thing to say but all he could find.

Crawley was trying to sit up, his hands carefully feeling his throat. Susan held him to her, her glare moderating.

'It don't matter now, Matthew. It just happened. A long time ago.'

She was trying to help Crawley to his feet. Matthew watched the manoeuvres dispassionately as though this was all happening on a screen and he, the watcher, stood apart from it all, unable now to feel any emotion as to whether the man lived, died, took his wife from him, or even sprang up to murder him on the spot. Nothing inside him seemed to care any more. Nothing mattered. What was it someone once said in the prison camp – a long-faced, miserable Aussie – does it matter if yuh die now or when yuh ninety; hundred years from now, no one'll remember yuh or care and yuh certainly won't care when it was yuh died? Nothing mattered.

So why not make it now rather than lingering on with memories of a love that had vanished? Quick. Easy. No time to think. A tall building, a few tablets sending one into endless sleep, a gas-filled room, a passing train. So many ways. And yet he knew he'd do none of those things. Like the coward he was, the coward he'd been in the prison camps, dreaming of going out in a blaze of glory taking half a dozen Japs with him but too weak-willed to do anything about it, he was weak-willed now; would live out his natural lifespan and take his memories with him to the grave. He wanted to weep. But he wouldn't let her see him weep.

He left the house, left Susan still cuddling her Geoffrey to her. In a daze he got back into the car and headed east towards his home, his parents and – an odd thought filtered into his head – Jenny Ross.

Chapter 28

'Look, you're going to have to make a decision very soon, Matthew.'

He heard her well enough but chose not to heed her. It would mean committing himself and he wasn't ready, couldn't see a time when he ever would be. Far preferable to keep his eyes closed, think instead of the sun bathing him with its heat, of sitting here enjoying his surroundings; anything but the making of decisions about signing those divorce papers.

High summer. The winter had been fierce and hard. The Big Freeze they'd called it, with everything, transport, power, everyday life, paralysed by deep snow drifts right into March, then devastating floods. Now summer was making up for it.

Jenny had become his constant companion since his return from the sanatorium; the night he'd thought he had killed that bastard Crawley seemed years ago instead of just a few months as he lolled now on a bench in Victoria Park. During that dragging eternity of waiting he met each day with hope of a letter from Susan that might contain a change of mind. Such a bloody forlorn hope. All that ever arrived was legal, concerning the divorce. He had finally

capitulated, the decree nisi having been granted with what
had struck him as indelicate haste. Now screeds of legal
correspondence followed, designed to drag as big a fee
from both parties as possible. Everyone was looking to
the main chance. What did they care how he spent days,
weeks, months, sick with desolation while it was all going
on? Now the decree absolute loomed.

Jenny was waiting for him to answer her, but he didn't
want to. She too was looking to the main chance. Why else
devote her time to him? He felt no swollen pride in the fact.
What the hell did she see in him? He had become a man
ravaged by circumstances, churlish, his thoughts invariably
centred on the past, on memories best forgotten but which
still persisted, emotions that tore him still with guilt and
remorse. Bob Howlett dying alone still haunted him; and
the sweet face that had lived in his head all through the
terrible years haunted him too. The once-loving face that
had hovered had grown twisted with loathing.

'Matthew, did you hear me?'

Yes, he had heard. He kept his eyes closed, pushed
away a moment of irritation at her persistence. He
needed her support more than he cared to admit; at times
he wasn't sure what he'd do without her. With her he
felt safe. When she wasn't with him, he felt lost. She
remained patient and understanding when he used her as
his sounding board to beat out his bad moments on, even
when he sometimes went too far. He would apologise and
she would accept his apologies, kiss his cheek lightly and
say it didn't matter.

But it did matter. He wasn't worthy of her love. She

had told him she loved him though had never said so again after that one time. He wished he could return her love, for her sake, but that would mean rejecting the feelings he had for Susan, and lying to Jenny, who didn't deserve to be lied to. Susan had become an obsession, a part of him he could not ignore.

'Matthew.'

He opened his eyes. 'I heard you.'

'Then you can't keep putting it off. You've got to start getting on with your life. I know all about getting on with one's life, Matthew. I've done it.'

The statement sounded vehement. Was it a hint that he might one day take up his life with her? He wished she wouldn't make those sort of comments. He loved Susan. But what was love? A bonding of two like souls, each helping the other without thought of self? Or was it this overwhelming, mindless desire for someone who selfishly destroyed? One endured of course, yet the other was all-consuming. What if he were to take Jenny on and Susan came crying back? Would he have strength enough to reject the one who'd torn him apart and cling to the one who'd been steadfast all these years without hope of gain? The thought frightened him, but he wasn't contemplating proposing marriage to Jenny, was he?

'Let's leave it,' he told her almost savagely. 'Just enjoy the afternoon, shall we?'

She was equally sharp. 'Yes. Shall we? If that's what you want.'

'That's what I want,' he snapped back, faintly surprised

at her tone. It wasn't like her. She was usually so mild-mannered.

He lifted his face to the sun and tried to forget it as she went quiet. Not moody, Jenny was never moody, but he could sense anger simmering inside her. This was a side of her he'd not seen before. An odd tingle of new respect for her went through him, warm as the sun on his face. He let the warmth soak in and tried not to think of Jenny or Susan or anything.

It was a sweltering summer. Temperatures had been soaring into the eighties; newspapers announced it as sizzling, with photos of eggs frying on pavements, toddlers naked by the sea, tarmac bubbling. Only the holiday-makers revelled in the heat. For himself, having known the humid sweat-bath of a Burmese jungle, this English summer could be comfortably endured lounging on a bench beside a shingle path. Victoria Park again looked beautiful, its railings restored, its lawns, where he'd been told ack-ack guns had once run up and down ploughing up the grass, once more verdant and immaculate. What had been allotments were now replanted with shrubbery and bright flowers.

It was peaceful sitting here, far from the problems the country faced. Food rationing was still going on, the government was still trying to repay America's Marshall Aid loan. Attlee talked of the country as being engaged in another Battle of Britain and the cost of cigarettes had risen to three shillings and fourpence. India, Ceylon, Pakistan and Burma all wanted to break away from British rule with resultant massacres; at home the rising cost of living plagued everyone.

It all came a poor second to his own problems, with this damned divorce business. For all his efforts trying not to think about it, he was. He felt so powerless even though he could stop it at any point. But soon it would be too late. It was as if he was being driven towards a cliff edge, unable to cry out, but he could watch the precipice drawing nearer, his life ceasing to exist. Why didn't he call a halt? He could still grab the wheel of his own fate and turn it from what they were all telling him was inevitable. Why didn't he? Because breaking this marriage *was* inevitable, if not now, then at some time. He couldn't *make* Susan love him, could never reawaken those feelings she had once had for him. But, dear God . . .

'I still love her, Jenny,' he said, and his voice broke.

Sitting beside him, Jenny knew he hadn't heeded a word she'd said. He remained lost in his own world, hoping all would come out the way *he* wanted it to come out. But it couldn't. Others were making sure this broken marriage did not mend, his parents, his solicitors, his wife.

Then there was herself – she too exerted an influence on him. She knew it from the way his face brightened when he saw her, though since that day in October he seemed to be holding her at bay. Before then their friendship had been easy. Now, when she came to his home, he would get up and go out into the garden or somewhere upstairs, anything to avoid being with her in the presence of his family. Yet he readily accepted the opportunity to be with her alone, as he was now.

'I expect you'll always feel that way about her,' she returned, studying a squirrel that had scurried down from a tree to investigate a bit of dry bread dropped by children going to feed the ducks. As it nibbled it kept one eye on the couple on the bench for a more likely morsel.

She was conscious of her voice sounding strained. 'But it'll serve you to no avail, you know. You do know, Matthew?'

She felt her heart shrink as he turned on her. 'What do you know about it?' Immediately he caught himself. 'I'm sorry, Jenny, I didn't mean that to sound like it did,' he said, then justified it by repeating himself in a different way. 'But you can't know how I feel about her.'

'Perhaps I do,' she countered softly, only to reap more bitter reaction.

'You sound like my mother.' This was accompanied by a cynical curl of his lips.

She had no reply to that. Something inside her was growing angrier by the second. Usually she curbed it, waited until he calmed down and tried to vindicate his hurtfulness, but this time her patience had no power and the anger exploded before she could catch it to hold it back. She turned on him, her grey-green eyes blazing.

'That's it, Matthew. Go on feeling sorry for yourself.' At her raised voice, the squirrel dropped its piece of stale bread and scurried back up the tree, but she did not see it go. 'I've just about had it up to here, Matthew. I do try to see your point of view. I do feel sorry for what's happened to you and I know I'm being unfair, that no one who's not suffered what you have can know what it was like, for all the stories and pictures we've seen. And now this on top of everything. But I'm only flesh and blood. Now do I sound like your mother? I want to help and I feel so useless, and I love you so much, Matthew. Yes I do know *exactly* what it's like to love someone who doesn't love you, when nothing can be done about it. I know it like mad.'

Tears were springing from her eyes. They rolled down her cheeks. 'I wish I was small and dainty and had someone to be crazy over me, as you are with *her*. But I'm not the sort of girl you fancy, am I? I've never been the sort of girl you fancy. Well, if she's the sort you fancy then you're welcome to her. That's what I say. But is that supposed to alter what I feel inside? You'd rather run after someone like her and let your heart be torn out of you while you grovel at her feet, pleading for her to come back and hurt you all over again. Well, honestly, Matthew, if that's what you want, I might as well just give up. No point me being your friend forever and ever. Damn what I feel.'

He was staring at her, the expression on his thin, handsome face one of confusion. Surely he couldn't be so naive as not to have some inkling of how she felt about him? She had said too much, had revealed her heart to him when she hadn't intended to. She felt exposed, but she was too angry with him to care. And now she fought to recover her composure, savagely sweeping the tears away with the back of her hand.

'What does it matter anyway? I've got a good career in nursing and that's all right with me. I don't suppose I'll ever marry, not now. I'm not the wife type. I'd only start bossing him about, whoever he'd be. I'm the bossy kind, you said so yourself. Like your mother. I suppose if I was like your wife you'd be letting me wipe the floor with you. I don't think I could ever bear that – from you.'

He was looking at her in a strange way, studying her, his dark brows drawn together. 'Jenny, I'm sorry. I didn't intend to upset you.' He was always being sorry.

She shrugged and looked away from him as he went on inadequately. 'You're the last person I'd want to hurt, you know that.'

Jenny said nothing, very much in danger of refuting the statement. He didn't seem aware of it.

'I've only been thinking of myself all this time. I never once stopped to consider how you feel in all this. Even when you said you loved me, I could think of no one else but Su . . .' he hesitated over the name, but plunged on. 'Susan. All I've ever done is abuse your friendship. Your real friendship. Using it and giving nothing back, especially knowing how you felt about me. Jenny, I wouldn't hurt you for the world. You're the only decent thing that has ever happened to me, and . . .'

As he broke off, she turned to see him still gazing at her, realised he hadn't once ceased looking at her, even though she had turned away from him. Now he put his hand out and laid it on her upper arm. She could feel the warmth of the hand penetrating the thin material of her summer dress.

He was drawing her gently towards him, his voice husky. 'I couldn't have gone on without you. I know the thought of her still consumes me, and I know I've got to fight it. But I know you're worth two of her, Jenny.'

His other hand took hold of her, he was pulling her

closer to him. When his face was inches away from hers, she felt his lips touch her cheek.

No, it was too much. He had no right. He was taking it upon himself to offer comfort with a kiss on the cheek. She made to turn her face aside from the insult of that friendly peck, the sudden move causing her lips unintentionally to brush his.

All at once she found herself unable to break away as the pressure of his lips on hers became instantly firm. In that second all her love for him poured out to encompass him. With a small choking sob, Jenny let her arms wrap themselves about his neck as if they had a will of their own, and to her astonishment his arms encircled her in response. The squirrel in the tree ceased scratching at the bark to look down at a young couple in a close embrace, the girl crying, the man holding her, kissing her gently now, and murmuring soft words of comfort.

'It's all right, Jenny. It's all right.'

'I'm sorry, Matthew. I shouldn't have . . .'

'No, you should. I've been damned stupid, selfish.'

'But you don't love me. You can't. You love . . .'

'I don't really know any more what love is. What I do know is I can't imagine being without you, Jenny. You've become part of my life.'

The squirrel, looking down, heard only a meaningless chatter of human sounds and went on exploring his own world, seeking food and, instinctively searching for a mate with whom to procreate his own species.

Below, if Jenny was expecting the words, 'I love you, marry me?' she was doomed to disappointment. The kiss

had been emotional but an accident. She knew that later
he would be embarrassed at having been carried away on
a wave of brief, profound affection. She knew that too.
She'd ruined everything in a weak, thoughtless moment.
In the meantime they would walk home together as though
nothing had happened.

What she didn't know about were the new feelings she
had awakened in him.

Jenny took the envelope her mother held out to her: 'It's
addressed to you, dear,' and stared at the unfamiliar
handwriting. She rarely received mail other than *The
Nursing Journal*. Her friends were local nurses with no
need to write, seeing them every day. Her first thought was
that it was from one of the old group in the QAs but the
postmark was local. It was the small uneven handwriting
that gave her the first clue as with the edge of a thumbnail
she slit open the flap to withdraw a single sheet of cheap,
blue-lined notepaper. She cast her eyes to the foot of the
letter, noting the name.

'Who's it from, dear?' queried her mother with interest.

'Matthew's wife. Why should she be writing to me?'

'Odd.' Mrs Ross moved to lean over her shoulder. 'She
won't be his wife for much longer. The divorce comes up
in two weeks' time, so I hear.'

Jenny nodded, already reading, ignoring the misspellings:

Dear Jenny, I thought I'd write to you becaus I
need some advise from you if its possible. Im ever
so worried and I don't know what to do. As you

know the devorce comes threw in a couple of weeks time and Geoffrey. Thats the man I am living with. Geoffrey is acting very strange. I think he's worried about the devorce but he is not as nice to me as he used to be. Im getting ever so worried. I wanted to talk to Matthew but I cant very well ask him direct after all this time and I was wandring if you could have a word with him on my behalf so as to pave the way so to speek. I know youve always been a good friend of his and perhaps you can act as a go between like. I will be waiting for your reply and hope you can help me. Thank you. Susan Ward.

'Well I never,' breathed Mrs Ross in Jenny's ear. 'That's a cheek if ever there was. You're more than friends with him nowadays from what you've told me.'

Jenny had told her about the incident in the park several weeks earlier, full of hope that in voicing it she could make love come true. What she hadn't mentioned was Matthew's reticence since then, just as she'd predicted but hadn't wanted to believe. His true feelings remained a mystery, leaving her alternately filled with hope and despair: perhaps he was battling within himself as to whom he needed most, perhaps needing to come to terms with it; or again perhaps his inane pursuit of that worthless cat dominated him still and he hadn't the heart to tell her she must forget what had happened. Maybe he'd been too taken up with the finalities of the approaching divorce to think of anything else as yet, but would once it was all over. Then again, maybe he still had hopes of the divorce never taking place and hadn't the courage to tell her that either. Time and time again a flood of anger would pour through her at the unfairness of being strung along. He was not man enough to tell her the truth and still her churning soul one way or the other.

This time she held it in, so as not to give him even more reason to fend her off. Outwardly they behaved as they had always done, still talked about all sorts of things – everything but the one thing that mattered to her. Her pent-up emotions were doing odd things to her. One minute she saw him as weak, the next she swept the thought aside in a fit of remorse, for whatever he was, she loved him. And he wasn't weak. He wasn't. He was merely terribly confused. Once this divorce was over he'd have to forget Susan.

But now she must hand him Susan's letter, stand by and watch his reaction; felt she knew already what it would be.

These closing hot days of summer they had continued to frequent the park together. He seldom wanted to go anywhere else, but now as they sat on a bench or on the lawn watching other late-summer sun-worshippers, picnicking families, children, people walking dogs, they didn't touch. They spoke of trivial things. Matthew never spoke of his wife now or the imminent divorce. It was as though neither existed and she hadn't dared bring up the subject lest she drive him further from her.

There seemed to be a dull, flat ache in her soul as she folded Susan's letter and put it back into its envelope.

'I'd better hand it to him straight away,' she said

defeatedly. It went without saying what his reaction would be. A ray of hope. Jenny would be forgotten in an instant as he embraced the marvellous knowledge that Susan at the eleventh hour wanted him to take her back. He would forgive her all she had done to him and Jenny Ross would be put aside, told of his wonderful good news, thanked for all she'd done for him, and forgotten.

'He'll be pleased,' she said simply as she slid the envelope into the pocket of her nurse's dress to hand to him on her way to work. Then she would hurry off before seeing his reaction and get on with her day, get on with her own life, as she had vowed so many times before. But this time it held all the characteristics of finality.

Chapter 29

It was Saturday night, nearly ten o'clock. Little Trevor, in his cot since eight, had waited for his father well past his bedtime, and Geoffrey's key was only now just turning in the street door lock.

She stood waiting for him, the whole of her slight, small body quivering with fury.

'What bloody time do you call this?' she attacked him as he came into the cluttered living room, still innocently pocketing his keys in the jacket he'd already taken off to drop over a nearby chair.

He looked at her astonished, his jovial, 'Hello, love,' frozen on his lips. 'You know I always see the boys on a Saturday.'

'Not until this bloody hour of the evening. And you already see them twice during the week too. You never used to. So what's so special about them now? You used to come home before eight so you could see your own son before he goes to bed.'

He glared at her now, his jacket hanging by its collar from one finger. 'They're my sons too, don't forget. I owe them some of my time.'

'Not every bloody day of the week.'

'It's not every bloody day of the week.' Angered now, he flung the coat at the chair, which it missed. It slid to the floor to lie in a crumpled heap. 'It's twice a week and once on a Saturday.'

'That makes three times,' Susan stormed, standing her ground on the rug before the empty firegrate. She had no intention of moving from the spot to welcome him or go off to get him cups of tea as once she always did whenever he came in the door. This time she was going to have it out with him, one way or the other.

'I'm not putting up with this, Geoffrey. Not for much longer. Why do you have to keep going to see them three times a week? It was four times last week.'

'Four?' he blazed at her.

'Yes, *four*. What about Monday? You went there on Monday as well.'

'For an hour, that was all. You're begrudging me one hour with my own boys, now?'

'It's one hour too many, Geoffrey. What about me waiting all hours God sends for you to come home and give me a bit of your time? I mean, I'm important to you too, aren't I? You used to think so. You used to be a lot different to what you are now. I need to have you here.'

'You've got me, haven't you? Nearly all the time.' He went and threw himself down in one of the pair of sagging fireside chairs. It creaked under the sudden violent weight. 'Don't start an argument, Sue,' he sighed. 'I'm tired.'

'And *I'm* tired,' she railed on at him. 'Tired of being a doormat for you. For you to come home any old time you please. And I suppose you expect to make love to me, as always, as if nothing's happened.'

'You like it.'

'That's got nothing to do with it. You come home from *her* and your blessed sons, and clamber on top of me and make love as if you've not had it for weeks. How do I know you haven't been making love to *her* as well?'

He sat bolt-upright. 'That's not fair, darling. You know I don't have nothing to do with Emma and she don't have nothing to do with me. It's just for me to see the boys, that's all.'

'What proof have I got of that?' she continued to blaze. 'And don't darling me straight after you've seen *her.* What's going on between you two?'

Geoffrey shot out of the chair and stalked about the room, flinging irritated, disbelieving glances at her. 'This is getting bloody silly. I thought our row in the week was bad enough, and over the same bloody thing. But you're going right over the top again. Nothing's going on between Emma and me. Can't you get that straight? She's just the mother of my sons and they live with her. Of course I have to see her when I go there, but she don't have nothing to do with me.'

'But you wish she did.'

'Of course not, darling. I love you. I left her for you and that's not changed.' His voice had grown softer, more persuasive. 'It's you I love, Sue, and no one else.'

'Huh!' She moved at last to the window to straighten the already moderately straight gold-patterned curtains. 'Love me? You don't care anything about me, only to get your oats, that's all you care about me. It's all I'm good for.'

'Don't be silly. And don't be selfish.'

'Selfish!' The curtains received a tug, almost dislodging the pelmet they hung from. 'Me? Selfish? I should think you're the one who's selfish, leaving me alone half the week.'

'You *are* bloody selfish, Sue, sometimes.'

'I'm not. I'm not selfish.'

This was how it was lately, arguments going round and round, silly and pointless, ending up unsolved unless she gave in, threw herself at him and burst into tears. Before, he would kiss her better, take her to bed to assuage his need with her. She adored being made love to in that way, the rougher the better, with her the object of his lust, the helpless recipient. But these last couple of weeks, he hadn't made love to her after any row; he had merely extricated himself from her pleas for him to forgive her and had gone sullenly to bed; he would be asleep or apparently so by the time she came to him. Any attempts to wake him up had been met with a deep snore and a mumble of protest. Many a night she had lain awake beside him, her eyes wet with what she hated to admit were self-induced tears. Her sniffling and snuffling sounded loud enough to have disturbed the devil, but not Geoffrey, even though to her mind he must have heard but ignored the noise. The next morning he would leave for work after breakfast, through which he said little but read the morning paper that fell through the letter box at six thirty. His departing peck on the cheek seemed a condemnation of her attitude of late and left her to weep silently the rest of the morning as she got his son from his cot to feed him.

Slowly she was coming to feel that their relationship was beginning to fall apart, that he was tiring of her. But why now? In less than a couple of weeks her marriage would come to an end. She couldn't let Geoffrey lose interest in her now, not after all that had happened. She was being silly of course. He hadn't lost interest in her. His lovemaking said as much, or had done until lately. It was her fault. She *was* being selfish. He did need to see his sons by his wife. Soon she would be his new wife when his own divorce came through. This wouldn't be for several months yet; Emma had only filed for it a little while ago.

Tomorrow she would have him all to herself, all day. She would make up for her foolish, groundless tantrum by being all sweetness and light, and on Monday would run to get him his evening tea, for that evening he'd be home at the proper time. Last Monday had been the exception, because of his middle son Percy's birthday.

Sunday passed blissfully. They made love in the afternoon, with Trevor safely asleep in his cot. She bit back the cries of ecstasy Geoffrey forced from her in case she awoke the child and put an end to the unbelievable climax to which her lover was capable of bringing her. And they made love again that night with her happy cries ringing out abandoned enough to wake the neighbours.

All Monday she went about the house, content that all was well again and waited for Geoffrey to come home from work. Five thirty came and went. Six o'clock. Seven.

Susan, watching the clock, the egg and bacon she'd cooked dried up in her efforts to keep it warm for him, began to seethe afresh. There was no reason for him to have been kept at work. It was obvious he had gone round again to where Emma and the boys still lived with her sister. But there was no birthday to celebrate this Monday. And hadn't she heard from Geoffrey last week that the youngest would be at a friend's birthday party this evening and that Percy and Malcolm were going off on a school coach trip to Southend and wouldn't be home until after seven thirty? And didn't Emma's sister do evening work in some nearby pub? If Geoffrey had gone round to Emma's tonight, he'd really blotted his copybook this time.

Sick at heart, Susan waited, put Trevor to bed and waited some more. It was nearly nine before Geoffrey came in. In the ensuing row, he ducked and dived like mad. He didn't admit it for one second but Susan knew he had been with Emma, really been with Emma; there was something in the look of him that showed he had. When she accused him outright, his protests were too violent to be true, so she *knew* he had.

It was then she began to be really frightened, knowing just what she had done and how her life could go. Were he to go back to his wife, what would she have left? Geoffrey's son – that was all. Suddenly she didn't want to be left just with Geoffrey's son. She didn't want to be the spurned mistress saddled with a baby. She could see it all looming before her like a great yawning canyon. She thought voluntarily of Matthew, for the first time in months. It was then that she wrote a scribbled, frantic letter to Jenny Ross in the hope that she would speak for her to him. Jenny had always been a saviour of lame dogs and desperate souls. She would not fail this desperate soul – for once in her life, Susan waxed poetic as she wrote her letter, then sat back to await the results, which she knew could only be to her advantage. Matthew would have her back in the blink of an eye, still madly in love with her as he was.

Susan rather liked that word, desperate. She said it over and over again to herself as she sealed her letter and went to post it. Her heart, though, still ached for Geoffrey and she prayed he'd have a change of heart and carry on their relationship as though nothing had happened. Then of course there would be no need for Matthew and no harm done because from past knowledge of Jenny, the girl would be very careful how she worded her errand and might even delay it in rehearsing the words she would use to him. There would still be time enough to rescind her plea. After all, Matthew had recovered, hadn't he? He was no longer the sick and ravaged person she imagined he had been after coming home. Look how he'd belted into poor Geoffrey. Geoffrey, the apparently healthier man, had been unable to defend himself. At the time she had hated Matthew, seeing a savage, embittered, degraded man. But thinking about it, his face, at the time twisted and suffused by fury, had still retained much of that which had attracted her to him that first time. Half crouched in rage as he'd been, he still looked tall and slim, a far cry from the sick wretch she had imagined. Memories of what he had been now flooded back. In time he would become that again and perhaps they would pick up the threads of those beautiful if brief months they'd had together before he'd gone away. She hoped so. That was if her and Geoffrey's affair was over, which in her heart she hoped was untrue. All she wanted in life was a stable, loving relationship with someone, to be looked after, to be loved, to be given security.

Matthew took little notice of the ringing of the doorbell. He and Dad had not long got up; both were washed and dressed and waiting for their breakfast, the nutty fragrance of toast creeping from the kitchen. He listened idly to his mother going to answer the door. Probably the postman. A parcel perhaps?

'Matthew. It's Jenny, here to see you.'

He stood up, curious, as she came in with his mother. She seldom came here on a Wednesday, and never in the morning, never so early, her nurse's coat, spattered by light, early-morning rain, showing she was in fact on her way to the hospital. She was looking a little strained.

'Anything wrong?' His first words showed his concern.

'I can't stay. I'm on my way to work.' She sounded breathless as if she'd been running, but the breathlessness seemed to have something to do as well with the strained look on her face. She was holding an envelope, holding it out in a way that did not exactly ask for it to be taken from her. 'This arrived for me in the post, but it has to do with you rather than me. I was going to pop it through your letter box but it needs some explanation why it was sent to me and not to you.'

'Shall I take your coat?' His mother eyed the rain-spotted garment with concern for her furniture lest Matthew's visitor sit herself down. Jenny shook her head quickly.

'I can't stop.' She was looking at him, her expression apologetic in a way, her high brow furrowed with concern the way it used to furrow when she had tended him in that first hospital in England.

'What is it, Jenny?' He ignored his father, who had also stood up sociably at Jenny's entrance, and came round the table towards her. Perhaps being nearer she might hand him the letter she said so concerned him.

'This isn't possible to break to you gently, Matthew. It's from your wife. I was supposed to explain, tell you what she wants. I suppose what she is hoping me to do is to . . .' She broke off with an impatient tut. 'Well, read it yourself. I can't be . . . I don't want to be her go-between. It's nothing to do with me, anyway.'

Thrusting the letter into his hands, she turned and with a little nod and a thank-you to his mother, allowed herself to be conducted out.

Left holding the envelope, he instantly recognised Susan's laboured handwriting. By the time his mother came back, eager to see what it was all about, he had the letter open, his eyebrows drawn together in a frown.

'What is it, dear?'

'As Jenny said,' his father's deep voice was deadened by the well-furnished little breakfast room, 'it's from Matthew's wife.'

'Well, what does she say? What does she want?'

'She wants to come and see me. I shall have to see her.'

'Matthew.'

'I want to hear her say this to my face.'

'You can't. You can't see her. The divorce case . . .'

'I have to.' Screwing the letter up, he thrust it into his trouser pocket and made out of the room.

'Your breakfast,' she called after him, but received no reply.

The night he'd attacked Crawley, his first glimpse of her in years had been a fleeting, distorted one, seen through a mist of rage. Now as he opened the door to her knock, she stood before him, as he remembered she had done years before that, still with the same petite build, the same blue eyes wide and timid. Perhaps she looked a fraction more mature but still vulnerable and unsure of herself, prompting a natural reaction in others to take her under their wing.

'I got your letter telling me to come here,' she began tremulously. 'I'm glad you wanted to see me.'

He didn't smile. He dared not. He stepped back to let her in and she followed him into the sitting room like a small, subdued dog at his heels. He closed the door and they stood facing each other in the filtered light of a drab September afternoon. The room was very quiet. They were alone, his mother reluctantly and full of disapproval of his request leaving them to themselves. It occurred to him that he hadn't yet asked Susan to sit down, but to do so would be an acceptance of her and he was wary of betraying how he felt looking at her. Seeing her again had resurrected that surge of adoration the sight of her had always brought and it alarmed him.

To cover the discomposure her nearness aroused, he said stiffly: 'You said in your letter you weren't happy.'

She nodded, catching the fuller part of her lower lip briefly between her small teeth, an endearing little habit that had always stirred his emotions to see. Matthew clenched his hands against them.

'So what did you want from me?'

She came forward a fraction, a small movement of appeal to that love he'd once had for her, an attempt to awaken it if it now slept. She couldn't know how easily the single movement could awaken it, for its sleep had never been total. Her eyes were glistening.

'I'm so sorry, Matthew, for everything I've done. I know I was wrong, but you were so far away and I didn't know if you was . . . oh, Matthew.'

Tears had begun trickling gently down her cheeks. He was in danger of being disarmed by them. He didn't want to look at them, so lowered his eyes, remembered all the crying he too had done; the pain remembered was becoming insufferable.

'Matthew, don't turn away. Look at me. I'm sorry. I really am.'

Now he looked up, surprised at his own reaction. What did she expect of him? That he'd take her in his arms, soothe away all the sorrow she was displaying, tell her it was all right, that he forgave her and wanted only to take her back as though nothing had happened? His whole being cried out that that was what he wanted to do. He felt his lip curl contemptuously with the knowledge of how easily he might, contempt for himself that he knew how close he was. But he had grown embittered. Her tears, they weren't for him. She wasn't hurting for him, only for herself, had always only ever thought of herself.

Rationality seemed to spear through his body, but its searing pain was his only salvation. He kept hearing Jenny saying, 'It's nothing to do with me.' But it was everything to do with her, rationality, security, trust. He could trust Jenny. He could never trust Susan – ever again.

When he did speak his voice seemed to be conveying every vestige of that agony spearing him. It was an effort to talk at all.

'I'm sorry too, Susan. I can't . . . I can't have you back. I know I can't. You see . . .' He stopped as her eyes opened wide with terror. His immediate instinct was to grab her to him to stop that awful look of desolation. Fighting it, he shut his own eyes so as not to see how she was looking at him.

'I need to trust someone,' he heard himself saying. With an effort he pulled himself together, willed himself to look at her while trying to keep the mirror of his soul closed to her. It made his stare harder than he intended. He saw her shrink back a little, the gesture almost destroying his resolve until he remembered again the agony she had caused him over the years of wanting her.

'You see,' he began again. 'It wouldn't be any good – not now.'

'Matthew, no!'

He pushed on, ignoring the cry. 'The first sign of

anything not going your way, any inconvenience, any outside temptation, and you'd be off again. It's not your fault. It's how you are. When we married, I'd no idea. All I knew was I loved you, adored you, thought you could do no wrong, that you were perfect. But it wasn't enough, was it? I couldn't hold you. I'll never be able to hold you.'

She had been gazing up at him, the dawning of what he was saying growing apparent in her gaze, but her protest came in a wail of disbelief. 'I don't know what you're saying, Matthew. I know I was wrong. I *am* sorry. I'll make it up to you. I will. I still love you. I'll make everything up to you.'

He wanted to counter, 'What about Crawley?' But that would be dragging it down to the level of a slanging match. Suddenly he wanted to be rid of her. He was beginning to feel unsteady, shaky, a dull nausea in the pit of his stomach. He wanted to sit down but he dared not.

'I want you to go.' His voice sounded hoarse, strangled.

'Matthew . . .' Her eyes suddenly hardened, narrowed with suspicion. 'Is it someone else?' He almost laughed. 'It's that Jenny Ross. You've fallen in love with her, haven't you? You don't want me now.'

He didn't reply. Every word she said seemed to be driving her further from him. He couldn't believe that he could ever *not* be in love with her. It would hover inside him, a small devil, to the end of his days ready to resurrect itself the second his guard was lowered. But at this moment he was merely beginning to feel sickened. That she could say Jenny's name with such contempt! Jenny could make six of her, ever willing to take on his burden of fears, his indecisions, and not complain. Yet his fear was that he'd burden her too much, more than she could stand. Not for himself, but for her. Was that true love? If it was, then Susan paled into insignificance beside it.

'I might've known.' Her words pierced through his thoughts, her tone contemptuous, covering the fear that consumed her.

He blinked. 'I think you'd better go, Susan. Back to Crawley – try to make the best of it. You can use your charm on him, Susan. You know how to do that, don't you? You're good at it. He won't be able to resist. As I once couldn't. You'll be all right. You'll always be all right.'

Bitterness rose up inside him without bidding, like some other self. He was astounded by his own words, their harshness. All at once the past had become another country. He held her look of disbelief, aware that his was arid.

She took a step or two towards him, her expression still one of abject pleading, but his arid stare remained a wall of glass. Realisation began to dawn on her and she gave a small defeated sob, turning from him like a rabbit released from a car's headlights. She had no idea how near she had come to shattering that fragile barrier.

Making blindly for the door, her sob breaking into full-blown weeping, she pulled it open, fleeing past his mother whom he saw standing just beyond. A bitter grin twisted his lips that she had been there listening to it all.

'She's gone then?' The stiff statement reached his

hearing, but he found himself incapable of answering her. What in hell's name had he done? Susan had been in his grasp and he'd thrust her away. For a moment there came an urge to run after her, but he let the moment pass.

Chapter 30

It was the dim light of October making her feel low. The days had begun rapidly to shorten, the promise of a long winter already dulling the sky. It had to be; people were usually affected by the weather. Even so, she should have felt brighter than this. After all, Matthew was now a free man.

Jenny looked across the dinner table at her mother. 'Matthew Ward's divorce came through last week, did you know?'

Mrs Ross smiled as she chewed, her fork engaged in selecting a piece of potato. 'He should feel easier now. I suppose you do too.'

Jenny's knife and fork lay idle each side of her plate, although she gripped them as though gripping a pair of lifelines. 'I suppose I do in a way.'

'You and he might spend more time with each other.'

'We already do.'

'You know what I mean.' Her mother hadn't once lifted her eyes from her plate. Jenny knew exactly what she meant. It was a pity Matthew didn't.

For days he had been moping indoors. Off duty this weekend, she'd gone over to his house yesterday, been heartily welcomed in by his parents, invited to stay for a bit of tea with them. But seeing Matthew's obdurate expression of moodiness, his apparent lack of joy at seeing her, wrapped up as he was in his own sullen grief of his lost marriage, she had felt a flush of anger at him and excused herself, saying she didn't want to leave her mother on her own on a Saturday night.

She hadn't gone across today at all. He could stew in his own morass of misery if that was what he wanted. Of course she ached to see him but she was no longer prepared to be his whipping boy whenever he felt like it. She had made up her mind about that. He was free now. Divorced. Nothing he could do about it. It was up to him to get on with his life. But she wished she was included in that life, and still had no idea whether she was or not.

'I'm sure I don't know what he's going to do,' she said to her mother, a little sharply.

'Are you going to see him after dinner?'

A ring of the doorbell interrupted an awkward denial. Jenny leapt up from the table. 'I'll go.'

She left her mother murmuring that she couldn't think who that could be on such an overcast Sunday afternoon and hurried to the door.

For a split-second her mind wouldn't work, having a problem placing the face. But already the name had burst from her lips in disbelief.

'Ronald!'

He looked awkward, a man faintly aged since she had last seen him. 'I remembered your address,' he began. 'I was going to write, but I was in the vicinity, attending a medical seminar, and I thought before going home I'd look you up. Hope you didn't mind.'

She could only stare at him. 'Er . . . no.'

He gave her a somewhat silly grin, slightly apologetic. 'I was at a bit of a loose end.'

'Oh.'

'I'm a free agent, you see. Nothing to rush back home for. Of course there's surgery in the morning, but it only takes a few hours in the car to get back to Bath, so I thought why not look up an old friend?'

'Oh.'

'My marriage broke up,' he continued by way of explanation for his unexpected appearance.

Jenny heard her mother's voice filter faintly from the dining room. 'Who is it, dear?'

Hastily she called back over her shoulder. 'An old friend, Mumsy.'

'Well, ask her to come in, dear. Don't let her stand on the doorstep.'

Jenny ignored the invitation but any moment her mother would come to see why.

'Look,' she said quickly, lowering her voice so that Mumsy wouldn't hear. 'Can you wait outside while I get my coat?' Somehow she didn't want to go through lots of introductions and explanations to Mumsy. 'We can take a walk and you can tell me about yourself and why you're here.'

He was looking embarrassed. 'Perhaps I'd better go, Jenny. I didn't mean to . . .'

'No,' she cut in. 'I'll only be a tick. I'd like to know

how you are.' After all, it was only polite. She couldn't turn him away.

She closed the door, gently so as not to seem rude, and hurried back along the hall. She felt flustered, not from renewed affection but by the fact that Matthew might have seen him at the door. Silly really – it could have been anyone. But he might see her walking with Ronald. What would he think? She felt suddenly unaccountably rebellious. What the hell did it matter what he thought?

'Didn't you ask her in, dear?' Her mother, coming from the dining room, regarded her a little bemusedly as Jenny quickly gathered her coat from the skeletal stand that held their everyday coats.

'I'm just going for a walk, Mumsy. Shan't be a tick.'

'It looks rather like rain. Silly going for a walk when you could have asked her in. I wouldn't have minded. You'd best take a brolly with you.'

To appease her, Jenny grabbed one of the two umbrellas sticking out at an angle from the guard rail around the foot of the coat stand.

'Don't be out too long, dear,' her mother's plaintive departing call followed her as she made towards the door. 'You don't want to get wet. And bring her in when you get back.'

'She has to get straight back home,' Jenny returned on the point of closing the door on her. And Ronald could go straight back too. Said he was divorced. If he had come here hoping to pick up where they had left off years ago, the cheek of it!

He was leaning on the gatepost looking somewhat

woebegone. As she reached him he straightened up, taking her arm and threading it through his as though it were his right, whether she objected or not. But it would have seemed rude to have shrugged away from him. He was only trying to be amicable and he did seem a little uncomfortable.

'It's so nice to see you again,' he was saying as he conducted her, guiding her before she realised it away from the main road from where he had obviously come. Still confused by him turning up like this out of the blue, it did not dawn on her until they had gone some way that this would not have been the route she would have consciously chosen. She took a quick glance up at Matthew's house as they passed it, but there was no sign of life. Jenny breathed a small sigh of relief.

'It's nice to see you again too,' she said.

'Well, as I was nearby.' He looked abruptly at her. 'You know, I was pretty broken up when you gave me up, Jenny. I really thought we had something going for us. I kept hoping. But I know you weren't the sort to play a chap along, so I had to decide to put it all out of my mind. I joined the Medical Corps, you know. That's where I met Penelope. We got married. We didn't see each other all that much. Then I came home unexpectedly one day and found her in bed with someone.'

'I'm sorry,' Jenny said as he paused.

'I don't know why I'm telling you all this,' he went on. 'After the divorce I began thinking about you again, wondering if you'd got married. I found out the hospital you're working in and that you were still single, and I thought there might still be a chance for you and me to, well, perhaps pick up where we'd left off. The war's over. Things are different now. Settled. I just hoped you might feel, well, perhaps a bit more ready to . . . well, us to, you know, start going out together again.'

So there had been a method in his coming here.

They had gone some distance when the first tiny droplet of rain made itself felt on the back of her hand. Jenny welcomed it with a stab of utter relief.

'It's started to rain. I'd best be getting back,' she said just a little too enthusiastically. She turned to him. 'Ronald, there is someone, you see. I'm going out with someone.'

It wasn't exactly an untruth, was it? She and Matthew. Friends. Not lovers. No proposal. But there was always hope. 'We're more or less going steady,' she said.

Working the rest of the week, there had been no chance to see Matthew. Most of the time, Jenny's mind was centred on Ronald Whittaker and the heartbreaking disappointment that had showed on his face when she had lied to him. Yes, it had been a lie – Matthew no more wanted her than he'd wanted his divorce. She found herself dreading her next evening off duty when she would have to pop over to see him, imagining his off-handed greeting. But she couldn't avoid going. They were friends.

She'd been so sorry for Ronald as he walked her back to her gate that she had leaned towards him and given his cheek a brief consoling peck, purely on impulse. He had read its message clear enough. He had taken her by surprise in catching her to him in a gentle hug. Not knowing how to break away and further hurt his feelings, she had stood thus in an embrace, half her mind thinking unkindly that the rain was getting heavier. He must have felt her tense. When he let her go, he smiled at her, such a sad smile.

'For old times' sake,' he'd murmured, then, 'Be happy, Jenny.'

With that he had walked away, leaving her standing there with tears misting her eyes, beginning to trickle down her cheeks, the spots of rain splashing them away.

She'd felt, still felt, oddly empty after his going. It created a strange sensation knowing he had walked into her life again, briefly, and as quickly walked out of it, leaving behind reawakened memories of that part of her life which felt as though it had never happened. She wondered what his world would be like, what he would do, who he would meet eventually to continue his life with? She would never know.

'Oh, Jenny, come in. I'm so glad to see you.'

Mrs Ward's expression was at once relieved and concerned. She had become a different woman lately. Jenny could almost read her mind, an ability few were privileged to possess. It invariably registered optimism whenever Mrs Ward's eyes fell upon her. It said: My future daughter-in-law, please God, as surely as if spoken aloud. This evening however, concern overrode the pleasure of seeing her as she bade Jenny to come in.

The evening was proving a busy one. For the first time since the war ended, Guy Fawkes Night was being wholeheartedly celebrated, the puny explosion of fireworks no longer conjuring recollections of wartime bombing raids.

Further down the road on a cleared-up bombsite, children had a large bonfire going. The stink of burning wood, rubber and old furniture and the acrid tang of saltpetre hung in the air. But Jenny no longer noted it, the look on Mrs Ward's face alarming her.

'Is anything wrong?' she asked as she was let in.

Mrs Ward lowered her voice, hovering with her in the spacious hallway. 'It's Matthew. Perhaps you can do something with him. He's hardly spoken two words to us and then only to snap at us. Even his father's becoming angry with him, and his father is normally a mild-mannered, understanding man. Neither of us know what to do with him.'

'What's wrong with him?' Jenny whispered back in the same conspiratorial undertone.

'We just don't know. He won't tell us. If we ask, he just snaps at us, tells us to mind our own B. business.' Mrs Ward never swore, not even in quoting. She loathed the mildest epithet in her hearing, much less her home. Jenny smiled to herself. She'd heard some ripe ones from Matthew before now; had heard some even riper ones from soldiers wounded and in pain. Mrs Ward should have been a nurse. That would have broadened her mind.

Jenny's smile, a tiny one that Mrs Ward hadn't even noticed though the hallway was brightly lit, vanished as fast as it had come and she turned her thoughts to what she was telling her.

'He's in his room. He must have seen you coming up

the path. But he hasn't even come down. I just don't know what's wrong with him.'

Jenny followed her into the lounge, returning Mr Ward's nod of welcome. He sat in an armchair by a low fire lit against the growing autumn damp, though it was not cold enough yet to warrant a larger blaze. He had been reading an evening paper, now folded on his knees. At Jenny's entrance he half rose then sat back down again. With a regular visitor, there was no call to stand on ceremony. His whole mien held a defeated look about it.

'Park yourself, Jenny,' he muttered, his terminology so like his son's, a breath of fresh air compared with his wife's self-conscious articulation.

'Is Matthew coming down?' Jenny asked as she sat herself on the sofa. It was him she had come to see, not his parents. The room had an odd atmosphere to it without him, almost as though he no longer lived here. She felt uncomfortable, an interloper.

'Hope so,' his father returned. 'Call him, Lilian, say Jenny's here.'

'He knows she's here,' she snapped.

'Then tell him again,' he snapped back.

It was unlike him. Jenny could sense the tension, the anger, the bewilderment that resided here, a tendency to bicker at the slightest provocation, something they'd never have done under normal circumstances. Yes, Matthew since returning home had been hard to deal with, the careless and debonair youth gone for good, in his place an embittered man tormented by evil memories. He was bound to be edgy and perverse. But not like this.

Jenny heard his mother call up but there was no reply. 'Should I try?' she said awkwardly as Mrs Ward came back into the room, her face tight with annoyance and embarrassment.

'You can if you like. Try knocking on his door.' It was a privilege Mrs Ward allowed no caller; to explore her upper floors was not their business. There was a significance in this acceptance. 'I think he might talk to you, tell you what the matter is with him.'

The newspaper rustled on Mr Ward's knees. 'You being a nurse, Jenny. If you can't pull him round, who can?'

What could she say? She nodded and got up from the sofa, wishing she was indeed wearing her uniform. It would make this confrontation with him official. Again perhaps not – it might drive him further away with whatever was worrying him. It had to be something dire. She couldn't think what.

Leaving them in the lounge she mounted the stairs and tapped lightly on the door his mother had indicated. His voice came muffled.

'It's open. We don't have keys to bedrooms in this house.'

Tentatively she pushed the door and came in, taking care to close it behind her, a signal that no one else would be an audience to whatever he said to her.

He was standing at the window gazing out, his back to her. With the light on and the curtains open, neither the lamplit road nor its lurid bonfire further down nor the flash of fireworks penetrated. Yet he seemed mesmerised by what was going on outside. Above that faint infiltration of wood smoke peculiar to Guy Fawkes celebrations, the room smelled slightly of cigarette smoke and she noted a nearly empty packet of cigarettes on the bedside cabinet next to a saucer acting as an ashtray with several butts in it. Jenny doubted whether there were any actual ashtrays in the whole house.

He shouldn't have been smoking; hadn't done so at least since his illness; it was detrimental to anyone recently recovered from such a condition. It spoke of rebellion, but what rebellion? She ignored the packet and sat on the foot of his bed looking at him across this rather spacious bedroom. Only the main bedroom in her house was nearly as large as this one. Hers was much smaller and the box room was exactly what it sounded like, a box room.

'Your mother said I could come up,' she began.

He didn't respond. He hadn't turned round to look at her at all. No use sitting here looking at someone's back. She might as well get up and go. His back had a very straight look to it. He did look very tall standing there, but not so painfully thin as he had been. He had put on a little weight at last and his shoulders seemed to have broadened again. Seeing them, she felt a thrill of love pass through her. She got up and went across to him.

'Matthew,' she whispered. She touched his shoulder, surprised and alarmed to have him shrug the shoulder away from her as though stung.

'Good God, Matthew, what is the matter?' The profile of his face in the light from the street lamps seemed chiselled in granite, exactly as his mother's sometimes appeared when in a dilemma.

There was nothing for it but to force him to turn away from the window where he seemed to be staring out, not at the celebrating children and the lingering parents, but at something entirely disconnected from them. The look he gave her on being turned to face her was no different, as though it were not she but someone else who stood there. Then he blinked, seemed to come back to himself, recognise who it was standing beside him.

'Jenny . . . Jenny . . . I don't want it to happen to me again. I don't want to be in love with someone and find they don't want me.'

So he was frightened of ever falling in love again. A sense of deadness began to grow inside her. He had made up his mind and was letting her down gently. There was a strange expression in his dark eyes, so dark they seemed to have buried themselves in the depths of his skull. There was a look on his face she couldn't understand. A silent request for her to leave, she guessed. He seemed in pain, his brows drawn together, his lips twisted.

'So if he's the one you really want.'

What was he talking about? 'Who?' she interrupted weakly.

'The chap you were out with last week.'

Oh, God, Ronald Whittaker. Matthew had seen them together, must have watched them come back, watched their embrace. It was imperative to explain. She started to but he wasn't listening, was still talking.

'I don't blame you, Jenny. What've I got to offer someone like you?'

'It's not like that, Matthew,' she blurted, but he still wasn't listening.

'I don't love you, Jenny, I just felt – watching you . . . I don't love you. You don't have to feel bound to me if there's someone else. I don't love you, you know. I really don't . . .'

Her heart plummeted in shock and misery. He stopped suddenly, his expression like one of desperation. It confused her. It also dawned on her that he was denying just too vehemently this love he was supposed not to have for her. What was it Shakespeare wrote? 'The lady doth protest too much, methinks.' Matthew too was protesting too much. He did love her.

From its downward flight, her heart was lifting up, a soaring bird within her breast.

'Oh, darling, it was someone I knew years ago. He came looking for me. I told him I felt nothing for him. And I don't. It was over long ago. He's married.' The lie tripped easily off her tongue. All she wanted was to hear Matthew translate into words that which was contorting his features. But she must be the one to say it, she knew. She didn't hesitate a single second.

'The only person I love is you, Matthew. It's always been you.'

She saw his brow clear, his eyes become brighter, his lips lose their tightness to quiver and part in a disbelieving, hesitant smile. Seconds later she was in his arms, hearing him whispering fiercely to her.

'You don't know how I felt seeing you, down there with someone else. You'll never know. That feeling of jealousy, like a huge black insect inside me, I wanted to tear it out. That was when . . .' A small ragged laugh, hardly a laugh at all but a sound, escaped him. 'That's when I knew. For the first time, I really knew.'

He didn't have to say it. She knew as well. All these years. All these wasted years. They were over. From now on she and Matthew would be able to look forward. There'd be times, of course, when sullenness overwhelmed him, old memories, old regrets maybe, the empty years of want raising their ugly heads in a dream, an unguarded moment. But she would be silent or encouraging, whichever his mood called for. There would also be the happy times, the loving moments, the quiet times.

'I love you,' she murmured, for the pair of them.

She felt him nod against her cheek before he kissed her, and knew he felt the same way about her. And it didn't matter that he did not put it into words.

Beyond the window a firework exploded in a protracted series of crackling – a jumping cracker. Perhaps in a little while she would suggest they take Mattie outside to see the fun. It would be Mattie's first time. She might be a little scared, but with a packet of hand-held sparklers Mattie could be gently coaxed into holding one to watch their fairy-like corona of sparks darting out like stars. This would soon inure her to the noise and the gleeful shouts as sky rockets whooshed up into the dark heavens.

It was in triumph that she and Matthew came downstairs and into the room where his parents waited in tense vigilance. It felt wonderful to witness their utter delight in seeing the smile on his face, his arm about her.

'We're taking Mattie out to see the fireworks,' he said simply, and for once his mother did not upbraid him for not calling his daughter Matilda.

Matilda sat half asleep in one of the armchairs, a little unnerved by the bangs and cracks outside. Jenny hadn't noticed her in the fraught moments earlier on, but now she was roused, still sleepy, and had her coat and hat put on her while Jenny made off down to a shop in Mare Street to buy the packet of sparklers. On the way she stopped off to tell her mother her news that Matthew had declared he loved her. Well, declared as much as he dared.

Matthew stood by the school railings, muffled in overcoat and scarf against the December cold, watching the children spilling out of the dim building into a sleet-spattered playground as the muffled echoes of the hand bell ringing home-time died away inside.

He thought of the night nearly four weeks ago, when he and Jenny had stood together with Mattie watching the fireworks and the bonfire, Jenny holding tightly on to her as she screamed in initial fright at the sudden noises, coaxing her to hold a sparkler by its thin stick between her small fingers until alarmed cries turned to squeals of delight.

At five years old, Mattie had suffered no fear of war. Her only trauma seemed to be the school where she had been started in September. She hadn't adjusted to it as well as she'd been expected to, and would throw herself into her grandmother's arms on coming out, saying she hated everyone there. The children were noisy and rough, the teachers frightened her; every morning she burst into tears, fighting every inch of the way as she was taken there, sometimes saying she felt sick, until on several occasions her grandmother relented and brought her home again.

Jenny had expressed concern. 'There's something worrying her.'

'Other kids cope,' Matthew had said.

'Mattie's not other kids, Matthew. She was taken from her mother, though she was too young to understand, and it must have been unsettling. She's only been with grandparents all this time. Then suddenly she had to adjust to a total stranger she is told is her father. And now she's whipped off to a school full of strangers and expected to cope. No, Matthew, she's not like other kids.'

For a moment the old ache had welled up inside him, thinking how like her mother Mattie was, wilful, at times almost uncontrollable, quick to burst into tears. Yet she could be so charming, endearing herself to everyone at first glance. She was so much like Susan, in ways and looks, that it tore him apart to watch her. Jenny was right, he often found himself actually avoiding her so as to lessen the pain it gave him.

'She'll just have to learn to adapt. We all have to learn that,' he had said, remembering that he too had had to adapt over the years after knowing only a youth full of being molly-coddled. It had come as a shock.

But Jenny had been firm. 'A child's view of things is different to ours. We know we have to put up with what comes, or go under. We learn to fight adversity. A child doesn't even know what adversity is, only that they're unhappy and can't understand why. It makes them behave oddly, and when we get confused by them, they get even worse in sheer frustration. There's something underlying all this. Something even she doesn't remember, but it's there lurking in the back of her mind. She needs a real parent, which is what you are.'

Now he was being a real parent, waiting for Mattie to come out of school.

He was remembering how Jenny had clutched Mattie to her as a banger went off nearby. The houses around them had danced and shivered in the shadows of the lurid flames leaping high into the air from the bonfire. Jenny had given a visible shudder. 'She's had enough of this. I think I have as well.'

They had walked back down the road towards his house, Mattie walking between them, each holding her hand. She had seemed happier away from the violent fun, enjoying the fireworks from a distance. Small rockets had streaked thinly up into the sky over the rooftops, dimmed by bright street lights before which the once practically touchable moon and the pure discs of stars receded, never again to be seen in their full glory by city dwellers in the way they had been during the years of blackout.

Walking back slowly, he had thought what a wonderful mother Jenny would make. And at his gate he had proposed to her and Jenny had said yes.

Recalling it all with a light feeling inside him, he waited for his daughter to emerge from the school exit.

First came the very young, protectively shepherded by a tweed-skirted, motherly teacher into the chill afternoon

already gathering into dusk. They were followed closely
by exuberant older children: girls in neat hats, precisely
buttoned overcoats and shiny strap shoes; boys with
caps askew, blazers and coats open and flying, socks
concertinaed and shoes with the mud of clogged playing
fields clinging to them, laces already coming unravelled.

Taking leave of their teacher, the younger children
ducked in and out of the bigger ones, seeking mothers who
stood in groups with craning necks to collect their offspring.

Matthew stood a little apart from them, the only man,
looking for his child. He saw her moving sedately among
the others – small neat figure in her blue overcoat, her
short dark curly hair peeping from under the small brim
of her blue school hat. Blue suited her, as it had suited her
mother.

Swallowing the lump that came into his throat, Matthew
called out to her. Catching sight of him, her face lit up,
but she walked across the playground and out of the gate
to him with all the nonchalance of one having survived
a traumatic experience and come off triumphant. The
first time ever, he calculated with pride in his daughter's
achievement.

She looked up at him with those great soulful blue
eyes, so like her mother's. 'Are *you* taking me home today,
Daddy?'

'Yes, Mattie,' he replied, love swelling within him as
he gazed down at her, that love filling every dark place her
mother's going had left inside him. She would fill it every
day from now on. She and Jenny between them. By them
he would survive. 'I'm taking you home.'

'Is Jenny going to be there?'

'Yes, she'll be there.'

Jenny had come over early. They had talked while his
mother had taken Mattie to school, for once without tears
with Jenny – he guessed he would always call her Jenny –
promising to bring her sweeties if she didn't cry. 'And next
week I'll go to school and wait for you to bring you home.
Is that all right?' And Mattie had squealed that it was and
had taken her grandmother's hand almost with enthusiasm.
Jenny was good for her, would always be good for her.

'And you should call her Jenny, not Jenny,' he said
solemnly. 'Or if you like, you could call her Mummy.'

Mattie thought for a moment, regarding him steadily. 'I
like Mummy, it's easier.'

Matthew felt a small pang for her. She had never truly
known her real mother, had she?

She was looking up at him, her mind gone entirely off
names. 'Can we go home now, Daddy? I'm cold.'

Home. He held her hand as he led her to the car, which
was warmer than having to walk in this weather. Home.
By Christmas it would be a new home, his and Jenny's
home, paid for from the trust money he'd been given
on his twenty-first birthday, put away to accrue interest
through the years, once intended for him and Susan. That
was in the past now. The rest of the money would go to
resuscitating the partnership – his father's wedding present
to him, saying he himself was too old to manage alone any
more. From now on the past would be put aside, only the
future of importance.

He held out a hand and felt the soft fragility of Mattie's

small fingers twine around his, trusting, possessive, confident of both present and future.

What of the future, he mused as they went towards the waiting car. Two weeks from now he would be married. In two weeks' time he would begin his life anew, perhaps regain a small part of what he had lost, after all those promises so carelessly made so long ago, so lightly taken for granted. He knew better now. He would make new promises to himself now; would never again take them all for granted, but he knew it would never again be quite the same.

Guiding his daughter to the car, he opened the rear door for her to scramble gratefully in. Then he went around the front, slid into the driver's seat, started the engine and pressed down on the accelerator with a force that made the thing roar wildly into life, driving off sharply enough to toss Mattie back into her seat with a delighted giggle.

Also by Maggie Ford:

The Servant Girl

She is the downstairs maid; he is the Master's son...

Forced to become a kitchen maid at Fortune Hall, Hetty Pearson strikes up an unlikely friendship with the younger son of the house, Richard.

But Hetty is just a poor servant girl: what hope does she have of either winning Richard's heart or escaping his older brother's more base attentions?

EBURY
PRESS

Also by Maggie Ford:

A Mother's Love

Can she escape the hardships of her past?

Growing up in London's tough East End, young Sara Porter has had to learn to take care of herself. Her mother resents her maternal responsibilities and has never shown her daughter the slightest bit of love.

Starved of affection, Sara vows not to let anyone get close and focuses instead on getting out of the East End. But still she hopes that one day she'll find a real family to call her own...

EBURY
PRESS

Also available from Ebury Press:

A Wartime Wife

By Lizzie Lane

Trapped in a marriage to the wrong man...

Struggling to make ends meet, Mary Anne Randall is offered no
help by her drunk and abusive husband. A pawnbroking business
run from the wash house at the back of her home is the only way
she can hope to keep her three kids fed and clothed.

But, as storm clouds gather over Europe, can Mary Anne break
free from her loveless marriage for what might be a last chance
at love...?

EBURY
PRESS

Also available from Ebury Press:

A Wartime Family

By Lizzie Lane

A scandalous woman?

Having left her abusive husband for very good reasons, Mary Anne
Randall finds herself judged harshly by her neighbours, especially
after she has the courage to risk a second chance at happiness.

But with the only man she has ever loved away fighting, Mary
Anne is less concerned by her tarnished reputation than with
keeping her children safe, as the bombs fall on Bristol – all too
close to home.

EBURY
PRESS

The Downstairs Maid

By Rosie Clarke

She is a servant girl...

When her father becomes ill, Emily Carter finds herself sent into service at Priorsfield Manor in order to provide the family with an income.

He will be the Lord of the Manor...

Emily strikes up an unlikely friendship with the daughters of the house, as well as Nicolas, son of the Earl. But as the threat of war comes ever closer, she becomes even more aware of the vast differences between upstairs and downstairs, servant and master...

If you like Downton Abbey you'll love this!

EBURY
PRESS

Like Mother, Like Daughter

By Maggie Hope

Sadie Raine has a bad reputation...

When she runs off with a Canadian airman, her two young daughters are left behind to pick up the pieces.

But Cath Raine is determined to rise above the local gossips. Only, when she meets the upper-class Jack on the grounds of his father's estate, she is tempted by the thought of an affair. Is she destined to follow in her mother's scandalous footsteps after all...?

EBURY
PRESS